'An enlightening and comprehensiv
creed in the living faith of the churcl
Nicaea to Constantinople, and the abiding significance of their creeds. An important read for anyone who wants to take their faith seriously.'
John Behr, Regius Professor of Humanity, University of Aberdeen, Scotland

'This is a very fine and, indeed, quite thorough introduction to the Nicene faith. Irving judiciously synthesizes revisionist scholarship of the past fifty years or so, jettisoning the hackneyed narratives of the past. The book masterfully sets the Nicene faith in its historical, theological and ecclesial context; charts its circuitous articulation in the fourth century in the course of extensive theological debate; and provides a nuanced account of the various theological positions in conflict with one another. But this volume provides even more: it is also a well-reasoned apologia for the importance of credal faith itself, rooted in the Great Tradition of the church. Addressed to Protestants and yet ecumenical in approach, this book should prove to be an excellent resource for Protestant, Catholic and Orthodox Christians alike.'
Mark DelCogliano, Associate Professor of Theology, University of St Thomas, Minnesota, USA

'The fourth-century trinitarian controversy was surely the most complicated and most important theological dispute in Christian history; yet from it came the most widely accepted consensus statement in the church: the Nicene Creed. The story of how such a universal statement could emerge from such a contentious debate is fascinating, but not for the faint of heart. Equally daunting is the relation between fourth-century trinitarian theology and modern theological discussions about God. Alex Irving is very well versed in both the ancient and modern discussions, and is in a marvellous position to explain both of them to interested readers. His work shows the way to a sophisticated and genuine appropriation of Nicene theology in the church today – an appropriation in which God's inner relations as Father, Son and Spirit hold pride of place and govern the way we understand the creation and redemption of humanity. If you are brave enough to dive into the deep waters of trinitarian theology, this book is just what you need.'
Donald Fairbairn, Robert E. Cooley Professor of Early Christianity, Gordon-Conwell Theological College, Charlotte, North Carolina, USA; author of *Life in the Trinity* and co-author of *The Story of Creeds and Confessions*

'The fourth century was a crucial time for the development of the mature doctrine of the Trinity, and that development is a classic example of the way that doctrines develop. Alex Irving is to be congratulated for giving us an up-to-date, reliable and readable (so far as the material allows!) account of this hugely important phase in the history of theology. Thoroughly recommended.'
Tony Lane, Professor of Historical Theology, London School of Theology

'The simple phrase "the Nicene Faith" is a helpful way of pointing to the doctrinal core of Christian belief. Yet the phrase condenses so much profound analysis, simplifies so many interpretive complexities and summarizes so much historical controversy that it requires some unpacking. Irving's book is the perfect guide to the depths beneath the motto.'
Fred Sanders, Associate Director of Torrey Honors, Biola University, La Mirada, California, USA

'This is a learned book, engaging with the whole range of scholarship on the subject of creeds in general and Nicaea in particular.

'It is also lucid and accessible. The reciprocity of Scripture and tradition is set out in a way that not only honours the primacy of Scripture but also gives weight to the human voice, the human reception and living in the reality of revelation. The trinitarian focus on revelation is a strong and persuasive way into a discussion on the role of creeds.

'The conclusion is a masterclass in theological method, drawing out the logic of the Nicene process. I would expect this book to make a regular appearance on reading lists in theology faculties and theological colleges.'
Jane Williams, McDonald Professor in Christian Theology, St Mellitus College, London

WE BELIEVE

Exploring the Nicene faith

Alexander Irving

APOLLOS (an imprint of Inter-Varsity Press)
36 Causton Street, London SW1P 4ST, England
Email: ivp@ivpbooks.com
Website: www.ivpbooks.com

First published 2021

British Library Cataloguing-in-Publication Data
A catalogue record for this book is available from the British Library.

ISBN: 978–1–78974–270–1
eBook ISBN: 978–1–78974–271–8

Set in Minion Pro 10.75/13.75pt
Typeset in Great Britain by CRB Associates, Potterhanworth, Lincolnshire
Printed and bound in Great Britain by Ashford Colour Press Ltd, Gosport, Hampshire

Produced on paper from sustainable sources.

Inter-Varsity Press publishes Christian books that are true to the Bible and that communicate the gospel, develop discipleship and strengthen the church for its mission in the world.

IVP originated within the Inter-Varsity Fellowship, now the Universities and Colleges Christian Fellowship, a student movement connecting Christian Unions in universities and colleges throughout Great Britain, and a member movement of the International Fellowship of Evangelical Students. Website: www.uccf.org.uk. That historic association is maintained, and all senior IVP staff and committee members subscribe to the UCCF Basis of Faith.

Teach me your way, O LORD,
that I may walk in your truth;
give me an undivided heart to revere your name.
I give thanks to you, O Lord my God, with my whole heart,
and I will glorify your name for ever.
For great is your steadfast love towards me;
you have delivered my soul from the depths of Sheol.
(Ps. 86:11–13)

Contents

Preface

This book started out as a teaching course delivered to twenty-two intrepid souls at St Stephen's Church, Norwich, in 2017–18, which I delivered alongside my friend David Humphreys. It then had a further outing at Norwich Cathedral as part of the Norwich Centre for Christian Learning programme under the leadership of Dr Gudrun Warren and the Revd Dr Peter Doll. My thanks go to each person who came to those sessions: the attention, questions, insights and prayers of each person are present in these pages.

This book has been written, almost entirely, during the coronavirus pandemic of 2019–21. One way or another, these months have reminded us that we – as created – are always teetering on the edge of nothingness. It is only the love of the Father through Christ in the power of the Spirit that keeps us from falling headlong back into the absence from which we were called.

My warm thanks go to the Revd Dr David Emerton, whose kindness and conscientiousness in helping me settle into a new role made it possible to finish this project. The warmth and understanding with which my family and I have been welcomed, even in these socially distanced times, has made our move far smoother than it might otherwise have been.

I am very grateful for the expertise, patience and hard work of Eldo Barkhuizen, who copy-edited this book. His attention to detail and theological acumen have significantly improved the quality of this work. Any errors that remain are wholly my own. My thanks also goes to the team at IVP, particularly Dr Philip Duce in his capacity as commissioning editor.

It is a presumptuous thing to offer a discussion of the Nicene Creed. But then, it is a presumptuous thing to speak about God and his works at all! We can do it only in the grace of Jesus Christ, the love of God and the fellowship of the Spirit. Each of us makes a contribution to the task of the church by holding on to and proclaiming the faith we have received. The invitation is only ever 'open your mouth, sinner, and speak'.

Abbreviations

Primary texts

Athanasius of Alexandria

AG	*Against the Greeks*
Defence	*Defence of the Nicene Definition*
Discourses	*Discourses Against the Arians*
Ep	*Epistle*
Incarnation	*On the Incarnation*
Synods	*On the Synods*

Basil of Caesarea

AE	*Against Eunomius*
Ep	*Epistle*
Spirit	*On the Holy Spirit*

Irenaeus of Lyons

AH	*Against Heresies*

Gregory of Nazianzus

Or	*Orations*

Hilary of Poitiers

Synods	*On the Synods*
Trinity	*On the Trinity*

Origen of Alexandria

Prin	*On First Principles*

Modern texts

CD	K. Barth, *Church Dogmatics*
DV	*Dei Verbum*, ed. W. M. Abbot SJ, tr. J. Gallacher, *The Documents of Vatican II: With Notes and Comments by*

	Catholic, Protestant and Orthodox Authorities (London: Geoffrey Chapman, 1967)
ECC	J. N. D. Kelly, *Early Christian Creeds* (London: Longmans Green, 1950)
NF	J. Behr, *The Nicene Faith: The Formation of Christian Theology*, vol. 2 (New York: St Vladimir's Seminary Press, 2004)
NL	L. Ayres, *Nicaea and Its Legacy: An Approach to Fourth-Century Trinitarian Theology* (Oxford: Oxford University Press, 2006)
RN	K. Anatolios, *Retrieving Nicaea: The Development and Meaning of Trinitarian Doctrine* (Grand Rapids, Mich.: Baker Academic, 2011)
SCC	D. Fairbairn and R. M. Reeves, *The Story of Creeds and Confessions: Tracing the Development of the Christian Faith* (Grand Rapids, Mich.: Baker Academic, 2019)
SCDG	R. P. C. Hanson, *The Search for the Christian Doctrine of God: The Arian Controversy, 318–381* (Grand Rapids, Mich.: Baker Academic, 1988)
WN	J. Behr, *The Way to Nicaea: The Formation of Christian Theology*, vol. 1 (New York: St Vladimir's Seminary Press, 2001)

General

Ep	*Epistle*
Epp	*Epistles*
Fr.	Fragment
Frs.	Fragments

Collections and journals

ACR	*Australian Catholic Record*
ANF	J. Donaldson and A. Roberts, *Ante-Nicene Fathers*, 10 vols., repr. (Grand Rapids, Mich.: Eerdmans, 1987)
CCR	*Coptic Church Review*
CH	*Church History*
CT	T. Mommsen and P. T. Meyer (eds.), *Theodosiani liber XVI cum Constitutionibus Simondianis et Leges Novella ad*

	Theodosianum Pertinentes, 2 vols. in 3 parts (Berlin, 1954). Translations can be found in P. R. Coleman-Norton, *Roman State and Christian Church: A Collection of Legal Documents to A.D. 535*, 3 vols. (London: SPCK, 1966)
EH	*Ecclesiastical History*
ETL	*Ephemerides theologicae lovanienses*
GCS	Die griechischen christlichen Schriftsteller
GOTR	*Greek Orthodox Theological Review*
HTR	*Harvard Theological Review*
IJCT	*International Journal of the Classical Tradition*
IJSC	*International Journal for the Study of the Christian Church*
IJST	*International Journal of Systematic Theology*
ITQ	*Irish Theological Quarterly*
JECS	*Journal of Early Christian Studies*
JEH	*Journal of Ecclesiastical History*
JRH	*Journal of Religious History*
JTS	*Journal of Theological Studies*
MT	*Modern Theology*
NPNF	P. Schaff and H. Wace (eds.), *Nicene and Post-Nicene Fathers of the Christian Church*, 2nd series, repr. (Grand Rapids, Mich.: Eerdmans, 1983–7)
PG	Patrologia graeca
PTMS	Princeton Theological Monograph Series
RÉAug	*Revue d'études augustiniennes et patristiques*
SJT	*Scottish Journal of Theology*
StPatr	*Studia patristica*
SVTQ	*Saint Vladimir's Theological Quarterly*
TD	*Theology Digest*
TJ	*Trinity Journal*
TS	*Theological Studies*
Urk	H. G. Opitz (ed.), *Athanasius Werke*, vol. 3, pt 1, *Urkunden zur Geschichte des arianischen Streites* (Berlin: W. de Gruyter, 1934)
VC	*Vigiliae christianae*
VE	*Vox evangelica*
ZAC	*Zeitschrift für antikes Christentum*
ZNW	*Zeitschrift für die neutestamentliche Wissenschaft*

Introduction

There are a number of excellent studies of the development of fourth-century theology and the theology articulated in the Nicene Creed.[1] Why, given this, is there a need for another one? The present work draws on this previous scholarship, and, while it sets out to articulate its own distinctive position in relation to this field of study, its primary purpose is to step into the discipline of constructive dogmatics in that it sets out to be a contribution to the ongoing task of the church's self-examination of its talk about God.[2] As a function of the church, the church's talk about God and its self-examination of that talk must be compatible with the nature of the church's existence in itself. The church does not have existence in itself and it does not have truth in itself. That which the church has is that which the church has received. Therefore, the core criterion of the church's self-assessment must be the extent to which it is not rooted in itself but is established upon and reaches beyond itself towards Jesus Christ in the power of his Spirit.[3] This function of the church, then, is an act of faith, derivative from the revelation of God;[4] and if it ceases to be obedient to this core criterion, then it ceases to be the distinctive voice of the church and begins to be the generic voice of humanity.

What is distinctive about the human voice of the church is that it participates in the eternal Son's confession of the Father. The church has true human existence *and a true human voice*, but not one that is separate from Jesus. This is a genuine human knowledge that is miraculously established. Therefore, the historic teaching of the church is integral to the contemporary task of the

[1] To name only a few: *NL* (L. Ayres, *Nicaea and Its Legacy: An Approach to Fourth-Century Trinitarian Theology* [Oxford: Oxford University Press, 2006]); *RN* (K. Anatolios, *Retrieving Nicaea: The Development and Meaning of Trinitarian Doctrine* [Grand Rapids, Mich.: Baker Academic, 2011]); *NF* (J. Behr, *The Nicene Faith* [New York: St Vladimir's Seminary Press, 2004]); *SCDG* (R. P. C. Hanson, *The Search for the Christian Doctrine of God: The Arian Controversy, 318–381* [Grand Rapids, Mich.: Baker Academic, 1988]); *ECC* (J. N. D. Kelly, *Early Christian Creeds* [London: Longmans Green, 1950]). Since the publication of the most recent of these volumes, there has been a host of high-quality scholarship, with which this present study engages.

[2] K. Barth, *Church Dogmatics: The Doctrine of the Word of God*, vol. 1, pt 1, ed. G. W. Bromiley and T. F. Torrance, tr. G. W. Bromiley (Edinburgh: T&T Clark, 1975), 11–17. Where I depend more exclusively on the scholarship of others it is indicated with a comment and a note in the bibliography.

[3] Barth, *CD*, 1.1, 4.

[4] Ibid. 17.

church's self-examination of its talk about God. To this end, the study of the development of Nicene theology is bracketed by broader considerations. First, the role of the tradition of the church considered from both historical and methodological aspects. Second, a consideration of the theological commitments of the Nicene confession, with particular attention to its central dialectic between God's non-transitive and God's transitive relations and how this informs our understanding of divine being and the gratuity of God in creating and redeeming.

Nicaea and the fourth century

If you have ever sat in a committee that has had to agree a shared statement, you will be aware that each phrase is pregnant with the discussion that produced it. These discussions are often informed by a wealth of history and a sense of purpose. Statements agreed by committees are rather like the tip of an iceberg in that respect. The statements that emerged from the councils of Nicaea (AD 325) and Constantinople (AD 381) are like this. The goal of this book is to draw out the theological discussions beneath the surface of the credal statement to facilitate further understanding of the meaning of the Creed. As such, it is the intention of this book to explore the Creed within its life-setting in the theological controversies and confessional atmosphere of the fourth-century church. To do so requires an awareness of the context of the confessional practice of the church that developed prior to (chapter 2) and in between (chapters 3–6) the councils of Nicaea and Constantinople.

The idea of a Nicene theology, as has been observed by Khaled Anatolios, does not refer to the historical event of the confession of Nicaea (325) itself 'but rather to that event as appropriated and interpreted by those who over the succeeding decades claimed to be . . . in continuity with its declaration of the consubstantiality of the Father and the Son'.[5] This is the appropriation and interpretation of the Nicene confession that would be validated at the Council of Constantinople (381). However, the delegates at Constantinople did not simply receive and reiterate the statement that emerged from Nicaea. The intervening decades saw significant developments in understanding. The phrase 'development of credal theology' may sound like a misnomer. After all, do creeds not articulate unchanging Christian belief? Does talking about belief in terms of 'development' not imply some level of the construction of Christian doctrine, whereby Jesus of Nazareth has been submerged under the Christ of

[5] Anatolios, *RN*, 1.

faith? However, when it comes to the Nicene faith, we are talking about a development. In part, this is a statement of demonstrable and historical fact. The credal statement we recite today was the product of two councils separated by some sixty years, decades characterized by intense thinking regarding the Christian doctrine of God. This reminds us that the Creed is not an abstract system of doctrine but is part of the living process by which the church receives and hands on the good news of God's saving love to us in Christ.

There are always some elephants in the room whenever the subject of creeds comes up. Given this, it is necessary to offer some thoughts that may encourage the reader that concerning ourselves credal theology is justifiable and worthwhile. First, there is a terminological barrier: What is a confession of faith? Second, there is the confusing reality that Christianity has several major creeds and they do not all share significant features such as provenance, structure or purpose. So, it is necessary to ask what the major creeds of the church are. Third, there are significant criticisms of credal theology. These come in implicit form from our culture, in more overt form from the philosophical movements that have contributed to that culture and in dramatically explicit form from dissenting theological traditions (both conservative and liberal). This raises the questions 'Why do the creeds provoke such resistance, and should Christians act upon these criticisms by refusing to come under credal authority, or (as is more likely) treat them with a mild neglect?' Fourth, we mostly encounter the creeds in the liturgy or in our early instruction in the faith. They are established norms, as unchallenged by most believers as the liturgy of the Eucharist. It does not immediately occur to us to ask about their justification: Why do the creeds exist, and would it matter if they did not?

What is a 'confession of faith'?

Jaroslav Pelikan observes that the confessional activity of the church has its 'origin in a twofold Christian imperative, to believe and to confess what one believes'.[6] This, though, does not ultimately rest on a body of doctrine, but on a *person*.[7] As Paul writes, 'if you *confess* with your lips that Jesus is Lord and *believe* in your heart that God raised him from the dead, you will be saved' (Rom. 10:9; emphases mine). The object of Christian confession is the crucified

[6] J. Pelikan, *Credo: Historical and Theological Guide to Creeds and Confessions of Faith in the Christian Tradition* (New Haven, Conn.: Yale University Press, 2003), 35. The subsequent discussion is heavily informed in ibid. 35–92.

[7] *SCC* (D. Fairbairn and R. M. Reeves, *The Story of Creeds and Confessions: Tracing the Development of the Christian Faith* [Grand Rapids, Mich.: Baker Academic, 2019]), 1.

and risen Jesus. In the act of confession, we express our belief that *this* person (and not some other) is Lord.[8] To affirm that Jesus is Lord carries with it a host of other commitments. On the kerygmatic level, it involves his incarnation, death, resurrection and ascension. On the theological level, it involves affirmations about the Son's relationship to the Father. For this reason, confessions of faith have tended to be compendiums of Christian doctrine, summaries of what is believed about Jesus.[9] A confession of faith is a commentary on the meaning of that primal Christian doxology that Jesus is Lord.[10]

This correlation between believing and confessing is built into the very meaning of the word 'creed', being an anglicized version of the Latin *credo*, 'I believe'. Accordingly, a dizzying array of Protestant confessions of faith are prefaced by the confluence of belief and confession.[11] For example, the Belgic Confession (1561) opens a direct allusion to Paul's language: 'we all believe in our hearts and confess with our mouths'.[12] The Christian church has historically recognized the necessity to *define* its beliefs. A confession is just such a definition: 'a technical term for the process of legislating what the church is required to believe, teach and confess'.[13] Confessions are formal statements by which the church has articulated what it believes about the person of Jesus Christ and our consequent identity as those who take his name. The purpose of such statements was expressed with clarity at the Council of Trent. In an introduction to the Nicene-Constantinopolitan Creed delegates at Trent made the following statement about the purpose of the creed:

> That this loving care of the council may both begin and continue by the grace of God, it determines and decrees first of all to begin with a creed of the faith. In this it follows the example of the fathers of the more revered councils who, at the beginnings of their proceedings, were accustomed to make use of this shield of all heresies, and in some cases by this means alone they have drawn unbelievers to faith, defeated heretics, and strengthened the faithful.[14]

Confessions of faith are described as having several functions in this passage: defending against deviant understandings, giving witness to non-believers,

8 Fairbairn and Reeves, *SCC*, 1.
9 Pelikan, *Credo*, 71–74.
10 C. R. Trueman, *The Creedal Imperative* (Wheaton, Ill.: Crossway, 2012), 135–136.
11 See Pelikan, *Credo*, 41–43.
12 *Belgic Confession*, 1. This and the following confessions are also cited from Pelikan's volume.
13 Pelikan, *Credo*, 1.
14 Trent, 3.

drawing back those who have fallen from truth and strengthening the body of Christ. So also, the Protestant confession the Wittenberg Articles of 1536 opens with the words 'we confess simply and clearly, without any ambiguity, that we believe, hold, teach, and defend'.[15]

'Faith' has both a subjective and an objective meaning. The Heidelberg Catechism of 1563 recognizes this nuance when it defines faith as 'not only a certain knowledge by which I accept as true all that God has revealed to us in his word, but also a wholehearted trust which the Holy Spirit creates in me through the gospel'.[16] Faith can refer both to the faith *that* one believes and also the faith *by which* one believes.[17] The latter aspect is the subjective aspect of faith. The former is the objective content of faith; that is, the activity of God in history in his saving self-revelation, which has been articulated in propositional form within the church. Both of these elements are present in the phrase 'confession of faith': it is a statement that *we believe* this *particular body of propositions* to be true.

The word 'confession' is no less complex. We are perhaps most used to this term in the sense of owning up to wrongdoing, or, in the formal liturgy, of confession and absolution. These are not the sense of the word when in the construction 'confession of faith'. A confession of faith is a public statement of belief, a witness to what one believes to be true. This carries a unique importance in Christian theology because at the centre of Christian belief is the witness of the incarnate Son to the Father by the power of the Spirit. For example, the letter to the Hebrews describes Jesus as the 'apostle and high priest of our confession' (Heb. 3:1). As apostle and high priest, Jesus is sent from the Father to humanity and represents humanity to God. It is thus before God and before the world that he proclaimed his faith. This is particularly evident in the Gospel of John, where Jesus is presented as the one sent from the Father to make the Father known: 'For this I was born, and for this I came into the world, to testify to the truth. Everyone who belongs to the truth listens to my voice' (John 18:37; see also John 3:34). This is the true confession.[18] All subsequent confessions of faith participate in Christ's and articulate the truth revealed in his person as we have received it from the apostles.[19] In this way,

---

15 Wittenberg Articles, 1.

16 Heidelberg Catechism, 21.

17 Pelikan, *Credo*, 49.

18 Such a focus on revelation as personal encounter predicated on God's self-disclosure has been a feature of much modern Catholic theology following the *Dei Verbum* of the Second Vatican Council. For a reception, see G. O'Collins, *Retrieving Fundamental Theology: Three Styles of Contemporary Theology* (London: Geoffrey Chapman, 1993), 48–62, esp. 52–56.

19 See also E. Schilebeeckx, *Christ the Sacrament of Encounter with God* (London: Sheed & Ward, 1963), 13–19.

to make a confession of faith is to give a public statement before God and before the world of the body of belief that has been given to the church by the apostolic preaching, which is ultimately rooted in the person of Jesus Christ. It is not surprising, then, that initiation into the church is a central source of confessions (e.g. catechism and baptismal confessions) as it is the means of participation in the life and mission of Christ. In this connection, Levering has recently argued a truly trinitarian account of revelation must account for the church's mediating role. Revelation is anchored in the Father's sending of the Son and Spirit through which the members of the church are enabled to receive and participate as witnesses in the divine mission of revelation and salvation.[20]

Such a construal of Christian confession is tied to a personal account of revelation centred not on the transfer of propositional information but on the self-revelation of God and its proper reception within our humanity completed in the person of Jesus. In my view, this is the proper foundation upon which to understand the relationship of Scripture and tradition (chapter 1). Revelation is an encounter by which God gives himself as the object of our knowing:

> The content of revelation is God's own proper reality. Revelation is not to be thought of as the communication of arcane information or hidden truths . . . Talk of revelation is not talk of some reality separable from God's own being, something which God as it were deposits in the world and which then becomes manipulable. Revelation is divine *self*-presentation; its content is identical with God.[21]

God establishes us as knowers of him both in Christ's human knowledge and in the guidance of the Spirit.[22] This gift of God's self is a 'treasure of revelation entrusted to the Church'.[23] This establishing of humanity as a dialogue partner establishes the knowledge of God held in the church in moral categories: we know in fidelity and in obedience to the gift of God's self that has been given.

---

[20] M. Levering, *Engaging the Doctrine of Revelation: The Mediation of the Gospel Through Church and Scripture* (Grand Rapids, Mich.: Baker Academic, 2014), 35–57.

[21] J. Webster, *Holy Scripture: A Dogmatic Sketch* (Cambridge: Cambridge University Press, 2012), 14; emphasis original. See also *DV*, 1–4 (pp. 112–114).

[22] K. Barth, *Church Dogmatics: The Doctrine of God*, vol. 2, pt 1, ed. G. W. Bromiley and T. F. Torrance, tr. T. H. L. Parker, W. B. Johnson, H. Knight and J. L. M. Haire (Edinburgh: T&T Clark, 1957), 65.

[23] *DV*, 26 (p. 128).

What are the major creeds?

There are three creeds:[24] the Apostles' Creed, the Nicene Creed and the Athanasian Creed. The Nicene Creed and the Chalcedonian Definition are closely related and were composed over what we now call the first four ecumenical councils. The Nicene Creed, confusingly, was ratified at the Council of Constantinople (381), and is a statement composed, at least in part, of a reaffirmation of the doctrinal commitments of the Creed of Nicaea (325), from which it takes its name. While the creeds of Nicaea and Constantinople are not the same confession,[25] there is enough theological continuity between them for them to be treated as a unity.

The First Ecumenical Council met in Nicaea in AD 325 and composed a confession describing the relation between the Son and Father (chapter 4), chiefly in response to the controversy between Arius and Alexander (chapter 3). The Second Ecumenical Council met in Constantinople in 381 following several decades of councils, theological disputes and political manoeuvres (chapters 5 and 6). At this council, the doctrinal content of the Creed of Nicaea was affirmed along with some significant developments, not least a significantly expanded statement on the Spirit's relation to the Son and Father (see Table 1 on p. 8).

The document we know as the Chalcedonian Definition is similar in that it was composed through two councils at which representatives from across the church were present (the Third Ecumenical Council in Ephesus in 431 and the Fourth Ecumenical Council in Chalcedon in 451). As with the First and Second Ecumenical Councils, these were called to formulate a response to a theological controversy. In the Chalcedonian Definition the question was not about the relation of the Son to the Father or the associated question of the relation of the Spirit to the Father and Son; this time, the question was over what it meant to say that God the Son became human.[26] As such, the Chalcedonian Definition is presented as an elaboration and clarification of the earlier Nicene Creed. It is a markedly different sort of statement from the Nicene Creed. The threefold structure is replaced by a focused Christological statement about the person of Christ. Ostensibly, the Chalcedonian Definition is not supposed to stand alone. As part of the proceedings of these councils, the Nicene Creed was read out, with the Chalcedonian Definition being a clarification of what is meant by the proposition that God the Son became human.

---

24 Five if a distinction is held between the Creed of Nicaea (325) and the Creed of Constantinople (381).

25 As is explained in chapter 6, the confession of Constantinople does not appear to use the Nicene statement as a base text.

26 See Fairbairn and Reeves, *SCC*, 80–108.

Table 1 The creeds of Nicaea and Constantinople

Creed of 325 (Nicaea)	*Creed of 381 (Constantinople)*
We believe in one God the Father All Governing, creator of all things visible and invisible.	We believe in one God, the Father All Governing, creator of heaven and earth, of all things visible and invisible.
And in one Lord, Jesus Christ the Son of God, begotten of the Father as only begotten, that is, of the essence [*ousia*] of the Father, God from God, Light from Light, true God from true God, begotten, not created, of the same essence [*homoousios*] with the Father,	And in one Lord, Jesus Christ, the only-begotten Son of God, begotten from the Father before all time, Light from Light, true God from true God, begotten not created, of the same essence [*homoousios*] with the Father,
through whom all things came into being, both in heaven and on earth;	through whom all things came into being;
Who for us humans and for our salvation came down and was incarnate, becoming human.	Who for us humans and because of our salvation, came down from heaven, and was incarnate by the Holy Spirit and the virgin Mary, and became human.
He suffered and the third day he rose, and ascended into the heavens.	He was crucified for us under Pontius Pilate, and suffered and was buried and rose on the third day, according to the Scriptures; and ascended to heaven, and sits on the right hand of the Father,
And he will come to judge both the living and the dead.	and he will come again with glory to judge the living and the dead.
	His kingdom will have no end.
And in the Holy Spirit.	And in the Holy Spirit, the Lord and life-giver, who proceeds from the Father, who is worshipped and glorified together with the Father and Son, who spoke through the prophets;
	And in one holy, catholic and apostolic Church. We confess one baptism for the remission of sins. We look forward to the resurrection of the dead and the life of the world to come. Amen.
But those who say, 'Once he was not', or 'he was not before his generation', or 'became to be out of nothing', or who assert that he, the Son of God, is of a different '*hypostasis*' or '*ousia*', or that he is a 'creature', or 'changeable', or 'mutable', the Catholic and Apostolic Church anathematizes them.	

Note: Both creeds are cited from D. Fairbairn and R. M. Reeves, *The Story of Creeds and Confessions: Tracing the Development of the Christian Faith* (Grand Rapids, Mich.: Baker Academic, 2019), 73 (modified by providing working English translations for transliterations of Greek terms).

The Apostles' Creed and the Athanasian Creed are slightly different from the Nicene Creed and Chalcedonian Definition. Neither is written by the ones to whom it is attributed. The Apostles' Creed was not written by the apostles but is an evolution of the confession of the church in Rome, which dates back at least to the middle of the second century (discussed in chapter 2). This confession did not assume its final form until the eighth century, which is the main reason why the claim that it is of apostolic authorship is dubious: if the apostles really composed it, it is desperately unlikely that it would have been subject to revision. Likewise, the so-called Athanasian Creed was almost certainly not written by Athanasius. The original text of the Athanasian Creed is in Latin, while Athanasius himself wrote in Greek. Also, the grammar and vocabulary used, as pointed out by Kelly, is characteristic of a later Latin than was standard in Athanasius' lifetime.[27] Theologically, it has been suggested the Athanasian Creed has more in common with the Latin theologians Ambrose of Milan and Augustine of Hippo than it does with the thought of the Alexandrian bishop.[28]

However, the thing that really establishes the Apostles' Creed and the Athanasian Creed as outliers is that *they were not composed at councils*. The Apostles' Creed is a confession of one local episcopal area that was attributed with especial significance ostensibly owing to the political priority of Rome and the primacy attributed to the episcopate of Rome. Meanwhile, the Athanasian Creed presents itself as a summary of Christian doctrine, which focuses well over half of its forty-two verses on trinitarian theology. Its purpose is, ostensibly, not for liturgical usage (it is too long and abstruse for regular recitation) but for instruction: 'a concise summary of orthodox teaching to be studied and mastered by the faithful'.[29] As such, it took no obvious passage through conciliar approval but represents at least part of the catechetical procedure of the church in Rome, perhaps in the fifth or sixth century.

Why are the creeds resisted?

For both theological and philosophical-cultural reasons there is resistance towards credal Christianity within some contemporary sections of the Protestant Church. Fairbairn and Reeves observe that these different trajectories coalesce in two major features of Western Protestant Christianity: biblicism

---

27 J. N. D. Kelly, *The Athanasian Creed* (London: A&C Black Publishers, 1964), 67–69.

28 Ibid. 24–33. For a shorter discussion of this, see M. Davie, *The Athanasian Creed* (London: Latimer Trust, 2019), 11–12.

29 Kelly, *Athanasian Creed*, 17.

and individualism.[30] The latter consists of individuals, alone with their Bible, resisting the siren call (or the oppressive orthodoxy) of the past in order to establish what they see of Jesus Christ in their personal reading of the Bible (or reason) alone. This is not a simple phenomenon, as the confluence of biblicism and individualism has a range of different influences within it.

Theological reasons

Ambivalence towards credal Christianity is a diverse phenomenon that has both conservative and liberal instantiations. On the conservative side, a dichotomy is sometimes drawn between the unique authority of Scripture and the validity of regulating its interpretation by the historic creeds. Daniel Williams observes that some evangelicals associate the tradition of the church with the institutional structure of the Roman Catholic Church and believe this to be 'antithetical to the absolute authority of the Bible'.[31] The principle of *sola Scriptura* can be applied in such a way to undermine any writings outside the biblical canon. Trueman wryly describes a pastor 'standing in the pulpit, seizing his Bible in his right hand, raising it above his head, and pointing to it with his left. "This," he declared in a booming voice, "is our only creed and our only confession."'[32]

It is important to note that this *does* intersect with a genuine Protestant sentiment. Protestantism was, in part, a reaction to an overreaching ecclesiastical authority that propounded as authoritative propositions and traditions alien to Scripture. It is within the Protestant consciousness to be sensitive to the undermining of the authority of Scripture by some supplementary authority. So, believers, eager to continue in what they believe to be a commitment to the unique supremacy of Scripture, can judge creeds and confessions of faith to be the tools of a corrupt religious system imposing extra-biblical beliefs upon the church. That is, of course, until it is realized that the Protestant churches have been prolific in their composition of confessions.

Even so, there is an idea that the Reformers rejected the tradition of the church in favour of unmediated access to Scripture, which alone stood as the sole authority, fully sufficient in and of itself. This is established on a crude dichotomy: the Roman Catholic Church had their tradition while the Reformers had Scripture. As has been documented in a host of other studies (and is discussed in chapter 1), this is a distortion of reality and is a misunderstanding

[30] Fairbairn and Reeves, *SCC*, 2.
[31] D. H. Williams, *Retrieving the Tradition and Renewing Evangelicalism: A Primer for Suspicious Protestants* (Grand Rapids, Mich.: Eerdmans, 1999), 18.
[32] Trueman, *Creedal Imperative*, 13.

of the point at issue in the Reformation. The contention of the Reformation was not Scripture versus tradition. Instead, the Reformation was about what really constitutes tradition and how it should be held in relation to Scripture.

However, this does not take us out of the woods just yet. Even if it is accepted that the historic teaching of the church does not supplement Scripture but provides parameters that guide our interpretation of Scripture, then what is to stop that body of beliefs being deployed as an a priori set of axioms, established before and independent of the reading of Scripture itself? In such a scenario, the edifice of credal and confessional language of the church would become a petrified forest, a body of beliefs separated from its evangelical foundation and imposed upon our reading of Scripture as an extrinsic framework that imposes its own logic upon Scripture. This is a problem unless the tradition of the church is, to some extent, treated as a mode of existence of the apostolic witness. That is a way in which the apostolic teaching persists in the church, not in the concentrated form of Scripture but in the diluted form of its reception by the worshipping communities the apostles established. In this way, that which is believed in the church retains its organic connection to the person of Christ (and so does not become an a priori abstraction) while also serving as the secondary partner to Scripture, at once regulating and confirming interpretations that are consistent with the apostolic intention. This view is developed further in chapter 1.

Another significant influence on a reticence regarding credal Christianity is liberalism. Integral to the liberal tradition and its antagonism to credal Christianity is a prioritization of the faith *by* which one believes over and above the faith *that* one believes. The focus of liberal Christianity falls on personal reception over and above doctrinal content. Friedrich Schleiermacher's *On Religion* (1799) is profoundly anti-dogmatic, interpreting religious meaning within a profoundly subjective locus characterized by sentiment.[33] This idea is developed in his later text *The Christian Faith* (1821) by his conception of theology as the reflection on the feeling of absolute dependence. That is, an analysis of the sense of oneself impacted by an external Whence, against which he or she can exert no counterinfluence.[34] With such a method, creeds and confessions do not constitute propositions of universal significance. Instead, they are bound to a particular time and are representative of a specific way of articulating the *sense of the divine*. Dogma discerned by consensus that has seemed to be true to the church therefore has no authority over the religious

33 F. Schleiermacher, *On Religion: Speeches to Its Cultured Despisers*, tr. J. Oman (San Francisco Calif.: Harper Torchbooks, 1958).

34 F. Schleiermacher, *The Christian Faith*, repr. (London: T&T Clark, 2016), 76–93.

consciousness of the individual.[35] This spirit undergirds an antithesis that continues to shape theological liberalism today: freedom instead of dogma.[36] A fine articulation of this perspective comes from the Anglian theologian Don Cupitt, who has argued that objective theism should be replaced by an autonomous spirituality.[37]

Culture and philosophy

Philosophical transitions are cultural transitions as much as they are intellectual transitions. In the Age of Enlightenment, the spirit of throwing off the dogmatism of the old and having the courage to determine veracity and virtue for oneself accompanied the most tumultuous revolts against the old order; for example, in the revolutions of the United States of America and France. So also within the church: as Pelikan observes, the 'consciousness of modernity' is characterized by 'discomfort' with the very idea of creeds.[38] By this Pelikan is referring, in part, to the antidogmatic spirit of the Enlightenment. Immanuel Kant defined the Enlightenment as the emergence of the rational individual, hostile to the imposition of tradition:

> enlightenment is *man's emergence from his self-incurred immaturity. Immaturity* is the inability to use one's own understanding without the guidance of another . . . The motto of enlightenment is therefore: *Sapere aude*! Have courage to use your *own* understanding.[39]

Creeds are, within this perspective, the most egregious of examples of the tyranny of the past. To reject them, in Kant's vision, is morally virtuous, a courageous break from immaturity and the taking up of responsibility.

Pelikan points to the impact this form of thought has had on the study of Christian history: the study of the history of doctrinal development does not provide greater insight into the person and work of Jesus Christ; instead, it drives the believer away from the purity of the gospel, submerging Jesus of Nazareth under the Christ of dogma. Such was the contention of the prevalent historical-critical biblical scholarship of the late eighteenth and nineteenth centuries, seeking to cut through the impositions the church had made on to

---

35 Pelikan, *Credo*, 491–492.

36 G. Bray, *Creeds, Councils and Christ: Did the Early Christians Misrepresent Jesus*, rev. edn (Nairobi: Mentor, 2009), 17–18.

37 D. Cupitt, *Taking Leave of God* (London: SCM Press, 1980).

38 Pelikan, *Credo*, 488.

39 I. Kant, *An Answer to the Question 'What Is Enlightenment?'*, tr. H. B. Nisbett (London: Penguin Books, 2009), 1; emphases original.

Christ in his presentation in Scripture to get to the genuine historical Jesus. For example, F. C. Baur maintained that the New Testament itself contained layers of interpretation and amplification that obscured the historical Jesus, concealing his ethical teaching, which was the true content of Christianity, under the apocalyptic folds of the apostolic interpretations. It is just such a thought that led to Thomas Jefferson's literally slicing the supernatural from the Gospels' presentation of Jesus in constructing his *The Life and Morals of Jesus of Nazareth* (1820).

This task of liberating Christianity from the theology of the church was taken up enthusiastically in historical theology. The iconoclastic church historian Adolf von Harnack argued in his fiercely Protestant *The History of Dogma* (1886–98) that the creeds and confessions of the church had stepped away from the true gospel of Jesus and had transformed it into a Greek philosophical system. The metaphysical concerns that characterize the credal search for doctrinal precision such as the constitution of the person of Christ and the introduction of the metaphysical language of 'essence' were deemed to be philosophical abstractions. Within this trajectory, Rudolf Bultmann contended that the Gospels were characterized by a perspective on reality that was incidental to the content of Jesus' person and message. In order for the inner logic of the gospel to be transposed into a format comprehensible to the modern mind, it needed to be 'demythologized'; that is, it had to be distilled from its encasing in an apocalyptic Jewish mindset and be rearticulated in a way that could confront the modern mind and call the latter to a moment of decision. Within this understanding, the error of credal Christianity is to mistake the mythological encasing for the true inner kernel of the Christian faith. As such, a doctrinal system was erected on precisely the elements that the true substance of Jesus' life and teaching needed to be abstracted from. In other words, credal Christianity has systematized the myth, rather than distilling truth from it.[40]

The philosophical developments of the later twentieth and early twenty-first centuries have been accompanied by a corresponding cultural shift, which is no less hostile to creeds. We might not, perhaps, have been prepared for just how far the philosophy of deconstruction has pervaded liberal societies. The criticism of that which exists beyond the subject – a shared idea of reason, value or truth – is manifestly hostile to credal Christianity. A postmodern society is, almost by definition, not going to be a credal society. One problem is the societal setting of meaning. For example, Paul Ricoeur in his *The Conflict of Interpretations* (1969) describes language as bound within the perspectives and

[40] See also Bray, *Creeds*, 23–24.

boundaries of the culture from which it emerged, which is incomprehensible within different cultures. Meaning cannot be divorced from the community within which it is shared.[41] The task of transferring meaning across radically different cultures is, therefore, complex at the very least. For Ricoeur, the absence of common ground requires the text to be deconstructed and rebuilt within a culturally relevant frame of reference: 'a world of the text for us to think about, while awaiting its complement, the *lifeworld of the reader*, without which the signification of the literary work is incomplete'.[42]

More recently, this antipathy towards the universality of truth – or at least to the incommunicability of meaning – has cross-pollinated with other modes of thought to create a philosophical and cultural movement that is incompatible particularly with credal Christianity. This is the growth of concern regarding *power* and the associated concern with group identity. Authority, orthodoxy and other concepts that demarcate or set transpersonal requirements are, at least, held in suspicion as the tools of a tyrannical hierarchy. Orthodoxy can be set aside within the new critical theory as not universally true, but as being an account of the priorities and beliefs of any particular group. To require that this be accepted beyond the parameters of that group is seen not only as ignorance of the role of the subject and the necessity of intersubjectivity in constructing meaning, but as being *morally reprehensible*.[43]

Why do creeds exist and would it matter if they did not?

There is a theological, cultural and philosophical onslaught against credal Christianity, such that the non-climactic continuity of the proclamation of the Nicene Creed week by week as an act of worship is not quite so obviously an insurgency against the norm. But that is what it is! A refusal to be swept along with the tides that would wash away this mode of existence of the apostolic gospel. However, this is a well-resourced and well-justified insurgency.

Reaction to the historical-critical method

The claims of the historical-critical method have come under significant scrutiny and its excesses have been pointed out both in the field of biblical

41 See P. Ricoeur, *The Conflict of Interpretations*, ed. D. Ihde (Evanston, Ill.: Northwestern University Press, 1974).

42 P. Ricoeur, *Time and Narrative*, vol. 2, tr. K. McLaughlin and D. Pellauer (Chicago, Ill.: University of Chicago Press, 1984–8), 160. Cited from D. Ihde, 'Text and the New Hermeneutics', in D. Wood (ed.), *On Paul Ricoeur: Narrative and Interpretation* (London: Routledge, 1991), 124–139; emphasis original.

43 See also Trueman, *Credal Imperative*, 30–31, 38–47.

scholarship and that of the history of doctrine. The proposition that the inner kernel of Jesus' teaching has been submerged within the dogmatism of the later church has been significantly muted in potency. Far from casting the gospel writers' presentation of Jesus off as ahistorical myth-making, their absolute centrality to an accurate assessment of the history of Jesus of Nazareth has been reasserted. So, likewise, in hermeneutics, the notion that the New Testament text needed to be deconstructed and reconstructed within a more appropriate cultural frame has itself been contested by affirmations of the necessity of grounding the meaning of a text within its own cultural frame of reference. Within the study of Christian history and the development of Christian doctrine, the force of von Harnack's thesis regarding the Hellenization of the gospel has been significantly dulled. Important twentieth-century studies from scholars including J. N. D. Kelly, G. L. Prestige and R. P. C. Hanson have demonstrated that, far from the early church deviating from some simple gospel of Nazareth, dressing it up in the garb of Greek philosophy, there is a profound continuity in which the apostolic gospel underwent assimilation into the mind of the church.[44]

Practice of confessions of faith in the New Testament

The observation that the Bible itself contains confessional statements is now approaching the level of a truism. Dogma, a body of beliefs judged to be correct by the consensus, is not antithetical or even alien to Scripture (see chapter 1). Instead, dogma is a genre contained within it. The people of God have made use of short, formulaic statements of their faith from the very beginning. As Pelikan points out:

> anyone, who in the name of the New Testament, declares an opposition to the very notion of creeds is obliged to come to terms with the priority – the chronological if not also the logical priority – of creeds within the teachings of Jesus himself and of his apostles.[45]

From the very beginning, the people of God have composed formulaic summaries of the faith. This movement towards set formulae became especially significant as the apostles neared death. Paul's letters to Timothy, for example, express a focused concern that Timothy should maintain conformity to the sound words he heard from Paul (2 Tim. 1:13). To assist him in doing so, Paul

[44] See also Bray, *Creeds*, 26–27.
[45] Pelikan, *Credo*, 130.

provides a variety of summaries of the faith (e.g. 2 Tim. 1:9–10).[46] Paul places a premium on his successor's conformity to a specific formulation of words: sayings that encapsulate the core of the apostolic teaching.

The bestowal of truth on human words

God has included *words* as a medium of self-revelation and has established humans – and our words – as agents in that revelation. As Bray has commented, 'the fundamental assertion of the Bible is that God can and does speak to mankind in a way which enables us to make an intelligent response'.[47] Likewise, responding to Hebrews 1:1–2, Levering writes that revelation includes its mediation through the believing community: 'God evidently intended for his revelatory words and deeds to be mediated by the people formed by his covenantal love.'[48]

In his early lectures, Karl Barth asked on what basis Christian theologians dare to speak about God. In terms of order of access, it is on the strength of the human words of the apostles.[49] But on what basis did *they* dare to speak about God?

> The prophets and apostles could no more talk about God than we can. Their witness, then, is this: *Deus dixit*, God has spoken. Scripture is the basis of preaching, but it, too, has a basis in a third thing even further back. It is the witness to revelation. But in this distinction between the historical witness and the revelation itself to which it bears witness, scripture itself as the words of the apostles and prophets is the Word of God, the permission and the command to speak about God.[50]

For Barth, the beginning of the knowledge of God is the act in which God speaks. It is this *actuality* that makes *possible* human speech about him. The speech of God is an act of generosity in which God, the speaker, enables the start of a series in which humans can speak of him. In his more mature writings, Barth would come to nuance this distinction between the historical witness and the incarnate Word of God. It is significant that Barth's principal theological work is entitled *Church Dogmatics* as opposed to *Christian Dogmatics*. Barth's very purpose was to challenge the proposition that theology

46 Trueman, *Creedal Imperative*, 72–79.

47 Bray, *Creeds*, 37.

48 Levering, *Engaging the Doctrine of Revelation*, 1.

49 K. Barth, *Göttingen Dogmatics: Instruction in the Christian Religion*, vol. 1, ed. H. Reiffen, tr. G. W. Bromiley (Grand Rapids, Mich.: Eerdmans, 1990), 51–53.

50 Ibid. 56.

is some act elevated above the activity of the church that can operate independent of the basic identity of the church.[51] This is important because the church is a creature of the Word of God; it exists in dependence and faith on the will of the Father to bring it into existence through Christ and in the power of the Spirit. Theology, along with the rest of the life of the church, cannot proceed apart from the church's faith in the act of the triune God, which always takes precedence. The act that God has undertaken is to speak his Word, and this Word of God encounters us in flesh, in Scripture and in proclamation. For the later Barth, the Word of God comes to us in a threefold form in which the inner foundation is the act of God, which is known to us through the human responses of Scripture and the preaching that draws on Scripture.[52] This means that God co-opts, as it were, human speech to be a vehicle of his own Word, including our human hearing and speaking in the act of God's revelatory, saving address to humanity.

If human speech is really included by God as a vehicle of the Word of God, then the teaching of the church is invested with an authority that returns us to Barth's question: On what basis do Christian theologians dare to speak about God? Alongside the Christological basis, there is a pneumatological basis. Yves Congar describes the Holy Spirit as the 'transcendent subject' of tradition, while the church is the 'historical subject' of tradition.[53] By this Congar means something surprisingly similar to Barth but parsed differently: God includes the tradition of the church in his act of revelation. Congar distinguishes between the stage of delivery, in which the Son becomes flesh, and the stage of transmission, in which the church makes its proclamation. The Spirit, for Congar, is 'ever active in this stage [transmission] to actualize the Word of God in the Church'.[54] The historical witness of the church, which evolves along with the society to which the witness is made, is enabled to contain revelation by the Spirit. In other words, the Spirit through whom the Word is incarnate in time is the Spirit through whom the Word is made present in the confessions of the church.

It is for this reason that Barth – drawing on Martin Luther – is able to say that

> dogmatics is possible only as a *theologia crucis* [theology of the cross], in the act of obedience which is certain in faith, but which for this very

---

[51] Barth, *CD*, 1.1, 12.

[52] Ibid. 88–120. See also Webster's discussion of this theme. J. Webster, *Barth* (London: Continuum, 2000), 55–57.

[53] Y. Congar, *The Meaning of Tradition*, tr. A. N. Woodrow (San Francisco, Calif.: Ignatius Press, 1964), 47–81.

[54] Ibid. 48.

> reason is humble, always being thrown back to the beginning and having to make a fresh start.[55]

This means that the task of the church's enquiry into its own proclamation is not simply the memorizing and repetition of dogmas; instead, it is an act of faith as we return again and again to the Word of God such that it may be received and responded to again by the words of the church. This absolute priority of the first event (being the self-revelation of God through Christ and by the Spirit) negates the second event (being the church's talk about God), but the second does not replace the first.[56] Instead, the second act remains a truly human statement, the truth of which has come from beyond the human realm of possibility, whereby to speak it and reflect upon it can only ever be an act of faith and obedience.[57] This highly personal approach to revelation is not discontinuous with the propositional character of God's self-communication. O'Collins, for whom the personal nature of revelation is essential to his 'fundamental theology',[58] considered it integral to revelation that God's revelation is transmitted, handed on 'through the community of the experience of God's revelation'.[59] The experiential basis is not incommunicable, but is able to be articulated in propositional form and passed on.[60]

Truth

Thomas F. Torrance held that the existence of truth independent from the mind who contemplates it is fundamental to knowledge. That is, something is what it is, and its nature is discovered, not imposed:

> The truth is that which is what it is and that which discloses what it is as it is. The concept of truth enshrines at once the reality of things and the revelation of things as they are in reality. Truth comes into view in its own majesty, freedom and authority, compelling us by the power of what it is to assent to it and acknowledge it for what it is in itself.[61]

In Torrance's view, truth belongs to reality. To know something is to know it 'according to its nature or reality, in terms of what it actually and really

55 Barth, *CD*, 1.1, 14.
56 Ibid. 12.
57 Ibid. 17.
58 O'Collins, *Retrieving Fundamental Theology*, 41.
59 Ibid. 44.
60 Ibid. 67.
61 T. F. Torrance, *Transformation and Convergence in the Frame of Knowledge: Explorations in the Interrelations of Scientific and Theological Enterprise* (Belfast: Christian Journals, 1984), 303.

is'.[62] This means that the truthfulness of human thought and statements is not determined by any other criteria (e.g. their inner coherence or their conformity to preset rules for what constitutes valid reasoning) than their conformity to what is there.

Christianity encourages a realist perspective towards truth: Jesus identified himself as Truth. To challenge the ontological status of truth is to challenge the existence of Jesus himself. Truth is not culturally defined or subjectively posited. It is within the fundamental convictions of Christianity that truth exists beyond the one who apprehends it and has its own content beyond that which is attributed to it. The doctrine of creation has also been fertile ground for Christian realism: God made the world, and it does not have existence only within the mind of the human knower. The doctrine of the Trinity, too, provides a strong realist bent to Christian thought, as the way God acts in space and time is the revelation of the way he exists as Father, Son and Spirit in eternity. The threefold structure of the saving events, in other words, is not a matter of human organization. Instead, God's saving self-revelation (his transitive relations) is by the will of the Father, through the Son in the power of the Spirit because it is firmly rooted in God's internal (non-transitive) relations:

> The truth of God is that he is who he is and that he reveals who he is as he is. The truth of God is the self-subsistent being of God in which he is open to himself in his being who he is, and in which he reveals himself to us as he is in his own reality . . . What God is towards men he is eternally in himself, and what he is in himself he is faithfully towards men.[63]

Among other things, this means that theology does not impose logical order upon revelation. The purpose of theology, within a realist mindset, is to expose the deep-lying logic of what God has shown us of himself; to have our mind conformed to the trinitarian structure of the way God has acted in creation because this, ultimately, is the patterning of our thought in accordance with the truth of God. This is why Torrance called the doctrine of the Trinity the 'ground and grammar of theology', for it is here that 'we find the knowledge of God reposing upon the final Reality of God himself, grounded in the ultimate relations intrinsic to God's own Being'.[64]

---

62 T. F. Torrance, *Incarnation: The Person and Life of Christ*, ed. R. T. Walker (Downers Grove, Ill.: IVP Academic, 2008), 202.

63 Torrance, *Transformation and Convergence*, 303.

64 T. F. Torrance, *The Ground and Grammar of Theology* (Belfast: Christian Journals, 1980), 158–159.

The Nicene Creed does not take its organization from the church or from theologians. Instead, it is shaped and determined by the trinitarian structure of God's revelation, which is ultimately determined by the existence of the one God as Father, Son and Spirit. For this reason, Fairbairn and Reeves describe the creeds as 'the grammar of Christian intimacy'.[65] This attractive phrase refers to the creeds as providing the rules for talk about God that is true of God. Creeds do not draw us away from Scripture: their purpose is to help us read Scripture better.

65 Fairbairn and Reeves, *SCC*, 3.

1
Tradition

Tradition and the gospel

The word 'tradition' can provoke a strong response. For some, tradition is the tyranny of the dead, a force that protects self-interested hierarchies. For others, tradition is a fusty form of conservatism, a set of customs that are done that way because that is how they have always been done. For others, tradition refers to the continuity of a way of life or an ethos, preserving that which is good and necessary from one generation to the next. Within Christian thought, tradition takes on a more specific meaning.[1] The tradition of the church is not mere conservativism; it is not only an ethos or way of life and – especially – it is not a callous elitism. Tradition, as derived from *traditio*, a Latin translation of the Greek *paradōsis*, means to 'hand over'. Alongside the use of the term to refer to Paul's heritage in Judaism (e.g. Gal. 1:14; Col. 2:8), Dunn identifies four categories of tradition in the Pauline corpus:

1 Kerygmatic tradition: the apostolic proclamation of the gospel (1 Cor. 15:1–3).
2 Church tradition: practices of the church instituted by Jesus that govern the activity of the worshipping community (e.g. 1 Cor. 11:23–25).
3 Ethical tradition (or the 'Jesus tradition'): guidelines for conduct and moral responsibilities derived from the example of Jesus (e.g. 1 Cor. 7:10; Phil. 3:17).

[1] There was a burst of attention to the concept of tradition and its use in early Christianity in the middle of the twentieth century. G. L. Prestige, *Fathers and Heretics* (London: SPCK, 1954); E. Fleeseman-van Leer, *Tradition and Scripture in the Early Church* (Assen: Van Gorcum, 1954); O. Cullmann, 'The Tradition', in *The Early Church* (London: SCM Press, 1956), 55–99; J. N. D. Kelly, *Early Christian Doctrines* (New York: Harper Torchbooks, 1958); R. P. C. Hanson, *Tradition in the Early Church* (London: SPCK, 1962); G. Florovsky, 'The Function of Tradition in the Ancient Church', *GOTR* 9 (1963), 181–200; A. C. Outler, 'The Sense of Tradition in the Ante-Nicene Church', in E. E. Cushman and E. Grislis (eds.), *The Heritage of Christian Thought* (New York: Harper & Row, 1965), 8–30; Y. Congar, *Tradition and Traditions: An Historical Essay and a Theological Essay* (London: Burns & Oates, 1966).

4 Tradition in the Pastoral Epistles: a consolidated body of propositional sayings that represent a sound summary of the content of the three other categories of tradition (1 Tim. 1:20; 2 Tim. 3:10 [kerygmatic tradition]; 1 Tim. 4:8; 6:3 [ethical tradition]; 3:1 [church tradition]).[2]

Tradition, in this broad sense, is the apostolic gospel, including how this informs belief, worship, praxis and ethics, as they have been received and passed on by the church. Athanasius referred to 'the actual original tradition, teaching and faith of the Catholic Church which the Lord bestowed, the apostles proclaimed and the fathers safeguarded'.[3] This describes the living process whereby the community established around and within the person of Jesus Christ handed on that which was entrusted to them by the apostles. Tradition, then, has two aspects. It refers both to the body of convictions that formed the content of the apostolic preaching and to the living act by which the church passes on that which has been received.[4] These two aspects form the basis of George Tavard's delineation of tradition with the categories transmission, development and memory.[5] This basic taxonomy is used here but developed slightly by the introduction of the category of the people of God.

Tradition and transmission

Eusebius of Caesarea described tradition as the succession from the apostles.[6] Similarly, the document *Dei Verbum* suggests, 'Tradition transmits in its entirety the word of God which has been entrusted to the apostles by Christ the Lord and the Holy Spirit.'[7] Tradition here refers to the act of handing on and to the object that is handed on.[8] That which is handed on is the apostolic preaching (the *kerygma*) concerning Jesus, and the act of handing it on takes place within the community of the church. Understood as transmission, then, tradition is

---

[2] J. Dunn, *Unity and Diversity in the New Testament: An Inquiry into the Character of Earliest Christianity* (London: SCM Press, 1977), 66–70.

[3] Athanasius of Alexandria, *Letters to Serapion*, 1.28. K. Anatolios, *Athanasius* (London: Routledge, 2004), 214–233.

[4] See also Congar, *Meaning of Tradition*, 125. Ferguson distinguishes between the active (the activity of handing over) and passive (the body of beliefs) senses of tradition that are handed over. E. Ferguson, *Paradōsis* and *Traditio*: A Word Study', in R. J. Rombs and A. Y. Hwang (eds.), *Tradition and the Rule of Faith in the Early Church: Essays in Honor of Joseph T. Lienhard* (Washington, D.C.: Catholic University of America Press, 2010), 3–29, at 4.

[5] See M. E. Alexander, 'G. H. Tavard's Concept of Tradition', in K. Hagen (ed.), *The Quadrilog: Tradition and the Future of Ecumenism* (Collegeville, Minn.: Liturgical Press, 1994), 287–311.

[6] Eusebius of Caesarea, *Ecclesiastical History*, ed. and tr. K. Lake, 2 vols. (Cambridge, Mass.: Harvard University Press), 1.1.1.

[7] *DV*, 9 (p. 117).

[8] G. O'Collins SJ, 'Revelation, Tradition and Scripture', in G. O'Collins SJ and M. Farrugia SJ (eds.), *Catholicism: The Story of Catholic Christianity* (Oxford: Oxford University Press, 2003).

the continual handing on of God's saving self-revelation in Christ, which was passed to us through the authoritative witness of the apostles. As Levering puts it 'tradition is the Church's faithful communication of the doctrines and practices of Christian faith across the generations'.[9]

The mechanism of this handing on is complex, including what the church does and also what the church is. The church is the community established by Christ and 'through her [God] communicates truth and grace to all'.[10] This takes place in the preaching of the church, its teaching and also in the life of the community as ways of being and worshipping have been received.[11] As Williams has put it, tradition as transmission involves 'the acceptance and the handing over of God's Word, Jesus Christ, and how this took form in the apostles' preaching' and in baptism, the Lord's supper and the worship of the Christian community.[12] This perspective reminds us that this is not the transmission of a museum piece, but is the ongoing presence of the kingdom of God today, shining out in the church's life, worship and witness.[13]

Congar has suggested that the tradition of the church needs to be understood within a broader view of transmission that has its origin in the will of the Father. The church is the recipient of a commission to guard the treasure of the apostolic witness to Christ. In this, the church is only part of a chain that extends to Jesus Christ's sending out the apostles as witnesses to his resurrection, which itself is rooted in the sending out of the Son from the Father in the power of the Spirit (John 17:18; 20:21). Christ himself is the one in whom God has revealed himself, and this revelation was entrusted to the apostles and, through the apostles, to the church.[14] For Congar, there is a flow of things being handed on from one to the other that ultimately ties the tradition of the church to the gospel itself.[15] The tradition of the church is the church handing on that which has been given to it: the gospel of the Son obeying the will of the Father by the power of the Spirit. Or, as Clement of Rome wrote, 'Now, the gospel was

[9] Levering, *Engaging the Doctrine of Revelation*, 140.

[10] *Lumen Gentium*, ed. W. M. Abbot SJ and tr. J. Gallacher, *The Documents of Vatican II: With Notes and Comments by Catholic, Protestant and Orthodox Authorities* (London: Geoffrey Chapman, 1967), 8 (p. 22).

[11] A World Council of Churches statement draws helpful distinctions: 'Tradition' is the Gospel transmitted from generation to generation in and by the church. On the other hand, 'traditions' refers to the differences between the different denominations. 'The Tradition' is the very life of the church as the body of Christ that has its source in the act of God in Christ and the Spirit. 'The Report of the Theological Commission on Tradition and Traditions', *Faith and Order Paper* 40 (Geneva: World Council of Churches, 1963), 105–112.

[12] Williams, *Retrieving*, 36.

[13] *Lumen Gentium*, 5, 8 (pp. 17–18, 22–24).

[14] See also Irenaeus of Lyons, *AH*, 3.5.1.

[15] Congar, *Meaning of Tradition*, 10–15.

given to the Apostles for us by the Lord Jesus Christ; and Jesus the Christ was sent from God. That is to say, Christ received his commission from God, and the Apostles theirs from Christ.'[16] This undergirds a fundamental unity of mind between Christ and his church, as Ignatius wrote, '[As Christ] represents the mind of the Father, so our bishops . . . represent the mind of Jesus Christ'.[17]

This perspective reminds us that the content of tradition does not *belong* to the church. While it may have its life within the people of God, it has its source beyond the people of God. A letter (probably from the second century AD) by an unnamed author makes this point very clearly:

> It is not an earthly discovery that has been entrusted to [the church]. The thing they guard so jealously is no product of mortal thinking, and what has been committed to them is the stewardship of no human mysteries. The Almighty Himself, the Creator of the universe, the God whom no eye can discern, has sent down His very own Truth from heaven, His own holy and incomprehensible Word, to plant it among men and ground it in their hearts.[18]

The object the church cherishes and passes on has come from outside itself and is held by the church as something *given* to it.[19] The tradition of the church is the apostolic gospel as it was passed to the first generation and believers and subsequently on through the various generations of the church. In his letters to Timothy, Paul encourages this apparently timid leader to 'guard the good treasure entrusted to you, with the help of the Holy Spirit' (2 Tim. 1:14). This good treasure is the gospel as Timothy received it from Paul. It is the apostolic witness to the act of God: the incarnation of God the Son, and his obedience in the flesh, death, resurrection and ascension.[20]

Tradition and the people of God

As the content of tradition is given to the church from beyond itself and yet has its life within the people of God, it has a very particular relation to the church as the people of God. The church possesses its tradition as a *gift* that is the ground of its existence. Therefore, the apostolic tradition establishes the

---

16 Clement of Rome, 'The First Epistle of Clement to the Corinthians', in A. Louth (ed.), M. Stamforth (tr.), *Early Christian Writings: The Apostolic Fathers* (London: Penguin Books, 1987), 42.

17 Ignatius of Antioch, 'The Epistle to the Ephesians', in Louth and Stamforth, *Early Christian Writings*, 3.

18 'The Epistle to Diognetus', in ibid. 7.

19 Webster challenges a collapse of Scripture into the tradition of the church. Webster, *Holy Scripture*.

20 See Pelikan, *Credo*, 383–388.

parameters of the church before the church establishes the parameters of tradition. As the second-century bishop Irenaeus of Lyons said, the church is given uniformity of belief by the tradition that has been given to it:

> The Church, though dispersed throughout the whole world, even to the ends of the earth, has received from the apostles and their disciples this faith: [She believes] in one God, the Father Almighty, Maker of heaven, and earth . . . and in one Christ Jesus, the Son of God . . . and in the Holy Spirit . . . The Church, having received this preaching and this faith, although scattered throughout the whole world, yet, as if occupying but one house, carefully preserves it. She also believes these points [of doctrine] just as if she had but one soul, and one and the same heart, and she proclaims them, and teaches them, and hands them down, with perfect harmony, as if she possessed only one mouth.[21]

Despite its multiplicity of locations and languages there is a unity to the one church, which is grounded in the reception of that which has come from beyond itself. If this were not the case, then the tradition of the church would be fully justified in receiving an institutional expression that is earthed in nothing beyond the church. That would be the basis of a shallow, inflexible dogmatism. Instead, our relation to tradition should be expressed less in terms of *servility* and more in terms of a corporate *fidelity*.[22] It is our corporate faithfulness to the gospel as we have received it. It is always open beyond itself to its fundamental content, which is the life and work of Jesus Christ as passed on to us by the apostles.

The second reason why tradition is best understood in relation to the category 'the people of God' is that revelation is inseparable from salvation. As Webster points out, God reveals himself in the economy of salvation in which 'God wills, establishes and perfects saving fellowship with himself in which humankind come to know, love and fear him.'[23] God's act in Christ is instantly a movement of revelation and of reconciliation.[24] In the same way *Dei Verbum*, reflecting on Ephesians 1:9, treats revelation and salvation as distinct but inseparable realities: 'through this revelation [God] speaks to [humans] as friends and lives among them, so that He may invite and take them into fellowship with himself'.[25]

21 Irenaeus, *AH*, 1.10–11.
22 Congar, *Meaning of Tradition*, 3.
23 Webster, *Holy Scripture*, 13.
24 Torrance, *Incarnation*, 77–79.
25 *DV*, 2 (p. 112).

Revelation, in other words, is not merely the giving of propositions to bridge the 'noetic divide' between us and God.[26] Instead, it is a *personal* act in which God communicates himself and establishes us in communion with him and with one another. For this reason, the only locus for theological thought is the people whom God has established in relation to himself.

Tradition is not controlled by the church, but is inseparable from the *people* who celebrate together the good news of Jesus Christ. It is that which is believed by the communities established by the apostles. In terms of historical order, these worshipping communities were the first repository of the apostolic teaching. As will be explored below, the belief and practice of these communities was integral to the interpretation of the apostolic writings. The communities lived out, consolidated and passed on the faith they received *by the practice of it.* In this way, Christian life and belief are 'corporate' and 'communal', 'something we receive and in which we are incorporated and take part'.[27] Tradition has its setting within the life of a community. So, while tradition has its ultimate ground beyond itself in the person and work of Christ, it is the gospel such as the people of God have received it, lived it and passed it on. The tradition of the church is the transmission of the faith we have received through the vitality of a living community.

The development of tradition

As it has its setting within a living community, tradition is not static. *Dei Verbum* recognizes this by referring to the ongoing presence of Christ in his church by the Spirit, through which there is progress in understanding:

> The tradition which comes from the apostles develops in the Church with the help of the Holy Spirit. For there is growth in insight into the realities and the words that have been handed down . . . For as the centuries succeed one another, the Church constantly moves forward toward the fullness of divine truth until the words of God reach their complete fulfilment in her.[28]

This growth in understanding is not the introduction of new revelation or some departure from the gospel. It is a growing intimacy with the truth revealed through Christ and by the Spirit. In part, this is inseparable from the telos of

[26] A. T. B. McGowan, *The Divine Spiration of Scripture: Challenging Evangelical Perspectives* (Nottingham: Apollos, 2007), 21.

[27] Congar, *Meaning of Tradition*, 29.

[28] *DV*, 8 (p. 116).

the church as an eschatological people.[29] The belief of the church has the character of waiting in hope and moving towards that belief's fulfilment. The role of *theology*, then, exists in a reciprocal relationship with tradition: theology is founded upon tradition,[30] but is also the mechanism of its further development. In part, this is indicative of the primacy of Scripture: theology does not have this reciprocal relationship with Scripture, which remains without development. However, dogmatics must always be *constructive* dogmatics.

John Henry Newman argued in his *Essay on the Development of Christian Doctrine* (1845) for the continuity in the gospel preached by the church from the first generation to the present day. The continuity, though, is not simple: there has been development in the church's understanding. However, this development is not indicative of a change in doctrinal content;[31] tradition develops as time moves on and new contexts adapt, giving rise to different modes of thought that provide insights into the truth we have received.[32]

> [the Scriptures] were intended to create an idea, and that idea is not in the sacred text, but in the mind of the reader; and the question is, whether that idea is communicated to him, in its completeness and minute accuracy, on its first apprehension, or expands in his heart and intellect, and comes to perfection in the course of time.[33]

Development takes place with regard to the idea located within the mind of the church. This idea developed at a remarkable pace in the early centuries, with a series of councils establishing doctrines we now view as foundational: the trinitarian formula of one God in three persons differentiated by modes of origin and the Christological formula of the union of two natures without confusion or separation in the person of God the Son incarnate. Orthodoxy has taken a historical course characterized by growing terminological precision by which to articulate with greater clarity the faith received from the apostles. These developments were lived responses to contemporary questions and controversies, in which followers of Christ drew on the intellectual resources of the world around them to gain a closer understanding of the truth they had received from the apostles.

---

29 *Lumen Gentium*, 48–51 (pp. 78–85).

30 *DV*, 24 (p. 127).

31 Newman gives seven tests of continuity in development. J. H. Newman, *An Essay on the Development of Christian Doctrine*, 2nd edn (London: James Toovey, 1846), 24–34.

32 See T. Tilley, *Inventing Catholic Tradition* (New York: Orbis Books, 2000).

33 Newman, *Development of Christian Doctrine*, 35.

As Robert Jenson put it, the church must be concerned by its identity across time. What is it that makes the church of today the same as the church of the apostles? For Jenson, the church is the community of the '*message* that the God of Israel has raised his servant Jesus from the dead'.[34] This same message must be heard and internalized by each new generation in each new cultural and historical situation.[35] This means that the contemporary church must have its say in receiving the inheritance of faith that has been passed down and exploring that inheritance and articulating it from the perspectives provided by that generation. The content of the tradition remains the same but the way in which it is articulated and passed on will be unique to the church's various circumstances today. Hanson used the image of a ship tied by a length of rope to a centre point: the wind and waves move the ship to different points of orientation to the centre point but it still remains tethered to its source.[36] The truth of the gospel does not change, for 'Jesus Christ is the same yesterday and today and for ever' (Heb. 13:8). However, as Williams describes, 'tradition has always functioned dynamically within the concrete moments of history, [so] its essential character involves the duality of conservatism and change'.[37] Tradition, in the aspect of its development, is a dialogue between that which has been received and the needs and concerns of any given present.

The development of tradition, then, is not an alteration of content. Instead, it is a growing insight into the deposit handed on to us by the apostles. The context and culture in which the people of God receive that faith does change and this provides new insights that give explicit expression to that which was believed implicitly until that point. The development of the Christian tradition, then, is not the introduction of new ideas; it is the application of new modes of thought through which that which is known implicitly within the corporate faith of the community is given more specific and conceptual formation:

> Tradition brings to the surface of consciousness elements previously imprisoned in the depths of faith and of its practice, rather than expressed, expounded and reasoned. So this conservative and protective force is also instructive and progressive. Looking lovingly toward the past, where its

---

[34] R. Jenson, *Canon and Creed: Interpretation: Resources for the Use of Scripture in the Church* (Louisville, Ky.: Westminster John Knox Press, 2010), 3; emphasis original.

[35] Ibid. 4.

[36] R. P. C. Hanson, *The Continuity of Christian Doctrine* (New York: Seabury Press, 1981), 83.

[37] D. H. Williams, *Evangelicals and Tradition: The Formative Influence of the Early Church* (Grand Rapids, Mich.: Baker Academic, 2005), xxiii.

> treasure is enshrined, tradition advances toward the future, where its victory and glory lie.[38]

In this sense, tradition involves conceptualizing that which is already known tacitly by faith. To engage with the tradition of the church, therefore, is to receive the inheritance of believers who have gone before us and who have faithfully received and passed on the faith of the church within their own moment. We bring the insights unique to our generation, owing to the questions of our age and, by so doing, that which is known in inchoate form is catalysed into explicit knowledge. Similarly, in a document discussing the formation of priests, the study of philosophy is recommended to facilitate 'dialogue with the [people] of their own day'.[39]

Tradition as memory

For some, tradition is euphemistic for the power grab of an ecclesial institution. To some extent, this is healthy. It is good to be aware of the darker orientations of our heart because we have got to know what we are up to! We have within us the capacity to prefer our doctrine and practices over their proper ground in the gospel. This is not a danger that knows denominational boundaries. The Protestant Church is as vulnerable to advancing its own traditions ahead of Scripture as is the Roman Catholic Church. The sin of loving our own institutions and schemas more than the gospel is no more at home in Rome than it is in Geneva, Wittenberg or Canterbury. There is, however, something unique to Protestantism, which is that it has a proclivity to allow suspicion of tradition to become wholesale *rejection*. Protestantism's very genesis was a reaction against the separation of church dogma and practice from the proper authority in Scripture. While the mainstream Protestants did not set about the total repudiation of the idea of a received faith, at its outer edges the 'Radical Reformation'[40] desired not simply to return to tradition properly integrated with
the apostolic witness in Scripture but a wholesale rejection of the idea that the apostolic gospel could be passed on by the church as an institution.[41]

---

[38] M. Blondel, 'Histoire et dogme: les lacunes de l'exégèse moderne', in *La Quinzaine* 56 (January and February 1904), 145–167, 349–373, 433–458.

[39] *Optatam Totius*, ed. W. M. Abbot SJ and tr. J. Gallacher, *The Documents of Vatican II: With Notes and Comments by Catholic, Protestant and Orthodox Authorities* (London: Geoffrey Chapman, 1967), 15 (p. 450).

[40] G. H. Williams, *The Radical Reformation* (Philadelphia, Pa.: Westminster Press, 1962).

[41] D. Janz, *Three Reformation Catechisms: Catholic, Anabaptist, Lutheran* (New York: Edwin Mellen Press, 1982), 133–140; A. McGrath, *Reformation Thought: An Introduction*, 2nd edn (Oxford: Blackwell, 1993), 135–136.

Some commentators see something similar to the extreme outer edges of the Protestant tradition in quarters of the contemporary evangelical church. Williams describes how tradition can be seen as inherently undermining the authority of Scripture, while statements such as creeds can be considered to be 'manifestations of a corrupted religious system or statements of ecclesiastical politics which were so culturally conditioned that they had no bearing for subsequent Christianity'.[42] Oden points to a culturally motivated separation from our past driven by the atmosphere of modernity which undermined the sense that the past could speak to our present, and argued that the evangelical church must return to its tradition to sustain it for the future.[43] Similarly, Mathison has argued that a cultural individualism has compromised the relationship between Scripture and tradition, leading to the impoverishing of evangelical theology and serving as a catalyst for a departure from Protestantism.[44] The current cultural atmosphere has not become any more conducive to encouraging listening to our past. Our current cultural moment prioritizes the right of self-determination predicated upon one's sense of oneself, directly antagonistic to any authority that may impose a standard.

In this context, it may be helpful to conceive of tradition as our *shared memory*. It is the collective act by which we call one another's minds to consider what God has done for us in Christ and to impress that experience upon each new generation. In this connection, Holmes has argued that to draw upon the heritage handed on to us is not an option we may or may not take up. Tradition is necessary to our identity as creatures and within the church. God made creatures to exist in time, and so, as creatures, we cannot abstract ourselves from a temporal sequence. We think as those who inherit very nearly two thousand years of history and cannot ignore that reality without disregarding a critical factor of what it is to be a creature.[45] Holmes also argues that our engaging with tradition is necessary because tradition is consistent with the very essence of the church as the body of Christ. We think as one communion of saints, in fellowship with those who came before us as we share together as those who have been included in Christ. We, the body of Christ, reflect on the gospel as we have received it from within – not from without.[46] McGrath approaches this from a different angle: our limitations as creatures. In order to be attentive to Scripture, McGrath argues, we need to recognize our intellectual

[42] Williams, *Retrieving*, 21.

[43] T. Oden, *After Modernity . . . What? Agenda for Theology* (Grand Rapids, Mich.: Zondervan, 1990).

[44] K. A. Mathison, *The Shape of Sola Scriptura* (Moscow, Ida.: Canon Press, 2001).

[45] S. R. Holmes, *Listening to the Past: The Place of Tradition in Theology* (Grand Rapids, Mich.: Baker Academic, 2002), 6.

[46] Ibid. 18–36.

and mortal constraints. If we are serious, McGrath suggests, about attending as faithfully as we can to Scripture, we must draw on the resource of our ecclesial heritage: 'we would be greatly assisted in the task of rendering a faithful and effective account of the biblical material if we were to draw on the rich witness of those who came before us'.[47]

Tradition and Scripture

Recognizing the risk of oversimplification, there are three very broad attitudes towards the relationship between Scripture and tradition: (1) tradition as supplementary to Scripture; (2) tradition as an ecclesial tool for the proper interpretation of Scripture; and (3) tradition as a mode of existence of the apostolic gospel, which regulates our interpretation of it.[48]

Tradition as supplementary

For some, tradition supplements that which is lacking in Scripture.[49] From this perspective, tradition is understood to be synonymous with the body of unwritten teaching of the apostles that is held within the community. Scripturally speaking, justification for this view is predicated upon a distinction Paul draws between the apostle's teaching in written and spoken form (2 Thess. 2:15). The *letters* of the apostles are occasional and orientated to specific problems. They are not intended to be exhaustive statements of Christian teaching and there is no systematic relating of the parts such that their aggregation provides an exhaustive account. Aside from this unwritten repository of apostolic teaching held in the corporate memory of the church, it is suggested the apostolic writings are incomplete. Scripture is seen not only as *formally insufficient* (in that it needs to be interpreted); it is seen to be *materially insufficient*, meaning that it does not contain every element of the apostolic teaching. As such, it requires completion from beyond itself in the practice and worship of the church, as the repository of the unwritten apostolic preaching. As Tony Lane comments, 'In practice, this attempt to find an apostolic foundation for ecclesiastical teaching was making the church herself, especially her life of worship, a source of doctrine.'[50]

---

47 A. E. McGrath, 'Engaging the Great Tradition: Evangelical Theology and the Role of Tradition', in S. Grenz and J. G. Stackhouse (eds.), *Evangelical Futures: A Conversation on Theological Method* (Grand Rapids, Mich.: Baker Books, 2000), 139–158, at 140.

48 A similar organization is suggested by Mathison, *Sola Scriptura*. Parallels are indicated in the footnotes.

49 'Tradition II', in ibid.

50 A. N. S. Lane, 'Scripture, Tradition and Church: An Historical Survey', *VE* 9 (1975), 37–55, 42.

It is a matter of significant dispute as to whether such a view was given formal articulation at the Council of Trent (1545–63) and whether it really has been the dominant character of Roman Catholic theology in the modern period.[51] The near-inclusion of the clause that the truth of the gospel was contained partly (*partim*) in Scripture and partly (*partim*) in unwritten form indicates that there was a significant body of opinion within the Council that Scripture and tradition contained complementary parts of the gospel and they needed to be taken together in order to be complete: Scripture and tradition as two equal but incomplete sources. However, the final formation of the clause strikes a compromise, referring to the truth of the gospel being contained in Scripture *and* in unwritten tradition, an ambiguity that allowed a variety of views to persist within Roman Catholic thought:[52] 'it remains permissible for a post-Tridentine Catholic to hold that all the truths of the Faith are to be found, if not formally expressed, then at least implied, in Scripture'.[53]

Tradition as a tool of interpretation

On the other hand, there is a view that tradition does not add to Scripture because in Scripture 'the universal Church of Christ has the most complete exposition of all that pertains to a saving faith'.[54] As such, tradition does not carry the authority of unwritten apostolic teaching held alongside Scripture.[55] However, this does not mean tradition can be jettisoned as an irrelevance: it carries authority as a guide in as much as it is found to cohere with the content of Scripture. Tradition, which is capable of being incorrect, is the church's corporate reception of the apostolic gospel. As such, even the most authoritative statements of the church's belief (such as the creeds formed at the early ecumenical councils) are assessed on the criterion of the degree to which they cohere with Scripture.[56] Tradition accepted on these terms becomes an

[51] For a helpful summary of this debate, see G. Moran, *Scripture and Tradition: A Survey of the Controversy* (New York: Herder & Herder, 1963).

[52] Examples of the softer interpretation that sees Scripture as containing all necessary to salvation that is complemented by tradition include J. R. Geiselmann, 'Scripture and Tradition in Catholic Theology', *TD* 6 (1958), 73–78; Congar, *Tradition and Traditions*, 165–166; H. Jedin, *A History of the Council of Trent*, tr. E. Graf, 2 vols. (Edinburgh: Thomas Nelson, 1967–71), esp. 2.52–98. Examples of the harder supplementary view include G. Ownes, 'Is All Revelation Contained in Sacred Scripture?', *Studia Montis Regii* 1 (1958), 55–60, and G. Moran, 'Scripture and Tradition: A Current Debate', *ACR* 38 (1961), 14–22.

[53] Y. Congar, 'Holy Writ and Holy Church', *Blackfriars* 41 (1960), 11–19, at 11.

[54] *Second Helvetic Confession*, 1.

[55] See J. Woodbridge, 'Role of "Tradition" in the Life and Thought of Twentieth Century Evangelicals', in C. Colson and R. J. Neuhaus (eds.), *Your Word Is Truth: A Project of Evangelicals and Catholics Together* (Grand Rapids, Mich.: Eerdmans, 2002), 103–146.

[56] T. George, 'Evangelical Reflection on Scripture and Tradition', in Colson and Neuhaus, *Your Word Is Truth*, 9–34.

invaluable tool in demarcating truthful from erroneous interpretations of Scripture.[57]

This is the view of the classical Reformers. John Calvin, for example, recognized the importance of standing within the *true* tradition of the church and insisted that the Reformed hermeneutic was more consistent with Christian tradition than was that of the contemporary Roman Church.[58] As Trueman puts it, '[Calvin] understood the Reformation not as Scripture versus tradition but as scriptural tradition versus unscriptural tradition'.[59] To Sadoleto (a Roman Catholic cardinal), Calvin wrote, 'our [Protestant] agreement with antiquity is far closer than yours, but that all we have attempted has been to renew that ancient form of the church'.[60] Correspondingly, Calvin had a high conception of the church as the mother of believers,[61] responsible for the teaching of believers in the faith as an accommodation to the reduced capacity of humanity. So important was this principle for Calvin that he wrote that any 'who refuses to be a son of the Church in vain desires to have God as his Father'.[62]

> Is not the Church the mother of believers? Does she not regenerate them by the Word of God, educate and nourish them through their whole life, strengthen and bring them at length to absolute perfection? For the same reason, also, she is called 'pillar of truth'; because the office of administering doctrine, which God hath placed in her hands, is the only instrument of preserving the truth, that it may not perish from the remembrance of [humanity].[63]

Consistent with this, in a section discussing the authority of councils, Calvin expresses his 'embrace and reverence as holy the early councils'. Crucially, though, their ultimate authority did not lie in the composition of the council itself, but in the grounds that councils 'contain nothing but the pure and genuine exposition of Scripture'.[64]

---

57 In Mathison's taxonomy, this is 'Tradition I'.

58 For more on this theme, see A. N. S. Lane, *John Calvin: Student of the Church Fathers* (Edinburgh: T&T Clark, 1999).

59 Trueman, *Credal Imperative*, 17.

60 J. Calvin, 'Reply to Cardinal Sadoleto', cited from J. C. Olin (ed.), *A Reformation Debate* (New York: Harper, 1966), 62.

61 J. Calvin, *Institutes of the Christian Religion*, ed. J. T. McNeill, tr. F. L. Battles (Philadelphia, Pa.: Westminster Press, 1960), 4.1. See also A. Irving, 'The Motherhood of the Church in John Calvin and Henri du Lubac', *IJSC* 18.1 (2018), 48–66.

62 J. Calvin, *Commentary on Galatians*, tr. W. Pringle (Grand Rapids, Mich.: Baker Books, 2005), 4.26, 141.

63 J. Calvin, *Commentary on 1 Timothy*, tr. W. Pringle (Grand Rapids, Mich.: Baker Books, 2005).

64 Calvin, *Institutes*, 4.9.8.

Similarly, the twenty-first article of the Church of England states that councils are capable of error and that their statements 'have neither strength nor authority unless it may be declared that they be taken out of holy Scripture'.[65] This does not indicate a disregard for tradition, but a Reformed distaste of tradition that had its ultimate source not in the gospel but in the church. For example, Richard Hooker held to the primacy of Scripture,[66] and recognized that the tradition of the church could err (and had done so in the case of his contemporary Roman Church) but did not see himself as involved in the creation of a new church, so much as a return to the consensus of faith shared by the church throughout its history.[67]

Rather than being a separate authority capable of justifying doctrines not found in Scripture, John Calvin saw tradition as having a 'critical ministering role',[68] one that saw tradition 'not as normative interpretation of Scripture nor as a necessary supplement to it but rather as a tool to be used to help the church to understand it'.[69] As such, it became a central tenet of Reformed theology to be deeply suspicious of private judgments regarding Scripture which deviated from the principle that individual passages needed, with the aid of the true inheritance of faith (with that inheritance defined as that which accords with Scripture), to be interpreted in the light of the whole.[70]

Tradition as a mode of the apostolic gospel

Finally, there is the view that Scripture and tradition coincide as different modalities of the apostolic gospel. They both have their source in the apostles' witness to Jesus, but are different modes by which that witness persists across time. The belief and practice of the church is coextensive with apostolic teaching also set forward in the Scriptures. In this view, tradition does not add to Scripture, but provides an authoritative *regulatory* framework for how Scripture should be interpreted. If a private interpretation of Scripture deviates from the interpretation held by the communities who hold the apostolic teaching in their corporate life, it has trespassed beyond the boundaries of the belief of the church and is, by definition, not apostolic.

Something very much like this appears to be the stance of the contemporary Roman Catholic Church as articulated in documents from the Second Vatican

65 *Thirty-nine Articles*, no. 21.

66 R. Hooker, *Of the Laws of Ecclesiastical Polity* (London: J. M. Dent, 1907), 1.13.2, 1; 5.8.2, 2.

67 Ibid. 4.9.1, 1. See also N. Atkinson, *Richard Hooker and the Authority of Scripture, Tradition and Reason: Reformed Theologian of the Church of England* (Milton Keynes: Paternoster Press, 1997), 38–45, 72–75.

68 McGrath, 'Engaging', 154.

69 Lane, 'Scripture, Tradition and Church', 43.

70 *First Helvetic Confession*, 29, 39.

Council. *Dei Verbum* identifies that God's revelation in Christ was transmitted by the witness of the apostles, and this apostolic witness comes in the form of written Scripture and the unwritten tradition of the apostles' preaching:

> Hence there exist a close connection and communication between sacred tradition and sacred Scripture. For both of them, flowing from the same divine wellspring, in a certain way merge into a unity and tend toward the same end. For sacred Scripture is the word of God inasmuch as it is consigned to writing under the inspiration of the divine Spirit. To the successors of the apostles, sacred tradition hands on in its full purity God's word, which was entrusted to the apostles by Christ the Lord and the Holy Spirit. Thus, led by the light of the Spirit of truth, these successors can in their preaching preserve this word of God faithfully.[71]

In this way, 'sacred tradition and sacred Scripture form one sacred deposit of the word of God, which is committed to the Church'.[72] However, this is not to say that Scripture and tradition are conceived of as identical in primacy. Instead, Scripture, as uniquely inspired by the Spirit has a distinctive and normative role in relation to the belief and praxis of the church. Tradition plays a role in supporting the primacy of Scripture: the church as the 'pillar and bulwark of truth' (1 Tim. 3:15). The church has received the apostolic tradition through which Scripture may be interpreted correctly. Therefore, the church is that which is able to interpret rightly and protect Scripture, which itself contains all that is necessary for salvation:

> The task of authentically interpreting the word of God, whether written or handed on, has been entrusted exclusively to the living teaching office of the Church ... This teaching office is not above the word of God but serves it, teaching only that which has been handed on, listening to it devoutly, guarding it scrupulously, and explaining it faithfully by divine commission and with the help of the Holy Spirit.[73]

Congar expresses something consistent with this when he writes that tradition is 'the communication of the entire heritage of the apostles, effected in a different way from that of their writings'.[74] For Congar, tradition is another mode of existence of the apostolic gospel: 'the saving gospel is contained entirely in

71 *DV*, 9 (p. 117).
72 Ibid. 10 (pp. 117–118).
73 Ibid.
74 Congar, *Meaning of Tradition*, 22.

the Scriptures as it is also contained entirely in tradition'.[75] In this, Congar sees tradition and Scripture at a point of fundamental harmony: they are passing on the same apostolic gospel, but in different ways. Therefore, 'Scripture contains, at least in the form of suggestion or principle, the entire treasury of truths which it is necessary to believe in order to be saved,'[76] and it is through the tradition of the church that Scripture is rightly understood.[77] Levering expresses a similar view: 'the content of divine revelation cannot be handed down, even in its Scriptural form, without being interpreted by the Church under the guidance of Christ and the Spirit'.[78] This best corresponds to the view of tradition in the early centuries of the church.

The reciprocity of Scripture and tradition

From the beginning, Scripture and tradition have coexisted in a relationship of reciprocity. This conviction is well expressed by Levering: 'it is not possible to conceive of Scripture, at any stage of its composition and collection into a canonical unity, outside of the liturgical community of the people of God'.[79] This grounding of Scripture within the church is reflected in Polycarp's comments to the church in Philippi:

> I am as far as anyone else of my sort from having the wisdom of our blessed and glorious Paul. During his residence with you he gave the men of those days clear and sound instruction of the word of truth. While he was there in person among them; and even after his departure he still sent letters which, if you study them attentively, will enable you to make progress in the faith which was delivered to you.[80]

The Christian community in Philippi inherited both Paul's teaching and the written text of his letter. These are not in tension but in reciprocity. This reciprocity was fundamental to the way in which believers identified and interpreted the repository of apostolic writings as they could be delimited by what was believed within the communities established and taught by the apostles. Scripture may well stand as the ultimate authority in all matters of faith, but it has never stood alone.

---

[75] Ibid. 42.
[76] Ibid. 116.
[77] See K. Rahner, 'Scripture and Tradition', *TD* 12.1 (1964), 3–7.
[78] Levering, *Engaging the Doctrine of Revelation*, 172–173.
[79] Ibid. 1.
[80] Polycarp of Smyrna, 'Letter to the Philippians', in Louth and Stamforth, *Early Christian Writings*, 3.

The apostles and tradition

Even in the most optimistic of analyses, there is a gap of some years between the events of God the Son's incarnate presence and the writing of the first apostolic texts. In this period, the apostles' witness to Christ became the body of an oral tradition 'passed on from teacher to pupil or from preacher to audience in an increasingly wide circle for some time before any of the oral tradition was put into writing'.[81] This apostolic gospel in the form of its being proclaimed (the *kerygma*) was its mode of existence prior to being committed to writing. The New Testament sometimes refers to this oral tradition as that which is handed on (*paradōsis*). Paul explicitly uses the word to refer to the content of that which has been received (1 Cor. 11:2; 2 Thess. 2:15; 3:6) but at other times this oral tradition is referred to more implicitly (John 21:20; Rom. 6:17; 1 Cor. 11:23; 15:1; 2 Peter 2:21).

This gap between the apostolic preaching and the commitment of the apostles' proclamation to writing means that the New Testament itself is couched within a pre-existing tradition.[82] The disciplines of form criticism and source criticism attempt to trace the sources of the biblical text in the shadowy world of theorized texts and oral traditions. They examine the complicated relationship between the biblical text and the apostolic communities who held the apostles' teaching. This fascinating line of inquiry has led to some important findings, such as the notion of some shared source ('Q') common to the Synoptic Gospels. However, its furthest extremes push too far in the direction that the Scriptures do not present us with a 'historical Jesus' but with a Christ dressed up in the hopes, fears and needs of the early Christian communities: a Christ created by the church, rather than a Christ received by the church. These extremities make Christians understandably suspicious of these methods, but, as Williams regrets, this has made some believers less aware of the reciprocal relationship between the apostolic writings and the apostolic teaching that formed the beliefs of the infant church before the emergence of the first apostolic texts.[83] This oral apostolic tradition would become the seedbed of the written apostolic witness in two ways: materially (in that it is the same content of the apostolic witness) and formally in distinguishing texts that are canonical from those that are not.

Materially speaking, the apostles established communities who consolidated their beliefs through practising those beliefs. They worshipped together,

[81] Hanson, *Tradition*, 8.
[82] J. Dunn, *The Oral Gospel Tradition* (Grand Rapids, Mich.: Eerdmans, 2013).
[83] Williams, *Retrieving*, 42–43.

confessed their faith together, were baptized and celebrated the Lord's Supper together. This internal culture of the church was shaped by the apostolic witness and would be drawn upon, consolidated and verified by the apostolic writings. For example, John is explicit in his Gospel that he is drawing from a reservoir of stories too many to be written down (John 21:25), but has chosen these events that circulated within the Christian communities in order that his audience might believe Jesus is the Son of God and have life in his name (John 20:30–31). By so doing, John validated these stories, consolidated their belonging within the Christian tradition and identified their meaning in relation to the life-giving purpose of God.

Paul, as a latecomer to the apostolic fold gives a unique insight into the creative relationship between the apostolic tradition already alive in the church and the apostolic writings. Paul writes, 'For I received from the Lord what I also handed on to you' (1 Cor. 11:23). He sees himself both as a recipient and as one who transmits. But Paul's reception of the gospel is not straightforward. As Dunn notes:

> On the one hand, [Paul] clearly expresses his gospel in the language of tradition handed over to him by his predecessors in the faith, while on the other he insists that his gospel came directly from God and not an inherited tradition.[84]

In Galatians, Paul is insistent that his gospel is not of human origin (Gal. 1:11–12) and did not require corroboration from the first disciples (Gal. 1:17) and did not need to be adapted or extended by them (Gal. 2:6). Clearly, Paul understood himself to be the recipient of a direct revelation that, to some extent, stood alongside the tradition taught by the other apostles. Paul earthed his authority in his personal encounter with Jesus Christ and the commissioning Paul received, which did not require any further corroboration (Gal. 1:15–16). On other occasions, however, Paul presents himself as the inheritor of a tradition already highly evolved within the Christian communities. For example, he describes what he has received in formulations that appear honed for repetition and transmission:

> For I handed on to you as of first importance what I in turn had received: that Christ died for our sins in accordance with the scriptures, and that he was buried, and that he was raised on the third day in

[84] Dunn, *Unity and Diversity*, 66.

> accordance with the scriptures, and that he appeared to Cephas, then to the twelve.
> (1 Cor. 15:3–5)

Dunn describes this as an example of *kerygmatic tradition*;[85] that is, a form of Christian proclamation about Christ that appears to have become a cornerstone of Christian instruction even within the first generation. In his letters to Timothy, Paul also draws upon stylized, perhaps even liturgical, statements that offer insights into the worshipping life of the apostolic communities (1 Tim. 2:5; 3:16) and refers to and verifies 'sayings' that have a liturgical character through reference to baptism:

> The saying is sure:
> if we have died with him, we will also live with him.
> (2 Tim. 2:11)

Ostensibly, there is a relationship here with Paul's developed theology in Romans 6 of baptism.

As Hanson notes, 'the Church from the earliest moment of its existence was a teaching Church',[86] and this 'continuous tradition of teaching within the Church, [was] often expressing itself in formulae',[87] short summaries of the doctrinal commitments of the apostolic gospel. As Bray helpfully describes, 'all the evidence suggests that it was a close-knit community which shared a comprehensive set of beliefs, even if these were not always set down in writing'.[88] There are far too many examples to consider here, but the New Testament is scattered with 'conventional summaries' of apostolic doctrine,[89] which had become, to some extent, established in the local churches (e.g. Rom. 8:34; 1 Tim. 2:5; 2 Tim. 2:8; 1 Peter 3:18).[90] One particularly interesting example of this form of instruction is Paul's formulaic statement regarding Christ's lineage and resurrection (Rom. 1:3–4). This closely knit, stylized theological statement bears parallels to an expanded formula used by Ignatius in his own pastoral instruction (see Table 2 on p. 40). This is an indication of a body of teaching within the communities established by the apostles that was passed down and used in the expression of and instruction in Christianity.

[85] Ibid. 66–67.
[86] Hanson, *Tradition*, 52.
[87] Ibid. 59.
[88] Bray, *Creeds*, 91.
[89] Kelly, *ECC*, 13.
[90] See Williams, *Retrieving*, 41–70.

Table 2 The parallel between Romans 1:3–4 and Trallians, 9

Romans 1:3–4	*Trallians, 9*
the gospel concerning his Son, who was descended from David according to the flesh and was declared to be Son of God with power according to the spirit of holiness by resurrection from the dead . . .	Christ was of David's line. He was the son of Mary; He was verily and indeed born, and ate and drank; He was verily persecuted in the days of Pontius Pilate, and verily and indeed crucified and gave up the ghost in the sight of all heaven and earth and the powers of the nether worlds. He was verily and indeed raised up again from the dead, for His Father raised him; and in Jesus Christ will His Father similarly raise us who believe in Him, since apart from him there is no true life for us.*

* Ignatius, 'The Epistle to the Trallians', in A. Louth (ed.) and M. Stamforth (tr.), *Early Christian Writings: The Apostolic Fathers* (London: Penguin Books, 1987), 9.

There remains a distinction between revelatory and immanent sources of Paul's reception of the gospel, which is unique for him as an apostle who began his apostolic ministry after the tradition had begun to take root in the apostolic communities. As such, he holds both sources of what he has received together within his own understanding of his apostolic ministry and authority. Clearly, there exists a fundamental compatibility between his ministry and authority such that he can establish his apostolic authority and interpretation of Jesus' death and resurrection on his unique encounter with Christ and still engage positively with the tradition that grew in the church. In this sense, Paul exemplifies the complex relationship the apostles had to the body of belief that had been established and expressed in the churches. The apostles were both the source of that body of belief held within the worshipping communities and the beneficiaries of it. They both established it and drew from it. This is well demonstrated in the Christ hymn of Philippians 2:5–11. This passage almost certainly pre-existed its use by Paul. It has the stylized form of a hymn or liturgical statement of faith. In citing from it, Paul both drew on this body of doctrine held by the worshipping community to guide his readers to a particular response and, by so doing, validated it as consistent with the apostolic gospel. However, the reciprocity does not end there. This statement, which appears to have emerged from the worshipping community, was described by Augustine as a 'rule for clearing the question [of the person of Christ] through all the Sacred Scriptures'.[91] If this reading is correct, then a hymn of the church,

[91] Augustine, *On the Trinity*, 1.7.

having been given apostolic validation, became a heuristic schema to determine the meaning of the apostolic writings.[92]

Formally, the belief about Christ held in the church served to set the boundaries between texts of genuine apostolic provenance and texts alien to that witness. The claim of apostolic authorship alone was insufficient, as many texts that styled themselves as authored by one apostle or another were soon in circulation (the pseudepigrapha): for example, the Gospels of *Thomas*, *Barnabas* and *Peter*. The beliefs and practices of the communities established by the apostles could act as a regulatory principle by which to determine which texts expressed the apostolic gospel and which did not:

> Canonicity was, from the beginning, a theological principle inherent to the church's Tradition; the 'canon' (i.e. the rule) of the church's faith was not a set of authoritative texts, but an authoritative teaching. Those texts which mirrored the canon (rule) of this faith, and had been received within the orthodox churches, were regarded as canonical.[93]

In other words, with the emergence of written texts the beliefs held within the church communities did not vanish as a source of authority. An unwritten body of beliefs and practices held by the communities established by the apostles regulated which texts were truly apostolic in origin and which were not.[94] As Kelly helpfully says, 'the testimony stood prior to the documents, and it would be more correct to say that the latter were valued precisely because they were held to enshrine the former'.[95] Scripture was seen to be Scripture on the grounds of its conformity to the church's body of beliefs and practice. Similarly, by drawing on the tradition of the church in their writings, the apostles consolidated and verified that tradition as a true reception of the apostolic gospel (e.g. Phil. 2:5–11). From the very beginning, Scripture and tradition were in a deep reciprocity, 'circulating in the Church side by side'.[96] This reciprocity continued as the apostolic age gave way to the post-apostolic age.

---

92 Pelikan, *Credo*, 135.

93 Williams, *Retrieving*, 45. See also Jenson, *Canon and Creed*, 33–41.

94 For a survey of the issues involved and a helpful overview of the scholarship, see J. J. Armstrong, 'From the *kanōn tēs alētheias* to the *kanōn tōn graphon*: The Rule of Faith and the New Testament Canon', in R. J. Rombs and A. Y. Hwang (eds.), *Tradition and the Rule of Faith in the Early Church: Essays in Honor of Joseph T. Lienhard* (Washington, D.C.: Catholic University of America Press, 2010), 30–47. See also J. T. Lienhard SJ, *The Bible, the Church, and Authority: The History of the Christian Bible in History and Theology* (Collegeville, Minn.: Liturgical Press, 1995).

95 Kelly, *Early Christian Doctrines*, 33.

96 Hanson, *Tradition*, 21.

After the apostles: the rule of faith

After the death of the apostles there was the urgent problem of establishing principles for valid interpretation of the apostolic texts. The urgency of this problem was due to the proliferation of texts claiming apostolic authority and the emergence of interpretative traditions that departed radically from the apostles' own teaching.[97] The problem, though, as John Behr describes, was a situation in which there was no authority by which individuals or groups could be identified as having departed from the apostolic teaching.[98] One such religious grouping (Gnostics) claimed a secret knowledge and tradition, supplementary to the apostolic writings, which had derived directly from the apostles' teaching. A Gnostic text, the *Gospel of Thomas*, claims access to 'secret words of Almighty God, which Lord Jesus Christ uttered and were scribed by his disciple Thomas'.[99] References to a secret tradition of Jesus' teaching passed on to individual apostles are scattered throughout texts of this sort.

How could the outer limits of what the church believed be established and maintained? On what terms could authentic Christian belief be differentiated from deviations from the apostolic preaching? Or, to put the matter in another way, how could true *catholicity* (belief in the whole gospel that is shared across the body of Christ, expressed in a common set of beliefs and practices) be distinguished from sects that laid claim to the apostolic tradition? Two important principles were established early on: (1) historical continuity with the apostles through the episcopacy, and (2) the doctrine preached and believed in the communities established by the apostles. The focus of this study is on the latter, but this cannot be held in isolation from the importance of the bishops, who were essential in demarcating the genuine apostolic tradition from deviations. Ignatius' letters offer a rich seam of thought regarding the centrality of the bishops and he instructs his readers to give 'your obedience to your bishop, as though he were Jesus Christ',[100] arguing that it is just this solidarity that will exclude 'wolves in plenty seeking to entrap the runners in God's race'.[101]

---

97 See E. Ferguson, '*Paradōsis* and *Traditio*: A Word Study', in R. J. Rombs and A. Y. Hwang (eds.), *Tradition and the Rule of Faith in the Early Church: Essays in Honor of Joseph T. Lienhard* (Washington, D.C.: Catholic University of America Press, 2010), 3–29.

98 J. Behr, *Irenaeus of Lyons: Identifying Christianity* (Oxford: Oxford University Press, 2013), 21–47. Rebecca Lyman provides an insightful and brief account of how the interaction with Gnosticism helped to shape an apostolic consciousness among the second-century believers. R. Lyman, *Early Christian Traditions* (Boston, Mass.: Cowley Publications, 1999), 37–61.

99 *The Gospel of Thomas*, 1, in A. Jacobs (tr.), *The Gnostic Gospels* (London: Watkins, 2006), 19.

100 Ignatius, 'Epistle to the Trallians', in Louth and Stamforth, *Early Christian Writings*, 2.

101 Ibid. See S. G. Hall, *Doctrine and Practice in the Early Church* (London: SPCK, 1991), 59–61; *DV*, 7.

Alongside this appeal for solidarity through obedience to the bishops, Ignatius also identifies genuine Christian belief in the form of the doctrinal content of Christianity in contradistinction to heresy.[102] His letters are characterized by frequent rebuttals of Docetism (the proposition that Jesus only *appeared* to be human). In his attempt to distinguish between genuine Christian doctrine about the person of Christ and false distortions, Ignatius appears to make use of already-existing Christian hymns:

> Very Flesh, yet Spirit too;
>   Uncreated, and yet born;
> God-and-Man in One agreed,
> Very-Life-in-Death indeed,
> Fruit of God and Mary's seed;
>   At once impassible and torn
> By pain and suffering here below:
> Jesus Christ, whom as Lord we know.[103]

This is the apostolic teaching that had taken root in the community and was beginning to be concretized as authoritative statements, delineating the tradition the community have received.

It was Irenaeus in his *Against the Heresies* that engaged in this task most fully.[104] In his reaction to Gnostic forms of exegesis, Irenaeus claims that the communities with a direct link to the apostles have interpretative primacy of the Scriptures. By contrast, Irenaeus presents Gnostic hermeneutics as the accommodation of Scripture to Gnostic pre-established opinions:

> Such, then, is their system [*hypothesis*], which neither the prophets announced, nor the Lord taught, nor the apostles delivered, but of which they boast that beyond all others they have a perfect knowledge. They gather their views from other sources than the Scriptures; and, to use a common proverb, they strive to weave ropes of sand, while they endeavour to adapt with an air of probability to their own peculiar assertions the parables of the Lord, the sayings of the prophets, and the words of the apostles, in order that their scheme may not seem altogether without support. In doing so, however, they disregard the order and the connection of the Scriptures, and so far as in them lies, dismember and destroy

102 Pelikan, *Credo*, 102.
103 Ignatius, 'Epistle to the Ephesians', in Louth and Stamforth, *Early Christian Writings*, 7.
104 See Behr, *Irenaeus*, 73–120.

> the truth. By transferring passages, and dressing them up anew, and making one thing out of another, they succeed in deluding many through their wicked art in adapting the oracles of the Lord to their opinions.[105]

Irenaeus' complaint is that Gnostic exegesis of Scripture was established on their own pre-existing framework and theosophical system, which they applied like a Procrustean bed to chop, stretch and shape words of Scripture to fit their own schema. To describe this, Irenaeus employs a term (*hypothesis*) derived from Hellenic rhetorical theory.[106] This refers to the '"overarching story" by which the scriptures were to be read and interpreted',[107] a broader schema or set of axiomatic principles in relation to which the constituent parts must be understood.[108] The problem with Gnostic exegesis, Irenaeus argues, is that it operates with a *hypothesis* alien to Scripture and the beliefs held by the apostolic communities. As such, the meaning of Scripture can be reconstructed just as a mosaic once organized in the form of a king can be reconfigured 'as to make them into the form of a dog or of a fox'.[109]

Irenaeus replaces the Gnostic *hypothesis* with a distinctively Christian 'general scheme of faith'.[110] In part, this is through Scripture alone for which Irenaeus provides a series of hermeneutical rules.[111] Individual texts must be understood in relation to the unity of the scriptural canon; namely, the Hebrew Scriptures and other apostolic writings.[112] Ayres offers the example of *Against Heresies*, 3.7, where Irenaeus, on the basis of broader familiarity with Paul's way of writing and theological commitments, refutes the Valentinian notion that Paul's reference to the 'God of this world' did not imply another deity.[113] This is an important principle to hold in mind before turning to think about the rule

105 Irenaeus, *AH*, 1.8.1.

106 For a discussion of the literary and rhetorical context of Irenaeus' use of *hypothesis*, see Behr, *Irenaeus*, 105–106, 112–113. See also D. W. Jorgensen, *Treasure Hidden in a Field: Early Christian Reception of the Gospel of Matthew* (Berlin: W. de Gruyter, 2016), 39–40. On the failures of Valentinian exegesis from Irenaeus' perspective, see E. Osborn, *Irenaeus of Lyons* (Cambridge: Cambridge University Press, 2001), 173–175.

107 F. M. Young, *Biblical Exegesis and the Formation of Christian Culture* (Cambridge: Cambridge University Press, 1997), 44.

108 Behr, *Irenaeus*, 112.

109 Irenaeus, *AH*, 1.8.1.

110 Ibid. 10.3. See P. Molodet-Jitea, 'The Preamble of the Gospel According to John – Its Significance in the Hermeneutical Conflict Between the Bishop Irenaeus of Lyons and the Gnostic School of Valentinus', *Hermeneia* 17 (2016), 134–145.

111 Laid out in P. S. Grech, 'The *Regula Fidei* as a Hermeneutical Principle in Patristic Exegesis', in J. Krašovic, *The Interpretation of the Bible: The International Symposium in Slovenia* (Sheffield: Sheffield Academic Press, 1998), 589–601, at 590–591.

112 Irenaeus, *AH*, 1.9.1–2. See also Behr, *Irenaeus*, 106–110; L. Ayres, 'Irenaeus vs the Valentinians: Towards a Rethinking of Patristic Exegetical Origins', *JECS* 23 (2015), 170.

113 Ibid. 172.

of faith. Irenaeus did not consider Scripture to be an impenetrable riddle that required some external standard imposed upon it to make it comprehensible. Instead, he held that Scripture could be interpreted in the light of its own internal coherence.

However, this is not all that Irenaeus has to say on the matter of regulating a true interpretation of the apostolic writings. Using the image of a person depositing money in a bank, he describes the apostles depositing their teaching in these communities as a *correlate* to the apostolic teaching being committed to writing.[114] For Irenaeus, apostolic teaching is maintained in the living voice of the church as well as in Scripture.[115] To demonstrate this, he conducts a thought experiment, asking how disputes would be solved if the apostles had not left any writings:

> Suppose there arise a dispute relative to some important question among us, should we not have recourse to the most ancient Church with which the apostles held constant intercourse, and learn from them what is certain and clear in regard to the present questions? For how should it be if the apostles themselves had not left us writings? Would it not be necessary in that case to follow the course of tradition which they handed down to those to whom they did commit the Churches?[116]

For Irenaeus, the community holds truth. The church is the recipient and guardian of the good treasure, which is the apostolic gospel. The church as the guardian of the apostolic witness is the authority that can determine which interpretations of the apostolic writings (and which writings) are consistent with the apostolic teaching and which are not.

The repository of this correct belief, Irenaeus argued, is held within the church, and it is set forward in the body of true belief received through baptism.[117] This is a condensed statement of genuine Christian doctrine that is normative for the interpretation of Scripture.[118] Tertullian, a contemporary of Irenaeus, takes a similar approach to Irenaeus. In his work *On the Prescription of Heretics*, Tertullian sets out to address the issue of who holds the authority when it comes to the interpretation of Scripture:

---

114 Irenaeus, *AH*, 3.4.1.

115 Ferguson, '*Paradōsis* and *Traditio*', 12.

116 Irenaeus, *AH*, 3.4.1.

117 Ibid. 1.9.4.

118 See also J. T. Lienhard SJ, *The Bible, The Church and Authority: The History of the Christian Bible in History and Theology* (Collegeville, Minn.: Liturgical Press, 1995), 42–58.

> With whom lies that very faith to which the Scriptures belong. From what and through whom, and when, and to whom, has been handed down that rule, by which men become Christians? For wherever it shall be manifest that the true Christian rule and faith shall be, *there* will likewise be the true Scriptures and expositions thereof, and all the Christian traditions.[119]

How do you determine which reading of Scripture is correct when there are no longer apostles to arbitrate? Like Irenaeus, Tertullian places the church at the centre as those who hold the apostolic teaching within the very life of their community: the community is the 'cistern of truth'.[120] The belief held by the churches established by the apostles becomes the key to regulate the beliefs drawn out of Scripture. This regulatory potential was mobilized through the development of the rules of faith: summaries and definitions of the body of beliefs held within the church.

Scripture, then, belongs alongside the general scheme of faith, which is 'the rule of truth which [the Christian] received by means of baptism'.[121] This rule (*kanōn*) is the broad tradition – including the belief, life and practices of the church[122] – that grounds the meaning of Scripture.[123] Like *hypothesis*, *kanōn* has a history in Hellenic thought. The term *kanōn* referred originally to a straight line against which the straightness of something else could be tested.[124] Within philosophy the term was used to denote the criteria of truth in relation to which the soundness of a proposition or an interpretation could be assessed.[125] Irenaeus promotes a distinctively apostolic *kanōn* in relation to which each passage of Scripture can be rightly interpreted. Although this ecclesial hermeneutic is not exhausted by doctrinal propositions, it certainly includes them.

119 Tertullian, *On the Prescription of Heretics*, 19, *ANF* 3; emphasis original.

120 Jenson, *Canon and Creed*, 16. See also Congar, *Meaning of Tradition*, 88–90.

121 Irenaeus, *AH*, 1.9.4. See also Irenaeus, *Proof of the Apostolic Preaching*, repr. (Pickerington, Ohio: Beloved Publishing), 1.7.

122 Osborn, *Irenaeus*, 145–146. Osborn provides a helpful definition: 'the canon of truth is the fullness of right belief found in scripture and tradition'. Ibid. 148. Young describes this holistic context for scriptural interpretation as a 'kind of counter-cultural *paideia*', a schooling orientated to an apostolic lifestyle and mindset for interpretation. F. M. Young, 'Interpretation of Scripture', in S. Ashbrook and D. G. Hunter (eds.), *The Oxford Handbook of Early Christian Studies* (Oxford: Oxford University Press, 2008), 845–863, at 850–851.

123 For a helpful discussion of the philosophical context of Irenaeus' use of *kanōn*, see Osborn, *Irenaeus*, 144. Osborn describes the prevalence of this term in Hellenic antiquity as a summary principle to enable objective analysis in a variety of different contexts. E. F. Osborn, 'Reason and the Rule of Faith in the Second Century AD', in R. Williams (ed.), *The Making of Orthodoxy* (Cambridge: Cambridge University Press, 2002), 40–42.

124 See J. T. Lienhard SJ, 'Canons and Rules of Faith', in P. M. Blowers and P. W. Martens (eds.), *The Oxford Handbook of Early Christian Biblical Interpretation* (Oxford: Oxford University Press, 2019), 55.

125 See P. M. Huby and G. Neal (eds.), *The Criterion of Truth: Essays Written in Honour of George Kerferd* (Liverpool: Liverpool University Press, 1989).

Irenaeus' rule of truth (set out in *Against Heresies*, 1.10.1[126]) is a propositional summary of the apostolic *kerygma*.

Irenaeus is certainly not the only Christian theologian to refer to a rule of faith.[127] This does not refer to a universally accepted creed, as such. Instead, it refers to the body of doctrine believed in the church that has been established by the apostles and handed down through the subsequent generations. Tertullian also referred frequently to the *traditio* as the content of the apostolic proclamation of the gospel against which deviating understandings could be established.[128] That is 'a rule of faith [that] has come down to us from the beginning of the gospel',[129] which is held by the church communities as the teaching given by the apostles. For Tertullian, this is the discipline of genuine Christian doctrine, and records several slightly different summaries of genuine Christian doctrine. One example of a rule of faith is as follows:

> Now, with regard to this rule of faith . . . there is one only God, and that He is none other than the Creator of the world, who produced all things out of nothing through His own Word, first of all sent forth; that this Word is called His Son, and, under the name of God . . . He sat at the right hand of the Father; sent instead of Himself the Power of the Holy Ghost to lead such as believe . . . will come with glory to take the saints to the enjoyment of everlasting life.[130]

This variety among even his own presentations of the rule of faith indicates that Tertullian did not consider the precise wording of the rule of faith to be fixed. However, the proximity of these passages in terms of their doctrinal content indicates that Tertullian was drawing on some unifying tradition of doctrinal coherence, organized around faith in God as Father, Son and Spirit. A range of examples of these from various authors contains some degree of variety owing to the theological priorities of each writer.[131] All of them, though, are condensed compendiums of Christian doctrine used as parameters by which to regulate private interpretations of Scripture. By this tool, the church was able to discern which interpretations of Scripture were truly apostolic and which were not.

---

126 See also Irenaeus, *Proof of the Apostolic Preaching*, 3, 6.
127 Irenaeus, *AH*, 1.1.20.
128 Tertullian, *Against Marcian*, 5.19.1, *ANF* 3.
129 Tertullian, *Against Praxeas*, 2, *ANF* 3.
130 Tertullian, *On the Prescription of Heretics*, 13, *ANF* 3.
131 These are helpfully laid out in Hanson, *Tradition in the Early Church*, 86–91.

The rule of faith and objectivity

The rule of faith was the opposite to the foreign regulatory schema imposed in a distorting fashion on Scripture by Gnostic hermeneutics. The rule of faith is a regulatory schema that is determined by the apostolic witness itself. The tradition of the church acts as a schema that regulates interpretation, which derives its structure from the reality it is talking about. The reality, Torrance wrote, is revelation: the full course of God's act from the Father through Christ and by the Spirit. The apostolic preaching derived its own structure and content from this act, and so also the tradition of the church is given its structure and content from beyond itself.[132] In this way, the tradition of the church takes its form from the pattern of God's activity in the world. It is not itself revelation; it is not in itself the direct testimony of the apostles. However, it is a pattern of understanding shaped by the reality with which it is principally concerned.

The significance of this is that the schema through which Scripture is interpreted is consonant with the content of Scripture. In this sense, the function of tradition charts closely with what Torrance would describe as objective thinking:

> Objective thinking certainly involves the disciplined control of our subjectivities lest they should be unwarrantably obtruded upon the object of inquiry and thus allowed to obstruct and distort our apprehension of it. This does not mean that once again the knowing subject is detached from the object of its knowledge, but rather that it enters into a close and active engagement with it, prepared and ready for whatever it may reveal in the give-and-take of investigation. Hence objective thinking lays itself open to the nature of reality of the object in order to take its shape from the structure of the object and not to impose upon it a structure of its own prescription. Objectifying or object-making thought, however, is the antithesis of this, for in it we 'make and mould' our objects of knowledge out of the stuff of our own consciousness. It is the activity in which the thing is 'known' only as it is coercively grasped and projected as an 'object' through an inflexible conceptual structure.[133]

It is the controlling of our subjective interpretations by a conceptual framework that itself is determined by the apostolic witness to revelation.

---

[132] T. F. Torrance, 'The Deposit of Faith', *SJT* 36 (1983), 1–28, esp. 6–8, 14–15.
[133] T. F. Torrance, *God and Rationality* (London: Oxford University Press, 2000), 9.

The purpose is to provide an interpretative framework in relation to which the apostolic writings may be properly understood. The worshipping communities established by the apostles are the ones who have preserved their witness intact and it is their belief that should regulate the way in which the Scriptures are interpreted. The point is that it is only from within the church that the Bible can be properly interpreted.[134] Scripture may well be materially sufficient and contain all we need to know for life and salvation, but it is interpreted from within a community of faith. As Georges Florovsky put it, tradition is 'Scripture rightly understood'.[135] Similarly, Jenson has proposed that tradition be understood as the '"critical theory" appropriate to the reading of Scripture'.[136] That is to say, the tradition provides the interpretative framework by which we can understand what Scripture is really saying. In this way, the biblical texts 'do not necessarily flaunt the sense they harbor',[137] but are interpreted in the light of what is believed by the worshipping community.

To put the case more strongly, Irenaeus and Tertullian considered the object of tradition to be the same as the object of Scripture in that they are modes by which the apostolic witness is perpetuated in the church.[138] The apostolic gospel delivered to the church inheres in both Scripture and the tradition of the church. Scripture and tradition stand in a reciprocal relationship wherein neither can fully stand without the other. Scripture, as the direct words of the apostles, enshrines the apostolic gospel in a particularly direct way, which is why it has primacy over the apostolic gospel *as it has been received by the church*. However, from the very beginning Scripture has been mediated by tradition.[139] This tradition, unlike Scripture, can become corrupted. The regulatory framework can become divorced from the apostolic teaching. It is in this sense that individually written rules of faith, which served to provide a regulatory framework for the interpretation of Scripture, would need to develop into the formal declarations of faith recognized as authoritative by the whole church: the ecumenical creeds, which would 'take over from the rule of faith the function of defining and summarizing the teaching of the Church'.[140]

134 Hanson, *Tradition*, 106.
135 G. Florovksy, 'The Function of Tradition in the Ancient Church', *GOTR* 9 (1963), 75.
136 Jenson, *Canon and Creed*, 7, 79–87.
137 Ibid. 79.
138 See Williams, *Retrieving*, 95–96; Hanson, *Tradition*, 109–117.
139 See Williams, *Evangelicals and Tradition*, 61–70.
140 Hanson, *Tradition*, 84.

2
Christian confessions in the second and third centuries

The conciliar creeds of the fourth century did not emerge out of a vacuum. By the fourth century a dense and diverse ecosystem of formal, confessional statements had already been developed. Alongside the rules of faith, liturgies of Christian initiation and eucharistic celebration are significant life-settings for the confessions of the church. This chapter explores the developing network of formal confessions in the second and third centuries and how this relates to the growing significance of confessional statements composed at councils.

The landscape in the second and third centuries is quite diverse. The confessions of Christian initiation included baptismal and catechetical confessions. The interrogatory baptismal confession is obviously associated with full sacramental inclusion and commitment to the church. Meanwhile, the declaratory confessions at the culmination of the catechetical process were concerned with instruction in the faith. Beyond this are differences in structure and content. Some confessions follow a three-clause structure, framing the statement of faith in accordance with the command to baptize in the name of the Father, Son and Spirit. Others, however, have a single-clause structure, focusing on the person and work of Christ. These Christological confessions tend to be kerygmatic in content. Over time, these different formats of confession were combined to form the three-clause structure with an expanded kerygmatic elaboration on God the Son incarnate.

There were also regional differences. Most obviously, the Latin-speaking West centred around Rome developed a different confessional identity from the Greek-speaking East. These different traditions developed along compatible but distinct lines, each with its own distinct theological character. There are further differences within these large blocks. Confessions of faith were regionally specific, with slight differences in wording and emphasis in different episcopal jurisdictions. The Eastern Church, for example, had a wealth of various confessions associated with catechetical schools and baptismal confessions of various locations. The Western Church appears to have had something approaching greater uniformity owing to the harmonizing influence of Rome.

Catechesis and baptismal confession

There is a close connection between the development of confessions and the initiation of new believers. In the process of initiation there were two related but distinct forms of confession. A central part of this process of instruction was learning through catechism, which culminated in the recitation of a formal declaration of faith prior to the rite of baptism. On some occasions, this is reflected in the liturgy of baptism that includes two specific moments: the baptism itself (where the candidate was asked three questions regarding his or her belief in the Father, Son and Spirit[1]) and, earlier in the rite, the candidate would be asked to declare his or her faith, not in the form of question and answer, but in reciting a formal declaration of the faith he or she had received.[2] Although clearly related, these two forms of confession do not share a common life-situation of the church. The declaratory confessions, 'conceived in the setting of their original purpose, were compendious summaries of Christian doctrine compiled for the benefit of converts undergoing instruction'.[3] On the other hand, the interrogatory statement of belief at the moment of baptism was a developing tradition with its roots in the command of Christ to baptize in the name of the Father, Son and Spirit. In other words, the public declaration of faith was *educational* (a demonstration of the fruits of the period of instruction), whereas the baptismal confession was more directly *sacramental* (the words with which the candidate was baptized and incorporated into the church).

Catechesis

The church, from the very beginning, was a teaching church. This process of instruction included both ethical and doctrinal catechesis. One of the earliest Christian catechisms was 'The Two Ways', which has been preserved in the first-century document the *Didache* and in an expanded form in the later text *Apostolic Constitutions*. 'The Two Ways' is a body of ethical instruction. Very importantly, in two of the sources in which this text is recorded it is immediately followed by baptismal rites, indicating that this ethical catechesis was part

1 Hippolytus, *Apostolic Tradition*, tr. B. S. Easton (Cambridge: Cambridge University Press, 1934), 21.1–20.

2 Cyril of Jerusalem, *Catechetical Lectures*, 19.2–9; 20.2–4; NPNF II.7.

3 Kelly, *ECC*, 50.

of the preparation of baptism.[4] This body of teaching includes stringent moral instruction: 'There are two Ways, a Way of Life and a Way of Death, and the difference between the two Ways is great.'[5] The purpose of this ethical catechism was to impress upon candidates for baptism the radically new way of life they were about to set out upon. Christian instruction, in other words, was not simply about developing a sound understanding of doctrine; it involved a commitment of one's life to the truth of that which had been received.

Candidates for baptism would also receive doctrinal instruction. Hippolytus' *Apostolic Tradition* (*c.*210) provides insight into the Church of Rome's worship and process of initiating new believers in the second century. Hippolytus describes that catechumens would spend a period of three years undergoing doctrinal instruction[6] before undergoing some form of examination of their conduct prior to their baptism.[7] Unfortunately, Hippolytus does not divulge the content of the doctrinal instruction. It could be, of course, that this is because the declaratory confession is largely the same as that which is confessed at the baptismal confession (see below).

Examples of formulaic summaries of the faith are embedded in longer texts and used for the purpose of instructing the readers. Frances Young refers to these examples as revealing a 'traditional "in-language"'[8] circulating in the Christian communities. Young's apposite phrase describes a situation in which summaries of the faith were not fixed formulae but rather familiar phrases and a common stock of doctrinal commitments indicative of a culture of orthodoxy. This 'in-language' most often occurs in two basic forms: (1) a three-clause structure, confessing faith in God as Father, Son and Spirit, and (2) as an expanded Christological statement.

Clement of Rome's (d. AD 99) letter to the church in Corinth includes a number of traditional summaries of the work of Jesus. For example:

> It was in love that the Lord drew us to Himself; because of the love he bore us, our Lord Jesus Christ, at the will of God, gave his blood for us – His flesh for our flesh His life for our lives.[9]

---

4 Williams, *Retrieving*, 77–78.

5 *The Didache*, in Louth and Stamforth, *Early Christian Writings*.

6 Hippolytus, *Apostolic Tradition*, 17.

7 Ibid. 20.1–4.

8 F. M. Young, *The Making of the Creeds* (London: SCM Press, 1991), 8.

9 Clement of Rome, 'The First Epistle of Clement to the Corinthians', in Louth and Stamforth, *Early Christian Writings*, 49.

Meanwhile, Ignatius' (d. AD 108) letter to the Trallians addresses the urgent problem of Docetic teaching. He urges his readers to 'take a fresh grip on your faith (the very flesh of the Lord) and your love (the life-blood of Jesus Christ)'.[10] Following this, Ignatius provides a definition of the Christian belief regarding the person of Christ. Importantly, Ignatius conveys several core Christological doctrines in a formulaic and repetitive format, coalescing on the necessity of Jesus' humanity to his saving work. That this is approaching the status of a formulaic statement to demarcate between the apostolic faith and deviations from it is suggested by the existence of a near-exact replica in another letter of Ignatius (see Table 3). Commenting on these passages, Kelly observes that 'the outline of the primitive Christological kerygma is visible through the loose folds of St Ignatius' polemical style'.[11] The similarity in these statements indicates an underlying confessional network of doctrines, which Ignatius is mobilizing in the act of equipping local communities to distinguish between genuine Christian belief and distortions of it.

The enigmatic text *Shepherd of Hermas* (*c.* AD 120–150) contains catechetical material embedded within a narrative. The text presents a dialogue between Hermas and the Shepherd, a divine teacher who instructs Hermas in 'lessons

Table 3 Similarities between the letters to the Trallians and Smyrnaeans

Letter to the Trallians	*Letter to the Smyrnaeans*
Close your ears, then, if anyone preaches to you without speaking of Jesus Christ. Christ was of David's line. He was the son of Mary; He was verily and indeed born, and ate and drank; He was verily persecuted in the days of Pontius Pilate, and verily and indeed crucified and gave up the ghost in the sight of all heaven and earth and the powers of the nether worlds. He was verily and indeed raised up again from the dead, for His Father raised him; and in Jesus Christ will His Father similarly raise us who believe in Him, since apart from him there is no true life for us.*	You hold the firmest convictions about our Lord; believing Him to be truly of David's line in His manhood, yet Son of God by the Divine will and power; truly born of a Virgin; baptized by John for his fulfilling all of righteousness; and in the days of Pontius Pilate and Herod the Tetrarch truly pierced by nails in His human flesh . . . so that by His resurrection He might set up a beacon for all time to call together His saints and believers, whether Jews or Gentiles in the one body of His Church.†

* Ignatius, 'The Epistle to the Trallians', in A. Louth (ed.) and M. Stamforth (tr.), *Early Christian Writings: The Apostolic Fathers* (London: Penguin Books, 1987), 9.

† Ignatius of Antioch, 'Epistle to the Smyrnaeans', in Louth and Stamforth, *Early Christian Writings*, in ibid. 1.

[10] Ignatius, 'Epistle to the Trallians', in ibid. 8.

[11] Kelly, *ECC*, 69.

which are to be disseminated for the instruction of the Church'.[12] The specific teaching of the Shepherd is communicated in twelve Mandates that are to be written down for the whole church.[13] The first of the Mandates is an injunction concerning belief, which includes a monotheistic statement: 'First of all, believe that God is One, even He who created all things and set them in order, and brought all things from non-existence into being, Who comprehendeth all things, being alone incomprehensible.'[14] This statement of the belief of the church comes in the form of instruction, suggesting its proper place as the opening part of catechetical instruction. It resonates with a liturgical character, doubtless invoking the Shema as the ancient creed of Israel (Deut. 6:4), transposed into Christian belief through Christ's teaching (Mark 12:28–31) and Paul's adaptation to include Jesus Christ in the category of the one God (1 Cor. 8:6).

Kelly goes so far as to suggest that in Justin Martyr's (d. AD 165) writings 'we for the first time come across what can plausibly be taken to be quotations of semi-formal creeds'.[15] His apologetic works written over the period AD 150–160 include both the three-clause confessions organized around the Father, Son and Spirit as well as more focused statements of belief concerning the person and work of Christ. One such example of a focused Christological statement in the context of the Son's authority over evil spirits is the following:

> For every demon, when exorcised in the name of this very Son of God – who is the First-born of every creature, who became man by the Virgin, who suffered, and was crucified under Pontius Pilate by your nation, who died, who rose from the dead, and ascended into heaven – is overcome and subdued.[16]

This summary of the work of Christ is free-standing and includes a more elaborate description of the core apostolic message about Jesus: that God the Son became a human, died and was resurrected. Justin also comments on the pre-existence of Christ as the 'first born'. While rudimentary, this does reflect an important strand in the church's confession of the Son's relation to the Father, being something that extends beyond and before the Son's incarnate life.

---

12 'Introduction', *Shepherd of Hermas*, tr. J. B. Lightfoot (London: Macmillan, 1891), 7.

13 Ibid. 1.[26].1 - 6.[49].5.

14 Ibid. 1.[26].1.

15 Kelly, *ECC*, 71.

16 Justin Martyr, *Dialogue of Justin, Philosopher and Martyr, with Trypho, a Jew*, 85.2. Several other examples are given in full at Kelly, *ECC*, 73–75.

Justin also refers to the three-clause structure of Christian belief with reference to the liturgical practice of the church. In a description of the eucharist, Justin explains the doxology is 'To the Father of the universe, through the name of His Son, and of the Holy Ghost.'[17] On other occasions, when the agenda is set by the accusations of others (and not by the church's own liturgical practice), Justin continues to parse the Christian faith by using the three-clause structure. For example, when responding to the charge that Christianity is atheism, Justin writes:

> we are not atheists, worshipping as we do the Maker of this universe . . . Our teacher of these things is Jesus Christ, who also was born for this purpose, and was crucified under Pontius Pilate, procurator of Judaea, in the times of Tiberius Caesar; and that we reasonably worship Him, having learned that He is the Son of the true God Himself, and holding Him in the second place, and the prophetic Spirit in the third.[18]

Here a kerygmatic summary of the death of Jesus is contained within a description of the relationship between the Father, Son and Spirit. This description of the three divine persons casts the Father, Son and Spirit in rank order.

Irenaeus' *Proof of the Apostolic Preaching* provides a much fuller example of the sort of content used in doctrinal instruction. The purpose of this text is to instruct its reader in the content of God's saving work, accomplished through the Son by the Spirit. Irenaeus' purpose is to 'show forth in brief the preaching of the truth for the confirmation of [the readers'] faith'.[19] It is a self-consciously didactic work, described by its author as a 'manual of essentials, that by little you may attain to much, learning in short space all the members of the body of truth'.[20] There are two very important sections with respect to the status of the confessions of faith in the second century. First, Irenaeus recapitulates the baptismal formula:

> Now faith occasions this for us; even as the Elders, the disciples of the Apostles, have handed down to us. First of all it bids us bear in mind that we have received baptism for the remission of sins in the name of God the Father and in the name of Jesus Christ, the Son of God, who was incarnate

[17] Justin Martyr, *The First Apology of Justin*, 65.3.

[18] Ibid. 13. The long ellipsis contains a description of Christian worship that is appropriate considering its belief in God as creator.

[19] Irenaeus of Lyons, *Proof of the Apostolic Preaching*, repr. (Pickerington, Ohio: Beloved Publishing, 2015), 1.

[20] Ibid.

> and died and was raised, and in the Holy Spirit of God. And that this baptism is the seal of eternal life, and is the new birth unto God.[21]

The parallel to the baptismal formula as recorded in the Gospel of Matthew is plain, with baptism being in the name of God the Father, Son and Spirit. There is a slightly expanded Christological statement within the three-clause structure, which became an increasingly common feature. It seems highly likely that, at some point, the free-standing kerygmatic Christological statements were joined to the three-clause baptismal confessions.[22] Importantly, this three-clause structure is deployed almost immediately in a more expanded presentation of core Christian doctrine:

> This then is the order of the rule of our faith, and the foundation of the building, and the stability of our conversation: God the Father, uncreated, beyond grasp, invisible, one God the maker of all; this is the first and foremost article of our faith. But the second article is the Word of God, the Son of God, Christ Jesus our Lord, who was manifested to the prophets according to the form of their prophesying and according to the method of the dispensation of the Father: through whom all things were made; who also at the end of the times, to complete and gather up all things, was made man among men, visible and tangible, in order to abolish death and show forth life and produce a community of union between God and man. And the third article is the Holy Spirit through whom the prophets prophesied and the patriarchs were taught about God . . . and who in the end of times has been poured forth in a new manner upon humanity over all the earth, renewing man to God.[23]

The baptismal confession has provided the structure for three articles of faith as Irenaeus elaborates upon them in this catechetical summary. The three articles set out in this statement go on to form the structure of the rest of the text. In other words, Irenaeus structures Christian doctrine in a form we now recognize as distinctively trinitarian, not ranking the persons but maintaining their clear differentiation.[24] Within this trinitarian structure, Irenaeus has included a loose statement of Christology.[25] Here the significance of including

---

[21] Ibid. 3.

[22] See also Kelly, *ECC*, 94–95.

[23] Irenaeus, *Proof of the Apostolic Preaching*, 6.

[24] E. Ferguson, 'Irenaeus' Proof of the Apostolic Preaching and Early Catechetical Instruction', *StPatr* 18.3 (1989), 127.

[25] See also Irenaeus, *AH*, 1.10.1.

a kerygmatic statement within the trinitarian structure begins to become clearer: Irenaeus described the work of God towards us in creation and redemption on the foundation of the eternal relations of the divine being.[26] This sophisticated coordination of the divine activity towards creation and the internal divine relations would become a key element of a distinctively Nicene approach to theology.

Baptismal confession

An important aspect of the development of a familiar body of doctrine and phrases was, of course, the liturgical tradition. This is clear in Paul's transmission of the apostolic tradition concerning the eucharist (1 Cor. 11:23–26). These liturgical practices contributed to a shared set of practices, statements and doctrines all of which fostered a unique Christian identity particularly well developed even in the first century. The *Didache* indicates that the eucharist had already been well established in a liturgical framework:

> And concerning the Eucharist, hold Eucharist thus:
> First concerning the Cup, 'We give thanks to thee, our Father, for the Holy Vine of David thy child, which, thou didst make known to us through Jesus thy Child; to thee be glory for ever.'
> And concerning the broken Bread: 'We give thee thanks, our Father, for the life and knowledge which thou didst make known to us through Jesus thy Child. To thee be glory for ever.
> As this broken bread was scattered upon the mountains, but was brought together and became one, so let thy Church be gathered together from the ends of the earth into thy kingdom, for thine is the glory and the power through Jesus Christ for ever.'
> But let none eat or drink of your Eucharist except those who have been baptised in the Lord's Name.[27]

A similar pattern can be observed with the developing liturgy of baptism. In Matthew's Gospel, Jesus' words of institution provide a threefold structure to baptism: 'Go . . . and make disciples of all nations, baptizing them in the name of the Father and of the Son and of the Holy Spirit' (Matt. 28:19). Confusingly, within the biblical material describing the practice of the apostles, baptismal rites do not explicitly follow this threefold formula. Baptism in the book of Acts is performed in the name of Christ alone (Acts 2:38; 10:47–48; 19:5) or the fact

[26] See also Fairbairn and Reeves, *SCC*, 31.
[27] *Didache*, 9.

of baptism is stated without further amplification (Acts 8:13, 38; 9:18; 16:15, 33; 18:8). Within Luke's narrative, the presence of *belief* is more highly prioritized than the precise formula of words accompanying baptism. For example, having heard Philip's exposition on the suffering servant from Isaiah and its fulfilment in Jesus, the Ethiopian eunuch believes and is baptized (Acts 8:30–39). However, there is no indication that there was any precise formulation of that confession of faith. Clearly, this is a lacuna that troubled the early believers, with a later addition to the story of the Ethiopian, accrediting to him a formal confession in Christ as the Son of God. This does not mean for certain that it was *not* the apostles' practice to baptize using the threefold formula. However, it is surprising that there is not greater specificity, given that the command of Christ was so explicit. Whatever the reason, unlike with the eucharist there is little evidence in the apostolic period of a well-established baptismal formula.

In the *Didache*, the formulation of the baptismal rite itself is given: 'baptise in the Name of the Father and of the Son and of the Holy Ghost'.[28] Similarly, Justin Martyr, in his description of the rite, implies that the command of Christ was reflected in the church's liturgy:

> there is pronounced over him who chooses to be born again, and has repented of his sins, *the name of* God the Father and Lord of the universe; he who leads to the laver the person that is to be washed calling him by this name alone. For no one can utter the name of the ineffable God; and if any one dare to say that there is a name, he raves with a hopeless madness. And this washing is called illumination, because they who learn these things are illuminated in their understandings. And *in the name of* Jesus Christ, who was crucified under Pontius Pilate, and *in the name of* the Holy Ghost, who through the prophets foretold all things about Jesus, he who is illuminated is washed.[29]

The formulaic repetition of 'in the name' indicates some level of formalization of the specific words used. Here, though, the bare bones have been filled out with specific doctrinal commitments regarding each of the persons. It should be noticed that the elaboration regarding the Son is reminiscent of the lone-standing Christological statements introduced above. This suggests that the process of combining the Christological statements with the three-clause structure of the baptismal command was already underway by the middle of

[28] Ibid. 7.1.
[29] Justin, *First Apology*, 1.61, *ANF* 1; emphases mine.

the second century. Tertullian also suggests that there was some doctrinal elaboration in the threefold structure of the baptismal confessions: 'then they were thrice immersed, making a somewhat ampler pledge than the Lord has appointed in the Gospel'.[30] Tertullian does not record the content of this fuller response. One possibility is the insertion of a kerygmatic statement regarding the incarnation, death and resurrection of Christ alongside other doctrinal comments regarding the Father and the Spirit. Another possibility is the addition of other objects of belief, such as the church, baptism, forgiveness of sins and the resurrection of the dead.

It is not until the third-century text of Hippolytus (AD 170–235), *Apostolic Tradition*, that a full account of the baptismal rite and confession is accessible. A conservative by disposition, Hippolytus was 'a stickler for ecclesiastical tradition' and this text records the practices of the Roman Church.[31] The purpose in writing was to 'address the churches, so that they who have been well trained, may, by our instruction, hold fast to that tradition which has continued up to now'.[32] Clearly, Hippolytus was not presenting innovations, but practices already well established by the time he came to write in around AD 215. Very importantly, Hippolytus shows the synthesis of the traditional three articles of the baptismal formula arising from the command of Christ and the more detailed kerygmatic Christological confessions:

> Let [the candidate] go over to the presbyter who baptizes and let the candidate stand in the water, naked, a deacon going with them likewise. And when he who is being baptized goes down into the water, he who baptizes him, putting his hand on him, shall say thus:
>
> 'Dost thou believe in God the Father Almighty?'
>
> And he who is being baptized shall say:
>
> 'I believe.'
>
> Then holding his hand placed on his head, he shall baptize him once. And then he shall say:
>
> 'Dost thou believe in Christ Jesus, the Son of God,
> who was born of the Holy Spirit and the virgin Mary,
> who was crucified in the days of Pontius Pilate,
> and was dead and buried,
> and rose again the third day, living from the dead,
> and ascended into heaven,

30 Tertullian, *The Chaplet*, 3, *ANF* 3.
31 Kelly, *ECC*, 89.
32 Hippolytus, *Apostolic Tradition*, 1.3.

and sat down at the right hand of the Father,
and will come to judge the living and the dead?'

And when he says:

'I believe',

he is baptized again. And, again, he shall say:

'Dost thou believe in the Holy Ghost, and the holy church, and the resurrection of the flesh?'

He who is being baptized shall say accordingly:

'I believe',

and so he is baptized a third time.[33]

Well before the opening of the third century an amplified confession of faith in interrogatory form had developed in Rome. This amplification came in two ways. First, there is a significantly developed Christology in comparison to the baptismal command. This appears to have come about through a synthesis between the kerygmatic confessions focusing on the person of Christ, his life, death and resurrection and the three-clause structure of the baptismal confession. Second, within the third clause, more doctrinal elements are added in advance of the command of Christ: belief in the church and in the resurrection.

Western and Eastern creeds

Alongside the variety in purpose and format, there were also regional differences between confessions. The basic regional difference is between the church in the West, centred around Rome and the church in the East. Undergirding this geographical distinction was a difference in dominant language (Latin in the West, Greek in the East). The Eastern and Western parts of the church had different confessional traditions. These different trajectories can be seen by comparing two reconstructions: the Old Roman Creed and the postulated Eastern Creed.

The Old Roman Creed

As Hippolytus' account of liturgical practice in Rome in the second and early third centuries indicates, the church in Rome was advanced in the development of a partially fixed declaration of faith that, combined with its claim to greater authority owing to its episcopal connection to Peter, 'became the ancestor of all other local creeds in the West'.[34] This partially fixed declaration of faith is

33 Ibid. 21.11–19.
34 Kelly, *ECC*, 101.

known as the Old Roman Creed. This confession was used across the Latin-speaking world in a variety of different formulations, owing to the unique conditions of each location. Very importantly, it was believed that this confession was directly related to the apostles' own composition.

A text of the Old Roman Creed does not exist. However, it has been reconstructed from a number of different sources. A significant source comes in the writings of the fourth-century figure Rufinus, who in his commentary on his own local confession of faith refers to where the confession of Rome differs. Confusingly, the title of this treatise is *A Commentary on the Apostles' Creed*. The suggestion is not that his local confession is the composition of the apostles and that the local confession of Rome deviates from this in a number of ways. Instead, the suggestion is that there is a family of confessions in the Latin-speaking West that derive from a confession composed by the apostles, which the regional confession of Rome maintained accurately, whereas other provinces (including Rufinus' own) modified their own local confessions to respond to a variety of heresies.[35]

It is from Rufinus that we have received the attractive idea that each of the apostles contributed one clause before parting for their separate missionary journeys. However fanciful, this does indicate that Rufinus understood himself to be commenting on the condensed body of beliefs composed by the apostles that was contained in the various local confessions in the Latin West. So, Rufinus' commentary demonstrates three important things. First, that there was a family of Latin creeds, all closely united in doctrinal content and structure but with some local variations. Second, that this family of creeds was believed to be the confession written by the apostles. Third, that the Old Roman Creed was viewed, at least by some, as closer to the original document 'composed by the apostles' (see Table 4 on p. 62).

It is very likely that what we know as the Apostles' Creed is the Old Roman Creed at a later stage of evolution. With respect to the Old Roman Creed and the Apostles' Creed of *c.*400, there are three minor changes, indicated by italics. The later version adds layers of clarification about the person of Jesus Christ and his relationship to the Father and to the church: he is the *only* Son of the Father and is 'our Lord'. Rufinus' view was that these additions were necessitated by the emergence of heresies in different regions in which this confession was used and proliferated. This implies that the exclusive word 'only' in relation to Jesus' Sonship was an addition to respond to inadequate understandings of the Sonship of Jesus. The addition of the clause 'the remission of sins', however, is

[35] Rufinus, *A Commentary on the Apostles' Creed*, 3. See Fairbairn and Reeves, *SCC*, 110.

Table 4 A family of Latin creeds

Old Roman Creed c.150	*Apostles' Creed c.400*	*Apostles' Creed c.700*
I believe in God the Father almighty;	I believe in God, the Father almighty,	I believe in God, the Father almighty, *creator of heaven and earth.*
and in Christ Jesus His Son, Who was born from the Holy Spirit and the Virgin Mary, Who under Pontius Pilate was crucified and buried, on the third day rose again from the dead, ascended to heaven, sits at the right hand of the Father, whence he will come to judge the living and the dead;	and in Christ Jesus, his *only* Son, *our Lord,* Who was born from the Holy Spirit and the Virgin Mary, Who under Pontius Pilate, was crucified and was buried, on the third day he rose again from the dead, ascended into heaven, sits at the right hand of the Father, whence he will come to judge the living and the dead;	And in Jesus Christ, his only Son, our Lord. He was *conceived* by the Holy Spirit, born of the Virgin Mary, *suffered* under Pontius Pilate, was crucified, *dead,* and was buried. *He descended to hell.* On the third day he rose again. He ascended into heaven, and is seated at the right hand of *God* the Father *Almighty,* thence He will come again to judge the living and the dead.
and in the Holy Spirit, the holy Church, the resurrection of the flesh.*	and in the Holy Spirit, the holy Church, the *remission of sins,* the resurrection of the flesh.†	I believe in the Holy Spirit, the holy *catholic* Church, *the communion of the saints,* the forgiveness of sins, the resurrection of the body, *and the life everlasting.* Amen.‡

* Cited from J. N. D. Kelly, *Early Christian Creeds* (London: Longmans Green, 1950), 102.

† Cited from D. Fairbairn and R. M. Reeves, *The Story of Creeds and Confessions: Tracing the Development of the Christian Faith* (Grand Rapids, Mich.: Baker Academic, 2019), 117.

‡ Cited from ibid.

more remarkable. This is not a clarification, but a wholly new proposition. If the Old Roman Creed really was the direct composition of the apostles, then (although conceivably it could have been subjected to clarification over time) the doctrinal content itself would not have been expanded.

The Apostles' Creed would come to assume its final form in the eighth century. The details of that development go beyond the parameters of this study.[36] However, this continuity indicates that this confession with its centre of gravity in the Western Church, and its authority – in reality – deriving from its association with the local Church of Rome (and so the Bishop of Rome) continued to exercise influence in the centuries after the conciliar confessions of the fourth century. There was in Rome and the surrounding Latin-speaking

36 See ibid. 109–125.

provinces, at least by the third century, and in all likelihood quite a lot earlier than that, a typical declaration of faith with a fairly settled body of doctrine with minor variation in the precise wording that persisted throughout the subsequent history of the church.

The Eastern Creed

Across the Eastern, Greek-speaking, Church, no single formula stands out as influential over its neighbours. Instead, different episcopal areas had their own confession of faith associated with their own catechetical school.[37] There is, however, significant overlap between these different confessions. Based on these commonalities, the nineteenth-century German scholar Hans Lietzmann reconstructed a prototypical 'Eastern Creed' that underlies the similarities that exist between the variety of local credal statements. However, even if Lietzmann's Eastern Creed is only a scholarly artefact, as a harmonization of the set of emphases and priorities characteristic of this body of declarations, it is a very useful resource (see Table 5).

There are commonalities between the Western and Eastern confessions. Both observe the threefold structure of the baptismal confession with an expanded

Table 5 The Old Roman Creed compared to the Eastern Creed

The Old Roman Creed	*The Eastern Creed*
I believe in God the Father almighty; And in Christ Jesus His only Son, our Lord, Who was born from the Holy Spirit and the Virgin Mary, Who under Pontius Pilate was crucified and buried, On the third day rose again from the dead, Ascended to heaven, Sits at the right hand of the Father, whence He will come to judge the living and the dead;	I believe in one God, the Father, the Ruler of all Maker of things visible and invisible. And in one Lord Jesus Christ, the only begotten Son of God. *Who was begotten from the Father before all worlds* *Through whom all things have come into being* Who for our salvation became man, suffered And rose again on the third day and ascended into heaven And will come again to judge the quick and the dead.
And in the Holy Spirit, the holy Church, the remission of sins, the resurrection of the flesh.*	And in the Holy Spirit. †

* Cited from Kelly, *ECC*, 102.

† The reconstructed Eastern Creed. Cited from G. Bray, *Creeds, Councils and Christ: Did the Early Christians Misrepresent Jesus*, rev. edn (Nairobi: Mentor, 2009), 103–104.

[37] For a full survey of the declarations of faith in Greek, see Kelly, *ECC*, 181–193.

Christological statement. There are also significant differences. These differences are sometimes characterized as practical versus speculative, as if the Eastern confession is characterized by theological conjecture as opposed to the Western statement of the events of Jesus' life. While this characterization is unsatisfactory, it does contain a kernel of truth. The Eastern creed does express a high theological mood that is somewhat looser than its Western counterpart on the core *kerygma*. For example, the Eastern credal tradition is more prepared to comment on the internal relations of the Son and Father, referring to the pretemporal existence of the Son alongside the Father as the one who is begotten from the Father, but does not consider it necessary to state that Jesus died!

However, it would be reductive to claim that the Eastern creed is 'theological', whereas the Western creed is a 'common-sense' statement of the salvific facts. It is true that the Western creed is characterized by greater historical specificity, but it also contains theological ideas not found in the East. Principally, the West recognizes the role of the Holy Spirit in the incarnation, recognizing more profoundly the unity of the Father, Son and Spirit in the one work of God.

The emergence of the conciliar creeds

The diversity of the confessional activity of the first three centuries did not simply disappear the morning after the Nicene Creed of 325 was composed. There is no evidence to suggest that it was supposed to disappear. Regional variety in the confessions of Christian initiation continued to be central to instruction and baptism throughout the fourth century. For example, Cyril of Jerusalem wrote his *Catechetical Lectures* in *c.*350, some twenty-five years after the Council of Nicaea, but makes no mention of it. Instead, the declaratory confession he offers instruction on is the confession of the church in Jerusalem.[38] Similarly, when given the task of writing an exposition of the creed, Rufinus did not comment on the Nicene Creed, but on the Latin confession common in the episcopal areas around Rome.[39] However, in the body of his exposition, Rufinus acknowledges theological challenges for which this local creed was ill-equipped and draws upon the theology of Nicaea to clarify the meaning of his traditional creed.[40] For Rufinus, then, the confession that has his primary allegiance is the Old Roman Creed in its form of existence in his diocese. The Nicene Creed served as a helpful elaboration, and not as a replacement. It was

[38] Cyril of Jerusalem, *Catechetical Lectures*, 17.
[39] See Williams, *Retrieving*, 165.
[40] Ibid.

not until the fifth century that the Nicene-Constantinopolitan Creed became more clearly established in a liturgical context.[41]

By the fourth century it was not new to make doctrinal decisions through the convening of a council accompanied by the production of a conciliar statement. This mechanism of governance was apostolic in origin. The Council of Jerusalem saw delegates from Antioch and Jerusalem convene to decide on the issue of whether Gentile Christians needed to adopt Hebrew customs for their full assimilation into the people of God, its findings being communicated by letter (Acts 15).[42] Eusebius also records that towards the end of the second century a council was called to respond to the emergence of Montanism, and its conclusions were circulated around the church.[43] Williams notes that by the third century, conciliar meetings took place on a nearly annual basis and it was becoming 'an essential feature of the way the church governed itself on a scale larger than the local congregation'.[44]

However, the Council of Antioch in 268 marks something of a transition in the role of councils in establishing doctrinal norms. At this council a long, theologically rich, confession was composed by a gathering of bishops in response to the doctrinal controversy surrounding Paul of Samosata (discussed further in chapter 3). Kelly describes this as a 'rehearsal or anticipation' of what would become the mature role of councils in composing authoritative confessions of faith, delineating genuine Christian doctrine from deviations beyond it.[45] This method of establishing the doctrine of the church became increasingly influential over the course of the fourth century, partly on account of Christianity's becoming the imperial religion. Constantine, for example, was present at the Council of Nicaea, impressing upon the delegates the significance of achieving one common doctrinal standard.[46]

The conciliar creeds would come to replace the rule of faith and become the *symbolon* of Scripture. A *symbolon* is a means by which the authenticity of something can be tested. This is well explained by Fairbairn and Reeves:

> think of a painting or tapestry, cut into two pieces, which are then verified by placing them back together again to show that they line up. We know that one piece is authentic because it matches the second.[47]

41 Ayres, *Nicaea*, 86; D. H. Williams, 'Constantine and the "Fall" of the Church', in L. Ayres and G. Jones (eds.), *Christian Origins: Theology, Rhetoric and Community* (London: Routledge, 1998), 117–136.

42 See also G. Bray, *Synods* (London: Latimer Trust, 2019), 4–9.

43 Eusebius of Caesarea, *Ecclesiastical History*, 5.16, 10.

44 Williams, *Retrieving*, 157.

45 Kelly, *ECC*, 207.

46 Ibid. Williams, *Retrieving*, 162.

47 Fairbairn and Reeves, *SCC*, 4.

So, as 'symbols' of the faith, the conciliar creeds stand as a pattern of belief (a mode of existence of the apostolic preaching) against which individual interpretations can be measured. Similarly, Hanson has argued that the conciliar creeds 'eventually [took] over from the rule of faith the function of defining and summarizing the teaching of the Church'.[48] In part, this is reflected by the presence of anathemas within conciliar confessions: from Antioch in 268 to Constantinople in 381 all confessions composed by councils included repudiations of perceived doctrinal deviations.

48 Hanson, *Tradition in the Early Church*, 84.

3
Arius and Alexander of Alexandria

The problem of categorization

It is notoriously difficult to find adequate categories to frame the controversies of the fourth century. A number of different models have described the different theological factions that contested for supremacy. One approach – encouraged by Athanasius in his polemical writings – is to use the Nicene confession of 325 as a boundary marker and to describe the theological groupings by their attitude to Nicaea. This approach is attractive for its clarity: on the one side the pro-Nicenes gathered around Athanasius and, on the other, the anti-Nicenes gathered around Arius and the 'Arians'. This view, however, has a number of problems.

First, the various factions do not cohere around the rallying posts in a way one would expect them to if this view were true.[1] As will be discussed in the next chapter, the doctrinal debates immediately following 325 did not take the Nicene confession as setting the agenda. Moreover, beyond its repudiation of Arius, it was not obvious how the Nicene confession was to be understood. The letter of Eusebius of Caesarea (discussed in the next chapter) indicates that there were significant differences in how the signatories understood important phrases.

Second, those who demurred with respect to the Nicene confession did not identify themselves as followers of Arius, or even demonstrate detailed knowledge of his writings.[2] They thought of themselves, not as intellectual descendants of Arius, but as faithful to Scripture and tradition.[3] In this connection, recent decades have seen something of a new perspective on Arius, in

---

[1] See Behr, *NF*, 21–36. For a short summary of recent scholarship, see D. M. Gwynn, *Athanasius of Alexandria: Bishop, Theologian, Ascetic, Father* (Oxford: Oxford University Press, 2012), 59–60.

[2] Ayres, *NL*, 2, 13–14.

[3] Hanson, *SCDG*, 123–128. See also J. T. Lienhard SJ, *Contra Marcellum: Marcellus of Ancyra and Fourth Century Theology* (Washington, D.C.: Catholic University of America Press, 1999), 31–33.

which Arius is conceived not as the founder of a theological school or as the architect of subsequent heretical thought that denies the divinity of Christ.[4] Instead, he was a representative of a far broader theological tradition the priorities of which emerged from antecedent theological concerns and would continue in marked tension with the Nicene confession.[5] In fact, as the dispute progresses, Arius cuts an increasingly marginalized figure, whose more extreme views were not shared widely. The very least that can be said is that the traditional understanding of an 'Arian' and a 'Nicene' camp does not account for the diversity and complexity of the fourth century.

If the fourth-century controversies cannot be framed around allegiance to either Nicaea or Arius, then how should they be? A broader view of the doctrinal disagreements is required to identify the theological priorities behind those who would come to oppose Nicene theology and those who would come to defend it. Some suggest that contesting doctrines of salvation are the best way to frame the disputes of the fourth century. In this view, the issue at hand is whether salvation is conceived of as humanity lifting itself up to heaven or God's descending to humanity. The former is associated with an idea of the Son as, in some sense, lesser than the *true* God who is able to suffer and die for the redemption of humanity and be adopted as the Son of God.[6] This view is attractive in that it establishes the dispute within categories closer to the surface of the Christian consciousness, and helpfully presents Arius and those sympathetic to him not as malevolent sophists, but as Christian theologians. This is often portrayed as an Arian Christology being representative of a gospel of ethical attainment, with Nicene Christology being associated with a gospel of divine descent.[7]

Others have suggested a geographical mode of categorization: a conflict between the 'Alexandrian' and 'Antiochene' schools. In this, the dispute is said to be between two contrary theological modes exemplified by Lucian of Antioch and Alexander/Athanasius of Alexandria.[8] Certainly, the impact of a 'Lucianite' form of theology is felt throughout the fourth century as a powerful alternative to Nicene theology. However, whether it is useful to organize the

[4] M. Wiles, *Archetypal Heresy: Arianism Through the Centuries* (Oxford: Clarendon Press, 1996).

[5] R. Williams, *Arius: Heresy and Tradition* (London: Darton, Longman and Todd, 1987), 1–25. See also Hanson, *SCDG*, 123–128; Ayres, *NL*, 11–20, 56–57; Behr, *NF*, 8–16; M. Slusser, 'Traditional Views of Late Arianism', in M. R. Barnes and D. H. Williams (eds.), *Arianism After Arius: Essays on the Development of the Fourth-Century Trinitarian Conflicts* (Edinburgh: T&T Clark, 1993), 3–30; M. Wiles, 'Attitudes to Arius in the Arian Controversy', in Barnes and Williams, *Arianism After Arius*, 31–43.

[6] R. C. Gregg and D. G. Groh, *Early Arianism: A View of Salvation* (Philadelphia, Pa.: Fortress Press, 1981). See also Fairbairn and Reeves, *SCC*, 47–48.

[7] Fairbairn and Reeves, *SCC*, 51–56.

[8] Lienhard, *Contra Marcellum*, 33–34.

dispute around 'Alexandrian' and 'Antiochene' schools is another matter. Arius himself, as is suggested below, emerges from a thoroughly Alexandrian milieu. Moreover, the exact character of Lucian's theology is not easy to discern and much is predicated upon Arius' description of himself as a 'Lucianite'.

A more historically useful category for the theological tradition that resisted the Nicene confession is 'Eusebian', named after both Eusebius of Caesarea and Eusebius of Nicomedia. This is a helpful designation because the theological differences between these two bishops are indicative of the breadth of the theological tradition that was uncomfortable with the Nicene confession. For this reason, the following reconstruction of the fourth century uses the label 'Eusebian' to describe the broad alliance of bishops who appear to be informed to some degree by Lucian and sought out alternatives to the Nicene confession. The clearest theological expression of this group is the Second Creed of the Dedication Council in 341 (see chapter 4). However, as the fourth century wore on, this broad alliance began to break down as their theological differences became increasingly clear, and by 360 the Eusebian alliance fractured into a range of smaller groupings (see chapter 5). For this reason, the utility of the category 'Eusebians' is specific to the period after the Nicene confession and up until the fracturing of this alliance throughout the 350s.

Given these difficulties, recent scholarship has categorized the fourth century through doctrinal commitments rather than personal allegiance. Lewis Ayres has suggested that the fourth-century debates revolved around two sets of theological trajectories:

1 the Father–Son relation wherein one trajectory emphasizes the *ontological sameness* of the Father and Son and the second one emphasizes the *ontological difference* between the Father and Son;
2 the question of the personal differentiation of the Father and Son, wherein one trajectory obscures their personal differentiation and the other emphasizes it.[9]

This second set of trajectories has been the focus of Joseph Lienhard. Lienhard organizes the theological controversies of the fourth century through a distinction between different ways of using the word *hypostasis*. He observes divergent 'miahypostatic' and 'dyohypostatic' (or 'trihypostatic') theologies.[10] The 'miahypostatic' grouping (including Marcellus and Athanasius) asserts that

[9] Ayres, *NL*, 41–42.
[10] J. T. Lienhard SJ, 'The "Arian" Controversy: Some Categories Reconsidered', *TS* 48 (1987), 415–437, esp. 420–427; Lienhard, *Contra Marcellum*, 35–46.

God is one *hypostasis*. This is a clear affirmation of monotheism, with the Father and Son conceived of as one concrete reality, emphasizing that the Son is God as the Father is God. This sameness is often accompanied by an utter distinction between God and creation, policed by the Son's generation *from the essence of the Father*, while creation is made from nothing *by the will of the Father*. Particularly in the case of Marcellus, this view was associated with the denial of the personal differentiation of Father and Son.[11] This view persisted throughout the fourth century: it was not until 362 that Athanasius would accept that there was a sense in which one could speak of God's three hypostases in a way that did not imply three distinct gods. Even then, Athanasius continued to prefer the miahypostatic construction until the end of his life.

The 'dyohypostatic' grouping gave a clear affirmation of the Father and Son as distinct and subsistent particulars or hypostases. This incredibly broad group includes Basil of Caesarea, Basil of Ancyra, Eusebius of Caesarea, Asterius and Arius. Central to this tradition is the commitment that the Father, Son and Spirit are distinct in *reality* and not only in the economy of God's activity or our conceptualization of it. This perspective involves a focus on the primacy of God the Father as the source of all things, and the Son is a distinct *hypostasis* who derives from the Father. A factor that would be significant in the fourth-century disputes was that this grouping was sensitive to any account of the generation of the Son that imposed materialistic ideas on the divine. The locus in which this was particularly problematic was in the question of the continuity of divinity between the Father and Son, with some members of this grouping rejecting the doctrine on the grounds that it implied the division of the divine essence. As such, it is not uncommon to find dyohypostatic theologians describing the Son as subordinate to the Father.[12]

Johannes Zachhuber observes the following commitments of the tradition that recognizes a multiplicity of hypostases:

1 it emphasizes the separate existence or 'subsistence' of the three Persons of the Godhead;
2 it employs to this end the term *hypostasis*;
3 also relevant is a particular kind of subordinationism.[13]

As will be suggested, those who affirmed the distinct subsistence of the Father, Son and Spirit did not *necessarily* think this entailed the ontological primacy

[11] Lienhard, *Contra Marcellum*, 42–43.
[12] Ibid. 38–42.
[13] Zachhuber, 'Basil', 65–85, at 66.

of the Father. Basil of Ancyra, for example, did not hold the subordinationist Christology of Arius. A more accurate way of accounting for the differences within this group of theologians may be through their diverse understandings of image-Christology (Williams gives this the elegant description of a 'pluralist *eikōn*-theology'[14]). This has to do with the terms of the Son's likeness to the Father (Col. 1:15; 2 Cor. 4:4): is it a likeness of essence, or one predicated on some other criterion (e.g. will)? Different theologians who asserted the plurality of divine hypostases answered this question very differently. DelCogliano has provided a helpful typology by which to organize the alternatives to image-Christology in the fourth century.[15]

1 A *participative* image-Christology, in which the Son does not share in the divinity of the Father by necessity, but rather contingently and by grace.[16] This is given its conciliar expression at the Council of Antioch (341).
2 A *constitutive* image-Christology in which the Son shares fully and necessarily the divinity of the Father of whom he is the image. This is given conciliar expression at the councils of Nicaea (325) and Constantinople (381) and broader theological argumentation by Alexander of Alexandria and Athanasius of Alexandria (although they did not recognize a plurality of divine hypostases). Within the dyohypostatic tradition, this position was held by Basil of Ancyra and Basil of Caesarea.

In other words, Lienhard's way of organizing the fourth century needs to be nuanced to recognize that theologians who recognized a plurality of divine hypostases coalesced with figures such as Athanasius on the ground of a constitutive image-Christology. This would be the ground on which the Nicene consensus was eventually established. The strength of Lienhard's method of categorization is that it reflects concrete historical groupings and accommodates the theological development of the fourth century. That is to say, it accommodates both the dispute between Marcellus and Asterius in the 330s and 340s and the stalemate caused by the Antiochene schism in the 360s and 370s. Moreover, Lienhard's mode of categorization further reminds us that the fourth century

14 Williams, *Arius*, 166.

15 See M. DelCogliano, 'Eusebian Theologies of the Son as the Image of God before 341', *JECS* 14.4 (2006), 459–484.

16 Young helpfully comments, 'in other words, there is no substantial difference between the way the Son is God's image and the way other creatures might come to image God'. F. M. Young, *God's Presence: A Contemporary Recapitulation of Early Christianity* (Cambridge: Cambridge University Press, 2013), 165–166.

is not the history of two monolithic blocks standing one against the another. Instead, alliances were formed between those with different theological priorities and modes of expression.

Khaled Anatolios has proposed a scheme that builds upon Ayres's and Lienhard's categorizations, developing their schemas along the lines set out by DelCogliano. For Anatolios, the question of the Son's sameness or difference is better framed as the mode of their unity: Is it a unity of being or of will? The former means that the Father and Son are necessary to each other in a unity that does not include contingency. The latter means that the unity of the Father and Son is in some sense volitional and the result of a purposive act.[17] This allows a way of further understanding the issues at play in the way in which the Son was understood to be the image of the Father. Within the trajectory of Arius, the Son images the Father in a *contingent* and *participatory* fashion, in which the Son is gifted a likeness to the Father. Within the trajectory of Alexander and Athanasius, the Son images the Father in a *necessary* and *constitutive* fashion whereby, by the generation of the Son from the essence of the Father, the divinity of the Father is communicated to the Son. This provides the perspective to appreciate nuanced differences between allied figures. For example, Eusebius of Caesarea, a significant ally of Arius, held an image-Christology different from that of Arius from which a significant distinct trajectory can be traced through to the homoiousian theologians who were so influential in the eventual pro-Nicene consensus (see chapter 5).

Theological tensions behind the Arian controversy

The controversy between Arius and Alexander (*c.*318–25) was the clash of two very different sets of theological priorities related to tensions within the theological tradition of Alexandria. For certain, the fault lines exposed in this controversy reached far deeper than these two individuals. Arius was not a callous disputant against established and clear orthodoxy. His account of the relation of the Father and Son was, however, a point of crisis for a variety of theological tensions that were already well established.[18]

Before Arius, two dominant accounts of the Father–Son relation attributed their unity to the exercise of volition. In these accounts, the Son's privileged relation to the Father is *contingent* as opposed to necessary. This contingency

[17] Anatolios, *RN*, 30–31.

[18] See also L. Ayres and A. Radde-Gallwitz, 'The Doctrine of God', in S. A. Harvey and D. G. Hunter (eds.), *Oxford Handbook of Early Christian Studies* (Oxford: Oxford University Press, 2008), 867.

is signalled by the Son's participation in the divine being through the application of will or through an understanding of the Son as the image of the Father in such a way that the Son does not share in the divinity of the Father. The first account concerns the network of relations between God the Father, the Son and creation. Specifically, this includes the issue of the Son's derivation as 'begotten' and how this compares to the making of creation. Is the begetting of the Son, in some sense, temporal and from nothing? Does the Son exist within the divine being by necessity (*in se*: 'in itself') or for the purposes of creation (*pro nobis*: 'on our behalf')? The second account concerned the question of the relationship between the humanity and divinity of Jesus Christ. Arius was born into a theological world replete with tensions. While he did not create them in a bolshy volte-face from an established orthodoxy, his doctrine did have the effect of bringing some of these issues into sharper relief.

God, the Word and creation

The theological tradition of the Egyptian city of Alexandria was characterized by deep internal tensions. Most pertinent here was the tension in the conception of the relationship between the Word and God in the context of God's relationship to creation. At one and the same time, the Word was understood to be integral to the life of God independent from creation and also to *become* a subsistent reality through the exercise of God's will to create and relate to creation. This duality ran throughout several generations of Alexandrian theologians and Arius would come to attempt to reconcile this tension in his own distinctive theological solution.

The duality described above raises a range of other theological problems. The Word is eternal and yet derived from God the Father. How should this be reconciled with the conviction that God is self-existent (*agen[n]ētos*)? Beyond this, is the Word an immanent property of the Father (e.g. his wisdom) or a distinct, subsistent reality?[19] These issues were made sharper as they intersected with the Word's explicit association with the work of creation, nested as it was within a Platonist assumption that the transcendent God relates to the material creation through the Word.[20] There was an understanding that the Word becomes active, or a clearly differentiated determinate being, in the exercise of the will of God to create. The Word is pulled towards two different ultimate grounds of being: one internal to the divinity (*in se*) and the other only for the purpose of creation (*pro nobis*). One way to understand Arius is to see him as

[19] G. L. Prestige, *God in Patristic Thought* (London: William Heinemann, 1936), 129.
[20] See Young, *Making*, 42.

having made an attempt to reconcile these dualities in a single and rigorously logical account.[21]

Philo of Alexandria (*c.*20 BC – AD 50) is often cited as an important forerunner of Arius on the grounds that he believed the Word to have two stages of existence: as a quality of the divine being (God's wisdom) and then as a distinct subsistent reality by an act of the divine will.[22] This interpretation has been challenged by Williams, who in turn argues that Philo connected the divine will to the divine nature, such that God's will to create is grounded in his inherently generative being.[23] The Word is the divine idea of which the created universe is the material representation.[24] The Word is, in some sense, made active as a distinct and subsistent entity *in the exercise of God's will to create*, but this cannot be identified as a result of God's will isolated from his nature. Something similar has been expressed more recently by Fr Georges Florovsky, for whom the intelligibility of created reality is a function of its being a copy (or ectype) of the divine idea.[25] This comparison is illuminating because Florovsky's broader argument is for the eternal and distinct subsistence of the Word in contrast to the contingent and temporal existence of creation. However, Philo's account can be understood as locating the Word as actualized in its distinct subsistence in connection to the relationship between God and creation. Philo's account of the Word is characterized by tension that he does not resolve. The Word is both true of God's life (*in se*) and yet given distinct subsistence for the sake of creation (*pro nobis*).

The tensions inherent in Philo's account of the network of relations between God, the Word and creation persist in Clement of Alexandria (*c.* AD 150–215). Clement inherited something of the idea of a duality between the Word as an internal property of the being of God and the Word as a distinct and subsistent entity that becomes distinct *for the purposes of God's relationship to creation.*[26] This is reflected in slippery passages that describe the subsistent Word as a 'child of the Word that is identical with God'.[27] The Word has different stages of existence, one internal to God as a property and the other as a subsistent reality.

---

21 Williams, *Arius*, 117–157.

22 H. A. Wolfson, *The Philosophy of the Church Fathers: Faith, Trinity, Incarnation*, vol. 1 (Cambridge, Mass.: Harvard University Press, 1956), 582–585.

23 Williams, *Arius*, 117–124.

24 For the relationship between Logos theology and Platonic ideas, see Wolfson, *Philosophy of the Church Fathers*, 257–286.

25 G. Florovsky, 'Creation and Creaturehood', in *Creation and Redemption: Volume Three in the Collected Works of Georges Florovsky Emeritus Professor of Eastern Church History* (Belmont, Mass.: Nordland, 1976), 43–78, at 61.

26 Williams, *Arius*, 127.

27 Cited from ibid. 127, n. 103.

Indeed, Clement later faced the accusation that he believed there to be two *Logoi*, one internal and necessary to the being of God, and the other a distinct individual who subsists as such by the act of God in creating and relating to that which he made.[28]

Just one generation before Arius, Origen of Alexandria (AD 184–253) attempted to reconcile some of these tensions by emphasizing the distinct and concrete individuality of the Son as well as describing a graded divinity.[29] Like Philo and Clement, Origen considered the Word to be that of God which is communicable to us. Unlike Philo and Clement, however, Origen is clear on the Word's eternal distinct existence.[30] The term he used to describe this was *hypostasis*: 'the only-begotten Son is God's wisdom hypostatically existing'.[31] As a *hypostasis* the Word not only has distinct existence in our conception but also in reality.[32] This is related to Origen's doctrine of the Son's eternal generation from the Father. In outlining this doctrine, Origen is careful to make clear the unique nature of this derivation as something *proper* (rather than accidental) to the divine being. Accordingly, he is careful not to introduce notions such as the following:

1 Sequence, which would mean that the Father is antecedent to the Son.
2 The materialist inference that the divine nature was divided[33] or changed.[34] On this account, Origen eschewed language that spoke about the Son's and Father's sharing in the divine nature, or of the Son's deriving from the essence of the Father.[35]
3 The suggestion that the Son is 'from something external to God's own substance, so that there was a time when the Son did not exist'.[36]

The following passage gives an example of Origen's cautious reception of the derivation of the Son from the Father.

28 Ibid. 127–128.
29 Prestige, *God in Patristic Thought*, 132. For a discussion of Origen's subordinationism, see ibid. 131–142.
30 For a fuller textual study of the occurrence of *hypostasis* in Origen, see I. M. Ramelli, 'Origen, Greek Philosophy, and the Birth of the Trinitarian Meaning of *Hypostasis*', *HTR* 105.3 (2012), 302–350, esp. 301–309. Ramelli draws out the philosophical and scriptural background of Origen's use of this term and identifies Origen as anticipating what would become Nicene orthodoxy in describing the Father, Son and Spirit as distinct in *hypostasis* but one in *ousia*.
31 Origen, *Prin*, 1.2.1, tr. G. W. Butterworth (Notre Dame, Ind.: Christian Classics, 2013).
32 Origen, *Commentary on John*, 10.37.212. Cited from Ayres, *NL*, 25.
33 Origen, *Prin*, 1.2.6.
34 Ibid. 4.4.1, 4.
35 Ayres, *NL*, 24.
36 Origen, *Prin*, 4.4.1.

> It is impious and shocking to regard God the Father in the begetting of his only-begotten Son and in the Son's subsistence as being similar to any human being or other animal in the act of begetting; but there must needs be some exceptional process, worthy of God, to which we can find no comparison whatever, not merely in things, but even in thought and imagination, such that by its aid human thought could apprehend how the unbegotten God becomes Father of the only-begotten Son. This is an eternal and everlasting begetting, as brightness is begotten from light. For he does not become Son in an external way through the adoption of the Spirit, but is the Son by nature.[37]

This passage is remarkable for the way it pre-empts many of the disputes of the fourth century. The alertness to improper ideas being imposed on to divinity through the proposition that the Son is begotten from the Father would prove to be a significant feature of the fourth century, particularly in the reception of the term *homoousios*. Moreover, Origen's clear-sighted distinction between the Son's extrinsic participation in divinity through adoption and his intrinsic belonging through generation would become a pillar of Athanasius' theological contribution.

To substantiate the unique status of the Son's derivation of the Father Origen applied the logic of correlate relations. If God is eternally Father, then there must eternally be the Son of whom he is the Father:[38] 'God was always the Father of his only-begotten Son.'[39] This means that the Son/Word does not have distinct existence *pro nobis* (as Williams characteristically puts it, he is not a 'cosmological convenience'[40]), but rather is true of the inner reality of what it is to be God. The way God exists is in the act of the Father's begetting the Son.[41] In other words, Origen positions the Father–Son relation as *constitutive of divine perfection*. Behr neatly summarizes the significance of this:

> [This] leads to the key theological insight, a fundamental principle of later Nicene trinitarian theology, that the relationship to the Son is constitutive of what it is to be God and, moreover, that the distinct subsistence of the

[37] Ibid. 1.2.4.

[38] Williams, *Arius*, 138.

[39] Origen, *Prin*, 1.2.2.

[40] Williams, *Arius*, 139.

[41] See P. Widdicombe, *The Fatherhood of God from Origen to Athanasius* (Oxford: Oxford University Press, 2001), 64–92.

> Son derives from the existence of God as Father rather than from his activity as creator.[42]

Another way Origen describes the Son's generation from the Father is through the notion that the Son is the brightness of the Father's light and image of the Father (Origen draws on John 1:5 and Heb. 1:3[43]):

> As therefore light can never exist without its brightness, so neither can the Son, who is called the 'impress' of the Father's 'substance', and his Word and Wisdom, be conceived as existing without the Father. How then can it be said that there was a time when the Son did not exist? For this is nothing else but to say that there was a time when truth did not exist, when wisdom did not exist, when life did not exist.[44]

Just as light has never existed without its brightness and an object always casts an image, so the Father has never existed without the Son, who is the wisdom and truth of the Father. This is an eternal imaging intrinsic to the nature of God.[45] As the image of the Father, the Son participates in all the Father is, reflects the Father perfectly[46] and is the revelation of the Father.[47] While this pre-empts Athanasius' image-Christology that would be central to the eventual Nicene consensus, it is here that Origen's thought begins to get more ambiguous. Origen establishes some distinction between the Son as image and the divinity of the Father. For example, he makes the following differentiation: the Son 'is an image of God's goodness, but not goodness itself'.[48] The goodness of the Son is a derivative goodness that has its source in the Father. It is the same goodness possessed in a different mode. In this sense, Origen's image-Christology would also inform the thought of Asterius.

This ambiguity is related to Origen's ideas of a graded divinity in which the Son is God in a reduced way. For Origen, the Son reveals the Father, but in such a way that the 'brightness falls softly on the tender and weak eyes of mortal man'.[49] In this connection, Origen could describe the Son as lower than the Father (and the Spirit as lower than the Son):

---

42 Behr, *WN*, 185. See also Ayres, *NL*, 27.
43 Origen, *Prin*, 1.2.7.
44 Ibid. 4.4.1.
45 Ayres, *NL*, 22.
46 Origen, *Prin*, 1.2.13.
47 Ibid. 1.2.8
48 Ibid.
49 Ibid. 1.2.7.

> The God and Father, who holds the universe together, is superior to every being that exists, for he imparts to each one from his existence that which each one is; the Son being less than the Father, is superior to rational creatures alone (for he is second to the Father); the Holy Spirit is still less, and dwells with the Saints alone.[50]

The purpose of this subordination of the Son is to enforce the transcendence of the Father as the font of divinity and the dependence of the Son on the Father whereby one does not posit two ingenerate beings.[51] This graded conception of divinity is the reason some think of Origen as the forerunner of Arius.[52] This, in the opinion of Fairbairn and Reeves, is of a piece with the Platonism of Origen's day, which gives shape to his soteriology as the descent of a lesser God to enable human souls to return to the highest divinity.[53]

It is in this context that Origen's occasional comments about the Father's willing the Son into existence should be understood.[54] This is difficult to reconcile with Origen's doctrine of eternal generation. However, the purpose of introducing volition into the doctrine of eternal generation is not primarily to ground the Son's existence in contingency but rather to emphasize that the Father alone is the uncaused origin.[55] This also intersects with Origen's alertness to the introduction of materialistic characteristics to divinity. To say the Son is begotten from the will of the Father is an alternative to the Son's generation from the essence of the Father, which may imply that the divine being can be divided or shared. As will be discussed in the next chapter, this would prove to be an influential argument of the anti-Nicene theologians of the fourth century and a primary motivation of describing the Son as begotten from the will (not the essence) of the Father. However, Origen's intention was not to undermine the necessity of the Son, but rather to *account for the eternity of the Son by using terms that did not undermine the unique status of the Father or the immateriality*

50 Ibid. 1.3.5.

51 See Behr, *WN*, 187–191.

52 B. Studer, *Trinity and Incarnation: The Faith of the Early Church* (Edinburgh: T&T Clark, 1994), 102–103; E. A. Clark, *The Origenist Controversy: The Cultural Construction of an Early Christian Debate* (Princeton, N.J.: Princeton University Press, 1992). Ayres challenges this assessment. Ayres, *NL*, 20–21.

53 Fairbairn and Reeves, *SCC*, 52–53. If this is the case, then this represents a tradition flowing from Justin Martyr, who understood the *Word* in a similar fashion to the second God of Platonism, who mediated between God and creation. See Behr, *WN*, 103–106. See also J. Dillon, *The Middle Platonists: 80 B.C. to A.D. 220*, rev. edn (Ithaca, N.Y.: Cornell University Press, 1996), 46. This aspect of Justin's thought is described briefly in chapter 2.

54 E.g. Origen, *Prin*, 1.2.6.

55 See Behr, *WN*, 193.

of the divine nature. It is important to be aware of this if the intentions of Arius and the later anti-Nicene theologians are not to be misunderstood.

Finally, Origen describes some intersection between the doctrine of eternal generation of the Son and the eternity of creation. He applies the same logic of correlate relations to the issue of cosmogony.[56]

> Now as one cannot be a father apart from having a son . . . so we cannot even call God almighty if there are none over whom he can exercise power. Accordingly, to prove that God is almighty we must assume the existence of the universe. For if anyone would have it that certain ages, or periods of time, or whatever he cares to call them, elapsed during which the present creation did not exist, he would undoubtedly prove that in those ages or period God was not almighty, but that he afterwards became almighty from the time when he began to have creatures over whom he could exercise power.[57]

Therefore, 'of necessity those things must always have existed, in virtue of which he is called [almighty]'.[58] Torrance diagnoses this as a 'failure to distinguish between the ontological and cosmological dimensions in his understanding of God as Father and as Creator'.[59] This is illustrative of the fact that, in Alexandrian theology, the status of the Son as derived from the Father and the status of creation are inextricably linked together. Origen's account of the eternity of creation came under severe criticism from Methodius of Olympia. Methodius, in a way that would give shape to part of Arius' thought, argued that to conceive of the cosmos as eternal alongside God was to establish it as a rival self-subsistent entity.[60] This would undermine the central claims of the uniqueness of God in his self-subsistence and so his ontological freedom. As Anatolios explains, 'God alone was unbegotten, sole existent, uniquely prior to everything that came to be through him.'[61] For this reason, Methodius insists on God's alone being ingenerate (*agennētos*), whereas creation is brought into being from nothing at a particular moment. In the working out of this doctrine, Methodius theorized an interval between the eternity of God and the coming

56 Anatolios, *RN*, 39.
57 Origen, *Prin*, 1.2.10.
58 Ibid.
59 T. F. Torrance, *The Christian Doctrine of God: One Being Three Persons* (London: T&T Clark, 2016), 208.
60 Williams, *Arius*, 168. See also Behr, *NF*, 38–48. For a consideration of a positive fourth-century reception of Origen, see Beeley's discussion of Pamphilus of Caesarea. C. Beeley, *The Unity of Christ: Continuity and Conflict in Patristic Tradition* (New Haven, Conn.: Yale University Press, 2012), 50–55.
61 Anatolios, *RN*, 39.

into being of creation.[62] That is, 'a quasi-time in which God existed before the world'.[63]

Methodius' concern was with the freedom of God and his uniqueness as the only ingenerate reality. However, in resisting a plurality of self-subsistent beings, he laid a question at the door of the proposition that something can derive from the Father and exist eternally. For example, Methodius describes the Father as the 'unoriginated origin', while the Son is the 'beginning after the beginning . . . the origin of everything else created'.[64] In Methodius' schema, there is some quasi-temporal sequence between Father and Son, suggesting that the interval between God and creation may also apply between the Father and the Son.[65]

What does all this have to do with the controversy between Arius and Alexander of Alexandria? In the view of Williams:

> the logical stresses of the Alexandrian Christian tradition finally proved intolerable [for Arius]: without wholly discarding the vocabulary and framework of metaphor going back to Philo, Arius attempts to cut the Gordian knot produced by those of his forbears.[66]

What is understood to be Arius' rigorously logical mind was uncomfortable with the cognitive dissonance of the Alexandrian tradition and he set about reconciling the tension by committing himself wholly to the understanding of the Word as existing *pro nobis*. This sets Arius on a trajectory in relation to his forebears, including a strongly subordinationist Christology (applying Methodius' notion of pretemporal sequence not to creation but to the Son) and apophatic theology, which emphasizes the unique freedom of the one unbegotten God.[67]

The humanity and divinity of Jesus Christ

A second set of tensions that would inform the Arian controversy was the issue of the humanity and divinity of Jesus Christ. Lucian of Antioch (*c.* AD 240–312) is a figure about whom little is known for sure. This is a frustration because

62 Behr, *NF*, 45–47.
63 Ibid. 48.
64 Cited from Hanson, *SCDG*, 83.
65 L. G. Patterson, *Methodius of Olympus: Divine Sovereignty, Human Freedom, and Life in Christ* (Washington, D.C.: Catholic University of America Press, 1997), 47.
66 Williams, *Arius*, 124.
67 Ibid. 175.

Arius defined himself as a 'Lucianist'.[68] Moreover, the fifth-century historian Philostogorius presents Lucian (not Arius) as the rallying point for those who resisted the Nicene confession.[69] What is known about Lucian comes from two secondary accounts of his thought. First, Epiphanius describes Lucian's doctrine of the incarnation as the Word's assuming a human body without a soul. The purpose of this, he writes, was 'in order that they might attach human passion directly to the Word'.[70] In other words, the full humanity of the incarnate Son was denied so that the sufferings and limitations of Jesus Christ might be attributed not to his human nature but to the attenuated divinity of the Word.[71] Second, the historian Sozomen records that the Second Creed of the Dedication Council (AD 341) was claimed to have been Lucianite in its theological commitments.[72] The fundamental convictions of this confession include a denial that the Son is identical in essence to the Father alongside a positive affirmation that the Son is distinct from the Father in reality, not only in our apprehension.

Williams suggests that Lucianite thought should be located within the broad category of image theology.[73] A distinctively 'Lucianite image Christology' subordinates the image (the Son) to the true object (the Father): the Son resembles the Father as the image does the reality, but does not share fully in the divinity of the Father.[74] This becomes increasingly explicit in those who would come to identify themselves with Lucian: Arius, Asterius and Eusebius of Nicomedia.[75] The Lucian tradition includes a network of connected convictions: the real distinct subsistence of the Father and Son, articulated in its subordinationist image-Christology, which means that the limitations of the incarnate Word do not need to be accredited to his humanity, but to the reduced deity of the Word.

On the other hand, there is the equally shadowy figure of Paul of Samosata, who, like Lucian, made an impact that lasted well into the fourth century.[76] Excerpts from the Council of Antioch (268/269) at which he was deposed are recorded by Eusebius.[77] Both Hilary of Poitiers and Athanasius record that Paul

---

68 Arius, *Letter to Eusebius of Nicomedia*, Urk 1, *NPNF* II.3; recorded in Thedoret, *Ecclesiastical History*, 1.4, NPNF II.3.

69 Cited from Ayres, *NL*, 57.

70 Epiphanius of Salamis, *Ancoratus: Die griechischen christlichen Schriftsteller* 25, 33. Cited from Behr, *NF*, 50.

71 Epiphanius of Salamis, 33–35. Cited from Hanson, *SCDG*, 79.

72 Sozomen, *Ecclesiastical History*, 3.5, *NPNF* II.2.

73 Williams, *Arius*, 162–167.

74 Ayres, *NL*, 57–58.

75 Williams, *Arius*, 163.

76 See Behr, *WN*, 207–235.

77 Eusebius of Caesarea, *Ecclesiastical History*, 7.30.

thought of the Word as a property or function internal to the being of God and not as a subsistent individual.[78] Very significantly given the developments that would unfold in the fourth century, Hilary records that Paul used the word *homoousion* to describe this doctrine: 'by attributing this title to God [Paul] had taught that He was single and undifferentiated, and at once Father to himself'.[79] The association of *homoousios* with Paul, Hilary explains, is the reason why it was so difficult to form a consensus around it: 'the Church still regards it as profane to exclude the different personal qualities, and, under the mask of the aforesaid expressions, to revive the error of confounding the persons'.[80] Similar explanations of the condemnation of the term *homoousion* at the council of Antioch are given by Athanasius and Basil of Caesarea.[81]

A second feature of Paul's thought is a distinction between the Word who exists eternally as a property or function of the divine being and the Son who has distinct subsistence only *pro nobis*.[82] Eusebius writes that '[Paul] does not confess that Christ is the Son of God and God before his generation in the flesh'.[83] Instead, it was this impersonal aspect of God's becoming manifest in the human being Jesus of Nazareth, who 'was not before Mary'.[84] In other words, the title 'Son' pertains only to the incarnate state of the Word. This aspect of Paul's theology is recorded in the minutes of the Council of Antioch: 'he says that Jesus is one and the other is the Word'.[85] Accordingly, Jesus Christ was a human anointed by this impersonal characteristic of divinity.[86] Through this anointing, Jesus Christ lived in such perfect harmony with the will of God that he was adopted as the Son of God.[87] Therefore, Paul conceived of the unity of the Father and Son not as a necessary unity of essence, but as contingent upon 'their agreement', their unity of will.[88] For Paul, then, it was true to say Jesus was 'from below',[89] 'in his nature he was a common man'[90] and God only in the sense that he was 'becoming God from man'.[91]

---

78 Athanasius, *On the Synods*, 45, NPNF II.4; Hilary of Poitiers, *On the Synods*, 81, NPNF II.9.

79 Hilary, *Synods*, 81.

80 Ibid. See also Young, *Making*, 44–45; Fairbairn and Reeves, *SCC*, 64; Hanson, *SCDG*, 69–72; Prestige, *God in Patristic Thought*, 202–203.

81 Athanasius, *Synods*, 43, 45; Basil of Caesarea, *Ep*, 52.1.

82 Athanasius, *Discourses Against the Arians*, 2.13; 3.51; 4.30; NPNF II.4.

83 Eusebius of Caesarea, *Ecclesiastical Theology*, 14, 1.14. Cited from Behr, *WN*, 215.

84 Athanasius, *Synods*, 45.

85 Cited from Behr, *WN*, 227.

86 For a presentation of the primary sources, see Behr, *WN*, 227–235.

87 Prestige, *God in Patristic Thought*, 115.

88 Athanasius, *Synods*, 45.

89 Eusebius of Caesarea, *Ecclesiastical History*, 7.30.11.

90 Ibid. 7.27.2.

91 Athanasius, *Synods*, 45.

Even though one might more naturally correlate Paul of Samosata to Marcellus of Ancyra (see chapter 4), there are points of contact between Arius and Paul. Specifically, the following convictions:

1. that the Son did not always exist (although for Paul, this is existence as a distinct particular);
2. that the Son's union with the Father is by will and adoption;
3. that the Father alone is God, whereas the Son is only so by grace.

These intersect with the points of contact that exist between Arius and Lucian. Like Lucian, Arius considers the Word to be the image of God, a reduced divinity, distinct in subsistence from the Father,[92] whose attenuated divinity is such that full humanity is not necessary in order to experience the various limitations of a created being.

The controversy between Arius and Alexander of Alexandria

The controversy between Arius and Alexander of Alexandria, which erupted in the latter years of the second decade (or the opening years of the third decade) of the fourth century,[93] is directly related to the tensions described above. The attempt to hold together the correlate eternity of the Father and the Son with the Son's derivative existence from the Father in the context of the Son's specific connection to the creative act of God was a complex theological problem that reached deep into the theological tradition of Alexandria. Arius and Alexander appear to have attempted to resolve these tensions in contradictory ways, precipitating the controversy that spilled out from Alexandria into the rest of the church.

There were other factors behind this controversy. For example, there was a degree of personal animosity between the two men. Arius, reportedly, considered himself passed over in favour of Alexander's being appointed Bishop of Alexandria in 313 and 'fell prey to the assaults of jealousy'.[94] Moreover, there were historical complexities of the role of the episcopate in the city of Alexandria.[95] However, Theodoret's fiercely antagonistic account of Arius as a

92 Williams has demonstrated that Arius would have considered Paul to be Sabellian. R. Williams, 'The Logic of Arianism', *JTS* 34.1 (1983), 56–81.

93 For an overview of the scholarship of the chronology of the controversy, see S. Parvis, *Marcellus of Ancyra and the Lost Years of the Arian Controversy 325–345* (Oxford: Oxford University Press, 2006), 69–72.

94 Theodoret, *Ecclesiastical History*, 1.1, *NPNF* II.3. See also Sozomen, *Ecclesiastical History*, 1.15.

95 See Behr, *NF*, 62; Beeley, *Unity of Christ*, 106–107.

troublemaker, implacably opposed to the truth of the gospel, is scarcely credible. The controversy began when Arius, a presbyter in Alexandria, took issue with Alexander's account of the coeternity of the Father and Son.[96] Against this, Arius insisted that the Father precedes the Son, believing Alexander's position to undermine the absolute divine being by implying two ungenerate principles. Beyond the absolute primacy of the Father, this also appeared to Arius to compromise the immateriality of the divine nature, attributing a physical idea of procreation or division to divinity.[97] This is complemented by reports of Arius' teaching, which included the doctrines 'that the Son of God was made out of that which had no prior existence, that there was a period of time in which he existed not; that, as possessing free will, he was capable of vice and virtue, and that he was created and made'.[98]

Arius wrote a statement of faith (discussed in detail below), presumably as a submission to a local synod to examine his theology. After examination of his thought, Arius was expelled from Alexandria.[99] He was reinstated by a synod held in Palestine from where he set about recruiting a number of senior bishops, many of whom were associated with the figure of Lucian of Antioch,[100] who wrote a number of letters to support his case. Among these bishops was Eusebius of Nicomedia, who had connections to the imperial house and who 'inaugurated a letter campaign' in support of Arius and against Alexander.[101] Athanasius reports that it was this 'Lucian Circle' that encouraged Arius to compose his famous work the *Thalia*.[102] Arius' cause was further bolstered by Asterius' *Syntagmation*, a text commissioned to articulate the theological tradition Arius represented. Alexander also appealed for broader support, including a significant letter to Alexander of Byzantium (*Hē philarchos*). He held a synod in Alexandria to condemn Arius, from which emerged an encyclical letter (known as 'One Body' [*Henos sōmatos*]), which responds to aspects of Arius' thought. With bishops rallying around contesting theological positions, a council, which met in 325 in Nicaea, was called to decide upon the issues under question.[103] The council decided in favour of the position represented by Alexander, and Arius was exiled.

96 Socrates, *Ecclesiastical History*, 1.5, *NPNF* II.2.
97 Williams, *Arius*, 84–86; Socrates, *Ecclesiastical History*, 1.5.
98 Sozomen, *Ecclesiastical History*, 1.15.
99 Socrates, *Ecclesiastical History*, 1.6; Sozomen, *Ecclesiastical History*, 1.15.
100 Epiphanius suggests that Arius studied under Lucian. See Hanson, *SCDG*, 5, n. 11.
101 Beeley, *Unity of Christ*, 107.
102 Athanasius, *Synods*, 15.
103 For a historical overview, see Behr, *NF*, 62–67, and Ayres, *NL*, 15–20.

Alexander of Alexandria

At most, two letters of Alexander remain: one to Alexander of Byzantium (probably quite early in the controversy, *c.*320/321[104]) and the encyclical letter from 100 North African bishops at the large synod held in Alexandria denouncing Arius.[105] These letters are both primarily concerned with describing and rejecting Arius' doctrine,[106] but it is still possible to discern something of Alexander's own theological perspectives.

Alexander's theology is most fully set out in his letter to Alexander of Byzantium (*Hē philarchos*) in which he complains of a conspiracy at work in Alexandria.[107] Arius is named as a conspirator against him and a summary of Arius' teaching is given. The central ideas Alexander attributes to Arius are as follows:

1 the one we know as the Son is created out of nothing;[108]
2 this coming into existence took place at some point and so there was a time when he did not exist;[109]
3 therefore, the Son is mutable;[110]
4 the meaning of the begotten is comparable to the origination of creation;[111]
5 therefore, he is not the Son of God by nature;
6 but was chosen to be so as a result of his perfect adherence to the Father's will, whereby 'his painstaking character suffered no deterioration' (it is a unity of will).[112]

In the encyclical letter (*henos sōmatos*) Alexander attributes the following additional doctrines to Arius:

[104] Recorded in Theodoret, *Ecclesiastical History*, 1.3. On the dating of this letter, see Williams, *Arius*, 50–61.
[105] Recorded in Socrates, *Ecclesiastical History*, 1.6, and Athanasius, *Defence Against the Arians*, *NPNF* II.435. For scholarship on date and authorship, see D. M. Gwynn, *The Eusebians: The Polemic of Athanasius of Alexandria and the Construction of the 'Arian Controversy'* (Oxford: Oxford University Press, 2006), 59–66. On authorship, the letter might well have been written by his eventual successor, Athanasius. See Williams, *Arius*, 50–54, and C. Stead, 'Athanasius' Earliest Written Works', *JTS* 39.1 (1988), 76–91. Stead considers the terminology of this letter – particularly its use of *ousia* – indicates Athanasius' authorship. C. Stead, *Divine Substance* (Oxford: Clarendon Press, 1977), 225. However, even if this is the case, it was sanctioned and signed by Alexander and so can be held as representative of his views. See also Parvis, *Marcellus*, 62–63.
[106] Gwynn, *Athanasius of Alexandria*, 62.
[107] Alexander of Alexandria, *Letter to Alexander of Byzantium (Hē philarchos)*, Urk 14, *NPNF* II.3. Theodoret, *Ecclesiastical History*, 1.3. The following references take their numbering from Urk 14.
[108] Alexander, *Letter to Alexander of Byzantium*, 11.
[109] Ibid. 22–23.
[110] Ibid. 11.
[111] Ibid. 19–21.
[112] Ibid. 13, 34.

7 that 'there was a period when [God] was not the Father';[113]
8 whereby the Son is a 'creature and work' of the Father.[114]
9 And was made for the purpose of bringing creation into being and 'would never have existed if God had not wanted to create us'.[115]
10 As the Son is entirely *pro nobis*, he is not proper to the Father but is 'alien to and other than the essence of God'.[116]
11 For which reason the Father is 'inexplicable' and 'invisible' to the Son.

Exegetically, Alexander complains that Arius and his allies focus on the passages of Scripture that describe the incarnate Son in human terms and then apply these to his pre-incarnate state ('they pick out every passage which refers to the dispensation of salvation'[117]), while ignoring the passages that refer to his divinity.[118] This tracks closely to the Lucianite theme of ascribing the limitations of the scriptural portrayal of Jesus not to the full humanity of Jesus, but to the attenuated divinity of the Son. Rejecting this, Alexander draws a distinction between that which belongs to the Son by nature and what is contingent upon his condescension to us.[119]

In contrast to Arius' thought, Alexander states his own conception of the Father–Son relation, which is characterized by what Ayres describes as their 'essential sameness'.[120] This is constituted by a real sharing of divinity rather than a non-substantial mirroring described above in relation to Lucian of Antioch. So, that which can be said of the Father, for example, that he is unchanging, can be said of the Son also.[121] Core to Alexander's thought are the two themes of correlate relations and the Son as the image of the Father. These ideas coalesce in Alexander's thought to mean that the generation of the Son is *intrinsic* to divinity.

As part of this, Alexander lays considerable stress on the eternally correlative relation of the Father and Son.[122] Attributing to Arius the doctrine that the Son

113 Alexander of Alexandria, *Letter to all Bishops (Henos sōmatos)*, 7, Urk 4b. Socrates, *Ecclesiastical History*, 1.6, NPNF II.2. The following references take their numbering from Urk 4b.
114 Alexander, *Letter to all Bishops*, 7.
115 Ibid. 9.
116 Ibid. 8.
117 Alexander, *Letter to Alexander*, 4.
118 Ibid. 4, 37.
119 See Behr, *NF*, 125.
120 Ayres, *NL*, 43–52.
121 Alexander, *Letter to all Bishops*, 14.
122 Beeley describes the theological overlap between Alexander and Origen. Beeley, *Unity of Christ*, 114–115.

was created out of nothing, Alexander argues for the eternal correlate existence of the Son with the Father.[123]

> The interval during which [Arius and his supporters] say the Son was still unbegotten of the Father was, according to their opinion, prior to the wisdom of God, by whom all things were created . . . Since the hypothesis implied in the phrase 'out of the non-existent' is manifestly impious, it follows that the Father is always Father. And He is Father from the continual presence of the Son, on account of whom He is called Father. And the Son being ever present with Him, the Father is ever perfect, wanting in no good thing, for He did not beget His only Son in time, or in any interval of time, nor out of that which had no previous existence.[124]

Arius' proposition that there is an interval between the Father and Son means that the Father was not always the Father, implying that there is something lacking in God prior to the generation of the Son. This is made more explicit as Alexander shifts his footing to argue that Arius' doctrine is tantamount to saying that there was a time when God existed without his wisdom and without the brightness of his glory:

> Is it not then impious to say that there was a time when the wisdom of God was not? Who saith, 'I was by Him as one brought up with Him: I was daily His delight?' Or that once the power of God was not, or His Word, or anything else by which the Son is known, or the Father designated, defective? To assert that 'the brightness of the Father's glory once did not exist' destroys also the original light of which it is the brightness; and if there ever was a time in which the image of God was not, it is plain that He Whose image He is, is not always: nay, by the non-existence of the express image of God's Person, He also is taken away of whom this is ever the express image.[125]

Alexander thus presents Arius' doctrine as destructive of the doctrine of God. Against this, Alexander returns to his main theme, which is the Son's unique relation to the Father, whereby the Son is *proper* to the Father. A similar line of argumentation is present in the encyclical letter. Referring to the Johannine doctrine that creation is made through the Word, Alexander writes:

123 Alexander, *Letter to Alexander*, 15.
124 Ibid. 24–26.
125 Ibid. 27–29.

> Who, hearing . . . that all things were made by him, will not abhor those who pronounce the Son to be one of the things made? How can he be one of the things which were made by himself? Or how can he be the only-begotten, if he is reckoned among created things? . . . How is he unlike the Father's essence who is his perfect image, and the brightness of his glory . . . ? Again, how if the Son is the Word and Wisdom of God, was there a period when he did not exist? For that is equivalent to saying that God was once destitute both of Word and Wisdom.[126]

By this mode of argumentation Alexander disqualifies any idea of sequence in derivation of the Son from the Father.[127] By describing the Father and Son in a necessary correlate relation,[128] Alexander presents the Father–Son relation as constitutive of divine perfection.[129]

This is closely related to Alexander's account of the Son as the image of the Father. Unlike Lucian, Alexander's image-Christology does not include the subordination of the Son through a non-essential likeness. For Alexander, the notion of image is used to denote the unity of nature between the Father and Son because the Son, as the image of the Father, shares fully the divinity of the one he reflects. The continuity between the image and the source is strengthened by Alexander's notion of the Son's generation out from the Father, whereupon he shares in the divinity of the Father:[130]

> We have learnt that the Son is immutable and unchangeable, all-sufficient and perfect, like the Father, lacking only His 'unbegotten.' He is the exact and precisely similar image of His Father. For it is clear that the image fully contains everything by which the greater likeness . . . And in accordance with this we believe that the Son always existed of the Father; for he is the brightness of His glory, and the express image of His Father's Person.[131]

As the image, the Son is the exact likeness of the Father,[132] whereby to posit division of essence between them is an absurdity.

---

126 Alexander, *Letter to all Bishops*, 13.
127 Beeley, *Unity of Christ*, 116.
128 Ibid. 115–116.
129 Anatolios, *RN*, 83. See also Widdicombe, *Fatherhood of God*, 130–132.
130 See D. A. Giulea, 'Divine Being's Modulations: *Ousia* in the Pro-Nicene Context of the Fourth Century', *SVTQ*, 59.3 (105), 307–337, at 309–311.
131 Alexander, *Letter to Alexander*, 47–48.
132 Ibid. 38.

Given that the Father–Son relation is unique and intrinsic to divine being, Alexander contrasts the eternal and necessary Sonship of the eternal Son to our contingent and adoptive sonship. Following a long discussion on the Son as the perfect image of the Father, Alexander draws the following inference:

> Hence it may be seen, that the Sonship of our Saviour has not even anything in common with the sonship of men. For just as it has been shown that the nature of His existence cannot be expressed by language, and infinitely surpasses in excellence all things to which He has given being, so His Sonship, naturally partaking in His paternal Divinity, is unspeakably different from the sonship of those who, by His appointment, have been adopted as sons.[133]

The Son is Son by nature not by grace. Therefore, his Sonship is not contingent on his 'being particularly diligent or working hard to progress morally', and cannot be lost.[134] Creation, on the other hand, is extrinsic to divinity and so, if we are to become the children of God, it is by the grace of adoption. Alexander's soteriological understanding, then, emphasizes our adoption as the children of God by participating in the one who is Son by nature.[135]

All of this raises the classic 'Arian' objection that if the Son is coeternal with the Father, does this not undermine the unique primacy of the Father as the sole unbegotten (see below)? Alexander's response to that criticism is to reject the proposition that either the Son is created or there are two unbegotten gods. Instead, Alexander identifies the Son as eternal and yet begotten from the unbegotten Father:

> These inventors of silly tales assert that we, who reject their impious and unscriptural blasphemy concerning the creation of Christ from the non-existent, teach that there are two unbegotten Beings. For these ill-instructed men contend that one of these alternatives must hold; either He must be believed to have come out of the non-existent, or there are two unbegotten Beings.[136]

Here Alexander is beginning to develop the contrast between the making of creation and the generation of the Son.[137] The Son is eternal, but this is not the

133 Ibid. 28–29.
134 Ibid. 34.
135 Ibid. See also Behr, *NF*, 129.
136 Alexander, *Letter to Alexander*, 46–48.
137 Ibid. 49.

same as saying he is unbegotten. Similarly, the Son is generate from the Father but this is not the same thing as to say he has a beginning. The clarification and consolidation of this idea that the Son is *eternally* derived from the Father would become central to Nicene orthodoxy.

Arius

Arius was probably from modern-day Libya and, we are told by Epiphanius, was an old man by the time the conflict with Alexander erupted. He was a highly regarded preacher in Alexandria,[138] and the leader of an ascetic community. Sozomen describes Arius as an expert logician,[139] and a characteristic of his thought was the attempt to reconcile tensions that existed in Alexandrian theology by taking one side of various dualities to their logical conclusion. In this way, he exposed and deepened fault lines that existed quite apart from him. It is for this reason that while Arius was the catalyst for the fourth-century disputes, he himself fades from significance after the Council of Nicaea. As is described in the following chapter, the notion of an 'Arianism' as a single coherent system perpetuated by disciples of Arius was a polemical construction of the fourth century to gather opponents of the Nicene confession under one unacceptable banner.[140] In reality, those who were dissatisfied with the Nicene confession were equally uncomfortable with aspects of Arius' theology and even distanced themselves from association with Arius.

Several of Arius' writings remain. There are three complete letters:

1 the credal letter to Alexander of Alexandria (*c*.321/322);[141]
2 an alliance-seeking letter to Eusebius of Nicomedia (*c*.321/322);[142]
3 a bland confession of faith seeking readmittance to the church following the Council of Nicaea.[143]

Extracts from his poetic work the *Thalia* are recorded by Athanasius in *On the Synods*, 15, and in *Against the Arians*, 1.5–6. The latter, however, is submerged in Athanasius' polemic (which reflects criticisms articulated in Alexander's encyclical letter[144]), whereas the former, seeing as they retain poetic metre,

138 Sozomen, *Ecclesiastical History*, 1.15.
139 Ibid.
140 See Williams, *Arius*, 82–90.
141 Recorded in Athanasius, *Synods*, 16.
142 Recorded in Theodoret, *Ecclesiastical History*, 1.4.
143 Recorded in Socrates, *Ecclesiastical History*, 1.26.
144 See Behr, *NF*, 135.

appear to be direct quotations.[145] There are also a number of other documents by authors sympathetic to Arius that are significant for a full appreciation of the issues involved in the Arian controversy.[146]

Scholarship in the nineteenth and early twentieth centuries tended to treat Arius as the architect of all subsequent heresy, recasting the gospel in the garb of rationalism[147] or Platonism.[148] As such, he has been presented as the archetypal heretic in relation to whom all other heresies can be coordinated.[149] More recently, revisionist scholarship, while recognizing the important influence of philosophical concerns on Arius' thought (such as his doctrine of pretemporal time and of a graded divinity in which the Son participates in the divine nature contingently as opposed to by necessity),[150] has noted the fact that Arius, steeped in Scripture and Christian tradition, was motivated by the religious concerns of worship and salvation as much as with the philosophical concerns of cosmology.[151] For example, Gregg and Groh present the case that Arius was motivated primarily by soteriological concerns in which the Son, who is changeable by nature, undergoes a process of moral advancement and assumes flesh to provide an exemplar and model for moral excellence by which we may also be adopted as the children of God.[152] However, as Ayres points out, this is reliant on Arius' teaching a direct adoptionistic Christology, similar to that of Paul of Samosata, for which there is no direct evidence.[153] Williams has been central to this reassessment of Arius, arguing that Arius was a theological conservative steeped in the theological and liturgical[154] commitments of Alexandrian Christianity (such as the unique primacy of the unbegotten and the nuanced account of the relationship between the Word and creation),[155] whereby his thought has connections with philosophical conjecture, but he cannot be considered an adherent of any one system.[156] Following the force of Williams's analysis, Arius is treated here as a Christian theologian.

145 Hanson, *SCDG*, 10.

146 For a discussion of the sources of the Arian controversy, see Williams, *Arius*, 48–61. These documents are included in the discussion below.

147 J. H. Newman, *The Arians of the Fourth Century* (Notre Dame, Ind.: University of Notre Dame Press, 2001), 1–38, 403–416, and Harnack, *History of Dogma*, 4.2–8, 38–49. Cited from Behr, *NF*, 132.

148 Gwatkin, *Studies of Arianism*, 17–28. Cited from Behr, *NF*, 133.

149 See Williams's analysis of this view. Williams, *Arius*, 2–11.

150 C. Stead, 'The Platonism of Arius', *JTS* 24 (1973), 85–100; Hanson, *SCDG*, 85–87; Anatolios, *RN*, 42–44.

151 C. Stead, 'The *Thalia* of Arius and the Testimony of Athanasius', *JTS* 29 (1978), 20–52; M. Wiles, 'In Defence of Arius', *JTS* 13 (1962), 339–347.

152 Gregg and Groh, *Early Arianism*, 15–30, 65. See also Hanson, *SCDG*, 27.

153 Ayres, *NL*, 55.

154 R. Williams, 'Angels Unawares: Heavenly Liturgy and Earthly Theology in Alexandria', *StPatr* (1997), 350–363.

155 Williams, *Arius*, 117–178.

156 Ibid. 230–232.

The driving force of Arius' complaint against Alexander is his concern to maintain the absolute and unique singularity of God. A significant aspect of this was the primacy of the term unoriginate/unbegotten (*agen[n]ētos*) in Arius' doctrine of God (see below for a discussion of this term). It is fundamental to the grammar of divinity that no being is more fundamental than the divine being (God does not derive being from beyond himself) and that there cannot be two absolute beings. In this connection, Arius rejected Alexander's doctrine of the Father and Son as coeternal and insisted on the singularity of the one unbegotten God.[157] In this, as Beeley points out, Arius can be understood as a deeply conservative thinker concerned to safeguard the transcendence of God, and the singularity of the absolute divine being.[158] So, there are aspects of Arius' thought that are unproblematic on the surface: the Son is not unbegotten; the Son is derived from the Father and receives from the Father; the Father alone is unbegotten. However, in his efforts to reject any notion of there being two ungenerate principles, Arius rejected the coeternity of the Son with the Father. The Son, Arius argued, is God only in a reduced sense, who, as begotten, has origin from nothing in some quasi-temporal period before the beginning of created time (meaning he is after the Father in terms of sequence). As such, the Son is a creature of the Father who images God in a non-substantial way. Instead, Arius thinks of the Son as changeable in nature, who is given, in response to his foreseen excellence of moral character, a unique share in divinity, whereby 'his divine status is a consequence of grace rather than nature'.[159]

Many of the doctrines attributed by Alexander are represented in Arius' own writings. Principally, Arius' view is that the divine nature is unique and incomposite (absolute). As such, the divine being is incommunicable and it is characteristic of Arius to present the Son as extrinsic to the being of God. This is demonstrated through a network of propositions: that God is not always Father; that the Son is not coeternal alongside the Father; that the Son's mode of origin is – to some extent – comparable to creation, meaning that the Son is brought into being from nothing at a particular point in pre-time, which is the groundwork of the infamous saying 'There was a time when the Son did not exist.' Of course, these contribute to the central doctrine of Arius' Christology, which is the radical subordination of the Son, who is unlike the Father in

[157] Stead, *Divine Substance*, 223–224.

[158] Beeley, *Unity of Christ*, 109. See also M. DelCogliano, *Anti-Eunomian Theory of Names: Christian Theology and Late-Antique Philosophy in the Fourth-Century Trinitarian Controversy* (Leiden: E. J. Brill, 2010), 115.

[159] Anatolios, *RN*, 17.

essence.[160] As extrinsic to the being of God, the Son is mutable and his sinless Sonship is not by necessity but rather by moral effort, aided by God owing to his excellence being foreseen. As external to the being of God, the Son does not know the Father fully.[161]

Williams offers a compact and comprehensive account of the major contours of Arius' thought, which is worth setting out here:

1 God alone is self-subsistent, *agenētos;* he is immaterial, and thus without any kind of plurality or composition; he is subject to no natural processes, no emanation, or diffusion of his substance.
2 He is entirely free, rational and purposive.
3 He initiates the creative process by freely bringing the Son into being, as a subsistent individual truly distinct from himself; he does this 'before all ages', yet there is a sense in which the Father exists prior to the Son, since the Son is not eternal, that is, not timelessly, self-subsistent.
4 By the will of God, the Son is stably and unalterably what he is, a perfect creature, not just 'one among others'; he is the 'inheritor' of all the gifts and glories God can give him, but since this is the effect of God's sovereign will, the Father's glory and dignity are in no way lessened by such a gift.[162]

Central to Williams's sketch of Arius' theology is the category of divine freedom: God is the sole source of all whose existence is self-subsistent and he acts in the utter freedom of a self-subsistent being to bring other things into existence.[163] Therefore, the Son cannot participate in the divine essence because that would compromise the freedom of God as the uniquely unbegotten source of all. Instead, the Son belongs to the category of that which is brought into being by the will of the Father. However, the Son is a pre-eminent member of the group of *things that have come to be*, as he is the one through whom God brought other things into being. As something that has come into being, the Son does not possess the divine nature by necessity, but rather in a transferred and contingent sense shares in the divine attributes by grace.[164]

160 Hanson, *SCDG*, 16–18.
161 See Athanasius, *Against the Greeks*, 1.6, *NPNF* II.4; *Synods*, 15.
162 Williams, *Arius*, 98. See also Stead, '"Eusebius" and the Council of Nicaea', *JTS* 24.1 (1973), 85–100, at 85–87.
163 Williams, *Arius*, 98.
164 Ibid. 222.

The unique unbegotten/unoriginate God and the meaning of 'begotten'

Arius' thought is characterized by an 'unflagging insistence on the utter singularity of the one unoriginated and unbegotten God'.[165] These terms – 'unoriginated' (*agennētos*) and 'unbegotten' (*agenētos*) – are similar but lexically distinct from each other. *Agennētos* is the privative adjective derived from the verb *gennaō* (I beget, I have given birth), whereas *agenētos* is the privative adjective derived from *ginomai* (I come into being). Up until the 350s, these terms were largely used synonymously.[166] This is represented in much of the modern literature by the cypher *agen(n)ētos*. The differentiation between these terms was an important aspect of the development of a trinitarian theology as it meant that both the Son and the Father could be described as 'unoriginate' (*agennētos*) but the Father alone is 'unbegotten' (*agenētos*).

At the time of the Arian controversy, it was not unusual for these terms to be elided. Dionysius of Alexandria, a forerunner of Alexander, considered *agen(n)ētos* to be a uniquely privileged descriptor for God.[167] To describe God as *agen(n)ētos* was taken as meaning that God is the one whose existence is self-grounded. It is similar in meaning to the category of divine aseity: God is entirely of himself and nothing of God's being is derived from beyond himself. It is not difficult to see how this intersected with the matter of the status of the begotten (*gen[n]ētos*) Son.[168] In this context, Arius understood Alexander's account of the coeternity of the Father and Son to be tantamount to asserting that there are two *agen(n)ētoi*. At best, this sounded to Arius like a Manichean dualism and at worst a form of ditheism.[169] As such, an affirmation of the unique and unbegotten God who alone is pure actuality from whom all else is derived as non-absolute is a common feature in the surviving writings of Arius and those of his sympathizers.

This aspect of Arius' thought is well demonstrated by his letter to Eusebius of Nicomedia (whom Arius describes as a 'fellow-Lucianist'[170]) in which he launches into an attack on the doctrine of the eternal generation of the Son. Arius identifies that he is refuting Alexander's proposition that the Father and

165 Anatolios, *RN*, 17.

166 Hanson, *SCDG*, 202–206. See also DelCogliano, *Anti-Eunomian Theory of Names*, 98–134.

167 DelCogliano, *Anti-Eunomian Theory of Names*, 106–108; A. Radde-Gallwitz, *Basil of Caesarea, Gregory of Nyssa and the Transformation of Divine Simplicity* (Oxford: Oxford University Press, 2009), 75–78.

168 DelCogliano considers this elision and the subsequent differentiation to be central to the development of Nicene logic. DelCogliano, *Anti-Eunomian Theory of Names*.

169 Anatolios, *RN*, 44.

170 Arius, *Letter to Eusebius of Nicomedia*, 5; Theodoret, *Ecclesiastical History*, 1.4. The following references include the location within Urk 1.

Son are coeternal and that the Father does not precede the Son.[171] In the course of the letter, Arius lays out his two reasons for rejecting this doctrine. First, it would imply that the divine nature is a material entity and so is capable of being shared such that the Son is either the offspring or a portion of God.[172] The divine being is a simple and spiritual reality, not a divisible material one, and therefore the Son must not be coeternal with the Father, but rather come into being after the Father and from non-being.[173] Second, the coeternity of the Son undermines the unique and solitary oneness of God as *agen(n)ētos*; the Son as *gen(n)ētos* exists as one with an origin and so cannot be unbegotten.[174]

Laying out his own doctrine, Arius argues that the Son – as begotten – cannot be absolute, as is the unbegotten (the *gen[n]ētos* is not the *agen[n]ētos*). This impression was made stronger in Arius' thought by the elision of unbegotten and unoriginate. For Arius the begotten Son is not true God because he has come into existence:

> But we say and believe, and have taught, and do teach, that the Son is not unbegotten, nor in any way part of the unbegotten; and that He does not derive His subsistence from any matter; but that by His own will and counsel He has subsisted before time, and before ages, as perfect God, only begotten and unchangeable, and that before He was begotten, or created, or purposed, or established, He was not. For He was not unbegotten. We are persecuted, because we say that the Son has a beginning, but that God is without beginning. This is the cause of our persecution, and likewise, because we say that He is of the non-existent. And this we say, because He is neither part of God, nor of any essential being.[175]

Arius' theological priority is ostensibly the unique primacy of God as *agen(n)ētos*. In his view, God (the Father) alone has no beginning, having existence grounded in himself. He has an unqualified priority in terms of causality as the uncaused origin of all else that is. The Son is begotten and so does not share the same absolute primacy. Moreover, owing to the elision of begetting and coming into being, the Son is taken as having a beginning. Therefore, being among those things that come from nothing, the Son might not have existed.

---

171 Arius, *Letter to Eusebius of Nicomedia*, 2.

172 Ibid. 5.

173 Ibid. See also Williams, *Arius*, 97.

174 See the excellent discussion of the priority of the name *agen(n)ētos* in Arius' thought at DelCogliano, *Anti-Eunomian Theory of Names*, 111–112. See also Athanasius, *Defence of the Nicene Definition*, 28, NPNF II.4.

175 Arius, *Letter to Eusebius of Nicomedia*, 5.

This establishes a division between the Father's and Son's modes of being: the Father is absolute and necessary, whereas the Son is contingent. From this, the following inference can be drawn: for Arius, while 'unbegotten' is intrinsic to the divine being (God is not God without this property), 'Father' is not.[176] 'Father' refers to a relationship extrinsic to the divine being, which Arius signified by attributing it to the will of God.

Arius' corresponding understanding of the meaning of 'begotten' is well set out in his credal letter to Alexander, which Athanasius and Hilary treat as the standard document expressing Arius' doctrine.[177] In this letter, Arius attempts to clarify his position, perhaps in advance of a synod to decide upon his orthodoxy. The letter opens by emphasizing the unique character of the one unbegotten God: 'We acknowledge one God, alone ingenerate [*agen(n)ētos*], alone Everlasting, alone Unbegun, alone True, alone having immortality.'[178] In this, the shape of Arius' comments to come are pre-figured: the Son is begotten and so is not God as the Father is God:

> And God, being the cause of all things, is Unbegun and altogether Sole, but the Son being begotten apart from time by the Father, and being created and founded before ages, was not before His generation, but being begotten apart from time before all things, alone was made to subsist by the Father. For He is not eternal or co-eternal or co-unoriginate with the Father, nor has He His being together with the Father, as some speak of relations, introducing two ingenerate beginnings, but God is before all things as being Monad and Beginning of all.[179]

Arius treats 'begotten' and 'created' as effective synonyms, interchangeable with each other, to describe the mode of the Son's origination from the Father. Accordingly, he describes the Son as 'a perfect creature of God'.[180] Like creation, the generation of the Son is not eternal and is the product of the will of God. Therefore, the Son is not from the Father; instead, the Son came into being from nothing at a particular moment, before which he did not exist. Unsurprisingly, then, Arius attributes the generation of the Son to the will of the Father: 'he made him subsist at his own will'.[181] The subsistence of the Son is the result of

176 Behr, *NF*, 136.

177 Athanasius, *Synods*, 16. See also Athanasius, *Discourses*, 2.19; Hilary of Poitiers, *On the Trinity*, 4.4.5, *NPNF* II.9.

178 Arius, *Credal Letter to Alexander*, Urk 6, NPNF II.4. Cited from Athanasius, *Synods*, 16. Subsequent references are from Athanasius, *Synods*.

179 Athanasius, *Synods*, 16.

180 Ibid.

181 Ibid.

God's purposive action and not the necessary relation of a correlate coeternity. By introducing this idea of contingence into the Father–Son relation, Arius locates the Father–Son relation as extrinsic to divine being.[182]

However, Grillmeier goes too far in his assessment that Arius' conception of the Father–Son relation is no different from the God–world relation.[183] Arius does, however, recognize that the generation of the Son is distinct from other extrinsic relations God is in. The Son is brought into existence through the will of God 'but not as one of the creatures'.[184] There are three important differences. First, the Son is brought into being in some quasi-temporal period before time began, drawing on Methodius' notion of some sequence between the Father and the generation of the Son whereby the Father is 'before the Son'.[185] Second, the Son is the instrument through whom God makes the rest of creation. Third, the Son is given some share in the glory of God, but as one who shares the divine nature or attributes by gift, not necessity.

Arius was also concerned by what he perceived to be a materialistic conception of divinity inherent in Alexander's doctrine of eternal generation. Accordingly, he resists the propositions that the Son is the offspring of the Father or that he is a portion of the divine nature. For Arius, the divine nature is not communicable or divisible. As begotten, the Son is not the unoriginated source of all and the divine nature cannot be communicated to him without introducing unhelpful materialistic connotations into speech about God. As such, Arius is comfortable with describing the Son as a distinct subsistent reality from the Father, which he describes by using the term *hypostasis*.[186]

The close doctrinal relationship between Arius and Eusebius of Nicomedia is well demonstrated by the latter's letter to Paulinus of Tyre,[187] which has been described as 'an Arian classic'.[188] To some extent, Eusebius recapitulates Arius' arguments against the coeternity of the Son: the unique status of the unbegotten and the materialistic undertones of the communication of divinity. For Eusebius, there cannot be two ultimate sources and the divine essence cannot be divided or shared. However, Eusebius develops these arguments by combining the divine essence with a more explicitly Lucianite

182 See also Widdicombe, *Fatherhood of God*, 144.

183 A. Grillmeier SJ, *Christ in the Christian Tradition: From the Apostolic Age to Chalcedon (451)*, vol. 1, tr. J. Bowden, 2nd rev. edn (London: Mowbrays, 1975), 231.

184 Athanasius, *Synods*, 16.

185 Ibid.

186 Ibid.

187 See Lienhard, *Contra Marcellum*, 77–78.

188 Stead, 'Eusebius', 86.

image-Christology. This is the basis upon which he rejects the doctrine that the Son is begotten from the essence of the Father.[189]

> We have never heard that there are two unbegotten beings, nor that one has been divided into two, nor have we learned or believed that it has ever undergone any change of a corporeal nature; but we affirm that the unbegotten is one and one also that which exists in truth by Him, yet was not made out of His substance [*ousia*], and does not at all participate in the nature or substance of the unbegotten, entirely distinct in nature and in power, and made after perfect likeness both of character and power to the maker.[190]

Like Arius, Eusebius describes the Son as 'created, established and begotten',[191] seeing this as something extrinsic to the divine being, which has no origin: 'If He had been from Him or of Him, as a portion of Him, or by an emanation of His substance, it could not be said that He was created or established.'[192] Given that it would become a central part of the Nicene confession, it is significant that Eusebius rejects the doctrine of the Son's being begotten from the essence (*ousia*) of the Father, recognizing that this would imply a necessary relation and continuity of divinity as outlined by Alexander. Commenting on Proverbs 8:22–23, Eusebius presents the generation of the Son as equivalent to the making of humans:

> But if the fact of His being called the begotten gives any ground for the belief that, having come into being of the Father's substance, He also has from the Father likeness of nature, we reply that it is not of Him alone that the Scriptures have spoken [Eusebius cites Deut. 32:18; Job 38:28; Isa. 1:2]. This expression does not imply that [a begotten thing] partakes of the nature of God, but simply that all things were formed according to His will. There is, indeed, nothing which is of His substance, yet every thing which exists has been called into being by His will. He is God; and all things were made in His likeness, and in the future likeness of His Word, being created of His free will.[193]

189 For a fuller discussion of this, see Williams, *Arius*, 64–65.

190 Eusebius of Nicomedia, *Letter to Paulinus of Tyre*, 3, Urk 8, *NPNF* II.3; Theodoret, *Ecclesiastical History* 1.5. The following references take their numbering from Urk 8.

191 Eusebius, *Letter to Paulinus of Tyre*, 4.

192 Ibid. 5.

193 Ibid. 5–8.

The Son is the image of God in the same way humanity is. Therefore, whatever 'image' may mean, it does *not* mean a likeness of essence. Alexander, according to Eusebius, has misunderstood the meaning of the Son's likeness to the Father as a likeness with respect to essence and has erred in coordinating this so closely to the Son's generation from the Father, which is not a unique relation. Instead, Eusebius insists that the Son is begotten *by the will of the Father.* As such, the Son does not participate in the nature of the unbegotten or in the divine attributes: he is the image of God but does not share in divinity. The point, then, of Eusebius' denial of the Son as begotten from the essence is clear: the Father does not share his unique position of primacy with the Son: 'that which is made did not exist before coming into existence; that which has come into existence has a beginning of being'.[194]

Asterius,[195] whose thought is reconstructed from recorded fragments of his *Syntagmation* (c.320–21),[196] like Eusebius of Nicomedia and Arius affirms the unique primacy of the one unoriginate (*agen[n]ētos*).[197] Importantly, Asterius describes the unoriginate as 'what was not made, but always is'.[198] As such, the Son, as begotten from the Father, does not share the primacy of the Father, which Asterius takes to disprove the continuity of essence between them.[199] In support of this, he denies that the Son is begotten from the essence of the Father, seeing generation to be by the will of the Father.[200] Moreover, any similarity between them is not on account of their same divinity, but of their harmony of wills.[201] In his image-Christology Asterius describes the Father–Son relation in which the Son's likeness of the Father is not ontological similarity.[202] In this connection, using the term 'hypostases',[203] Asterius describes the Father and Son as two distinct realities.

194 Athanasius, *Synods*, 17. See Stead, *Divine Substance*, 226–227; Lienhard, *Contra Marcellum*, 79–82.

195 Short biographical details can be found in Lienhard, *Contra Marcellum*, 89–91.

196 Athanasius claimed that Arius consulted this work. Athanasius, *Defence of the Nicene Definition*, 8.1. See also M. DelCogliano, 'How Did Arius Learn from Asterius? On the Relationship Between the *Thalia* and the *Syntagmation*', *JEH* 69.3 (2018), 477–492. The importance of this observation is that it locates Arius within the Lucianite theological tradition, rather than his being a leader of a distinct 'Arian' group.

197 Frs. 12 and 3. Cited from DelCogliano, *Anti-Eunomian Theory of Names*, 120. The fragment numbering refers to Markus Vinzent, *Asterius von Kappadokien*. See DelCogliano, *Anti-Eunomian Theory of Names*, 120, n. 103.

198 Fr. 7. Cited from Lienhard, *Contra Marcellum*, 93.

199 Fr. 74. Cited from DelCogliano, *Anti-Eunomian Theory of Names*, 120.

200 Frs. 16, 18, 20. Cited from DelCogliano, *Anti-Eunomian Theory of Names*, 121.

201 Fr. 14. Cited from Lienhard, *Contra Marcellum*, 94. See also Athanasius, *Discourses*, 1.29–34.

202 Fr. 90. Cited from Lienhard, *Contra Marcellum*, 97.

203 Fr. 63. Cited from Lienhard, *Contra Marcellum*, 96.

Eusebius of Caesarea

Eusebius of Caesarea (263–339)[204] provides an important example of a figure involved in the early stages of the Arian controversy, whose theological priorities overlapped those of Arius with regard to the rejection of the doctrine of eternal generation, but whose overall theological vision was quite different from Arius'. Some, from an assessment of his thought, have set out to rehabilitate Eusebius' being wholly shaped by his association with Arius.[205] This distinction between Eusebius and Arius is significant because it demonstrates that, after Arius, the 'Eusebian' faction, which included Eusebius of Caesarea and Asterius, was not a monolithic group and a persuasive case can be made that Eusebius of Caesarea makes an important contribution to the eventual character of Nicene orthodoxy.[206]

In his early works, Eusebius articulates the divinity of Christ with considerable clarity. His *Ecclesiastical History*, focused on the history of the passing down of orthodox doctrine, which centres on the divinity of Christ, is not a straight historical work as we might understand it.[207] Arius' controversy with Alexander took place while Eusebius was writing two significant texts, *Preparation for the Gospel* and *Proof of the Gospel* (314–23). In these texts, Eusebius seeks to present Christianity as superseding pagan culture (in response to Porphyry's *Against the Christians*). Central to the themes of these works is the divinity of Christ against the denials of that doctrine,[208] and therefore the suitability of ascribing glory to him,[209] alongside a pronounced anti-modalistic theology in which he affirms the real and distinct subsistence of the Son from the Father.[210]

Within the parameters of the dispute between Alexander and Arius, Eusebius affirms the unique relation of the Son to the Father indicated by the term 'begotten'. As begotten, the Son receives the divinity of the Father[211] and is properly the object of human worship.[212] Therefore, the Son is the image of the Father and is able to reveal the Father.[213] In this way, Eusebius appears to have

204 A short biography can be found at Lienhard, *Contra Marcellum*, 70–73.

205 S. Inowlocki and C. Zamagni (eds.), *Reconsidering Eusebius: Collected Papers on Literary, Historical and Theological Issues* (Leiden: E. J. Brill, 2011).

206 Beeley, *Unity of Christ*, 49. Beeley contends that Eusebius has been subjected to repeated misunderstandings that have obscured his contribution. See also Williams, *Arius*, 172–173, and Hanson, *SCDG*, 52–53.

207 Beeley, *Unity of Christ*, 59.

208 Eusebius of Caesarea, *Ecclesiastical History*, 1.2.23; 4.22.

209 Ibid. 1.2.6–7; 1.3.10; 4.15.

210 Ibid. 1.2.14.

211 Eusebius, *Proof of the Gospel*, 5.4.14. Cited from Beeley, *Unity of Christ*, 72.

212 Eusebius of Caesarea, *Ecclesiastical History*, 1.2.3–4; 1.3.10.

213 Eusebius of Caesarea, *Preparation for the Gospel*, 7.15. Cited from Beeley, *Unity of Christ*, 70.

a constitutive image-Christology as opposed to the participative view of Arius and his namesake in Nicomedia.[214] Eusebius of Caesarea's view would become core to Nicene orthodoxy and central to Athanasius' own Christology: the salvific and revelatory efficacy of Christ arising from the divinity he has received from the Father.[215]

However, Eusebius does appear to hold to the priority of the Father in such a way that compromises the eternity of the Son. In a letter written to Alexander, Eusebius distances himself from Arius' proposition that the Son comes into being from nothing, insisting instead that this denies the coeternity of the Son. For Eusebius there is one unbegotten source, and

> if it were not he alone who exists eternally, but the Son also exists eternally, how indeed could one who exists beget another who already exists? It would have to follow that there would actually be two who exist eternally.[216]

Likewise, Eusebius is also able to describe the Father as pre-existing the Son on the grounds that only the Father is unbegotten.[217] This appears to import some idea of sequence (if not temporality) into the relation of the Father and Son. Likewise, in his letter to Euphration of Balena, Eusebius describes a subtle subordination. The Son, as caused by the Father, is lower in the chain of primacy (not coeternal), and so inferior to the Father:[218] 'for one is indeed the first and the best and leads to / proceeds from the second, both in order and in honour'.[219] While subordinate to the Father in the chain of causation, the Son has primacy over creation, which is created through him.[220]

Eusebius' conception of the Father–Son relation appears, then, to be something of an outlier. He stresses the continuity of divinity inherent in the Son's being begotten from the Father, while denying the coeternity of the Father and Son. The element of his thought that introduces this tension is that Eusebius locates the generation of the Son within the will (as opposed to essence) of the Father,[221] which, while this generation is related to the divine nature,[222] is not the necessary relation described by Alexander. So, while Eusebius does not

214 Stead has pointed to the theological differences between Eusebius of Nicomedia and Eusebius of Caesarea particularly on the question of the meaning of the Son's generation from the Father and in their different roles in the Council of Nicaea. Stead, 'Eusebius', 85–100.

215 Eusebius of Caesarea, *Ecclesiastical History*, 1.2.2; 5.1.

216 Eusebius of Caesarea, *Letter to Alexander of Alexandria*, 4, Urk 7.

217 Eusebius of Caesarea, *Proof of the Gospel*, 4.3. Cited from Beeley, *Unity of Christ*, 91.

218 Eusebius of Caesarea, *Letter to Euphration of Balena*, 2, Urk 3.

219 Ibid. 1. See also Lienhard, *Contra Marcellum*, 74–75.

220 Williams, *Arius*, 102.

221 Eusebius of Caesarea, *Demonstration of the Gospel*, 4.3. Cited from Anatolios, *RN*, 60.

222 Ibid. 4.1.

consider the generation of the Son to be the same as God's act of creation, it is still a purposive act undertaken in accordance with God's will.[223] In other words, Eusebius inserts contingence into the Father–Son relation. Correspondingly, he envisages some form of sequence in the Father–Son relation, with the Son's being 'after' the Father (at least in terms of order of being, if not in time).[224] A function of Eusebius' prioritization of the will of the Father in bringing the Son into being is that Eusebius is insisting in rejecting the proposition that the Son is begotten from the essence of the Father.[225] For Eusebius, such a proposition is inextricably linked to a material conception of the divine essence as something that can be divided or apportioned.

Eusebius was a unique figure. Like Arius, Eusebius did attribute the generation of the Son to the will of the Father,[226] but is eager to describe this relation in such a way that it accounts for a substantial degree of sameness between them. In this connection, Eusebius was able to describe the generation of the Son from the Father through the analogy of the sun and its light,[227] which seems to imply some idea of the communication of divinity from the Father to the Son in relation to derivation itself (as opposed to being a contingent gift given subsequently):

> [the Son] completely preserves the living and vivid spiritual image of the one God, being made in all things like the Father, and bearing the likeness of his actual divinity. Thus he is the only Son and the only image of God, endued with the powers of the Father's unbegotten and eternal essence according to the example of likeness, and fashioned to the utmost accuracy of likeness by the Father himself.[228]

For Eusebius, then, the Son is the image of the Father in that his very essence is derived from the Father to be the manifestation of the Father. This undergirds a stronger account of the Son as the mediator of the Father to humanity than that found in Arius.[229] Eusebius, in straddling the party lines, helps us to

223 Eusebius of Caesarea, *Letter to Alexander*, 2–3.

224 Stead, *Divine Substance*, 231.

225 For example, Eusebius of Caesarea, *Demonstration of the Gospel*, 3.13. Cited from Stead, *Divine Substance*, 232.

226 Ayres, *Nicaea*, 59. Ayres notes from *Demonstration of the Gospel*, 4.3.13, that Eusebius was concerned to avoid materialist ideas of the divine essence. See also Anatolios, *RN*, 63.

227 Eusebius of Caesarea, *Ecclesiastical Theology*, 1.8.2–4. Cited from Ayres, *NL*, 58.

228 Eusebius of Caesarea, *Demonstration of the Gospel*, 5.4. Cited from M. DelCogliano, 'Eusebian Theologies of the Son as the Image of God Before 341', *JECS* 14.4 (2006), 459–484, at 472–473.

229 Eusebius of Caesarea, *Ecclesiastical Theology*, 3.21.1. Cited from DelCogliano, 'Eusebian Theologies of the Son', 475.

identify more closely the difference between a constitutive image-Christology and a participatory image-Christology.[230]

The reduced God

Arius' *Thalia* is a dramatic text for the way the internal tensions of Alexandrian thought were reconciled by attributing to the Son an attenuated form of divinity. For example, Arius asserts that the Son exists only *pro nobis* and as such is not the true God who is transcendently beyond creation, but rather God in a reduced or attenuated sense:

> God Himself then, in His own nature, is ineffable by all men.
> Equal or like Himself He alone has none, or one in glory.
> And Ingenerate we call Him, because of Him who is generate by nature.
> We praise Him as without beginning because of Him who has a beginning.
> And adore Him as everlasting, because of Him who in time has come to be.
> The Unbegun made the Son a beginning of things originated;
> and advanced Him as a Son to Himself by adoption.
> He has nothing proper to God in proper subsistence.
> For He is not equal, no, nor one in essence with Him . . .
> There is full proof that God is invisible to all beings;
> both to things which are through the Son, and to the Son He is invisible . . .
> Thus there is a Triad, not in equal glories. Not intermingling with each other are their subsistences.
> One more glorious than the other in their glories unto immensity.
> Foreign from the Son in essence is the Father, for He is without beginning.
> Understand that the Monad was; but the Dyad was not, before it was in existence.
> It follows at once that, though the Son was not, the Father was God.
> Hence the Son, not being (for He existed at the will of the Father), is God Only-begotten,
> and He is alien from either . . .
> At God's will the Son is what and whatsoever He is.
> And when and since He was, from that time He has subsisted from God.
> He, being a strong God, praises in His degree the Superior.
> To speak in brief, God is ineffable to His Son.

230 Young, *God's Presence*, 165–166.

For the Son does not know His own essence, for, being Son, He really existed, at the will of the Father.
What argument then allows, that He who is from the Father should know His own parent by comprehension?
[25] For it is plain that for that which has a beginning to conceive how the Unbegun is, or to grasp the idea, is not possible.[231]

Many of the ideas already discussed are present here: the unique and absolute primacy of God as unbegotten (lines 1–4, 15); the begetting of the Son as a function of the will (not the essence) of the Father (lines 17, 19); the Father has primacy over the Son and the Son has primacy over creation (line 6); the Son is alien in essence from the Father and does not possess anything that is proper to God (lines 8–9, 14); the eternity of the Father and the 'temporal' beginning of the Son (and so the Son did not exist before he was begotten) whereby God existed aside from the Son (lines 15–16); and the three unequal subsistent realities (hypostases) that are alien in essence to one another (line 12).

The Son is adopted by the Father (line 7),[232] emphasizing the non-necessity of the Father–Son relation: this is not a relation of being (as per the correlate relations of Alexander and Origen), but a relation established through a purposive act. The Son is extrinsic to divinity and is given some degree of participation in the properties of divinity by the gift of the Father.[233] This is what DelCogliano describes as a 'participative' approach to the Son as the image of God: the Son manifests the Father not because he shares in the essence of the Father but because he participates by grace in certain attributes of God.[234]

Arius presents the Son as the mediator of our knowledge of and worship of the unbegotten God (lines 3–5). Yet, as extrinsic to the being of the Father, the Son reveals God only to a limited degree. This is the source of a pronounced apophaticism in Arius' thought. The Son does not have perfect knowledge of God, but only a limited knowledge according to the measure possible for the Son as a finite being (line 22).[235] The Son reflects the being of God in a dim way through his own created glory.[236] The Son's ignorance of the Father is a focal point that illustrates his reduced divinity because it is a function of the Son's

231 Recorded in Athanasius, *Synods*, 15. As this is an abridged citation, the lines refer to their appearance here for ease of internal reference. They do not refer to the presentation in Athanasius' own record.

232 See Athanasius, *Defence of the Nicene Definition*, 6.

233 See Athanasius, *Discourses*, 1.9; Williams, *Arius*, 106.

234 DelCogliano, 'Eusebian Theologies of the Son', 462.

235 See Athanasius' description of Arius' notion of the Son's participation in the Father. Athanasius, *Discourses*, 1.5–6, 9.

236 See Williams, *Arius*, 64–65, 105–106.

having a beginning and thus being of finite span, who is unable to comprehend the eternal and infinite (line 25). This is one of Arius' most distinctive doctrines, not shared by his supporters and the later anti-Nicene theologians.[237]

The record of Arius' *Thalia* in Athanasius' *Discourse Against the Arians* is more difficult to distil from its polemical setting. It is full of Athanasius' own interjections and inferences:

> The mockeries which [Arius] utters in [the *Thalia*] repulsive and most irreligious, are such as these: 'God was not always a Father.' but 'once God was alone, and not yet a Father, but afterwards He became a Father.' 'The Son was not always;' for, whereas all things were made out of nothing, and all existing creatures and works were made, so the Word of God Himself was 'made out of nothing,' and 'once He was not,' and 'He was not before His origination,' but He as others 'had an origin of creation.' 'For God,' he says, 'was alone, and the Word as yet was not, nor the Wisdom. Then, wishing to form us, thereupon He made a certain one, and named Him Word and Wisdom and Son, that He might form us by means of Him.'[238]

The theological commitments of this list of quotes from the *Thalia* are, by now, familiar. They are put more explicitly here, however, than elsewhere. For example, the statement that God 'became' the Father is attributed to Arius. This is probably a *reductio ad absurdum*, a polemical conclusion drawn from Arius' doctrine of the beginning of the Son, rather than a direct quotation. Even if this is the case, Arius does effectively make this point by decentring the eternal correlative relation of Father and Son when he asserts that the designation 'Father' is incidental to the divine nature, favouring instead, the term 'unbegotten'. The reversal of this point would be a central aspect of the distinctive Nicene theology.

Closely connected with the 'Father' being incidental to the divine nature is the doctrine attributed to Arius that the Son is brought into existence *for the purpose of creation*. The existence of the Son is contingent on the will of God to create, whereby the Son is entirely *pro nobis* and not *in se*.[239] With regard to the tension latent within the Alexandrian theological tradition, Arius' solution is to establish the generation of the Son exclusively in connection with his mediatorial function. This is substantiated through Athanasius' later claim that

237 See a fuller discussion in Williams, *Arius*, 64–65, 97–98.

238 Athanasius, *Discourses*, 1.5.

239 For Asterius, the Son is brought into being for the purposes of creation through an intermediary. Athanasius, *Discourses*, 2.24.

Arius posited a distinction between the wisdom immanent to God and the Son.[240] The wisdom that is an internal attribute of God is the quality by which he begets the distinct subsistence, the Son, who is called 'Wisdom' only to the degree that he has a unique relationship with this internal attribute of God. The significance of this distinction, Athanasius argues, is to distinguish between the Son as a power of God and the 'great power' intrinsic to God's nature.[241]

Athanasius also attributes to Arius the Lucianite doctrine that, in becoming incarnate, the Son assumed a human body without a soul. This is of a piece with Arius' tendency to attribute the limited conditions of the incarnate Son to the attenuated divinity of the Son, rather than to the human nature he assumed into union with himself:[242]

> Why do they, fabricating earth-born deceits, make much of proving that the Christ assumed a body without a soul? [It is] so that if they are able to corrupt any [to think] that these things are to be defined thus, then, by attributing changes of affection to the divine Spirit, they might easily persuade them that the mutable is not begotten of the immutable nature.[243]

In the view of Hanson, the idea that the limitations, weaknesses and even sufferings of the incarnate Christ were attributed to his reduced divinity rather than to the conditions of his incarnate state is the heart of Arianism: irrevocable proof of his inferiority as the begotten Son.[244] For Hanson, it is integral to the soteriological logic of 'Arianism' that a death which has salvific qualities must be the death of one more than human, but the true God is unable to suffer and die. Therefore, the saving death must have been that of a reduced God, more than human but less than the true God.

Finally, Athanasius attributes to Arius the doctrine that the Son was not unchangeable or glorious by nature but rather 'as foreknowing that he would be good, did God by anticipation bestow on him this glory, which afterwards, as man, he attained from virtue'.[245] The Son remained steadfast by the pre-emptive action of God and so their shared glory is a unity brought about by their unity of will, not a unity of being: it is a moral, not a substantial, unity:

240 See Williams, *Arius*, 117.
241 Athanasius, *Discourses*, 1.5.
242 See Hilary, *Trinity*, 7.6.
243 Eustathius of Antioch, 'On the Soul Against the Arians'. Cited from Behr, *NF*, 146.
244 Hanson, *SCDG*, 106–122.
245 Athanasius, *Discourses*, 1.5. See also Hanson, *SCDG*, 21.

> Moreover he has dared to say, that 'the Word is not the very God;' 'though He is called God, yet He is not very God,' but 'by participation of grace, He, as others, is God only in name.' And, whereas all beings are foreign and different from God in essence, so too is 'the Word alien and unlike in all things to the Father's essence and propriety,' but belongs to things originated and created, and is one of these. Afterwards, as though he had succeeded to the devil's recklessness, he has stated in his *Thalia*, that 'even to the Son the Father is invisible,' and 'the Word cannot perfectly and exactly either see or know His own Father,' but even what He knows and what He sees, He knows and sees 'in proportion to His own measure,' as we also know according to our own power. For the Son, too, he says, not only knows not the Father exactly, for He fails in comprehension, but 'He knows not even His own essence;' – and that 'the essences of the Father and the Son and the Holy Ghost, are separate in nature, and estranged, and disconnected, and alien, and without participation of each other;' and, in his own words, 'utterly unlike from each other in essence and glory, unto infinity.' Thus as to 'likeness of glory and essence,' he says that the Word is entirely diverse from both the Father and the Holy Ghost. With such words has the irreligious spoken; maintaining that the Son is distinct by Himself, and in no respect partaker of the Father.[246]

It is here that Alexander's complaint that Arius deploys a Lucianite hermeneutical strategy in which Jesus' human limitations are taken as evidence of his attenuated divinity is most clearly at work.[247] The incarnate Son's lack of knowledge (e.g. Mark 13:32) is attributed to his limited sharing in the divine nature. In Athanasius' polemic, this would be interpreted as indicative of an incoherent soteriology and epistemology: as one whose own Sonship is by grace, the Son cannot draw us to share by grace what he shares by nature,[248] and as one who is external to the divine being, he cannot reveal God to humanity fully and finally.

246 Athanasius, *Discourses*, 1.6.
247 Behr, *NF*, 148–149.
248 Ibid. 146.

4

'Begotten from the essence of the Father': from Nicaea to Constantinople (1)

There is an idea that the Council of Nicaea (325) established Christian orthodoxy, which was assailed by various heretical factions before its triumphant reassertion at the Council of Constantinople (381). In part, the problem with this view is that it treats trinitarian belief as if it were separate from the *process* of theological development through which it became established. As Behr has pointed out, such a conception threatens to sever Christian belief about the Trinity from its roots as obedience to God's self-revelation and transpose it instead to the realm of abstract dogma.[1] The linear vision of the fourth century is also historically untenable. It was in the shifting parameters of the controversy and the waxing and waning fortunes of the respective theological alliances that the logic of the Christian doctrine of God was progressively discerned. For this reason, part of the story of the fourth century is the development of a terminology around which a theological consensus could be formed. The following three chapters set out this complex route from Nicaea to Constantinople. The focus of this study falls on the theological convictions expressed by individual theologians and at the significant councils that met throughout the middle decades of the century.

The defeat of Arius

The beginnings of the anti-Arius consensus: the Council of Antioch (AD 325)

At the beginning of AD 325, some months before the general Council of Nicaea, a smaller council of fifty-six bishops met in Antioch for the business of electing

[1] Behr, *NF*, 3–8.

a new bishop.[2] While gathered, they took the opportunity to compose a statement against Arius. The statement follows the familiar three-clause structure, but only the clause on the Son and the following anathemas are included here:

> [We believe] in one Lord Jesus Christ, only begotten Son, begotten not from that which is not but from the Father, not as made but as properly an offspring, but begotten in an ineffable, indescribable manner . . . who exists everlastingly and did not at one time not exist . . . He alone is the express image, not as if He might have remained unbegotten from the Father, nor by adoption . . . but the Scriptures describe him as validly and truly the begotten Son, so that we believe Him to be immutable and unchangeable, and that He was not begotten and did not come to be by volition or by adoption . . . but in a way which passes all understanding . . . we confess Him to have been begotten of the unbegotten Father . . . He is the express image, not of the will or anything else, but of His Father's very substance . . .
>
> We anathematize those who say . . . that the Son of God is a creature [*genēton*] or has come into being or has been made and is not truly begotten, or that there was when He was not . . . Furthermore, we anathematize those who suppose that He is immutable by His own act of will, just as those who derive His birth from that which is not, and deny that He is immutable in the way the Father is. For just as our Saviour is the image of the Father in all things, so that in this respect particularly He has been proclaimed the Father's image.[3]

This confession draws on ideas familiar to us now through Alexander and anticipates themes that would be reiterated at Nicaea. It appears to respond directly to the confession Arius had submitted to Alexander some years previously, particularly in its repudiation of the Son's coming into existence by the will of the Father. Three convictions are characteristic of Alexander's thought.[4] First, the Son's ineffable generation from the Father, which negates the proposition that the Son came into being from nothing and had no existence prior to being brought into existence. In this way, the confession begins to form a primitive contrast between the different modes of derivation proper to the Son

[2] Kelly, *ECC*, 209.

[3] Cited from Kelly, *ECC*, 210.

[4] See Behr, *NF*, 68. Parvis argues that there is a close relationship between this creed and Alexander's letter to Alexander of Byzantium. Parvis, *Marcellus*, 79–80.

and to creation. Second, the Son is true of the Father (it is a necessary relation) in contrast to the Son's relation to the Father being by adoption (a contingent, volitional relation). Third, the identification of the Son as possessing the attributes of divinity in terms of his immutability, which undergirds a constitutive image-Christology in which the Son is the same essence as that which he reflects.

The anathemas include direct repudiations of core doctrines of Arius: that the Son is among those things which have come into being from nothing by the will of the Father and that his immutability is an appearance caused by his strength of will.[5] While the anathemas do not explicitly repudiate a participative image-Christology, the final clause does indicate an understanding of Christ as image in such a way that he is immutable, indicating his continuity of divinity with the Father (it articulates a nascent constitutive image-Christology). In this, even though it is not stated with clarity in the statement itself, something of a recognition of a broader difference between two different ways of understanding the Son as the image of the Father is beginning to be articulated.

The Council of Nicaea

In an effort to put an end to the controversy between Arius and Alexander, the emperor Constantine (who had converted to Christianity some ten years previously[6]) summoned a gathering of bishops in the city of Nicaea.[7] While there are no surviving minutes (*acta*) of the proceedings at Nicaea, there are some sources of evidence.[8] Both Socrates and Eusebius record the Council's international nature.[9] Clearly, what made Nicaea remarkable in the eyes of its commentators was its universality.[10] On 20 May 325, some three hundred bishops gathered and, as Eusebius describes in celebratory detail, the emperor in purple and gold took his seat to adjudicate the council,[11] and delivered an opening address in which he urged the bishops to overcome their theological

[5] Hanson, *SCDG*, 150.

[6] Socrates, *Ecclesiastical History*, 1.2; Sozomen, *Ecclesiastical History*, 1.3–6. For a historical study of the life of Constantine with particular attention to his conversion to Christianity, see T. D. Barnes, *Constantine and Eusebius* (Cambridge, Mass.: Harvard University Press, 1981), 1–80.

[7] Eusebius of Caesarea, *Life of Constantine*, 3.6, tr. G. Hall, *Eusebius: Life of Constantine* (Oxford: Clarendon Press, 1999).

[8] Eyewitness reports come from Eustathius, Athanasius and Eusebius of Caesarea. A record of Eustathius' report of the council can be found in Theodoret, *Ecclesiastical History*, 1.7. Eustathius was of the understanding that the Nicene confession was a resounding defeat for Arius and his supporters. See also Ayres, *NL*, 88–92, and Hanson, *SCDG*, 152–162.

[9] Eusebius of Caesarea, *Life of Constantine*, 3.7–8; Socrates, *Ecclesiastical History*, 1.8.

[10] See Kelly, *ECC*, 212.

[11] Eusebius of Caesarea, *Life of Constantine*, 3.10.

disunity.[12] It was Constantine's intention for this gathering of bishops to reach a theological consensus to unite the whole church.

In a letter explaining his own actions at the Council of Nicaea, Eusebius of Caesarea notes that he read a confession (probably the baptismal confession of Caesarea) affirming that the Son is begotten from the Father.[13] Eusebius reports that the council received this confession positively, and that Constantine himself affirmed its doctrinal commitments, advising the delegates to subscribe to it with the single insertion of *homoouios*.[14] Whether or not Eusebius is implying that his confession was used as the base text for the Nicene confession, he is making the claim that, upon entering the council, his doctrine was compatible with the confession the council eventually composed.[15] Ostensibly, Eusebius had two reasons for doing this: first, to distance himself from his associations with Arius, and, second, to prepare the way to return to his diocese claiming that his doctrinal commitments at the beginning of the council were not compromised in affirming the Nicene confession. This is indicative of the pressure those associated with Arius were under at the beginning of the council.[16]

After lengthy, and apparently rancorous,[17] discussion, an agreement was reached such that the bishops were 'united as concerning the faith'.[18] It appears to be certain that theological choices made at the council were taken with the purpose of ostracizing Arius.[19] Athanasius, present at the council as part of Alexander's entourage, would later describe that the terms chosen were calibrated particularly to 'do away with the irreligious phrases of the Arians'.[20] Along with the specifications that the Son is from the *essence* of the Father and is 'true God from true God', the term Athanasius highlights as particularly unacceptable to those who sympathized with Arius is *homoousios*, the assertion that the Son is of identically the same essence as the Father. While the reality is more complex than Athanasius' account recognizes (a softer interpretation of the meaning of *homoousion* was available as demonstrated by the letter of Eusebius of Caesarea, discussed below), Socrates records that five delegates,

12 Ibid. 3.12; Sozomen, *Ecclesiastical History*, 1.19; Theodoret, *Ecclesiastical History*, 1.6.

13 Eusebius of Caesarea, *Letter to the Diocese of Caesarea*, 3, NPNF II.4. All numbering is with reference to the record of this letter in this volume.

14 Ibid. 4.

15 Ayres, *NL*, 89; Kelly, *ECC*, 211–226.

16 See also Ayres, *NL*, 89.

17 Eusebius of Caesarea, *Letter to the Diocese.*

18 Eusebius of Caesarea, *Life of Constantine*, 3.13.

19 Ayres, *NL*, 90.

20 Athanasius, *Defence of the Nicene Definition*, 19. The impression that the dice were loaded against the Arian faction before the Council of Nicaea sat is strengthened by the preparations prior to the council. See T. G. Elliot, 'Constantine's Preparations for the Council of Nicaea', *JRH* 17.2 (1992), 127–137.

including Arius and Eusebius of Nicomedia, would not accept the settlement on the grounds that they objected to the term *homoousios*, considering it to intrude materialistic notions on to the divine being.[21] All five were deposed and Arius' writings were declared heretical.[22]

The conciliar letter coming from this council was from the emperor himself claiming that the conclusions of the council were such that 'no room was left for further discussion or controversy in relation to the faith'.[23] This letter identifies the Nicene council as an unequivocal condemnation of Arius' doctrine:

> the impiety and guilt of Arius and his adherents were examined into, in the presence of our most religious emperor Constantine: and it was unanimously decided that his impious opinion should be anathematized, with all the blasphemous expressions he has uttered, in affirming that the Son of God sprang from nothing, and that there was a time when he was not; saying moreover that the Son of God, because possessed of free will, was capable either of vice or virtue; and calling him a creature and a work.[24]

Constantine delivered a closing address to the bishops focused particularly on the unity of the church with the injunction to maintain harmony.[25]

The Nicene confession

Hanson and Ayres consider the confession composed to be a 'window onto the complexity of the early fourth-century theological debates' but it cannot be understood as a definitive turning point in the search for the Christian doctrine of God.[26] Its significance, they suggest, lies in its refutation of Arius and in providing a statement around which a consensus could form, rather than in providing a positive account of Christian belief. Certainly, the Nicene confession is not a full expression of what would become trinitarian theology.

[21] Socrates, *Ecclesiastical History*, 1.8. See also Theodoret, *Ecclesiastical History*, 1.6. These concerns are itemized below.

[22] Sozomen, *Ecclesiastical History*, 1.21.

[23] Eusebius of Caesarea, *Life of Constantine*, 1.17.

[24] Socrates, *Ecclesiastical History*, 1.9. Socrates records several letters from Constantine to encourage assent to the Nicene confession. See also Sozomen, *Ecclesiastical History*, 21; Theodoret, *Ecclesiastical History*, 1.9.

[25] Eusebius of Caesarea, *Life of Constantine*, 3.21–23.

[26] Ayres, *NL*, 91–92; Hanson, *SCDG*, 172. The confession could have claimed the Son was '*eternally* begotten from the essence of the Father' but does not do so. Nor does the confession address the question of whether it is appropriate to speak of three hypostases and what might be meant by such terminology.

Moreover, the diversity of theological opinions between co-signatories of the confession belies any sense of uniformity: the confession was signed by Alexander, Marcellus and Eusebius of Caesarea, among whom there were significant theological differences. This, as Ayres suggests, renders the original Nicene theology as a 'fluid and diverse phenomenon'.[27]

However, acknowledging this should not obscure the fact that the confession does articulate doctrinal commitments that would be determinative for subsequent Christian thought. A distinctive 'Nicene' theology is beginning to be expressed within the Nicene confession, and this is not wholly submerged under the political folds of Constantine's ambition to achieve unity at any cost. The heart of this distinctively Nicene theology is the link it establishes between the Son's generation from the essence of the Father and the designation of the Son as *homoousios* to the Father: it is because the Son is from the essence of the Father (and not from his will, or from nothing) that there is continuity of divinity between the Father and Son. This provides the grounding logic of what would become trinitarian theology: *the Son (and the Spirit) derive from the Father in a way that only God can.*

The confession of Nicaea appears to have used a characteristically Eastern creed as its base text.[28] If this is the case (and we can consider the prototypical Eastern confession set out in chapter 2 as indicative of the document that was modified), then several technical phrases are added to clarify the meaning of the Son's generation from the Father and to repudiate Arius:

> [We believe] in one Lord Jesus Christ, the Son of God begotten of the Father, the only-begotten (that is, of the essence of the Father) God of God; Light of Light, true God of true God, begotten not made, identically the same essence as the Father; through whom all things were made (both in heaven and on earth).

First, in the immediate parenthetic clarification of what is meant by only-begotten,[29] the Son is said to be begotten *from the essence of the Father.* While

[27] Ayres, *NL*, 99.

[28] See also Kelly, *ECC*, 217–230. Kelly rejects the claim made by Eusebius that the base text is the local confession of Caesarea owing to several significant discrepancies. Parvis argues differently. Parvis, *Marcellus*, 85–86. Either way, the point is that a base text was modified by anti-Arian additions. For a summary of the scholarship around the Nicene confession, see W. Kinzig and M. Vinzent, 'Recent Research on the Origin of the Creed', *JTS* 50.2 (1999), 535–559.

[29] Skarsaune has argued that the syntax of this opening phrase is irregular, indicating that the modifier 'only-begotten', strengthening the appearance of anti-Arian phrases, was inserted into a pre-existing credal confession. O. Skarsaune, 'A Neglected Detail in the Creed of Nicaea (325)', *VC* 41 (1987), 34–54.

this phrase was not newly composed at Nicaea,[30] its introduction here is a 'deliberately formulated counterblast to the principal tenet of Arianism'.[31] Athanasius describes how this crucial clause was added so as not to allow any room for manoeuvre for Arius.[32] It is attractive to consider that Athanasius himself was the one to suggest this clarification. This phrase is used in *Henos sōmatos* (which is considered by many to be Athanasius' earliest theological work). Moreover, the generation of the Son from the essence of the Father continued to be a central part of his theology throughout his life.[33]

Whatever its provenance, this phrase is included as a repudiation of Arius' doctrines that the Son is different in essence from the Father, being begotten from nothing by the will of God for the purposes of God's relation to creation.[34] The inclusion of this phrase within the Nicene confession affirms the necessity of the Father–Son relationship: it is true of the Father's very being that the Son is begotten from him. In other words, any notion of *contingence* is excluded from the Father–Son relation.[35] This has three implications:

1 It means that the Father–Son relation constitutes divine perfection.
2 It establishes the Father–Son relation as necessarily true of God *in se* and not true only *pro nobis*.
3 To be begotten from the essence involves the continuity of divinity from the Father to the Son.

This, in other words, introduces the doctrine of eternal generation to church dogma: the generation of the Son is not extrinsic to the divine being and is not contingent on any other factor but is an eternal act of the internal life of God. This means that the Son is *proper* to the Father and the undivided divinity of the Father is communicated to the Son. The distinction between Father and Son is not a product of God's extrinsic relations to creation: the Son is not begotten for the sake of God's creative work, and the Son is not begotten at the moment of his birth from Mary. Instead, the Son is eternally distinct

[30] Ayres, *NL*, 97. The phrase had formerly been criticized by Origen, Eusebius of Caesarea and Eusebius of Nicomedia, who argued that it implies something like human procreation, which would carry biological implications for divine being. See also K. Giles, *The Eternal Generation of the Son: Maintaining Orthodoxy in Trinitarian Theology* (Wheaton, Ill.: IVP Academic, 2012), 91–120. See also S. R. Holmes, *The Quest for the Trinity: The Doctrine of God in Scripture, History and Modernity* (Wheaton, Ill.: IVP Academic, 2012), 56–81.

[31] Kelly, *ECC*, 235.

[32] Athanasius, *Defence of the Nicene Definition*, 19–20.

[33] Parvis argues for Athanasian provenance. Parvis, *Marcellus*, 87–88. See also Beeley, *Unity of Christ*, 122–123.

[34] Athanasius, *Discourses*, 1.9.

[35] See Behr, *NF*, 156.

within the life of God as the one who is timelessly begotten from the essence of the Father.

Second, the Creed uses a series of images piled one upon the other to describe the Son's generation from the Father: 'God of God, Light of Light, true God of true God'. Clearly, this is a targeted rebuttal of Arius' doctrine that the Son's derivation from the Father entails the Son's ontological inferiority (the Son is not true God of true God). More broadly, this clause continues the trajectory set in the Council of Antioch earlier in 325 by targeting a participative image-Christology that rejected the proposition that the Son was brought into being from nothing.[36] In this respect, the Nicene statement is reminiscent of the image-Christology of Alexander in which the Father as source and the Son as image are characterized by ontological continuity. The Son is God who comes out from God; he is the brightness that has eternally shone from the light; he possesses fully the divine nature as true God, which he reflects. In passing, while it was not their focus, these remarks also exclude ideas about divine emanation, which include layers of divine beings (*aeons*) emanating out from the supreme God.[37] The Nicene confession sets out that the Son is derived from the Father in an incomprehensible and immaterial manner that is intrinsic to divine being, which includes the communication of divinity from the Father to the Son.

Third, the generation of the Son is contrasted to the making of creation [*gennēthenta ou poiēthenta*]. This makes explicit that which is implicit in the proposition that the Son is begotten from the essence of the Father. Significantly, the word used for 'made' is the same as the term used in the first clause of the confession to describe God's act of making creation [*poiētēn*]. This is a direct response to Arius' credal letter, which treats creating and begetting as effective synonyms. In emphasizing this distinction between begetting and making, the Nicene confession makes a very important clarification: the begetting of the Son is *intrinsic* to the divine life, whereas the making of creation is *extrinsic*. These spatial metaphors are intended to be ways of describing (1) the Father–Son relation in terms of necessity, being of the divine perfection, and (2) the God–creation relation in terms of contingence not integral to God's own being. The significance of this is that, while the Son is derived from the Father, he did not *begin to exist*. The Son is timelessly derived from the Father

36 Ayres, *NL*, 4–5.

37 The philosophical substructure of such ideas comes from Plotinus, who conceived of the First Principle being the source of the second Principle, with the latter being ontologically inferior to the former. E. P. Meijering, 'The Doctrine of the Will and of the Trinity in the Orations of Gregory of Nazianzus', *God, Being, History: Studies in Patristic Philosophy* (Amsterdam: Elsevier, 1975), 103–113.

without sequence. In this way, the central paradox of trinitarian theology is introduced: the Son is both begotten and absolute.

Fourth, the anathemas against Arius' thought strengthen the close association between the twin doctrines of the Son's generation from the essence of the Father and his identity of essence with the Father:

> And those who say, 'there was once when he was not', and 'before being begotten he did not exist', and 'He came into existence from nothing' or who assert that the Son of God is of [*ek*] another *hypostasis* or *ousia*, or mutable or changeable – these the Catholic and Apostolic Church anathematizes.[38]

Several things should be noted about these anathemas:

1 The first three phrases explicitly rejected are all distinctive of Arius himself. These doctrines are not all shared by Arius' contemporary sympathizers.
2 The three elements of Arius' teaching explicitly repudiated are those that contravene the central Nicene claim that the Son is eternally from the essence of the Father.
3 The proposition that the Son is of a different *hypostasis* or *ousia* of the Father is repudiated. Understanding what this phrase is intended to repudiate is not easy. In part this is because there is some confusion over whether *ousia* and *hypostasis* are being used synonymously or not (it was not until Basil of Caesarea's work later in the century that they would be clearly differentiated and *ousia* had a technical meaning of the divine essence and *hypostasis* the distinct subsistence). Even so, Stead lays out two possibilities. First: this proposition rejects the idea that the Son is of a different essence from the Father. In this case – given the apparent equation of *ousia* and *hypostasis* – the anathema could be understood as rejecting the distinct subsistence of the Son also. Second: acknowledging the force of the preposition *ek* (out from), this proposition rejects the idea that the Son is derived from some other *hypostasis* or *ousia*. Stead considers the second option to be most likely, engaging as it does with the associated cosmological question of the derivation of the Son, rejecting any proposition that thinks of the Son as being begotten from some other source than the Father.[39] The point of this anathema, in other

[38] Cited from Behr, *NF*, 155.
[39] Stead, *Divine Substance*, 233–236.

> words, is *not* to reject that the Son is a distinct subsistence from the Father.[40] Instead, it is to reject the doctrine that the Son has an origin outside the Father and so should be understood as reinforcing the central Nicene doctrine, which is that the Son is from the essence of the Father. Similarly, Behr has argued that the intention of this anathema, by negating its alternative, is to safeguard the proposition that the Son is begotten from the Father, and so is of one essence with the Father.[41] That is to say, the Son is not from a different reality than the Father and is of one essence with the Father. In my view, this second possibility is most likely as it makes the most sense of the following denial of the Son's mutability: the Son is immutable because he shares the divinity of the Father, begotten, as he is, from the Father's essence.

The final clarification of the meaning of begotten from the essence of the Father is the inclusion of the term *homoousios*.[42] *Homoousios* is a compound word consisting of *homo* (meaning 'same') and *ousia* (often translated 'essence'). *Ousia* is a term that had a long philosophical history prior to its adoption by Christian theologians. This itself was cause for concern, with the accusations that alien forms of thought were being imposed upon the Scripture and tradition of the church.[43] Moreover, by late antiquity *ousia* had acquired a whole range of possible meanings,[44] with the context in which it was used being central in discerning its meaning.[45] This complexity was not made less acute by introducing *ousia* into Christian theology![46] It is not beyond possibility that the term was chosen precisely because its elasticity suited Constantine's political concerns of alienating Arius while establishing a broad consensus.

Unsurprisingly, the conceptual range of *homoousios* is broad. In his conceptual analysis of the term *homoousios*, Stead lays out several different possible meanings:[47]

1. The Father and Son are one individual. This sense is unsatisfactory in that it obscures the reality of the distinctions between the persons.

---

40 Ibid. 241.

41 Behr, *NF*, 158.

42 Ayres argues that *homoousios* was never intended as a stand-alone term, but needs to be understood as a qualification of 'from the essence of the Father'. Ayres, *NL*, 95–96.

43 Athanasius, *Defence of the Nicene Definition*, 21.2.

44 Stead lists seven senses of *ousia*. Stead, *Divine Substance*, 131–156.

45 Kelly, *ECC*, 243.

46 For a discussion of the introduction of *ousia*-language into theology, see Stead, *Divine Substance*, 157–189.

47 Ibid. 247–251; Kelly, *Creeds*, 243–244; Hanson, *SCDG*, 190–202.

Moreover, it is possible that this use of *homoousios* had already been repudiated at the Council of Antioch in 268. See below.

2 The Father and Son are aspects, parts or expressions of one common, anterior and impersonal essence as if divinity were the basic 'stuff' from which the Father and Son were made. This is the sense that Arius and other detractors of the Nicene confession often attributed to it. This sense is unsatisfactory because it attributes physicality to the divine essence and because it renders the Father and Son as common descendants of some third entity, rendering them sons and brothers in relation to an anterior essence. This sense of *homoousios* was consistently attributed to the Nicene confession by its detractors and rejected by its defenders. The most effective defence on this account was provided by Basil of Caesarea (see chapter 6). It is unlikely that this sense of *homoousios* was intended given that it is possible that it, too, was repudiated at the Council of Antioch in 268. See below.

3 A common divinity of the Father and Son that is not antecedent to the Father and Son but is instantiated within them. This could be understood in a generic sense whereby the Father and Son are members of a common class. However, this sense of the term does not necessarily need to be parsed using the logic of generic universals. Instead, it can be deployed using the filial language of continuity of divinity from the Father to the Son, begotten from the essence of the Father. This is the sense, particularly in its non-generic formulation, that would be championed by Athanasius.

An important aspect of understanding the intended meaning of *homoousios* is forming a judgment over which theological traditions were formational to its inclusion.[48] Much has been made of the suggestion that *homoousios* is indicative of the influence of Western theological ideas communicated through the central figure of Constantine's senior theological advisor Ossius of Cordoba.[49] In favour of this view is Athanasius' comment that Ossius was the one to propose the term *homoousios*.[50] If this is the case, it could appear that theology of a Western character with its strong focus on the unity of the divine nature was particularly

48 For a summary of the scholarship, see Stead, *Divine Substance*, 250–251. P. A. Beatrice has made the case for its provenance in the Arian controversy. P. A. Beatrice, 'The *Homoousion* from Hellenism to Christianity', *CH* 74 (2002), 243–272.

49 For a discussion of Ossius' role at the Council of Nicaea, see Kelly, *ECC*, 251–253. Ever since Theodor Zahn's account of Marcellus of Ancyra in 1867, the notion that Western influence was determinative of the Nicene confession has received much support. This account has been questioned in Stead, *Divine Substance*, 250–255. More recently, Ulrich has questioned the priority of Western theological concerns over the Nicene confession. For a discussion of this scholarship, see J. Ulrich, 'Nicaea and the West', *VC* 51 (1997), 10–24.

50 Athanasius, *History of the Arians*, 42. Cited from Kelly, *ECC*, 251–252.

influential at Nicaea. This view is attractive as it has some explanatory force: the assertion of the one divinity of Father and Son against the subordinationism of Arius.

However, the introduction of the term *homoousios* must address the tensions that arise within the Alexandrian tradition, which Arius had attempted to resolve in his own distinctive way. Within this context, the identification of the Son as *homoousios* is to describe the Son not as a cosmological convenience, but as one whose divinity is in continuity with the Father. This sense can be located fairly squarely as a direct contradiction of Arius' claim in the *Thalia* that the Son is not of one essence with the Father. Locating *homoousios* as emerging from an Alexandrian (rather than a Western) theological milieu also makes best sense of the logic of the credal statement itself: *homoousios* qualifies what is meant by the central claim that the Son is begotten from the essence of the Father. Therefore, its intention is to say that the Son has no origin outside God, is eternally out from the Father's essence and so is identically the same essence as the Father. In this connection, it has recently been argued that Alexander was influential in the adoption of the term *homoousios*.[51] In other words, the third of Stead's options is the most likely account of the meaning of *homoousios* once the slight nuance regarding filial over generic language is accommodated.

The controversial status of *homoousios*

The theological history of *homoousios* is complicated. Paul of Samosata is recorded as having claimed the Son is *homoousios* with the Father and that this was part of the reason that he was condemned at the Council of Antioch (268). It is not clear in what sense Paul of Samosata used the term, with conflicting answers arising from Athanasius,[52] Basil of Caesarea[53] and Hilary of Poitiers.[54] Athanasius and Basil claim that Antioch (268) was not repudiating the doctrine of the Son's identity of essence to the Father. Instead, they suggest that Paul of Samosata used *homoousios* to refer to some antecedent essence beyond the Father and Son from which they are both derived.[55]

51 M. Edwards, 'Alexander of Alexandria and the *Homoousion*', *VC* 66.5 (2012), 482–502. Others consider Alexander to have been either indifferent to the *homoousion* (Hanson, *SCDG*, 140; Stead, *Divine Substance*, 223) or even to have been cajoled into accepting it (T. D. Barnes, 'Review of N. Lenski [ed.], *The Cambridge Companion to the Age of Constantine* [Cambridge: Cambridge University Press, 2006]', *IJCT* 14 [2007], 197). Some consider that Alexander and Ossius had agreed in advance of the Council that *homoousios* should be included. See Barnes, *Constantine and Eusebius*, 215.

52 Athanasius, *Synods*, 43.

53 Basil of Caesarea, *Ep*, 52.1.

54 Hilary, *Synods*, 81, 86–88.

55 See Kelly, *ECC*, 247–248.

On the other hand, Hilary claims that Antioch (268) rejected a use of *homoousios* that implied God was an undifferentiated monad. In Hilary's view, it was not the identity of essence that was being objected to, but its use by Paul of Samosata to suggest that the Father and Son are one subsistent reality. Whether he used the term *homoousios* to refer to an anterior impersonal essence (as Athanasius and Basil understood to be the case) or to refer to an undifferentiated divine monad (Hilary's view), we may never know. Yet, the significant consequence of this was that the use of the term *homoousios* in the Christian doctrine of God *had been condemned at a church council.* This was, to say the very least, awkward for the Nicene confession and its later defenders. It was also a gift for those hostile to the Nicene confession, who would use this fact to their advantage.[56] At the very least, *homoousios* was a term that could be associated with importing materialist ideas upon divinity and obscuring the distinction between the Father and Son.

Both these senses of *homoousios* are present in the theological discussion in the decades before and after Nicaea. The skirmish between Dionysius of Alexandria (*c.*200–265) and Dionysius of Rome (d. 268) illustrates how the term could be associated with improper ways of relating the divine essence with the distinct subsistences of the Father and Son.[57] Dionysius of Alexandria initially rejected the term *homoousios* on the grounds that it implied the eradication of the distinction between the Father, Son and Spirit.[58] Eager to halt the growing influence of Sabellianism in one of his provinces,[59] Dionysius laid great stress on the personal distinction between Father and Son,[60] going so far as to declare that the Son is 'in essence alien from the Father'.[61] This amounted to something Basil of Caesarea would later liken to – what we would call – corrective oversteer.[62]

On the other hand, the complaint of Arius and those who sympathized with him was that to use *homoousios* implied the divine nature is some quasi-physical stuff that could be divided.[63] The assumption is that any similarity between distinct things must have a material or, in the case of the Son's derivation from the Father, biological basis.[64] In his letter to Alexander, Arius used the word *homoousios* to describe an unacceptable account of the Father–Son relation,

56 Epiphanius, *Panarion*, 4.15.1–2. Cited from Hanson, *SCDG*, 193.
57 Kelly, *Creeds*, 246–247.
58 For a summary of the scholarship, see Hanson, *SCDG*, 191–193.
59 Athanasius, *On the Opinions of Dionysius*, 5, NPNF II.4.
60 Athanasius, *Defence of the Nicene Definition*, 25.
61 Athanasius, *Opinions*, 4.
62 Basil, *Ep*, 9.2.
63 Williams, 'Logic of Arianism', 197–198.
64 See Ayres, *NL*, 94–95.

whereby the Son is a part of the divine essence that has been subtracted from the Father:

> [The Father] begat an only-begotten Son before time and the ages . . . and that he made him subsist at his own will . . . but not as one of the creatures; offspring, but not as one of the other things begotten; nor as Valentinus pronounced that the offspring of the Father was an emanation; nor as the Manicheans taught that the offspring was a one-in-essence-portion [*meros homoousion*] of the Father.[65]

By describing the Son as from the will of the Father, Arius denies the proposition that the Son is from the essence of the Father, which he believes implies the divisibility of the divine essence. Arius' concern, it would appear, is not that the *homoousios* would obscure the distinctions between the divine persons, but that it would intrude materialistic notions into how divinity is understood.[66]

Arius' is the concern that appears to have been more pertinent at the Nicene Council. In his letter explaining his decision to assent to the Nicene confession, Eusebius of Caesarea records Constantine's interpretation of the *homoousion*:

> [Constantine] interpreted as not in the sense of the affections of bodies, nor as if the Son subsisted from the Father in the way of division, or any severance; for that the immaterial, and intellectual, and incorporeal nature could not be the subject of any corporeal affection, but that it became us to conceive of such things in a divine and ineffable manner.[67]

According to Eusebius, Constantine was clearly concerned to give an interpretation of the term *homoousios* that excluded a materialist understanding of the divine essence. Apparently, he was less concerned with providing a positive account of its meaning. Eusebius uses this imperial reticence to justify an interpretative sleight of hand whereby he had his own subordinationist take on the Nicene confession (see below).[68]

The past of *homoousios* was undeniably chequered prior to its adoption at Nicaea. This raises the question as to why this contentious term was used in the Nicene confession. Eusebius of Caesarea suggests that the aspect that appealed to Constantine was its flexibility. Athanasius rejects this view, explaining that,

65 Arius, *Letter to Alexander*, 2–3.
66 See also Stead, *Divine Substance*, 243–244.
67 Eusebius of Caesarea, *Letter to the Diocese*, 4.
68 Behr, *NF*, 159.

while a scriptural designation would have been preferable, all of these phrases had been co-opted by Arius and his followers and given a subordinationist interpretation, which would effectively make their use meaningless. The *homoousion*, Athanasius argues, was essential to 'collect the sense of the Scriptures' in a way that would show the difference between their view and Arius'.[69] The different assessments of Athanasius and Eusebius raise the question of what the Nicene Council achieved.

What did the Council of Nicaea achieve?

One of the curiosities of the fourth century is that an event which appeared to be so momentous dropped into the background almost immediately after it was over. Eusebius of Nicomedia was reinstated to his episcopal seat after issuing a letter of recantation.[70] Even Arius' exile did not last long. Having written an insipid statement of faith, which avoided the central themes of the controversy,[71] Constantine instructed Arius' readmission to communion, but he would never be a significant figure again as Alexander and his successor, Athanasius, refused to restore him to ministry in Alexandria, and he died before a council in 336 had decided upon his future.[72] Even Athanasius, in his significant polemical work *Discourses Against the Arians* (*c.*339–43) does not mention Nicaea, while his two major works of the 330s, *Against the Gentiles* and *On the Incarnation* do not mention the Arian controversy at all.[73] It was not until the 350s and his *Defence of the Nicene Definition* that he came out in full and detailed support of the Nicene confession.[74] Meanwhile, in the Latin-speaking parts of the church there was no available translation of the Nicene confession until 356, when Hilary of Poitiers provided one in his *On the Synods*.

This relative silence concerning Nicaea may be because the Nicene confession is so directly aimed at resolving the controversy surrounding Arius and Alexander. It is orientated to the exclusion of Arius' distinctive theological settlement of the tensions inherent in the Alexandrian tradition, not to address the subtler divergent theological trajectories. The Nicene confession successfully rebutted Arius, but there was still a diverse range of incompatible image-Christologies, and the problem of miahypostatic/diohypostatic theological

69 Athanasius, *Defence of the Nicene Definition*, 20.

70 Socrates, *Ecclesiastical History*, 1.14.

71 See ibid. 1.26. Eusebius of Nicomedia also wrote a letter of recantation with a featureless acceptance of the *homoousion*. Eusebius of Nicomedia, *Letter of Recantation*, Urk 31, *NPNF* II.2; Socrates, *Ecclesiastical History*, 1.14.

72 Socrates, *Ecclesiastical History*, 38; Sozomen, *Ecclesiastical History*, 29.

73 See Wiles, 'Attitudes to Arius', 31–43.

74 Kelly, *ECC*, 257.

constructions. Moreover, as the century goes on, it becomes increasingly clear that, within these broad ways of framing the theological controversies of the fourth century, there were diverse traditions within each grouping. For example, not all who asserted a plurality of divine hypostases held complementary image-Christologies, and not all who rejected a plurality of divine hypostases conceived of God's unity in the same way.

The fact that the Nicene confession was directly orientated to the challenge posed by Arius has three implications. First, Kelly suggests that the Nicene confession was a political document aimed at securing unity among the bishops.[75] As a statement designed to unite bishops in a common condemnation of Arius and his theology it was successful. Therefore, the issue for which it was primarily composed was closed. Its authority was focused on a specific scenario with a definitive set of doctrinal issues at stake. It could hold authority only if the heresy of Arius were reinvigorated, which is the primary reason why Athanasius labelled his opponents 'Arian', as only then could he apply the full force of this council against them. In this way, he made his interpretation of the Nicene confession the only viable option and pushed his opponents to the already-repudiated margins (see below and in chapter 6).

Second, as a function of its political utility, the Nicene confession is open to a variety of interpretations. Constantine appears to have been more concerned that people should sign the confession than that they should understand it in the same way.[76] As such, it was assented to by both those who held to something like a modest participative image-Christology and by those who held a constitutive image-Christology more like Alexander's. For this reason, Parvis describes Nicaea as a 'dismal failure'.[77] While this may be an overstatement (the confession did satisfactorily repudiate the extreme doctrines of Arius), that figures with such wildly different theological priorities were able to approve the Nicene confession suggests that it was treated almost as an empty cypher into which almost anyone could import his own meaning does not speak well for its efficacy. This is illustrated by Eusebius of Caesarea's letter to the church in Caesarea. While he had no difficulty acknowledging and agreeing with the Nicene condemnation of Arius' more extreme and distinctive doctrines,[78] there were plenty of phrases in the Nicene confession that were awkward for Eusebius, and he had to demonstrate significant hermeneutical ingenuity to make

[75] Ibid. 255–262.

[76] Ibid. 261–262. For an analysis of Constantine's ongoing involvement in matters related to the Nicene confession, see T. G. Elliot, 'Constantine and "the Arian Reaction After Nicaea"', *JEH* 43.2 (1992), 169–194.

[77] Parvis, *Marcellus*, 83.

[78] Eusebius of Caesarea, *Letter to the Diocese*, 8–9.

conceptual space for himself.[79] As such, he is eager to demonstrate that he interrogated the meaning of phrases that might have been taken to mean a continuity of divinity predicated on a materialist or biological understanding of the divine essence:

> On their dictating this formula, we did not let it pass without inquiry in what sense they introduced 'of the essence of the Father,' and 'one in essence with the Father.' Accordingly questions and explanations took place, and the meaning of the words underwent the scrutiny of reason. And they professed that the phrase 'of the essence' was indicative of the Son's being indeed from the Father, yet without being as if a part of Him. And with this understanding we thought good to assent to the sense of such religious doctrine, teaching, as it did, that the Son was from the Father, not however a part of His essence.[80]

The proposition that the Son is from the essence of the Father was acceptable to Eusebius once it was clarified that it did not imply the division of divinity. Similarly, Eusebius qualified his acceptance of the claim that the Son is *homoousios* with the Father by stressing that it did not impose a materialist conception of divinity.[81]

> And so too on examination there are grounds for saying that the Son is 'one in essence' with the Father; not in the way of bodies, nor like mortal beings, for He is not such by division of essence, or by severance, no, nor by any affection, or alteration, or changing of the Father's essence and power . . . but because 'one in essence with the Father' suggests that the Son of God bears no resemblance to the originated creatures, but that to His Father alone Who begat Him is He in every way assimilated, and that He is not of any other subsistence and essence, but from the Father.[82]

This is not a positive account of the meaning of *homoousios*, preferring instead to define it by contrast to the utter dissimilarity between God and creation. Similarly, Eusebius does not go so far as to identify the Son in an eternal

---

79 Ayres, *NL*, 91.

80 Eusebius of Caesarea, *Letter to the Diocese*, 5.

81 Ayres, *NL*, 90. It could be that Eusebius considered the Council of Antioch (324) to have been sufficient in condemning the extremes of Arius' doctrine. M. Edwards, 'The First Council of Nicaea', in M. M. Mitchell and F. M. Young (eds.), *The Cambridge History of Christianity* (Cambridge: Cambridge University Press, 2006), 552–567.

82 Eusebius of Caesarea, *Letter to the Diocese*, 7.

correlative relation to the Father, describing God's essential Fatherhood not as indicative of the Son's coeternity, but rather of God's generative potential.[83] A consummate survivor, Eusebius took every inch of space provided by Constantine to interpret the confession in a way compatible with his own complex Christology.[84] In the light of this, Ayres's comment describes the situation well: '[this] demonstrates the extent to which the promulgation of *homoousios* involved a conscious *lack* of positive definition of the term'.[85]

Eusebius also sought to carve out some middle ground in which the generation of the Son, while not explicitly attributed to the will and purposive act of the Father, did not imply the eternal correlation of the Father and Son:

> we also accepted the phrase 'begotten, not made,' since the council asserted that 'made' was a term used to designate other creatures which came to be through the Son, to whom the Son had no similarity. So according to their reasoning, he was not something made that resembled the things which came to exist through him, but was of an essence which is too high to be put on the same level as anything which was made. The divine sayings teach us that his essence was begotten from the Father, and that the mode of his being begotten is inexpressible and unable to be conceived by any nature which has had a beginning of its existence.[86]

For Eusebius, the clause 'begotten, not made' does not pertain to the Son's coeternity but rather to the Son's difference from creatures. This is indicative of a certain apophaticism in Eusebius' account of the Son's generation from the Father. Its conceptual content, for Eusebius, does not make a positive statement about the Father–Son relation but rather in differentiating between the Son's and creation's mode of derivation. In this way, Eusebius interpreted the Nicene confession in a manner consistent with his position that the Son has primacy in relation to creation but the Father has primacy in relation to the Son.[87] It is telling, however, that Eusebius does not comment on the clause 'true God of true God', which makes a positive statement about the Father–Son relation.

With this distinction in place, Eusebius writes approvingly of the anathemas against Arius, accepting that the propositions that the Son was begotten temporally from nothing are unscriptural.[88] However, the distinction between

---

83 Ibid. 10.
84 Anatolios, *RN*, 19, 63–64.
85 Ayres, *NL*, 91; emphasis original.
86 Eusebius of Caesarea, *Letter to the Diocese*, 11.
87 Anatolios, *RN*, 60.
88 Eusebius of Caesarea, *Letter to the Diocese*, 15–16.

the Son's generation and the making of creation is not held to imply the eternal generation of the Son. Instead, while recognizing God is eternally Father, Eusebius interprets the doctrine of eternal generation in terms of *potentiality*:

> At this point in the discussion, our most pious Emperor maintained that the Son existed before all ages even according to his divinely inspired begetting, since even before the act of begetting was performed, in potentiality he was with the Father, even before he was begotten by him, since the Father is always Father, just as he is always King and always Savior; he has the potentiality to be all things, and remains exactly the same forever.[89]

Eusebius' attempt is to affirm the pre-existence of the Son in such a way that does not imply his eternal generation. The logic of this position is a theological construction that does not operate on Arius' dialectic of eternal existence and making from nothing, but rather on necessary existence (the Father) and that which is brought into being by the will of the Father (the Son and creation). In this way, Eusebius constructs an interpretation of the Nicene confession that at one and the same time recognizes the repudiation of Arius while not requiring a full-throated affirmation of the Son's co-divinity with the Father. This indicates that the Nicene confession allowed divergent theological traditions to coexist after its promulgation.

Third, on account of its supposed pliability and inelegant parenthetic clauses, the Nicene confession was never suitable for liturgical usage. As suggested in the last chapter, local confessions remained in use for instruction and initiation well through the fourth century. It also lacks in appropriate confessional balance. It has a significantly inflated, cumbersome and highly technical Christological clause with only a brief comment on the Spirit's acting as a placeholder. As such, the laity or even the presbytery would have had little functional familiarity with the Nicene confession.

Fighting in the dark? (335–51)

The decades following Nicaea are often presented in a way that is summed up by Socrates' well-known statement 'it seemed not unlike a contest in the dark; for neither party appeared to understand distinctly the grounds on which they

---

89 Ibid. 16.

calumniated one another'.[90] Hanson suggests that the different theological trajectories were not yet formed or their terminological modes of expression sufficiently sophisticated, such that this period was a

> search in the fog, a situation when ignorant armies clashed by night . . . It was not a history of the defence of an agreed and settled orthodoxy against the assaults of open heresy. On the subject which was primarily under discussion there was not yet any orthodox picture.[91]

While there is truth to this, it is not beyond possibility to identify what the major doctrinal issues were in this period.

Identifying the disputants and the dispute

It is not possible at this point to talk of a pro-Nicene faction and an anti-Nicene faction, because all were, nominally at the very least, its signatories. The main protagonists were not disputing the Nicene statement, but interpreting and relating it to their own theological priorities in very different ways.[92] However, in the period immediately after the Nicene confession, it is possible to organize the controversy along the following lines:

1. Those who affirmed the distinct hypostatic existence of the Son (diohypostastic tradition) alongside either a softer constitutive image-Christology than Nicaea or a participative image-Christology. This faction was gathered around Asterius, Eusebius of Nicomedia and Eusebius of Caesarea, and is denoted here as the 'Eusebian faction'.
2. Those who rejected the application of *hypostasis* to refer to the Son's discrete subsistence (miahypostatic tradition) held alongside a strong constitutive image-Christology, who were comfortable with the Nicene confession. This faction was gathered around Athanasius and Marcellus, with a powerful ally in the diocese of Rome.

These factions were not monolithic. Against the Athanasian polarizing narrative that conceived of pro-Nicene orthodoxy and the Arians, it is appropriate to differentiate between extreme and moderate factions within the Eusebian alliance, with Eusebius of Caesarea holding something closer to a constitutive

---

90 Socrates, *Ecclesiastical History*, 1.23.
91 Ibid.; Hanson, *SCDG*, xviii.
92 Behr, *NF*, 27–28; Kelly, *ECC*, 241.

image-Christology than others.[93] Likewise, within the faction gathered around Athanasius and Marcellus there were differences regarding the best way to describe the unity of the divine being in relation to the distinct subsistence of the Father and Son. Athanasius' association with Marcellus and the lingering suspicion of their shared commitment to a miaphypostatic theology continued to cause problems throughout the fourth century, especially in Antioch.[94]

The 'Eusebian Alliance'

During the 330s, Eusebius of Caesarea's attention turned to Marcellus, against whom he strengthened his insistence on the reality of the distinction between the Father and Son prior to the incarnation. His two major theological works of this period are *Against Marcellus* and *Ecclesiastical Theology* (337–9).[95] In these texts, he continues the emphasis from his earlier thought; namely, that the divinity of the Father is communicated to the begotten Son,[96] which undergirds the Son's revelatory and salvific work alongside his personal distinction from the Father.[97] As such, the Father–Son relation is foundational to the inner logic of the gospel, whereby the proposition that the Son is not differentiated from the Father in reality (a doctrine attributed to Marcellus) is ruinous of the gospel itself.

Lienhard describes Eusebius' efforts in this post-Nicene period in the following way: '[he] tried to steer a course between "Arianism" as he understood it, and the errors of Marcellus'.[98] To this end, he rejected core doctrines of Arius, such as the Son's being brought into existence from nothing.[99] However, eager to maintain the absolute primacy and singularity of God as the one *agen(n)ētos*, Eusebius describes the Son as 'neither unoriginate nor unbegotten',[100] thereby equating the quality of eternity with the unbegotten Father alone and introducing some notion of sequence into the Father–Son relation. The Father alone is absolute and does not derive any aspect of his being from beyond himself. The Father and Son, then, are clearly distinct from each other, which Eusebius described by asserting that there were two unequal hypostases within the Godhead:

[93] There were significant differences between Eusebius of Caesarea and Asterius, particularly in their image-Christologies. DelCogliano, 'Eusebian Theologies of the Son'. Asterius conceived of the Son as image in a participatory way, while Eusebius held something closer to a constitutive view. For a further indication of this diversity within the Eusebian faction, see M. Crawford, 'On the Diversity and Influence of the Eusebian Alliance: The Case of Theodore of Heraclea', *JEH* 64.2 (2013), 227–257.

[94] This is discussed in chapter 6 with respect to the Antiochene schism.

[95] See also Beeley, *Unity of Christ*, 77–90.

[96] Eusebius of Caesarea, *Ecclesiastical Theology*, 1.11. Cited from Beeley, *Unity of Christ*, 87.

[97] Eusebius of Caesarea, *Ecclesiastical Theology*, 1.13; 2.21. Cited from Beeley, *Unity of Christ*, 86.

[98] Lienhard, *Contra Marcellum*, 108.

[99] Eusebius of Caesarea, *Ecclesiastical Theology*, 1.10.4. Cited from Lienhard, *Contra Marcellum*, 109.

[100] Eusebius of Caesarea, *Ecclesiastical Theology*, 2.6.1. Cited from Lienhard, *Contra Marcellum*, 110.

> [the church] does not teach two unbegottens or two unoriginates, as we have often said, or two essences that exist side by side in equality of honor, and hence not two gods; but she teaches one first principle and God, and the same as the Father of the only-begotten and beloved Son.[101]

Eusebius writes the following credal statement to articulate his understanding of the Son:

> [The church] teaches the only-begotten Son of God, Jesus Christ, begotten of the Father before all ages. He is not the same as the Father. He exists and lives and truly coexists as Son in himself. God from God, light from light, life from life. By unutterable and unspeakable words, words wholly unknown to us and incomprehensible, he was begotten of the Father for the salvation of the universe. He subsists, not like the rest of begotten things, nor does he have life as the things begotten through him do; but he alone was born of the Father himself and is life itself.[102]

This statement envisages the Father–Son relation as, to some extent, unique and unknowable, stressing the difference between the generation of the Son and the making of creation. However, Eusebius also elides the generation of the Son with the making of creation, by describing creation as 'the rest of begotten things'. The centre of gravity in Eusebius' statement locates the Son as divine with the Father – albeit a secondary form of deity who lacks eternity, whose generation is for the purposes of salvation – but there is also an uncomfortable tension in which the Son is also located with creation as among the things brought into being, even if the Son's coming into being is laced with the unknowability of divinity. To describe the Father–Son relation, Eusebius frequently used the idea of an object and its image.[103] As the image of the Father, the Son is like the Father (which was often described in terms of the light and its radiance[104]), but subordinate to the Father as the source is greater than that which is derived from it. Importantly, Eusebius applies this doctrine of the Son's

101 Eusebius of Caesarea, *Ecclesiastical Theology*, 2.23.1. Cited from Lienhard, *Contra Marcellum*, 111–112.

102 Eusebius of Caesarea, *Ecclesiastical Theology*, 1.8.2–3. Cited from Lienhard, *Contra Marcellum*, 114–115.

103 See Lienhard, *Contra Marcellum*, 118, n. 54.

104 It is for this reason that some see the division between Eusebius of Caesarea and others in the Eusebian faction who held to a more explicitly participative image-Christology as a precursor of the division between the heterousian and homoiousian factions in the middle decades of the fourth century. See e.g. S. Parvis, 'Joseph Lienhard, Marcellus of Ancyra and Marcellus' Rule of Faith', in R. J. Rombs and A. Y. Hwang (eds.), *Tradition and the Rule of Faith in the Early Church: Essays in Honor of Joseph T. Lienhard* (Washington, D.C.: Catholic University of America Press, 2010), 89–108, at 90.

diminished divinity to the mediatorial status of the Son.[105] This is a strikingly Lucianite theological move.

Asterius became the central theological force of the Eusebian faction in the 330s and 340s. He was repeatedly characterized by Athanasius as an advocate – and even the teacher – of Arius.[106] He was the focus of a theological attack from the opposing faction and would be a significant voice in the Council of Antioch of 341 at which his participatory image-Christology was given precise conciliar expression. Asterius continued and strengthened Arius' insistence on the primacy and singularity of God with the quality of being unbegotten becoming the central characteristic of divinity. The Son, as begotten by the will of the Father, is not intrinsic to the divine being and is a creature inferior to the Father, brought into existence to be the one through whom creation was brought into being.[107] As such, he does not share in the attributes of the Father by essence, but rather these are bestowed upon him contingently by the will of the Father.[108]

Like Eusebius, Asterius distanced himself from Arius' more extreme positions. For example, he replaced Arius' contention that God became Father with something like Eusebius of Caesarea's notion of potentiality: God can eternally be described as Father because he eternally possesses generative power.[109] Accordingly, Asterius deployed a characteristically Lucianite image-Christology of the Son as 'unchanging image of the essence and will and power of the glory [of the Father]'.[110] In a similar vein, Asterius stressed that the Son is the 'unchanging image of the substance and will and glory and power of the Father',[111] in a marked departure from Arius' notion of the incomparability of the Father and Son.

Marcellus and Athanasius

On the other side of the dispute was the alliance of Marcellus of Ancyra (born *c.*280) and Athanasius. There was significant overlap between the theologies of Athanasius and Marcellus, particularly in their opposition to the subordinationist Christology they considered to be inherent to the Eusebian faction and in their common conviction that the Son is eternally proper to the Father, which is the reason they both resisted describing the Son as a distinct *hypostasis* from

105 Eusebius of Caesarea, *Ecclesiastical Theology*, 2.17.7. Cited from Lienhard, *Contra Marcellum*, 120.
106 Athanasius, *Discourses*, 1.30, 32; 3.2; *Synods*, 20.1; *Defence of the Nicene Definition*, 8, 20.
107 Anatolios, *RN*, 19, n. 16, 54.
108 DelCogliano, 'Eusebian Theologies of the Son', 464–465.
109 Anatolios, *RN*, 57.
110 Cited from Anatolios, *RN*, 58.
111 Anatolios, *RN*, 19, n. 14.

the Father.[112] Marcellus emerges as the central figure in the post-Nicene controversies because of his distinctive conception of the unity of the Father and Son,[113] which led to his teaching that 'the existence of the Son of God commenced when He was born of Mary, and that His kingdom would have an end'.[114] He was a partisan participant at the Council of Nicaea,[115] but was always cool towards the Nicene confession.[116] Marcellus continued his forthright resistance to the subordinationist diohypostatic tradition with his lost work *Against Asterius* (*c.*330). This text was responded to by Eusebius of Caesarea in his *Against Marcellus* and *Ecclesiastical Theology*, from which most fragments of Marcellus' writings survive in the form of citations. With the theological consensus in the East closer to the diohypostatic perspective of the Eusebians, Marcellus was deposed at the Council of Constantinople in 336, having been judged to have fallen 'into the opinions of Paul of Samosata',[117] after which he sought refuge in Rome. Marcellus wrote to Julius of Rome expressing his theological convictions, using the Old Roman Creed and not the Nicene confession as indicative of his views, and was subsequently vindicated at the Council of Rome in 341.[118]

Marcellus' thought is characterized by a concern to preserve the unity of God, which has been understood as monistic.[119] For Marcellus, the unity of God is often the 'unity of a personal subject'.[120] It is commonly said that, for Marcellus, the Word is not a subsistent, personal reality but a property internal to God:

> the Logos himself alone was united to God; and this [united being] was eternal and unbegotten, and was one and the same thing as God, called by the distinct names of Father and Son, but one in *ousia* and *hypostasis*.[121]

---

112 See also Ayres, *NL*, 106. On Athanasius' reluctance to condemn Marcellus on account of their significant agreement regarding the Son as intrinsic to the Father, see J. T. Lienhard SJ, 'Did Athanasius Reject Marcellus?', in Barnes and Williams, *Arianism After Arius*, 65–80.

113 For discussions of Marcellus, see Ayres, *NL*, 62–69; Hanson, *SCDG*, 217–235; Lienhard, *Contra Marcellum*, 49–68.

114 Sozomen, *Ecclesiastical History*, 2.33.

115 Hanson, *SCDG*, 217.

116 This may be because the phrase 'God from God, Light from Light' permitted Eusebius to maintain his doctrine of the distinct *hypostasis* of the Son. Parvis observes that Marcellus used the Old Roman Creed (not the Nicene Creed) to demonstrate his orthodoxy in his letter to Julius of Rome and at the Council of Serdica. Parvis, *Marcellus*, 91–92.

117 Sozomen, *Ecclesiastical History*, 2.33.

118 Ibid.

119 Anatolios, *RN*, 19. See also J. T. Lienhard SJ, '*Ousia* and *Hypostasis*: The Cappadocian Settlement and the Theology of "One Hypostasis"', in S. T. Davis, D. Kendall SJ and G. O'Collins SJ (eds.), *The Trinity: An Interdisciplinary Symposium on the Trinity* (Oxford: Oxford University Press, 2002), 100–122, at 111–112.

120 Lienhard, *Contra Marcellum*, 53–54.

121 Fragment of Marcellus of Ancyra, Eusebius of Caesarea in *Against Marcellus*, 1.1.4, ed. M. Vinzent *Markell von Ankyra: Die Fragmente; Der Brief an Julius von Rom.*, supplements to *VC* 39 (Leiden: E. J. Brill, 1997). Cited from Hanson, *SCDG*, 224, n. 80.

Elsewhere Marcellus is recorded as having asserted that the Word is no more distinct from God than a human word is from the speaker.[122] As such, Marcellus is commonly understood as falling within the miahypostatic tradition which rejects the proposition that God has his life as three hypostases.

However, a one-sided assessment of Marcellus' thought does not account for the continuing support and loyalty of Athanasius throughout the fourth century, which resulted in infuriating stalemates in the search for a pro-Nicene consensus. More sympathetic treatments of Marcellus' doctrine recognize in Marcellus a rather more mainstream theological figure.[123] Typically, these theological and historical re-evaluations of Marcellus rely less on their presentation as fragments by his theological enemies and draw instead on the confession of faith he set out in his letter to Julius to defend himself against accusations of heresy.[124] With his continuing stress on the unity of God, he refers to God as one 'indivisible' reality,[125] a mode of expression which courted the accusation from Eusebius that for Marcellus 'there are three Names to be found in the one *hypostasis*' (the distinction between Father, Son and Spirit is *conceptual* as opposed to *actual*).[126] However, Marcellus can be understood as simply advocating for the indivisibility of the one God:

> We have learned from the divine Scriptures that the Godhead of Father and Son is undivided. For if someone separates the Son, that is the Word, from God Almighty, it is necessary for him either to think there are two Gods . . . or to confess that the Word is not God, which also itself is seen to be alien to the orthodox faith.[127]

It can be inferred that Marcellus considered speaking of a plurality of divine hypostases to be either compromising monotheism or the divinity of the Son.[128] It is for Marcellus' insistence on this point that he and Athanasius were in theological alliance.

However, others contend that Marcellus recognized plurality most clearly in God's economic activity, rather than in his internal reality. The plurality emerging from singularity is the temporary expansion (or 'dilation') of the

[122] Fr. 87. Cited from Anatolios, *RN*, 19.
[123] Lienhard, *Contra Marcellum*; Parvis, *Marcellus*, esp. 30–37; A. H. B. Logan, 'Marcellus of Ancyra and the Councils of 325: Antioch, Ancyra and Nicaea', *JTS* 43.2 (1992), 428–446.
[124] Parvis, 'Marcellus' Rule of Faith', 94–101.
[125] Recorded in Epiphanius, *Panarion*, 72.3.1. Cited from Hanson, *SCDG*, 23.
[126] Eusebius of Caesarea, *Ecclesiastical Theology*, 3.4.159. Cited from Hanson, *SCDG*, 226.
[127] *Letter to Julius*. Recorded in Epiphanius, *Panarion*, 73.2.2. Cited from Parvis, 'Marcellus' Rule of Faith', 96.
[128] See also Hanson, *SCDG*, 229–230.

divine being for the purposes of creation and salvation, which ultimately reverts to the stillness of the undifferentiated divine being.[129] For example, in reference to John 16:13, Marcellus explains that 'in this text we have a plain reference to the monad which expands to form a triad while in no way allowing itself to be divided'.[130] This begins with the work of creation. This undifferentiated stillness (or 'silence')[131] gives way to temporary differentiation as the Word 'came forth from the Father in order that everything should come into existence through him'.[132] It is in connection to the incarnation that Marcellus attributes the relation of having been begotten. It is this temporal begetting, then, that establishes the incarnate Word as a distinct subsistent reality.[133] This, then, does not undermine divine singularity, for 'the Godhead would appear to be extended simply by activity (*energeia*), so . . . the Monad is genuinely indivisible'.[134]

For Marcellus, it appears that the dilation to plurality in outward actions will be reconciled into a return to singularity, which is the driving force behind Marcellus' distinctive eschatology. A doctrine that is frequently attributed to Marcellus is that the Son's kingdom is only temporary, and that his rule will come to an end and be given over to the Father, who is the true single Lord.[135] At this point, the Word will divest himself of human flesh, and return to an undifferentiated oneness with the Father.[136] This doctrine of the termination of the Son's kingdom to be replaced by the one rule of God was distinctive to Marcellus, and was quietly missed out of his statement to Julius of Rome.[137] In this way, the plurality of God's saving action resolves finally into the singularity and eternity of the divine unity.

Perhaps the best that can be said in a study such as this is that Marcellus' clear doctrine of the indivisibility of the one Godhead, true of both Father and Son, was the reason why he enjoyed the consistent support of Athanasius; however, he was perceived (either rightly or wrongly) to undermine the reality and eternity of the distinct subsistence of the Father and Son.

129 Ayres, *NL*, 69. However, Lienhard has suggested that this is an inference from Marcellus' writings, with emphasis on its distorting his polemic concern, which was to object to the pluralistic language in the Eusebians' doctrine of God. Lienhard, *Contra Marcellum*, 56–57.

130 Cited from Ayres, *NL*, 66.

131 Hanson, *SCDG*, 227.

132 Ibid. 225, n. 90.

133 Ibid. 227. This is challenged at Parvis, 'Marcellus' Rule of Faith', 98.

134 Eusebius of Caesarea, *Ecclesiastical Theology*, 2.4.102. Cited from Hanson, *SCDG*, 228, n. 109.

135 Lienhard suggests this is a misreading and that what is handed over is a partial victory and a partial kingdom, which is to be fully integrated with the rule of the Father. Lienhard, *Contra Marcellum*, 64–66.

136 See also Ayres, *NL*, 66–67.

137 Hanson, *SCDG*, 231.

The construction of the 'Arians'

Towards the end of the 330s the label 'Arian' began to be applied to the Eusebian faction by their opponents. The purpose of this designation was to undermine the claim of the Eusebians that they held a legitimate interpretation of the Nicene confession and to define them not as advocates of *apostolic* doctrine, but of *Arius'* doctrine. As such, the label 'Arian' was frequently used in contrast to the description 'Christian'. One of the earliest examples of this comes in Julius of Rome's letter to the Council at Antioch in 341, which had gathered for the purpose of dedicating a church building (for which it is often referred to as the Dedication Council). This council met in the context of uncomfortable relations between Rome and the Eastern Church on account of Athanasius and Marcellus. Both Marcellus and Athanasius had been deposed from their respective sees in different circumstances, only to be vindicated by a council held in Rome earlier in 341. Julius addressed the Eastern bishops who had gathered at Antioch as 'Arian'. This deeply provocative action was informed by Athanasius and Marcellus.

Athanasius and the 'Arians'

An example of the polemic that informed Julius' letter comes from Athanasius' *Discourses Against the Arians.* Here Athanasius presents the dispute as between two factions: the Christians and the 'Arians':

> when Alexander of blessed memory had cast out Arius, those who remained with Alexander, remained Christians; but those who went out with Arius, left the Saviour's Name to us who were with Alexander, and as to them they were hence-forward denominated Arians. Behold then, after Alexander's death too, those who communicate with his successor Athanasius, and those with whom the said Athanasius communicates, are instances of the same rule; none of them bear his name, nor is he named from them, but all in like manner, and as is usual, are called Christians . . . Thus, though Arius be dead, and many of his party have succeeded him, yet those who think with him, as being known from Arius, are called Arians.[138]

Inevitably, this is an immense oversimplification which was not undertaken in error but for its polemical value.[139] If Athanasius could portray the diverse body

[138] Athanasius, *Discourses*, 1.3, NPNF II.4.

[139] Ever since Stead's important essay (C. Stead, 'Rhetorical Method in Athanasius', *VC* 30 [1976], 121–137), criticisms of Athanasius' polemical strategies have become more common. For example, Gwynn, *Athanasius of Alexandria*, 76–82.

of theologians and bishops who were dissatisfied with the Nicene confession as 'Arian', then the inevitable corollary is that *any* reticence towards the Nicene confession is not within the bounds of orthodoxy. However, it is evident that it was possible to demur from the Nicene confession and not be an advocate of Arius' doctrine.

The theological character of Athanasius' polemic is considered in chapter 6. This chapter considers the ecclesio-political aspect of his polemic. Athanasius, Bishop of Alexandria following the death of Alexander (d. 326), led a diocese still torn by the Meletian schism (as soon as Athanasius replaced Alexander, the Meletians began agitating against Athanasius[140]) and the Arian controversy, over which he refused to compromise amid the constant speculation up until his death in 336 that Arius would be reinstated.[141] Athanasius first used the term 'Arian' or 'Ariomaniac' in his Easter Letters of 338 and 339 in which he delivers the reminder to the church under his care to persevere in its confession on the full divinity of the Son.[142] Importantly, he identifies such a confession as integral to the Easter faith: 'if He were a creature, He would have been holden by death; but if He was not holden by death, according to the Scriptures, He is not a creature, but the Lord of the creatures'.[143] Behr suggests that this letter indicates the ongoing influence of Arius' theological ideas within the diocese of Alexandria itself.[144] However, it is striking that in his description of these lingering views, no mention is made of Arius' more distinctive doctrines such as the Son's coming to being from nothing.[145] These 'Arians', in other words, might well have been characterized by a body of beliefs more like those of the moderates within the Eusebian faction than those of Arius.

The controversy that surrounded Athanasius and brought about his deposition at the Council of Antioch (339) was not doctrinal. Instead, accusations were made against his conduct by an influential group led by Eusebius of Nicomedia (who had become Eusebius of Constantinople in 338).[146] Athanasius

140 The Meletian schism refers to a dispute between Meletius of Lycopolis and Peter of Alexandria that was over the question of readmittance or ordination of lapsed believers through the Diocletian persecutions (303–312), but might also have reached deeper into a challenge of the authority of the Bishop of Alexandria, resulting in two parallel church bodies. See Anatolios, *Athanasius*, 5–6. For the Meletians' agitation against Athanasius, see Hanson, *SCDG*, 249–258.

141 Anatolios, *Athanasius*, 12.

142 Athanasius, *Epp*, 10.9; 11.10; NPNF II.4.

143 Athanasius, *Ep*, 11.13.

144 Behr, *NF*, 23.

145 Athanasius, *Ep*, 10.9.

146 That this was a cabal led by Eusebius of Nicomedia is certainly the view of Socrates, *Ecclesiastical History*, 1.23, 27–28, 30–35; Theodoret, *Ecclesiastical History*, 1.25–26. This was Athanasius' second exile. The first followed the Council of Tyre (335), at which similar accusations against him – including the charges of sexual impropriety and sorcery – were led by Eusebius of Nicomedia. Sozomen, *Ecclesiastical History*, 2.31; Theodoret, *Ecclesiastical History*, 1.28. See also Anatolios, *Athanasius*, 12–13;

considered this an 'Arian' conspiracy against him. He called a council in Alexandria in 338 that produced an encyclical letter in which Athanasius is defended against the charge that he secured his position as bishop by murder and intimidation.[147] This letter describes these accusations as part of a conspiracy of 'the Arian madmen' to remove him from office,[148] whom Athanasius names as 'Eusebius [of Nicomedia/Constantinople] and his fellows'.[149] However, through an alliance with the dissident Meletian clergy, the conspiracy was successful and Athanasius was deposed and exiled in 339.[150] When his appeal to Constantine failed owing to Eusebius of Nicomedia/Constantinople's continued slurs against him,[151] Athanasius sought refuge in Rome,[152] where he was able to forge alliances with significant political and ecclesiastical figures, including Marcellus.[153]

Marcellus was significant in emboldening Athanasius in the latter's growing willingness to use the designation 'Arian'.[154] In his three *Discourses Against the Arians* (composed during his exile in Rome between *c.*339 and 343[155]), Athanasius describes a cabal of theologians dedicated primarily to Arius' thought. He describes the continuity of Arius' doctrine as 'Arianism',[156] and its teachers as 'professors of Arius's madness'.[157] Significantly, he distinguishes between 'Arianism' and genuine Christianity, with the former described as a sect that has supplanted Christ with Arius,[158] and also as holding beliefs inconsistent with the received rule of faith.[159] Observing that the Eusebian faction did not hold Arius' more extreme doctrines, Athanasius claims that this was not a fundamental difference in their core shared doctrine but was an example of their vacillating and inconsistent thought, indicative of the impossibility of their joint position.[160]

(note 146 *cont.*) *Athanasius: The Coherence of His Thought* (London: Routledge, 1998), 86–87; Hanson, *SCDG*, 259–273.

147 Athanasius, *Defence Against the Arians*, 1.3–5, 9. An estimate of Athanasius' character is not straightforward. See Hanson, *SCDG*, 239–242.

148 Athanasius, *Defence Against the Arians*, 1.6. Hanson points to evidence of a concerted effort of Eusebius of Nicomedia to pack episcopal positions with those sympathetic to his theological convictions. See Hanson, *SCDG*, 274–284.

149 Athanasius, *Defence Against the Arians*, 1.6. See Gwynn, *Eusebians*, 51–57.

150 Recorded in Sozomen, *Ecclesiastical History*, 2.25.

151 Ibid. 2.28; Socrates, *Ecclesiastical History*, 35.

152 Socrates, *Ecclesiastical History*, 2.17.

153 Behr, *NF*, 163; Marcellus, *Contra Marcellum*, 137–138.

154 Behr, *NF*, 25–26; Anatolios, *Athanasius*, 87.

155 On composition, see Anatolios, *Athanasius*, 19, n. 75.

156 Athanasius, *Discourses*, 1.1.

157 Ibid. 2.1.

158 Ibid. 1.2–4.

159 Ibid. 2.11–17.

160 Ibid. 1.30–34.

This tactic of identifying disquiet with the Nicene confession with Arianism is one that Athanasius would use again and again. As Wiles's wry observation describes, 'the dead Arius was not even a whipping boy but the whip'.[161] This was an unfortunate tactic of Athanasius', as it grouped all who demurred from the Nicene confession together under an association with Arius' extreme subordinationism. Gwynn has demonstrated how Athanasius' policy of polarization coloured both the fourth century and subsequent assessments of it, giving the impression of two monolithic and opposed factions, one gathered around Arius and the other around Nicaea.[162] As the subsequent decades proved, it was possible to have misgivings about the precise wording of the Nicene confession while holding doctrinal commitments closely corresponding to it. As such, in the 350s Athanasius would have to back-peddle from his earlier intemperate remarks.

Marcellus and the 'Arians'

Marcellus was already in Rome following his being condemned for heresy at the Council of Constantinople in 336.[163] Julius wrote to the Eusebian faction to call them to a council in Rome in 340 for the purpose of investigating the accusations made against Athanasius and Marcellus. In their reply, which took a year to come, the Eusebian faction declared the previous condemnations of Athanasius and Marcellus were satisfactory, warning of schism if the church in Rome continued to defend these controversial bishops.[164] Prior to the Council of Rome, Marcellus wrote to Julius to defend his own orthodoxy while describing his opponents as those who reject Nicaea and 'still persist in their former errors'.[165] The error, Marcellus specifies, is to teach that the Son is another *hypostasis*, distinct from the Father,[166] and that the distinction between them includes not attributing eternity to the Son,[167] but conceiving of their relationship as involving some form of sequence. Marcellus also describes the Eusebians by using the terms of the Nicene anathemas, thereby accusing them of being Arians.[168] The council, in which Athanasius and Marcellus were

161 Wiles, 'Attitudes to Arius', 27.

162 Gwynn, *Eusebians*, 170–244.

163 For the complex events surrounding this and Athanasius' exile, see Parvis, *Marcellus*, 135–158. For Athanasius' exile in Rome, the establishment of common cause with Marcellus and their influence on Julius, see T. D. Barnes, *Athanasius and Constantius: Theology and Politics in the Constantinian Empire* (Cambridge, Mass.: Harvard University Press, 2001), 47–62.

164 Recorded in Socrates, *Ecclesiastical History*, 2.17.

165 Recorded in Epiphanius, *Panarion*, 72.2–3. Cited from Behr, *NF*, 25.

166 Lienhard, '*Ousia* and *Hypostasis*', 113.

167 Lienhard, *Contra Marcellum*, 141–142.

168 Ibid. 142.

vindicated, was finally held in 341. This caused consternation among the Eusebian party, who saw this as an illegitimate intervention by an overreaching Church of Rome into matters already decided at earlier councils.

Relations were stretched to breaking point when, following Marcellus' lead, Julius described the opponents of Marcellus as 'Arian' in his long letter to the Eusebians explaining the Council of Rome's decision to vindicate Athanasius and Marcellus.[169] In this letter, Julius accuses the Eusebians of attempting to subvert the Nicene confession, reflecting the influence of Marcellus and Athanasius. Julius also affirms the orthodoxy of Marcellus, identifying him as a pro-Nicene bishop.[170] This is significant, as *Julius was identifying orthodoxy solely by opposition to Arius.*[171] This letter is indicative of the categories in which Athanasius, Marcellus and their allies in Rome were thinking at the time: two parties, the Nicene orthodox and the 'Arian' heterodox, were gathered around the Eusebians.[172]

Following this letter, the controversy can begin to be loosely defined with a geographical referent: a Western miahypostatic perspective informed by Athanasius and Marcellus in contrast to an Eastern diohypostatic perspective gathered around Eusebius of Caesarea, Eusebius of Nicomedia and Asterius.[173] Indeed, given that after the death of Constantine in 337[174] the empire was divided between East and West, with different emperors favouring different solutions to the doctrinal divides depending on conviction (or the prevailing attitude among the bishops of that area), these geographical terms of reference became increasingly serviceable in the fifth and sixth decades of the century.

Refusing the label 'Arian'

The designation 'Arian' was hotly denied by the Eastern bishops. The response to Julius' letter to the Council of Antioch argues, 'We have not been followers of Arius – how could Bishops, such as we, follow a Presbyter? – nor did we receive any other faith beside that which has been handed down from the beginning.'[175] Not only is allegiance to Arius an inversion of proper church order, but also the Eastern bishops consider themselves consistent with the

169 Athanasius, *Defence Against the Arians*, 1.21–36. See Socrates, *Ecclesiastical History*, 2.22–23.
170 Athanasius, *Defence Against the Arians*, 1.32.
171 See also Lienhard, *Contra Marcellum*, 139.
172 See also ibid. 140.
173 For more on this controversy causing divisions between the Eastern and Western halves of the empire, see Ayres, *NL*, 109. As Van Dam points out, language in the Roman Empire was connected to ideas about the imposition of power, culture and religion. See R. van Dam, *The Roman Revolution of Constantine* (Cambridge: Cambridge University Press, 2009), 184–216.
174 Socrates, *Ecclesiastical History*, 1.39.
175 Athanasius, *Synods*, 22; Socrates, *Ecclesiastical History*, 2.10.

tradition of the church, not the beliefs of any individual. For Williams, the proposition that there was any such thing as 'Arianism', meaning a single coherent system that traced its roots to the thought of Arius, is a fantasy created by the polemic of Athanasius and Marcellus.[176] Similarly, as Barnes observes, 'if one does not *assume* Arius' influence it suddenly becomes very difficult to *prove* Arius' influence' on later generations.[177] Arius was not the architect of a tradition. Instead, he was an isolated representative of a broader theological trajectory.[178]

If it is incorrect to describe the faction who opposed Athanasius and Marcellus as 'Arian', then how might this coalition be described? Williams describes a 'pluralist *eikōn* theology', following from the image-Christology of Lucian of Antioch.[179] This is a helpful categorization, particularly when held alongside Anatolios's suggestion of gathering anti-Nicene theologians around their preference for describing the relation of the Father and Son as a unity of will. This broad theological trajectory had several different expressions, of which Arius was a particularly radical example. On the other extreme of this grouping was Eusebius of Caesarea, who thought of the Son as image in a way that had areas of overlap with a constitutive image-Christology. So, while this grouping can be defined around a shared clarity regarding the distinct subsistence of the Son, there were differences among them as to how to understand the Son as image of the Father.

The differences within this theological grouping would become increasingly exposed in the 350s. For some, any deference to the Nicene confession would be dropped altogether in a return to the doctrine that the Son is unlike the Father in essence. For others, the distinct hypostatic existence of the Son would be articulated in a way that recognized the continuity of divinity between Father and Son. In this connection, it is Williams's view that the two characteristics of this trajectory (that the Son is a distinct *hypostasis* from the Father and the Son resembles the Father as his image) existed in tension with each other (How can the Son perfectly reflect divinity without possessing the divine nature?), which would cause this faction to fray with those who prioritized the Son's essential imaging of the Father becoming convinced that a Nicene affirmation of the unity of being was the better way to uphold that doctrine.[180] However, this is to pre-empt the content of chapters 5 and 6.

176 Williams, *Arius*, 82–83.

177 M. R. Barnes, 'The Fourth Century as Trinitarian Canon', in L. Ayres and G. Jones (eds.), *Christian Origins: Theology, Rhetoric and Community* (New York: Routledge, 1998), 47–67, at 54; emphases original.

178 Williams, *Arius*, 166.

179 Ibid.

180 Ibid.

Councils of terminological confusion

The confession-making activity of the 340s demonstrates the extent to which the major protagonists were yet to understand fully the nature of the dispute and also the limited linguistic tools available to them at this point.[181] In the view of Anatolios, this confusion is best represented by the two councils of Antioch (341) and Serdica (343), where the central term *hypostasis* is used in two utterly contrasting ways, with the former eager to resist Marcellus and the latter the ontological distinction between the Father and Son (which is the Nicene usage).[182] This terminological confusion contributed to the mistrust between the two sides, with the Eusebians seeing the Athanasian-Marcellian side as obscuring the distinction between Father and Son and seeing the Eusebians as separating the Son from the Father with regard to essence.

The Council of Antioch (341)

The first of the councils in this period is that of Antioch in 341, at which a group of around ninety bishops, including Eusebius of Constantinople (formerly, Nicomedia), Asterius and Acacius of Caesarea (the successor of Eusebius following his death in *c.*339) gathered in Antioch to dedicate a newly built church (hence it is known also as the 'Dedication Council').[183] Parvis describes how this gathering was a 'breath of fresh air to the Eastern theological scene'. With Athanasius and Marcellus exiled (temporarily at least) they could turn to a positive articulation of their own theological convictions.[184] Given the developing tactic of associating them with Arius, this represented a significant opportunity to articulate a genuine alternative to the Nicene confession, one that better reflected their priorities: the real subsistent distinction of Father and Son and a more participative account of the Son as image of the Father. This gathering also provided the occasion to respond to Julius' letter and the slur that they were disciples of Arius.

Several confessions of faith are associated with this council.[185] How these confessions should be held in relation to the Nicene confession is an important question on which Athanasius and Hilary of Poitiers took different views. While they were not set as attempts to *replace* the Nicene confession, there would be no point in composing them unless it was understood that the

181 In Athanasius' view, the conciliar activity of the middle decades of the fourth century was inherently a rejection of the Nicene confession. See Athanasius, *Synods*, 6.

182 Anatolios, *RN*, 20–21.

183 Ayres, *NL*, 117. On the delegates of this council, see Parvis, *Marcellus*, 163–164.

184 Parvis, *Marcellus*, 164.

185 All of them are recorded in Athanasius, *Synods*, 22–25.

meaning of the Nicene Creed needed to be tightened in a certain direction. The delegates of the Dedication Council were vociferous in their rejection of the label 'Arian' along with its implicit suggestion that they were meeting in defiance of Nicaea. In the view of Hilary of Poitiers, the primary purpose of the delegates who met in Antioch in 341 was not to smuggle 'Arian' doctrine into the confessional basis of the church, but to respond formally to the restoration of Marcellus at Rome by stressing the real (and not merely nominal) subsistence of Father, Son and Spirit.[186] The less conciliatory Athanasius, however, viewed all councils of this period as intrinsically anti-Nicene, with the single goal of steering church doctrine towards a position more sympathetic with Arius.[187] Athanasius' assessment might well have been provoked by the fact that the *homoousion* is excluded in each statement ratified by the council, which (by the time of his writing in the 350s) he saw as a deliberate volte-face from Nicaea. However, excluding *homoousios* was not unusual for the time. Even those who would be its staunchest defenders in the 350s, owing to its controversial associations were not motivated to insist upon it in the two decades following 325 (including Athanasius himself!).

The first confession (the First Creed of Antioch), to which is attached the indignant refusal of the designation 'Arian', is a fairly bland statement. It avoids the controversial term *homoousios* altogether and affirms the Son's coexistence with the Father and rejects Marcellus' most distinctive doctrine with a statement of the Son's everlasting kingdom.[188] Another confession associated with this council (called the Third Creed of Antioch) was not composed by the council but was proposed by Theophronius of Tyana and subsequently accepted by the council as orthodox. This confession also avoids the term *homoousios* but affirms that the Son is 'perfect God from perfect God',[189] and again contradicts the distinctive Marcellian idea of the Son's finite reign. However, it is distinctive in its assertion that the Son was 'with God in subsistence [*pros ton theon en hypostasei*]',[190] in an emphatic repudiation of miahypostatic doctrine. This is reiterated in the anathemas that name Marcellus along with Paul of Samosata, indicating that the target of the Third Creed of Antioch was the *homoousios* when interpreted in a modalist fashion.[191]

186 Hilary, *Synods*, 31–33.

187 Athanasius, *Synods*, 6–7.

188 Ibid. 22. Ayres, *NL*, 119.

189 Athanasius, *Synods*, 24.

190 Ibid.

191 The ongoing influence of the Council of Antioch (268) on the theological debates of the fourth century has been well sketched by Giulea: a precedent was set for using *ousia* and *hypostasis* interchangeably to denote the discrete subsistence of the three. D. A. Giulea, 'Antioch 268 and Its Legacy in the Fourth-Century Theological Debates', *HTR* 111.2 (2018), 192–215. Giulea sees, then, an older third-century orthodoxy as

The Second Creed of Antioch is recorded by Hilary as the only confession officially ratified at this council, and so it is often described in short hand as the Dedication Creed.[192] It has also been known as the Lucianite Creed,[193] which Lienhard describes as a 'classic statement of Eusebian theology'.[194] Included below are its sections on the relationship of the Father and Son, its recounting of the baptismal commands and the anathemas.

The Father–Son relation:

> And in One Lord Jesus Christ, His Son, Only-begotten God, by whom are all things, who was begotten before all ages from the Father, God from God, whole from whole, sole from sole, perfect from perfect, King from King, Lord from Lord, Living Word, Living Wisdom, true Light, Way, Truth, Resurrection, Shepherd, Door, both unalterable and unchangeable; exact Image of the Godhead, Essence, Will, Power and Glory of the Father.[195]

The baptismal commands:

> our Lord Jesus Christ enjoined His disciples, saying, 'Go ye, teach all nations, baptizing them in the Name of the Father, and the Son, and the Holy Ghost'; namely of a Father who is truly Father, and a Son who is truly Son, and of the Holy Ghost who is truly Holy Ghost, the names not being given without meaning or effect, but denoting accurately the peculiar subsistence [*hypostasin*], so that they are three in subsistence [*hypostatei tria*], and in agreement one.[196]

The anathemas:

> Holding then this faith . . . we anathematize every heretical heterodoxy. And if any teaches, beside the sound and right faith of the Scriptures, that time, or season, or age, either is or has been before the generation of the Son, be he anathema. Or if any one says, that the Son is a creature as one

(note 191 *cont.*) shaping the perspective of some of the Eusebians, particularly on the question of the Son's real distinction from the Father, which could be described in the language of two *ousiai*. See also D. A. Giulea, 'Reassessing Arianism in the Light of the Council of Antioch 268', *ETL* 95.1 (2019), 63–96.

192 Hilary, *Synods*, 29.

193 Claims that it is based on a 'Lucianite Creed' that pre-dated 341 are without evidence.

194 See Lienhard, *Contra Marcellum*, 169.

195 Athanasius, *Synods*, 23.

196 Ibid.

> of the creatures, or an offspring as one of the offsprings, or a work as one of the works . . . or if he teaches or preaches beside what we received, be he anathema.[197]

There is clear daylight between this confession and Arius' theological convictions. The more radical elements of Arius' thought are included in the anathemas (e.g. that the Son is begotten from nothing), and, as an alternative to the *homoousios*, a number of scriptural designations that pertain to the Son's unity with the Father are given. A 'true-blue' Arian,[198] of course, could not accept the statement that the Son is the exact image of the Father with the associated titles ('Light, Way, Truth') indicative of the Son's being the revelation of the Father. As such, the confession bears a closer resemblance to the theology of Asterius (who was present). As for its repudiation of Marcellus, the confession contains a pointed clarification that the baptismal command does not refer to three *names*, but to three subsistent realities (hypostases).

However, this statement is not compatible with the Nicene confession. The confession leaves room for the three distinct subsistences to be conceived of as in a graded Trinity, where the unity is not ontological (and thus necessary) but rather by volition (*symphōnia*) and is thus contingent:[199] 'Eusebius of Caesarea would have been deeply pleased to read' this unity predicated on agreement.[200] This allowed for aseity to be applied to the Father alone. So, while this confession excludes the farther reaches of Arius' doctrine, it does provide the conceptual space for the subtle subordination of the Son to the Father through its participative image-Christology wherein the Son as image does not derive from the essence of the Father.[201] Indicative of this is the absence of central elements of the Nicene confession, such as the Son's being begotten from the essence of the Father and the contrast it draws between the begetting of the Son and the making of creation.[202] As such, this confession establishes a Eusebian, anti-Marcellian theology within a credal statement: the Father, Son and Spirit are distinct hypostases who are not equal in honour.[203]

Hilary provides a nuanced assessment of this confession, commenting that 'perhaps this creed has not spoken expressly enough of the identical similarity

---

197 Ibid.
198 Hanson, *SCDG*, 287.
199 Anatolios, *RN*, 20.
200 Lienhard, *Contra Marcellum*, 169.
201 Hanson argues for the direct influence of Asterius. Hanson, *SCDG*, 288–299. See also Ayres, *NL*, 119.
202 See also Gwynn, *Athanasius of Alexandria*, 83–85.
203 Lienhard, *Contra Marcellum*, 170.

of the Father and the Son',[204] but recognizes that their primary concern was with Marcellus and the doctrine that 'in spite of Nicaea, presumed to attribute the three names to the Father'.[205] Hilary's reception can be read as a recognition that the Dedication Creed made a contribution to Nicene Christianity, by pressing for greater clarity on the real distinct subsistence of Father and Son.[206] Hilary also finds much in this confession that he approves of, particularly in its presentation of the Son as God begotten of God, with at least some continuity of divinity indicated by the attribution of changelessness to him.[207] In conciliatory mood, then, Hilary concludes that 'this Council by dividing the three substances, which it did to exclude a monad God with a threefold title, did not introduce any separation of substance between the Father and the Son'.[208] Hilary's somewhat warm reception of the Second Creed of the Dedication Council is part of a broader effort at alliance building between the pro-Nicene faction and the moderate Eusebians, who found in this confession precedent for their conviction that the Son is like the Father with regard to essence (*homoiousios*). This is developed in chapter 6.

Athanasius was in a less conciliatory mood. Commenting on the fourth confession associated with this council, he wrote, 'thinking that their composition was deficient still, and fluctuating in their own opinions', and drew up a fourth confession (The Fourth Creed of Antioch) after the council had been closed.[209] As Kelly notes, this final confession has the air of an attempt at 'rapprochement between the bishops gathered at Antioch and the diocese of Rome'.[210] Lienhard describes this confession as a 'mild form of the Eusebian theology'.[211] Despite its extra-conciliar provenance, this confession would become the base text for several other confessions over the course of the next decade:

> We believe in one God the Father Almighty . . .
>
> And in His Only-begotten Son, our Lord Jesus Christ, who before all ages was begotten from the Father, God from God, Light from Light, by whom all things were made in the heavens and on the earth, visible and invisible, being Word, and Wisdom, and Power, and Life, and True Light; who in the last days was made man for us . . . whose Kingdom endures

204 Hilary, *Synods*, 31.
205 Ibid.
206 See Ayres, *NL*, 121.
207 Hilary, *Synods*, 33.
208 Ibid.
209 Ibid. 25.
210 Kelly, *ECC*, 273.
211 Lienhard, *Contra Marcellum*, 171.

> indissolubly into the infinite ages; for He shall be seated on the right hand of the Father, not only in this age but in that which is to come And in the Holy Ghost, that is, the Paraclete . . . He sent forth after His ascension into heaven, to teach them and to remind of all things; through whom also shall be sanctified the souls of those who sincerely believe in Him.
>
> But those who say, that the Son was from nothing, or from other subsistence [*hypostasis*] and not from God, and, there was time when He was not, the Catholic Church regards as aliens.[212]

As Hanson observes, what this confession leaves out is more significant than what it affirms.[213] The controversial language of *hypostasis* is not used to refer to the distinct subsistence of the Father, Son and Spirit. Where *hypostasis* is used in the anathemas, its intention is synonymous with essence (*ousia*), following the usage of the Nicene confession. Similarly, the word *ousia* and other words related to it – such as *homoousios* – are omitted altogether. The statement that the Son is begotten from the Father (not from nothing) and that the Son is God in the mode of coming out from God appear to be muted condemnations of Arius' doctrine, but are a long way from the Nicene assertion that the Son is begotten *from the essence* of the Father. There is also an anathema against the other doctrine characteristic of Arius regarding the quasi-temporal origin of the Son. The confession is characterized by a lengthy assault on Marcellus' doctrine of the Son's time-limited reign. In other words, this is a statement more articulate on what it rejects (Arius and Marcellus) than on what it affirms. As such, while it defined the conceptual area yet to be agreed on, it acted rather like a blank slate upon which the various factions were able to modify in the direction of their various theological priorities. It is probably for this reason that for the next fifteen years it served as the basis for a number of other confessions.

The Council of Serdica (343)

An attempt at a rapprochement between the Eastern and Western factions was undertaken at the Council of Serdica in 343,[214] but it proved to be a disastrous failure. Theodoret reports that some 250 bishops were in attendance, including Athanasius and Marcellus. Upon hearing that Athanasius and Marcellus were

212 Athanasius, *Synods*, 25.

213 Hanson, *SCDG*, 292.

214 For the broader political context, see Ayres, *NL*, 122–124. The dating of the Council of Serdica is disputed. See Parvis, *Marcellus*, 210–218. For a full historical study of this council, see Barnes, *Athanasius and Constantius*, 71–82.

to be present after their reinstatement following the Council of Rome, the Eastern bishops (whom the fiercely partisan Theodoret describes as 'the Arian faction') considered the Council void and refused to attend.[215]

Meanwhile, the Western delegates who remained at the Council of Serdica composed their own confession of faith, which is a very long (and rude) statement against the theological priorities expressed in the Dedication Creeds.[216] This document is, in reality, more of a polemic against the Eusebian faction, whom it continues to describe as 'the Arians' and perpetuating a 'madness', using inexcusable methods in furthering the Arian cause.[217] By contrast, the letter is full of praise for Athanasius and Marcellus. Its principal doctrinal concern is with the attribution of three hypostases to God, which it repudiates. The way in which this repudiation is phrased indicates terminological confusion:

> we have been taught, and we hold the catholic and apostolic tradition which teach, that the Father, the Son, and the Holy Ghost have one essence [*ousia*], which is termed substance [*hypostasis*] by the heretics. If it is asked, What is the essence of the Son?' we confess, that it is that which is acknowledged to be that of the Father alone; for the Father has never been, nor could ever be, without the Son, nor the Son without the Father.[218]

The attribution of distinct subsistence (*hypostasis*) has been understood as synonymous with the term used to describe the divinity of the Father, Son and Spirit (*ousia*). As such, in the terminology as it is understood at Serdica, one divine *hypostasis*/*ousia* is common to the Father and Son. With such an understanding the proposition regarding the distinct hypostases of the Father, Son and Spirit was conceived of as tritheistic or – more likely – as subordinating the Son and Spirit to the Father. Clearly, the varying use of *hypostasis* in the different confessions agreed at the Dedication Council did not help the delegates of Serdica understand the intention of the opposing party. Even so, it is not reading too much into this confession to observe there was less than eirenic willingness to assume the worst possible meaning. However, there is some acuity in the complaint that the Eusebians understood the unity of the Father and Son to be a 'concord and harmony which prevail[s] between the Father and

215 Theodoret, *Ecclesiastical History*, 2.6.

216 Recorded at ibid. 2.6. In the view of Parvis, this confession might have been written by Marcellus. Parvis, *Marcellus*, 239–245.

217 Lienhard, *Contra Marcellum*, 145–148.

218 Theodoret, *Ecclesiastical History*, 2.6.

the Son'.[219] Against this volitional unity, the doctrinal emphasis of the Serdican confession falls heavily on the singularity of divinity: 'We confess that God is; we confess the divinity of the Father and of the Son to be one.'[220] This was not intended in such a way as to deny the distinct reality of the Father and Son. The statement also clearly indicates: 'We do not say that the Father is Son, nor that the Son is Father; but that the Father is Father, and the Son of the Father Son.' However, the way in which the Father and Son are distinguished from each other is not stated in this document.[221]

The Serdican confession also contains a focused attack on the Eusebian understanding of the Son, describing their doctrine as extrinsic to genuine Christian belief:

> For those who separate the Son from the substance and divinity of the Father, and alienate the Word from the Father, ought to be separated from the Catholic Church, and alienated from all who bear the name of Christians.[222]

> We declare those men excommunicate from the Catholic Church who say that Christ is God, but not the true God; that He is the Son, but not the true Son; and that He is both begotten and made; for such persons acknowledge that they understand by the term begotten, that which has been made.[223]

These comments sharpen the Western objection to the Eusebian faction: they diminish the divinity of the Son (the Son is not true God); they elide the Son's relation to the Father with our adoptive relation to the Father (the Son is not true Son); and they elide the generation of the Son with the making of creation. By contrast, the Western bishops affirm the eternal relation of the Father and Son, whereby the Son is *proper* to the Father. They refuse that the Son is a lesser divinity whose attenuated divine properties mean that he can mediate between God and creation in a chain of being.[224] Significantly, this begins to clarify the distinction between the generation of the Son and being brought into existence. These points are central to Athanasius in his *Discourses Against the Arians*, which was written at around the same time as the Serdican confession.

219 Ibid.
220 Ibid.
221 Kelly, *ECC*, 278. Parvis, *Marcellus*, 242–243.
222 Theodoret, *Ecclesiastical History*, 2.6.
223 Ibid.
224 See also Lienhard, *Contra Marcellum*, 150.

Clearly, something had gone wrong. What had been intended as a process of reconciliation had 'turned into an explosion'.[225] It should, though, be noted that the Council of Serdica does make some concession to the Eusebian faction with a rejection of the time-limited reign of Christ. Moreover, some progress was made in that it was now clear that each side was not understanding the other and that the principal reason for this was the imprecise use of technical terminology, specifically *hypostasis*.

The Long-Lined Creed (345)

Further efforts to reconcile the divided factions were made throughout the rest of the 340s.[226] One significant concession was in a council drawing together both Eastern and Western bishops that adjudged Photinus (a significant ally of Marcellus[227]) 'held the heresy of Sabellius the Libyan, and Paul of Samosata, [and] they immediately deposed him'.[228] Sozomen describes Photinus' theology in the following way:

> He acknowledged that there was one God Almighty, by whose own word all things were created, but would not admit that the generation and existence of the Son was before all ages; on the contrary, he alleged that Christ derived His existence from Mary.[229]

However, further attempts at doctrinal consensus had to wait until the so-called 'Long-Lined Creed' (*ekthēsis makrōstichos*) (345) from a further council in Antioch. This text is a composite document: its base text is the Fourth Creed of Antioch (341) and it is supplemented by longer anathemas composed by the Eusebian bishops after the walkout at Serdica (343) and supplemented by seven explanatory notes designed to elucidate the doctrine expressed.[230] This

225 Hanson, *SCDG*, 306–307.

226 Ibid. 306–314; Ayres, *NL*, 126–127.

227 Lienhard, *Contra Marcellum*, 220.

228 Socrates, *Ecclesiastical History*, 2.29. The downfall of Photinus appears to have been orchestrated prior to the council opening. In the view of Hilary, this was part of Athanasius' establishing distance between himself and Marcellus. See Parvis, *Marcellus*, 249. Lienhard, however, suggests that Athanasius' departure from Marcellus at this point was only temporary, intended to push Marcellus back into a more mainstream position. Lienhard, 'Did Athanasius Reject Marcellus', 65–80; *Contra Marcellum*, 154–156. Parvis sees Marcellus himself as benignly in control of the events, allowing certain aspects of doctrine to be attributed to him such that he could be eased out of the controversy, allowing for more 'moderate' figures to move towards reconciliation. Parvis, *Marcellus*, 250–251. This elegant suggestion goes some way to explaining how Marcellus maintained so deeply into the fourth century the personal loyalty of Athanasius and other pro-Nicene theologians, but not the younger pro-Nicenes such as Basil of Caesarea.

229 Sozomen, *Ecclesiastical History*, 4.6.

230 Recorded in Athanasius, *Synods*, 26, and Socrates, *Ecclesiastical History*, 2.19.

text marks a maturing of Eusebian theology. Its repudiation of Marcellus and Photinus is expressed in such a way that it is clear their complaint is not with their monotheism, but with the way they obscure the real subsistence of the Son. It is also a temperate document, calmly setting forward their own theological convictions. It makes two significant conciliatory steps to the faction surrounding Athanasius. First, it takes steps to clear up the misconception that the assertion of three hypostases was tritheism. Second, although it is clearly trying to avoid all language regarding *ousia* (and so *homoousios*), the confession does attempt to demonstrate the continuity of divinity between the Father and Son.[231]

The anathemas of the Long-Lined Creed begin to identify the parameters of the dispute more clearly. The final anathema also clarifies that the real doctrinal disagreement between the moderate voices of either faction was not really on tritheism, modalism or the ontological subordination of the Son. Instead, the persisting disagreement was over the nature of the Son's generation from the Father and whether it contained any element of contingence: Is the Son image in a participative or constitutive manner? Continuing straight on from where the Fourth Creed of Antioch stopped, the additional anathemas say the following:

> But those who say, (1) that the Son was from nothing, or from other subsistence and not from God; (2) and that there was a time or age when He was not, the Catholic and Holy Church regards as aliens. Likewise those who say, (3) that there are three Gods: (4) or that Christ is not God; (5) or that before the ages He was neither Christ nor Son of God; (6) or that Father and Son, or Holy Ghost, are the same; (7) or that the Son is Ingenerate; or that the Father begat the Son, not by choice or will; the Holy and Catholic Church anathematizes.[232]

In Kelly's view, this creed is wholly 'eirenical' in intention.[233] Certainly, anathemas 1–5 are concerned with clarifying what the affirmation of three hypostases does not mean. These begin with the, by now standard, distancing from the extremities of Arius' doctrine (notes 1 and 2). Importantly, this is held alongside a reassertion of the unique primacy of the Father as unbegotten: 'Yet we must not consider the Son to be co-unbegun and co-ingenerate with the Father . . . But we acknowledge that the Father who alone is Unbegun and Ingenerate, has

231 Ayres, *NL*, 127.
232 Athanasius, *Synods*, 26.
233 Kelly, *ECC*, 277.

generated [the Son] inconceivably and incomprehensibly to all.'[234] In this way, the document demonstrates a capacity to distinguish between the Son as derived from the Father as begotten and those things brought into being from nothing. In other words, the Son is not unbegotten, but neither is he brought into being. This distinction – drawn here by the supposedly 'Arian' Eusebians – would become a major hallmark of Nicene Christianity, which recognizes the Son to be both begotten and unoriginate.

Note 3 sets out to explain in terms less open to misinterpretation that they do not intend tritheism. Importantly, it attempts to set out the belief in three distinct subsistences without the use of the term *hypostasis*:

> Nor again, in confessing three realities and three Persons, of the Father and the Son and the Holy Ghost according to the Scriptures, do we therefore make Gods three; since we acknowledge the Self-complete and Ingenerate and Unbegun and Invisible God to be one only, the God and Father of the Only-begotten, who alone hath being from Himself, and alone vouchsafes this to all others bountifully.[235]

The Father, Son and Spirit are recognized as distinct in reality, not only in name. However, this clear affirmation of the personal subsistence of each of the three is distanced from the proposition that there are three gods. The oneness of God is attributed to unique and solitary monarchy of the Father, whereby the one divinity is identified with the person of the Father. The Father alone is the ingenerate divinity and has life in himself, which he *gives*. Problematically from a Western perspective, it is left unclear as to whether the life the Father gives to the Son is different from the life he gives to creation. As Ayres suggests, the language of the Father giving life is ambiguous. While it forestalls any notion of two ingenerates, it does allow for the perspective that the Son is, in some sense, secondary to the Father.[236] While note 5 does assert the divinity of the Son, the development of a sophisticated Nicene theology would require the more careful integration of the divinity of the Son with his derivation from the Father.

Notes 5–6 consolidate previous objections to Marcellus' doctrine. First, the doctrine of the Word's pre-personal existence as a property of the Father: 'we abhor . . . those who make a pretence of saying that He is but the mere word of

[234] Athanasius, *Synods*, 26.
[235] Ibid.
[236] Ayres, *NL*, 128.

God and unexisting, having His being in another'.[237] Second, the proposition that the Father, Son and Spirit are one reality. Significantly, included within these repudiations of Marcellus is a positive account of the Father–Son relation. On the one hand, the confession goes to some lengths to stress the eternal coexistence of the Father and Son: 'We, on the contrary, regard Him not as simply God's pronounced word or mental, but as Living God and Word, existing in Himself, and Son of God and Christ; being and abiding with His Father before ages.'[238] The attribution to the Son of the property of life in himself is significant in that it asserts that *the Son is not among those things which have come into being.*

Note 7, however, presents greater difficulties for theological consensus:

> those who irreverently say that the Son has been generated not by choice or will, thus encompassing God with a necessity which excludes choice and purpose, so that He begat the Son unwillingly, we account as most irreligious and alien to the Church . . . For we, knowing that God is absolute and sovereign over Himself, have a religious judgment that He generated the Son voluntarily and freely.[239]

Ostensibly, something of the old concern with two ingenerate principles that reaches back to the beginning of the controversy is at work here.[240] In this connection, the claim is made that 'God is absolute and sovereign over Himself.'[241] God is not determined in his being from something beyond himself, nor is he determined by some ontic fatalism whereby he must be this or that. Therefore, the generation of the Son is not inherent to divinity itself such that the Son might be thought of as necessarily and eternally correlate to the Father. A thinly veiled criticism of the Nicene assertion that the Son is begotten from the essence of the Father follows by anathematizing those who do not attribute generation to the will of the Father. If the Son is begotten by the will of the Father, then an element of contingence is inserted into the Father–Son relation whereby the Son is not in a necessary relation to the Father. Aware that this was likely to be a contentious proposition, the confession sets out to clarify that attributing the generation of the Son to the will of the Father does not mean that the generation

237 Athanasius, *Synods*, 26. The anti-Marcellian polemic is expanded in notes 4–10 and 19–22 of the Council of Sirmium (351). The Council of Sirmium is, once again, the Fourth Creed of the Dedication Council with twenty-eight elucidatory notes.

238 Athanasius, *Synods*, 26.

239 Ibid.

240 See the twenty-sixth note of the Council of Sirmium (351). Athanasius, *Synods*, 27.

241 Ibid. 26.

of the Son is considered as equivalent to the making of creation and refusing the inference of any interval between Father and Son ('the Father embosoming the Son, and all the Son hanging and adhering to the Father, and alone resting on the Father's breast continually'[242]). What is in view here is a participative image-Christology that tends towards the continuity of divinity. Quite how, however, the derivation of the Son can be attributed to the Father's will without introducing contingence into the Father–Son relation is not explained.

Accordingly, the attempt to ascribe the generation of the Son to the will of the Father so as to preserve the absolute singularity of the Father involves the subordination of the Son, with the Father 'alone being Head over the whole universe wholly, and over the Son Himself, and the Son subordinated to the Father'.[243] Clearly, this is not intended to be the same as the ontological subordination of Arius but as a relational ordering in which the Son derives his being from the Father (and as such, aseity cannot be attributed to the Son). But, equally clearly, the theological priorities of the Eusebian faction contrasted sharply with those of the Nicene confession: while the former stressed the unique status of the unbegotten Father and maintained that primacy by inserting some degree of contingence into the Father–Son relation, the latter prioritized the continuity of divinity and eternity of the Father and Son.[244] By the end of the 340s, what was required was an account of the compatibility between the unique monarchy of the Father and the full and necessary continuity of divinity between the Father and Son. The contribution of the moderate elements of the Eusebian faction in developing such a theological construction (and so to the eventual Nicene settlement) should not be missed. However, the Long-Lined Creed does not contain such an account: there remains a tacit rejection of the eternal generation of the Son from the essence of the Father that is the only ground of their perfect continuity of divinity.[245]

242 Ibid.
243 Ibid.
244 Ayres, *NL*, 126.
245 Ibid. 129.

5

'The Son is like the Father': from Nicaea to Constantinople (2)

The rise of 'Neo-Arianism' (351–62)

The 350s are characterized by a theological assault on the Nicene confession bolstered by a political will to establish consensus around a different formulation of the relation of the Father and Son.[1] The emergence of a more extreme alternative to the Nicene confession served to highlight the differences within the Eusebian faction, leading to its eventual fracturing. Over the course of a complex civil war (351–3) Constantius rose to full control of the whole empire.[2] Like Constantine, Constantius understood the political importance of the doctrinal unity of the church and so was motivated to support theological formulations that could command consensus.[3] Prior to becoming sole emperor, Constantius had ruled over the Eastern half of the empire. Consequently, he was more familiar with the participatory image-Christology of the Eusebians and favoured a variant of just such a Christology as that which could achieve a broad consensus.

The Council of Sirmium (351)

The Council of Sirmium is indicative of this change in circumstances. The council was held – with Constantius present – in the diocesan seat of Photinus, the ardent ally of Marcellus. The purpose of the council was to examine the doctrine of Photinus, which was conducted through a debate between Photinus and Basil of Ancyra (who himself had replaced the deposed Marcellus at the Council of Tyre in 336).[4] The council deposed and exiled Photinus, replacing

---

1 Fairbairn and Reeves, *SCC*, 68.

2 See Hanson, *SCDG*, 315–325, and Ayres, *NL*, 133–134.

3 Behr, *NF*, 84.

4 Sozomen, *Ecclesiastical History*, 4.6; Socrates, *Ecclesiastical History*, 2.29. See also Hanson, *SCDG*, 325; Ayres, *NL*, 134.

him with the 'anti-Nicene' figure Germinus.[5] Other significant casualties of this council included Marcellus and Athanasius, who were both sent into exile.[6]

The creed produced at this council, the First Sirmium Creed, is the Fourth Creed of the Dedication Council that replaced the explanatory notes of the Long-Lined Creed with twenty-seven additional anathemas.[7] These anathemas focus on the core doctrine of Photinus and its associated theological implications. Note 19, for example, explicitly repudiates the doctrine that the Father and Son are one person, with many of the preceding notes denying associated propositions such as the unbegotten being born from Mary (note 10). Importantly, note 6 connects *ousia*-language with the doctrine of the divine essence dilating and contracting:

> 6 Whosoever shall pretend that the essence of God is dilated or contracted, be he anathema.
> 7 Whosoever shall say that the essence of God being dilated made the Son, or shall name the dilation of His essence Son, be he anathema.[8]

As Ayres helpfully points out, this suggests that the term *ousia* was perceived by the authors of this confession as potentially problematic.[9] Notes 24–25 continue to try to walk the fine line traced out in the Long-Lined Creed in identifying the relationship between the generation of the Son and the will of the Father:

> 24 Whosoever shall say that the Son of God at the will of God has come to be, as one of the works, be he anathema.
> 25 Whosoever shall say that the Son has been generated, the Father not wishing it, be he anathema. For not by compulsion, led by physical necessity, did the Father, as He wished not, generate the Son, but He at once willed, and, after generating Him from Himself apart from time and passion, manifested Him.[10]

This confession is somewhat more sophisticated than its predecessor. First, it is explicit in differentiating between the Son's generation by the will of the Father and the bringing into existence of creation from nothing. In this way, a radical

5 Hanson, *SCDG*, 325–326.
6 Behr, *NF*, 84.
7 Recorded in Athanasius, *Synods*, 27; Socrates, *Ecclesiastical History*, 2.30.
8 Athanasius, *Synods*, 27.
9 Ayres, *NL*, 135.
10 Athanasius, *Synods*, 27.

contingence is not imported into the Father–Son relation. Second, it is more nuanced in delineating the relationship between the Father's will and the generation of the Son. Rather than an explicit statement that the Son is begotten at the will of the Father, it is stated that the Son's generation is not an ontological necessity. Ostensibly, the concern here is with rendering divinity the servant of higher causal laws. However, the relationship is still described in terms of sequence with a quasi-temporal reference to the period 'after' the generation, indicating the sequential primacy of the Father.

The defence of the Nicene Creed

Over the course of the 350s, as Constantius' authority over the Western half of the empire was consolidated, the attempts to persuade the Western bishops to accept the Creed of Sirmium were stepped up. It was this that led to the Western bishops' growing attention to the Creed of Nicaea. The 325 creed was becoming a point around which to rally in opposition to the policies of Constantius and the decrees of Sirmium. In this connection, Athanasius and Hilary of Poitiers wrote extensively in this decade to define the meaning of the Nicene Creed and to identify it as a true expression of the tradition of the church, while (Athanasius in particular) presented the creed-making activity of the 340s and 350s as part of one 'Arianizing' tradition.

However, the political momentum was against them, with political and even military pressure exerted on all to subscribe to the doctrinal content of the confession of Sirmium (351).[11] In 356, Athanasius was chased from Alexandria by troops, from where he went into hiding in the Egyptian desert.[12] Even Ossius, the theological advisor of Constantine in 325 – who by this point would have been well into his nineties – was detained for one year and coerced into signing an anti-Nicene doctrinal statement, described as the 'blasphemy of Sirmium' in 357, which described the Son as like the Father and excluded all *ousia*-language (discussed below).[13] Meanwhile, an emboldened theological grouping led by Aetius and Eunomius, who were antagonistic to the Nicene confession, became increasingly influential. These figures asserted that the Son is unlike the Father in essence.

However, it is not quite so simple as the emergence of two camps becoming internally uniform, standing in opposition to the other. The emergence of an

---

[11] Athanasius, *History of the Arians*, 40–41; Sozomen, *Ecclesiastical History*, 4.11. See also Behr, *NF*, 84–85.

[12] See Anatolios, *Athanasius*, 25–27.

[13] Athanasius, *Synods*, 28. This doctrinal statement is considered below in connection with the council of Antioch (357).

extreme and explicit form of subordinationism served as a catalyst to expose further the pre-existing distinctions within the Eusebian faction.[14] The more moderate Eusebian bishops affirmed God's three hypostases but were virulent on the perfect resemblance of the Son to the Father. They could not accept subordination as described by Aetius and Eunomius, on the grounds that it undermined the perfect likeness of the Father and Son. The growing significance of a more extreme anti-Nicene theological perspective began to clarify where the doctrinal differences were and also the terms on which a lasting consensus could be formed. As Williams suggests, this provided an opening Athanasius could exploit to convince the more moderate members of the Eusebian faction that the Nicene account of the Father–Son relation was more suitable as a way of upholding the perfect similarity of the Father and Son (this alliance-building effort is described in chapter 6).[15]

Rival factions

It is common for studies of this period to give a schema for understanding the different factions by their attitude to the Nicene proposition that the Son is *homoousios* with the Father.[16] This is, to a degree, an artificial framework as individual theologians would not necessarily recognize themselves as members of a wider group, other, of course, than seeing their perspective as the received tradition of the church. However, as a way of delineating the major theological trajectories, it is a useful heuristic tool.

Identical according to essence

The faction gathered around the figure of Athanasius rallied around the Nicene confession in the 350s, giving full support to the doctrine of the *homoousios*. A brief consideration of the thought of Hilary of Poitiers serves as a helpful orientation to this perspective.[17] While Athanasius set about interpreting and defending the Nicene confession in the Greek-speaking Eastern part of the church, Hilary did likewise in the Latin-speaking Western part. Many of the central themes found in Hilary are found also in Athanasius and so the following discussion anticipates and introduces some central ideas of Athanasius' thought.

[14] Behr, *NF*, 87.
[15] Williams, *Arius*, 166.
[16] See Fairbairn and Reeves, *SCC*, 67–68; Anatolios, *RN*, 20–23.
[17] For biographical information on Hilary, see Hanson, *SCDG*, 459–471; Ayres, *NL*, 177–178.

The accent of Hilary's thought falls heavily on the Son's generation from the essence of the Father.[18] This is the foundation of both the essential unity of the Father and Son and their personal distinction:

> the Son is the perfect image of the Father: there under the qualities of an identical essence, the Person of the Son is not annihilated and confounded with the Father: there the Son is declared to be image of the Father in virtue of a real likeness, and does not differ in substance from the Father, whose image He is: there on account of the life which the Father has and the life which the Son has received, the Father can have nothing different in substance (this being implied in life) from that which the Son received to have: there the begotten Son is not a creature, but is a Person undistinguished from the Father's nature there, just as an identical might belongs to the Father and the Son, so their essence admits of no difference: there the Father by begetting the Son in no wise degenerates from Himself in Him through any difference of nature: there, though the likeness of nature is the same in each, the proper qualities which mark this likeness are repugnant to a confusion of Persons, so that there is not one subsisting Person who is called both Father and Son: there, though it is piously affirmed that there is both a Father who sends and a Son who is sent, yet no distinction in essence is drawn between the Father and the Son, the Sent and the Sender: there the truth of God's Fatherhood is not bound by limits of time: there the Son is not later in time.[19]

As generate from the essence of the Father, the Son is distinct from the Father but cannot be divided from him in terms of their essence. The mode of the Son's derivation from the Father includes both the continuity of divinity and the distinction of their persons.[20] Given the miahypostatic/diahypostatic disputes in the first half of the fourth century, this is a significant position to adopt.

Similarly, in *On the Trinity* Hilary argues that the generation of the Son from the Father means that the Son receives the divinity of the Father,[21] on account of which their difference is not 'a matter of words rather than reality' and also the Son's derivation is contrasted to that of a 'creature made out of nothing'.[22] Ayres observes that Hilary's strategy is to define orthodoxy as falling between

[18] See also Ayres, *NL*, 179.
[19] Hilary, *Synods*, 27.
[20] Hilary, *Trinity*, 7.25. See also Hanson, *SCDG*, 478–479.
[21] Hilary, *Trinity*, 2.3.
[22] Ibid. 2.4.

the extremes of subordinationism and modalism.[23] In this connection, the following statement is a good example of the way Hilary attempts to maintain identity at the level of essence alongside their distinct subsistence as Father and Son: 'God the Father and God the Son are One altogether, not by confusion of Person but by unity of substance.'[24]

In developing this line of thought, Hilary maintains the logic of the Nicene confession with its clarifications of what is meant by the Son's deriving from the essence of the Father:

> For He is the offspring of the unbegotten, One from One, true from true, living from living, perfect from perfect; the Power of Power, the Wisdom of Wisdom, the Glory of Glory, the Likeness of the invisible God, the Image of the Unbegotten Faith.[25]

The same logic is present in less compressed form in the following passage:

> The Son draws life from the Father Who truly has life; the only-begotten from the unbegotten, Offspring from the Parent, Living from Living. As the Father has life in Himself, even so gave He to the Son to also have life in Himself. The Son is perfect from Him that is perfect, for He is whole from Him that is whole . . . There is distinction, for They are Father and Son; not that Their Divinity is different in kind, for Both are One, God of God, One God only begotten of One God unbegotten. They are not two Gods, but One of One.[26]

It is axiomatic for Hilary that the Son, as begotten from the Father, shares the one divinity of the Father, and, if he does not, then he is not properly to be called Son.[27] In defence of this perspective, Hilary was able to use the argument of the eternal correlation of Father and Son.[28]

> For where a father is the source of being, there also is birth; and further, where the Source of being is eternal, the birth also is eternal: for since

[23] Ayres, *NL*, 180–181; Hilary, *Trinity*, 6.9–19.

[24] Hilary, *Trinity*, 4.42.

[25] See ibid. 2.8.

[26] Ibid. 2.11; 7.14–17, 28–30, 31.

[27] Ibid. 2.8. See also M. Weedman, *The Trinitarian Theology of Hilary of Poitiers* (Leiden: E. J. Brill, 2007), 181–183. Weedman demonstrates the close connection in Hilary's thought between the Son's generation from the Father and the continuity of divinity between them.

[28] Hilary, *Trinity*, 1.28; 2.3; 9.57.

> birth comes from the source of being, birth which comes from an eternal source must be eternal ... But if that which has been born from the Eternal is not born eternal, it will follow that the Father also is not an eternal source of being. Therefore if any measure of eternity is wanting to Him Who has been born of the eternal Father, clearly the very same measure is wanting to the Author of His being.[29]

Every aspect of Hilary's presentation treats divine generation as intrinsic to divine being. In this connection, Hilary posits a strong distinction between creation and the eternal generation of the Son:[30] as the Son is generate from the essence of the Father, 'then the Son has by nature everything that the Father has, including eternity'.[31] On this basis, Hilary rejects Arius' doctrine that the Father and Son are one by harmony of will or activity, but not by nature.[32] Indeed, the Son's engagement with the same work as the Father is not seen as *constitutive* of their unity, but as *indicative* of their unity of nature.[33] However, it is also the basis of their distinction, as the Father as the source of life and divinity is not the same as the Son who receives.[34] This is connected to Hilary's image-Christology, which he considered to undergird the distinction of the Father and Son – as something cannot be its own image[35] – and also their identity of nature, for an image contains the essence of the original.[36]

Given the eternal correlation of the Father and Son and the continuity of divinity between them, Hilary argues that the Son is *homoousios* with the Father. His positive reception of this term is nuanced by denying certain possible interpretations of it. Hilary rejects the idea of succession,[37] or some anterior essence or material underlying the Father and Son in relation to which they would be brothers.[38] Instead, *homoousios* is to be understood in terms of the continuity of the Father's divinity: 'God's nature did not produce a nature unlike itself: but the Son begotten of God's substance has derived the essence of His nature by virtue of His origin, not from an act of will after the manner of creatures'.[39] In this connection, Hilary suggests there is no

29 Ibid. 12.21.
30 Ibid. 7.14.
31 Weedman, *Trinitarian Theology*, 183. See also 187.
32 Hilary, *Trinity*, 8.5–6; *Synods*, 19.
33 Hilary, *Trinity*, 7.19. See also Ayres, *NL*, 182–183.
34 Hilary, *Synods*, 14.
35 Ibid. 13.
36 Ibid. 13, 15. For the connection between eternal generation and image-Christology, see Weedman, *Trinitarian Theology*, 101–102.
37 Hilary, *Trinity*, 7.39; Hanson, *SCDG*, 479–480.
38 Hilary, *Synods*, 71.
39 Ibid. 58.

great difference in doctrine between those who assert the Son is identical in essence to the Father (*homoousios*) and those who consider the Son to be *like* in essence to the Father (*homoiousios*) because 'no likeness exists where there is no equality of nature'.[40] This was a strategy for rapprochement that was carried forwards also by Athanasius and is explored in greater detail in the next chapter.[41]

Significantly, Hilary's advocacy of the *homoousios* is the basis of his soteriology. It is because the Son is in perfect and essential unity with the Father that, through his gratuitous union with us at the incarnation, he is able to facilitate our union with the Father:

> The world is to believe that the Son has been sent by the Father because all who shall believe in Him will be one in the Father and the Son . . . So now all are one in glory, because the glory given is none other than that which was received: nor has it been given for any other cause than that all should be one. And since all are one through the glory given to the Son and by the Son bestowed upon believers, I ask how can the Son be of a different glory from the Father's, since the glory of the Son brings all that believe into the unity of the Father's glory?[42]

For Hilary, this is parsed through an understanding of the sacraments, through which the believer is incorporated into the body of the incarnate Son, sharing in his filial relationship to the Father and so sharing in the glory of God the Father.[43]

Unlike in essence

On the other side of the spectrum was an explicit subordinationist account of the Father–Son relation. This group asserted that the Son is alien in essence (hetereousian) to the Father. This faction, led by Aetius and Eunomius, are often described as 'neo-Arians'.[44] Socrates describes Aetius as one who 'agreed in doctrine with Arius, and maintained the same opinions', who formally

[40] Ibid. 76, 88.

[41] Ibid. 81, 86, 88–91.

[42] Hilary, *Trinity*, 8.12.

[43] Ibid. 8.16.

[44] This name was given by T. A. Kopecek, *History of Neo-Arianism* (Washington, D.C.: Catholic University of America Press, 1979). For biographical details of Aetius and Eunomius, see Hanson, *SCDG*, 598–603, 611–617. Anatolios suggests that the reason Eunomius achieved greater notoriety is that Aetius presented his thought via logical analysis, whereas Eunomius presented his thought within a more explicit credal framework. Anatolios, *RN*, 69–70. Socrates, in particular, presents Aetius as a poor philosopher, who had not engaged at all with the tradition of the church. Socrates, *Ecclesiastical History*, 2.35.

distanced himself from Arius' thought only for his ecclesial survival.[45] While true in part, this is misleading in as far as their doctrine is different from that of Arius on some key points. However, there is significant overlap in that they reinvigorated Arius' old argument regarding the subordination of the Son on account of the unique primacy of the unbegotten (*agen[n]ētos*).

Aetius and Eunomius departed from Arius' apophatic theology, holding instead a clear doctrine that the knowledge of God's very essence is accessible, revealed as it is through the divine name unbegotten (*agen[n]ētos*). As it is the *name* unbegotten that uniquely manifests divinity itself,[46] the Father alone is understood to be God. The Son, as begotten, is held to be extrinsic to divinity, which this faction described with *ousia* language: with respect to the Father, the Son is 'unlike in essence'.[47] This faction is well introduced by a section from a letter of an unnamed author:

> By reason of his birth the Son is less and is confessed [to be so]. He does not consequently preserve likeness to the unbeginning in respect of *ousia*, but preserves the full will of God, bearing it in his own existence; so he preserves his likeness, not according to *ousia* but according to the principle of truth.[48]

Throughout the 360s and 370s Aetius and Eunomius established separate episcopal areas in regions where their support was strong, some of which survived well into the fifth century.[49]

There is only one remaining work of Aetius, the *Syntagmation* (The *Little Treatise*, *c.*359),[50] outside which there are a few fragments by which to gain an assessment of his thought. The *Syntagmation* is a dense logical argument consisting of a series of thirty-seven propositions answering Athanasius' *Defence of the Nicene Definition*.[51] The purpose of this work is to demonstrate by means

45 Socrates, *Ecclesiastical History*, 2.35. Sozomen, *Ecclesiastical History*, 4.12.

46 DelCogliano describes two broad theories regarding the relationship between names and realities in late antiquity: the *naturalist* view, where there is a natural correspondence between names and reality, and the *conventionalist* view, where names are references to reality with no constitutive connection to them. DelCogliano locates the heterousian theory of names and naming with the naturalist view. DelCogliano, *Anti-Eunomian Theory of Names*, 49–97.

47 See Anatolios, *RN*, 21.

48 Recorded in Epiphanius, *Panarion*, 73.21.2. Cited from Hanson, *SCDG*, 604. See also L. R. Wickham, 'The Syntagmation of Aetius the Anomean', *JTS* 19 (1968), 532–569.

49 Ayres, *NL*, 146.

50 Recorded in Epiphanius, *Panarion*, 76.11.1–76.12.37, and Pseudo-Dionysius, *The Trinity*, 28.1173–1201. On the dating of the *Syntagmation* see Kopecek, *History of Neo-Arianism*, 1.226–227.

51 Aetius is described 'in dependence on the precepts of Aristotle's categories'. Socrates, *Ecclesiastical History*, 2.35.

of logical analysis that the Son is unlike the Father in essence.[52] Aetius conceived of divine being as an undifferentiated and still Monad, which could have no intrinsic generation on the grounds that this would render divine being mutable.[53] It is intrinsic to the absolute divine being (the unbegotten) that it cannot change, as that would imply the passive potentiality whereby it is not truly absolute. Moreover, 'the ingenerate (*agennēton*) cannot be like the generate (*gennētō*)',[54] because to be ingenerate is indistinguishable from the simple divine essence and to be generate is extrinsic and alien to it: 'If God can really turn himself into a generating agency, what he generates cannot possibly possess his whole *ousia* because it is generated and not generator.'[55] As Radde-Gallwitz observes, Aetius' goal is to force a dilemma: 'no thing can be both generate and ingenerate in the same respect'.[56] Ingenerate and generate cannot both be attributed to God. For Aetius, then, the notion that the divine being is inherently generative, moving outward from itself to share its life with another is a misnomer. To be generate is conceptually alien to divinity. As such, Aetius resisted the application of the name 'Father' to divine being, as it implies generation is intrinsic to divinity, favouring the designation 'Unbegotten'.[57]

This is related to the central philosophical conviction of neo-Arianism, which is that names directly signify essence: 'things which are dissimilar in nature are stated dissimilarly, and conversely things which are stated dissimilarly are dissimilar in nature . . . Therefore the Son is dissimilar to the Father.'[58] A difference in names *necessarily* indicates a difference in essence, such that the difference in names of the unbegotten and the begotten is indicative of their difference in nature which is underscored by the respective property that underlies these designations: unbegotten and begotten. The proposition that a name is intrinsic to and revelatory of essence is related to Aetius' remarkably non-Arian doctrine of the knowledge of God. Given God's self-naming, we are afforded complete knowledge of God: 'with such entire clarity do I know God and so fully do I know him and am acquainted with him, that I do not know myself better than I know God'.[59] Combined with the static view of divine being described above, Aetius views that God is known by the name he has revealed

[52] Hanson, *SCDG*, 607.

[53] Recorded in Pseudo-Dionysius, *Trinity*, 10. Cited from Hanson, *SCDG*, 603–604.

[54] Recorded in Epiphanius, *Panarion*, 76.6.1. Cited from Hanson, *SCDG*, 606. See also Radde-Gallwitz, *Transformation of Divine Simplicity*, 90.

[55] Aetius, *Syntagmation*, 8. Cited from Hanson, *SCDG*, 608. For a discussion of the history of the designation of God as ingenerate, see Radde-Gallwitz, *Transformation of Divine Simplicity*, 67–86.

[56] Radde-Gallwitz, *Transformation of Divine Simplicity*, 95.

[57] Ayres, *NL*, 146.

[58] Recorded in Basil of Caesarea, *Spirit*, 2.4. Cited from Hanson, *SCDG*, 606.

[59] Recorded in Epiphanius, *Panarion*, 76.4.1–2. Cited from Hanson, *SCDG*, 606.

and not in a filial self-giving that includes us in the mutual knowledge of the Father and Son. This, as Hanson observes, lends to Aetius' theology a rationalistic character.[60] Similarly, Socrates suggests that Aetius' strict adherence to a syllogistic mode of reasoning meant that 'he was unable to comprehend how there could be generation without a beginning, and how that which was begotten be coeternal with him who begat'.[61]

There are more sources from which an estimation of Eunomius' doctrine can be retrieved.[62] At its heart is a very similar network of convictions to Aetius', specifically the twin doctrines that the name 'unbegotten' reveals the divine essence, whereby the begotten Son is unlike the Father in essence.[63] A version of the doctrine of divine simplicity looms large in Eunomius' thought. All that can be said of God must be identical to the divine essence.[64] If not, God would be composed of a variety of parts, upon which he is dependent, mitigating against his absolute primacy. On these grounds, Eunomius argued that when we call God 'ingenerate', we are not simply naming a human conceptualization of God, but the divine essence itself.[65] Therefore, the name 'Son' and the relation of begetting cannot be said truly of God, on the grounds of divine simplicity: that all claims about and titles of God must be predicated on the essence of the single God.[66] The very essence of God is indicated by the name 'unbegotten', and therefore that which is begotten is by definition extrinsic to divinity.[67] Alongside this, Eunomius held a clear doctrine of the incommunicability of divine being: '[the unbegotten] has no sharer of his Godhead, nor participator of his glory nor joint possessor of his authority'. Given these propositions, the generation of the begotten Son cannot be intrinsic to divine being. The Son, then, who comes into existence by generation does not share in the glory of the unbegotten Father, because 'He could never come into contact with generation, so as to communicate his own nature to something generated.'[68]

In this way Eunomius objected to the cornerstone of the Nicene confession: that the Son is begotten from the essence of the Father and is God as the

60 Hanson, *SCDG*, 611.

61 Socrates, *Ecclesiastical History*, 2.35.

62 Eunomius' *Apology* survives. Fragments of Eunomius' rejoinder, *Second Apology*, are recorded by Gregory of Nyssa in his *Against Eunomius*. Also Eunomius' *Confession of Faith* is recorded by Gregory of Nyssa. For a summary of the scholarship on the dating of these works, see Hanson, *SCDG*, 618, n. 83. A useful summary of Eunomius' teaching can be found in Radde-Gallwitz, *Transformation of Divine Simplicity*, 50–57.

63 Anatolios, *RN*, 69.

64 Radde-Gallwitz, *Transformation of Divine Simplicity*, 112.

65 Eunomius, *Apology*, 8.1–3. Cited from Radde-Gallwitz, *Transformation of Divine Simplicity*, 97–98.

66 Radde-Gallwitz, *Transformation of Divine Simplicity*, 97.

67 Hanson, *SCDG*, 625.

68 Eunomius, *Apology*, 8. Cited from Hanson, *SCDG*, 622.

Father is God. For Eunomius, this contravenes the basic grammar of divinity. It asserts that something can be derived from another and be absolute. Eunomius considers this a non sequitur: if the divine essence is commensurate with being ingenerate, then it is illogical to say that which is generate is identical in essence to God.[69] Furthermore, from Eunomius' perspective, it introduces causality into divine being and so the proposition that the divine being is capable of undergoing change. Instead, Eunomius argues that the Son is 'begotten before all things by the will of its God and Father'.[70] In service of this doctrine, Eunomius applies the distinction between divine being and divine willing, identifying all causality as belonging to the will rather than the being of God.[71] Anatolios considers this to be the 'climactic expression' of the tradition that relates the Father and Son through the category of divine will, as opposed to by being.[72] For Eunomius, divine being is eternal, unchanging, transcendent over all causality, while divine will and action are temporal and external to divine being.[73] Correspondingly, Barnes has demonstrated how Eunomius interrupted the normal metaphysical sequence from essence to action by excluding the notion of essence having an essential capacity (*dynamis*) that is manifested in the corresponding activity.[74] The coming into existence of the Son, then, as a product of the will of the unbegotten cannot be intrinsic to divinity, for causality has no place in Eunomius' conception of divine being.[75]

The Son as begotten exists by virtue of the Father's will.[76] For Eunomius, this is not continuous with divinity.[77] To assert that the generation of the Son is internal to divine being would be to introduce causality into divinity, thereby eradicating the transcendent freedom of God from the chain of causality and collapse divine willing and action into divine being:

> We . . . do not consider it unhazardous to have to unite the action to the essence. We recognize that the divine essence is without beginning, simple, and endless, but we also recognize that its action is neither without

[69] Eunomius, *Apology*, 9, 11. Cited from Ayres, *NL*, 147.
[70] Eunomius, *Apology*, 12. Cited from Anatolios, *RN*, 75.
[71] Eunomius, *Apology*, 15. Cited from Ayres, *NL*, 147.
[72] Anatolios, *RN*, 78.
[73] Ibid. 74.
[74] M. R. Barnes, *The Power of God: Dynamis in Gregory of Nyssa's Trinitarian Theology* (Washington, D.C.: Catholic University of America Press, 2016), 188–191. Cited from Anatolios, *RN*, 74.
[75] Anatolios, *RN*, 74.
[76] S. M. Hildebrand, *The Trinitarian Theology of Basil of Caesarea: A Synthesis of Greek Thought and Biblical Truth* (Washington, D.C.: Catholic University of America Press, 2009), 43.
[77] Anatolios, *RN*, 73–75.

> beginning nor without ending ... There is no need, therefore, to accept the half-baked opinions of outsiders and unite the action to the essence.[78]

It is perfectly proper, then, to describe the Son as a creature, for his being begotten is alien to the unbegotten and incommunicable divinity: the Son is unlike the Father with regard to essence. However, as the image of the Father, the Son is unique among creatures. The scriptural attribution of the Son's likeness to the Father is ascribed, then, not to an essential likeness, but to the activity of the Son in which there is harmony between the will of the Son and the Father. In his obedient activity the Son reflects the Father's will: 'it is not with respect to the essence but with respect to the action (which is what the will is) that the Son preserves his similarity to the Father'.[79] It is only in the sense that he reveals and accomplishes the Father's will, then, that the Son can be said to reveal the Father. Moreover, the Son's obedience becomes the dominant soteriological category as the Son actualizes the saving will of God on creation.[80] This carries a significant corollary for Eunomius' doctrine of God: the name 'Father' is not properly spoken of divinity in itself, but rather only of God's extrinsic relation to the Son. It is a term to describe God's mode of action and bears no relation to divine being itself.[81] The Nicene approach to theology is the exact reverse of this.

The difference in essence between unbegotten and the begotten is consolidated by Eunomius' philosophical understanding of the relationship between name and reality, in which the name is not a human convention but is given directly by the reality for true knowledge of it.[82] Therefore, as with Aetius, name is directly revelatory of essence, whereby we are afforded knowledge of the divine essence. However, the name 'Father' is not revelatory of essence. Instead, 'unbegotten' is the name that manifests divinity, indicative of God's being uncaused, one, incomparable, indivisible and free. Part of the story of the emergence of trinitarian theology, per se, is the rejection of the driving theological claim that divine simplicity means that names and titles can only be predicated essentially of God in favour of a different view of divine simplicity that accommodated the capacity for absolute and relative predication in theology.[83]

78 Eunomius, *Apology*, 23. Cited from Anatolios, *RN*, 75.
79 Eunomius, *Apology*, 24. Cited from Anatolios, *RN*, 76.
80 Anatolios, *RN*, 76.
81 Ibid. 75.
82 For an assessment of the philosophical roots of this, see Hanson, *SCDG*, 630–632, and Anatolios, *RN*, 73.
83 This is the thesis of Radde-Gallwitz, *Transformation of Divine Simplicity*. DelCogliano helpfully traces this perspective into the Eusebian tradition. M. DelCogliano, 'Basil of Caesarea and the Primacy of the Name "Son"', *RÉAug* 57 (2011), 45–69, at 48–53.

Like according to essence

Third, there was a faction characterized by a suspicion of the materialistic implications of the *homoousion*. However, this group were equally concerned to uphold the essential likeness between the Father and Son. This grouping conceived of the Son as *like* the Father *according to essence*. This doctrine is often described using the phrase *homoios kata ousian*, or *homoiousios*,[84] of which the latter has become a standard term of reference. This perspective is most commonly associated with the senior episcopal figure of Basil of Ancyra, who, as Ayres describes, 'was heir to a tradition in eastern theology that strongly emphasized the Son's nature as image and revealer of the Father'.[85]

The theological convictions of this group are best represented in the doctrinal statement contained within a synodal letter emerging from a small council of bishops Basil called in Ancyra (358), among whose number were Eustathius of Sebaste (who will reappear when our story comes to Basil of Caesarea's defence of the divinity of the Spirit) and George of Laodicea.[86] Ostensibly, this council was prompted by the need to make a statement in response to the growing influence of Aetius' theology arising from events in Antioch in 357 (see below) and the growing authority of the homoians expressed in the Creed of Sirmium (357) (see below). As such, Basil is seen to be intervening on the basis of the exclusion of *ousia*-language and in favour of the essential likeness between the Son and the Father.[87] This document, written by Basil, aligns itself with the statement of faith produced at the Dedication Council. This is almost certainly a reference to the Second Creed of the Dedication Council given its proposition that the Son is the exact image of the *ousia* of the Father and the clear acknowledgement of the three hypostases.

It is no surprise therefore to find in this statement a strong anti-modalist emphasis on the Son as the image of the Father, who, as the image, makes the

[84] The earliest recorded instance of this phrase in use comes from Hilary, *Synods*, 11 (358).

[85] Ayres, *NL*, 150.

[86] This statement is recorded in Epiphanius, *Panarion*, 73.2.1. See also Hilary, *Synods*, 13–28. DelCogliano considers George of Laodicea to have made several significant contributions to the eventual pro-Nicene consensus, which – given his early schooling in the Eusebian tradition – indicates just how much the 'constitutive' image-Christology within the Eusebian tradition contributed to Nicene theology. These include George's use of the idea of individuating features, his distinction between *ousia* and *hypostasis* and his focus on the divinity of the Spirit. In this connection, DelCogliano describes George as a 'grandfather of pro-Nicene theology'. M. DelCogliano, 'The Significance of George of Laodicea in the Fourth Century Trinitarian Debates', *StPatr* 46 (2010), 307–311. See also M. DelCogliano, 'George of Laodicea: A Historical Reassessment', *JEH* 62.4 (2011), 667–692. An alternative view is Zachhuber, 'Basil', 65–85.

[87] Weedman holds that Basil of Ancyra's thought in these areas significantly influenced Hilary of Poitiers in his own response to the Creed of Sirmium (357). Weedman, *Trinitarian Theology*, 97–100.

Father known.[88] In this connection, Basil 'emphasizes the ineffable depth of the Father's self-gift in generating the Son'.[89] This element of his thought is best demonstrated in an idea that is central to Basil's thought: the distinction between the creator–created relation and the Father–Son relation the language of essence maintains. The argument goes that, if the Son is not like the Father with regard to essence, then he is no different from creation and the Father–Son relation is collapsed into the God–creation relation.[90] The crux of this argument is that the Father–Son relationship includes some communication of essence,[91] which is not the case in the creator–creature relation: 'the begetting of a living being that is like in *ousia* because every father is thought of as a father of an *ousia* that is like his'.[92] As such, to deny that the Son is like the Father in essence is to say that his mode of generation is no different from that of creation. A corollary of this is that the Father is not truly 'Father' but is instead only creator.[93]

This view is set against the neo-Arian claim that the Son is unlike the Father in essence, rejecting (1) that the Son is only like the Father in activity and arguing instead that the Son is like the Father in both activity and essence,[94] and (2) the temporal coming into existence of the Son.[95] Moreover, it is set clearly against the doctrine that likeness of essence obscures personal differentiation, because the Son, as derived from the Father, is differentiated from him.[96] An argument that would be used again by Basil of Caesarea (one-time deacon to Basil of Ancyra) was used in this connection, which is that something cannot be the same as that to which it is like.[97] Clearly, there is a concern to distance the doctrine of the Son's being like the Father in essence from any materialistic associations, explicitly rejecting any suggestion that the generation of the Son is by emanation or change in the Father.[98] In this connection, the anathemas also make a distinction between likeness of essence and identity of essence in the course of which *homoousios* is explicitly rejected as tautologous for identical in essence.[99] Sozomen suggests that the central complaint against *homoousios*

---

88 See Behr, *NF*, 88–89.
89 Ayres, *NL*, 150.
90 Epiphanius, *Panarion*, 74.4.3. Cited from Hanson, *SCDG*, 353.
91 Hilary, *Synods*, 16.
92 Epiphanius, *Panarion*, 74.4.2. Cited from Hanson, *SCDG*, 352–353.
93 For Basil of Ancyra's influence on Basil of Caesarea see DelCogliano, *Anti-Eunomian Theory of Names*, 182–184.
94 Hilary, *Synods*, 19–20 (Anathemas 6 and 7).
95 Ibid. 24–25 (Anathemas 10–11).
96 Ibid. 14 (Anathema 2).
97 Ibid. 13.
98 Ibid. 21.
99 See also Hanson, *SCDG*, 355–356.

was that it intruded material ideas on to divine being and that the emperor Constantius was 'deceived' by the argument that *homoousios* 'properly belongs to corporeal beings, such as men and other animals', whereas *homoiousios* 'appertains exclusively to incorporeal beings'.[100] However, it would be incorrect to conclude that this faction is incompatible with the pro-Nicene faction. The emergence of a pro-Nicene consensus was the gradual reconciliation of the homoiousian and homoousian factions, which is described in the next chapter.

Like

Finally, there was a faction who avoided *ousia* language in its account of the Father–Son relation, preferring instead to describe the Son as 'like' (*homoios*) the Father. The possible range of meaning in this designation is significant and so theologians who could advocate for it formed a broad and diverse faction, which is one reason why this option was attractive to political leaders. However, the primary motivation of the designation was not to form a broad consensus, but rather to remain within the parameters of that which could be said of the Father–Son relation from the Scriptures alone.[101] Often this grouping is described as the *homoian Arians* owing to the fact that the designation of the Son as like the Father included the primacy of the Father over the Son. Hanson identifies twelve homoian confessions,[102] not all of which can be discussed here. However, this perspective is most clearly and influentially articulated in the Second Creed of Sirmium (357), which is discussed below.

Acacius of Caesarea (the successor to Eusebius of Caesarea[103]) followed Eusebius theologically,[104] rejecting the creation of the Son from nothing, but advocating a more subtle subordination based on the Son's generation by the will of the Father and attributing the Son's likeness not to the continuity of divinity from the Father to the Son, but in terms of the harmony of will and activity between the Son and Father.[105] While there is some evidence that Acacius, depending on political circumstances, vacillated in his opinions,[106] the following statement is indicative of core homoian ideas:

100 Sozomen, *Ecclesiastical History*, 3.18.
101 Hanson, *SCDG*, 561.
102 For a list and discussion of these sources, see Hanson, *SCDG*, 558–578.
103 Socrates, *Ecclesiastical History*, 2.4.
104 Hanson, *SCDG*, 579–580.
105 Anatolios, *RN*, 20–21, 71. On Acacius, see Lienhard, *Contra Marcellum*, 182–186.
106 Acacius was the signatory of a letter endorsing *homoousios* and criticizing those who affirm the Son is only like the Father. For this reason, Socrates suggests that he and his followers were ready 'to accommodate their opinions to those invested with supreme authority'. Socrates, *Ecclesiastical History*, 3.25.

> The image bears the characteristics of the original in itself and also provides a difference, a difference as a likeness . . . Therefore the Son is an image of the Father, living [image] of the Living One in movement, in activity, in power and will and glory, not devoid of life nor of movement, deriving its existence and delineation from another, and itself not being in motion in itself or through itself. And he is the exact image so that the exact resemblance does not present a Father, but precisely a Son.[107]

There is a strong focus on the similarity of the Son to the Father with respect to the scriptural designation of the Son as the image of the Father. However, this is complemented by a recognition that the very designation of the Son as image implies the Son's difference from the Father. This may sound similar to the correlation of similarity and difference used by Basil of Ancyra, but the parameters for similarity and difference are significant. Like his predecessor Eusebius, Acacius recognizes similarity in the categories of will and power as opposed to likeness with regard to essence. These doctrinal commitments were given powerful voice in the late 350s, which were the years of homoian ascendency.

Homoian ascendency

The late 350s and early 360s were a period in which the homoian faction were in the ascendency owing to the potential of this vague descriptor to form a broad consensus. However, the viability of a genuine consensus established on this term was hamstrung by the perception that the description of the Son as like the Father was motivated by a strident subordinationist Christology. This is certainly the perspective given in Basil of Ancyra's letter in which he writes of the growing influence of Aetius in the city of Antioch under the episcopacy of Eudoxius.[108] As Ayres observes, there was a strong sense that 'those shaping Constantius' policies during the 350s were pushing an agenda that was strongly and intentionally subordinationist'.[109]

The Council of Sirmium (357)

The appointment of Eudoxius as the Bishop of Antioch following the death of Leontius in 357 is indicative of the antagonism to the Nicene confession in this

[107] Recorded in Epiphanius, *Panarion*, 72.10.2. Cited from Hanson, *SCDG*, 583.
[108] Sozomen, *Ecclesiastical History*, 4.12–13. The concern that homoian doctrine may be an entry point for a more explicit subordinationism is also indicated by the letter of Constantius condemning Eudoxius of Antioch. Sozomen, *Ecclesiastical History*, 4.14.
[109] Ayres, *NL*, 150.

period. Eudoxius is described as a student of Lucian, who followed Asterius closely,[110] and was soon joined in Antioch by Aetius and Eunomius. A small council was called in 357 to endorse a statement of faith written earlier that year in Sirmium.[111] This doctrinal statement is explicit regarding the unique primacy of the Father and the exclusion of essence-language, and in its condemnation of both *homoousios* and *homoiousios*, leading Hilary to describe it as the 'blasphemy of Sirmium':[112]

> It is evident that there is one God, the Father Almighty, according as it is declared over the whole world; and his only-begotten Son Jesus Christ, our Lord, God, and Saviour, begotten of him before the ages. But we ought not to say that there are two Gods . . .
>
> But since it troubles very many to understand about that which is termed *substantia* in Latin, and *ousia* in Greek; that is to say, in order to mark the sense more accurately, the word *homoousion* or *homoiousion*, it is altogether desirable that none of these terms should be mentioned: nor should they be preached on in the church, for this reason, that nothing is recorded concerning them in the holy Scriptures; and because these things are above the knowledge of mankind and human capacity, and that no one can explain the Son's generation . . . But no one can doubt that the Father is greater in honor, dignity, and divinity . . . And no one is ignorant that this is also catholic doctrine, that there are two persons of the Father and Son, and that the Father is the greater: but that the Son is subject, together with all things which the Father has subjected to him. That the Father had no beginning, and is invisible, immortal, and impassible; but that the Son was begotten of the Father, God of God, Light of Light; and that no one comprehends his generation, as was before said, but the Father alone.[113]

Hilary observes that the 'object of the authors was to proclaim the Father to be the one and only God of all things, and deny the Son to be God'.[114] Following Hilary's assessment, Hanson describes it as an 'Arian creed'.[115] There is a clear

110 Philostogorius, *Ecclesiastical History*, 4.4. Cited from Behr, *NF*, 87.

111 Socrates, *Ecclesiastical History*, 2.30; Sozomen, *Ecclesiastical History* 4.12. See also Hanson, *SCDG*, 343–347. It appears that this is the statement that Ossius was compelled to sign through torture. Socrates, *Ecclesiastical History*, 2.31; Sozomen, *Ecclesiastical History*, 4.6.

112 Hilary, *Synods*, 11.

113 Socrates, *Ecclesiastical History*, 2.29. See also Hilary, *Synods*, 11; Athanasius, *Synods*, 28.

114 Hilary, *Synods*, 10.

115 Hanson, *SCDG*, 346.

strategy to avoid ditheism by isolating the Father as true God who has life in himself while the Son has derivative existence. This focus on the unique glory and primacy of the Father and the subordination of the Son is reminiscent of Arius' own theological settlement.[116] The injunction against the term *homoousios* and the moderate *homoiousios* on the basis of *ousia*-language being alien to Scripture is, in effect, a renouncement of the Nicene confession. As Kelly suggests, the agnosticism regarding the Son's generation leaves the door open for the radical doctrine of Arius that the Son was made from nothing,[117] but the Sirmium confession does not explicitly make that proposition.

This was an effective call to arms for those sympathetic with the 325 Creed of Nicaea. For example, Hilary explains that this confession was the primary catalyst for his *On the Synods*.[118] It was also at this point that Athanasius set out on his own presentation and defence of Nicene theology. The confession of Sirmium not only sparked a resurgence in efforts to establish the Nicene confession as a rallying point, but also marked a point of no return for the Eusebian alliance. There was now clear light between the various theological dispositions within the Eastern bishops.[119] In this sense, the temporary ascendency of a homoian theology with a strong heteroousian bias served to clarify the differences between perspectives that were more difficult to see before.[120] At this point, then, the broad coalition of the Eusebian alliance began to fracture into the diverse strands of homoian, heteroousian and homoiousian.

The homoiousian alternative: the Council of Ancyra (358)

With the exclusion of *ousia*-language, those who advocated the *homoiousios* were now isolated from their traditional allies. Basil of Ancyra summoned a council in Ancyra in the winter of 358 out of which a synodal letter (discussed above) was written. This statement includes an appeal to ratify the Second Creed of the Dedication Council – a statement also effectively repealed by the Sirmium confession – as representative of Basil's and his associates' views.[121] Basil believed that this statement would be able to command a consensus

116 Ibid.

117 Kelly, *ECC*, 286.

118 Hilary, *Synods*, 2, 7–9. Hilary organizes this text in rhetorical, not chronological, order, placing the Creed of Sirmium in the position of greatest visibility.

119 D. Davis, *The First Seven Ecumenical Councils (325–787): Their History and Theology* (Collegeville, Minn.: Liturgical Press, 1983), 95–96.

120 See also Ayres, *NL*, 144–149.

121 Epiphanius, *Panarion*, 73.2–11. Cited from Kelly, *ECC*, 288.

between those who prioritized the distinct hypostatic existence of the Father and Son and those who prioritized their likeness in essence.

For a brief period, it seemed this might be the case and Basil is described as having 'great influence' over the emperor.[122] Constantius seized upon the opportunity provided by this middle path between the homoian and homoousian factions by excluding the radical homoousian and heteroousian factions.[123] Eudoxius, Aetius and Eunomius were put into exile and a confession (the third Creed of Sirmium) was composed. Unfortunately, this confession is now lost, but the imperial letter indicates that it articulated the homoiousian theology of Basil,[124] and probably contained an anathema against the use of the term *homoousios*.

The reassertion of homoian theology: the 'Dated Creed' (359)

An avenue for a lasting agreement appeared to be opening up between the homoiousian and homoian factions. To this end, Constantius intended to call a general council,[125] but settled instead to hold two separate councils, which were duly called, one in the Western city of Rimini (Arminium) and the other in the Eastern city of Seleucia (supposedly the plan for one general council in Nicomedia was disrupted by an earthquake[126]). Eager to achieve consensus, Constantius had a statement composed that could be presented to both councils. This confession is known as the 'Dated Creed' by its detractors on account of its date of composition (23 May 359[127]) being attached to the statement, which suited the accusation that it was a theological innovation inconsistent with the received tradition.[128]

The Christological section of the confession was intended to be acceptable to both the homoian and homoiousian factions by excluding *ousia*-language in such a way that excluded the more extreme heteroousian and homoousian factions.[129] The Christological section of the creed is as follows:

122 Sozomen, *Ecclesiastical History*, 4.15.

123 Philostogorius, *Ecclesiastical History*, 4.8. Cited from Behr, *NF*, 89. See also Ayres, *NL*, 152–153.

124 The imperial letter arising from this council is recorded in Sozomen, *Ecclesiastical History*, 4.14. This imperial letter includes a repudiation of Eudoxius and Eunomius and a statement that Constantius had always believed the Son to be like the Father in essence. See Hanson, *SCDG*, 357–362; Behr, *NF*, 90.

125 Sozomen, *Ecclesiastical History*, 4.16. Cited from Ayres, *NL*, 157.

126 Socrates, *Ecclesiastical History*, 2.39; Sozomen, *Ecclesiastical History*, 4.16.

127 Socrates, *Ecclesiastical History*, 2.37.

128 Recorded in Athanasius, *Synods*, 8. For a historical study of the composition of this creed and its passage to promulgation, see Barnes, *Athanasius and Constantius*, 144–151.

129 See also Behr, *NF*, 90.

> [we believe] in one only-begotten Son of God, before all ages, before all beginning, before all conceivable time, and before all comprehensible thought, begotten without passion: by whom the ages were framed, and all things made: who was begotten as the only-begotten of the Father, only of only, God of God, like to the Father who begat him, according to the Scriptures: whose generation no one knows, but the Father only who begat him.[130]

A diplomatic explanatory note explains that the term *ousia* was excluded because 'not being understood by the people [it] has caused offense on account of the fact that the Scriptures do not contain it'.[131] The justification given for the exclusion of *ousia*-language is *pastoral* rather than theological,[132] meaning that its continued use in theological circles is not ruled out. This, then, is not a repudiation of the Nicene confession per se, but it does quarantine it, ensuring that its terminology will not be given liturgical expression.

The description of the generation of the Son as 'God of God' is of a piece with the repudiation of Aetius, Eunomius and Eudoxius and appears to have been intended to appeal to the image-Christology of Basil of Ancyra. As such, this confession is a homoian creed that looks to bake in a prophylactic against explicit subordinationism. Even though the embargo against *ousia*-language was repeated ('in future no mention should be made of substance in reference to God'[133]), it was obviously hoped that – while this would be unacceptable to the pro-Nicene faction – enough had been said to address the theological priorities of the homoiousian faction.[134] In this way, the confession was intended to be acceptable to the theological priorities of both the homoians and the homoiousians.

This was a miscalculation. As we have seen, *ousia*-language was central to the theological logic of Basil of Ancyra. As such, he had some difficulty in signing this confession, explaining that in doing so he meant that the Son is like the Father 'in all things, and not just in will, but in essence and in existence'.[135] This unease with the homoian doctrine of the Dated Creed led to Basil's writing a longer defence of homoiousian theology in collaboration with George of Laodicea.[136] They argue that homoian theology has a centre of gravity

130 Socrates, *Ecclesiastical History*, 2.37. Athanasius, *Synods*, 8.

131 Socrates, *Ecclesiastical History*, 2.37.

132 Hanson, *SCDG*, 365.

133 Socrates, *Ecclesiastical History*, 2.37.

134 Hanson, *SCDG*, 364.

135 Recorded in Epiphanius, *Panarion*, 73.22. Cited from Kelly, *ECC*, 291. See also Ayres, *NL*, 158.

136 Epiphanius, *Panarion*, 73.12–24. The authorship of this letter is uncertain (see Hanson, *SCDG*, 365–366) and here it is treated as a joint work of Basil and George.

that pulls towards a heteroousian position, and so it is necessary to retain the qualifier that the Son is like the Father with regard to essence.[137] This is a significant argument as it pre-empts the argument Athanasius would make that an alliance with the homoousian faction would emerge as the only route for the homoiosian faction to secure the meaning of the Son's essential likeness to the Father.

Beyond this, the letter also includes a defence of *ousia*-language in theology on the grounds that, while the term is not found in Scripture, the meaning of this term is the sense of the Scriptures.[138] Again, this pre-empts the arguments that would be made by the pro-Nicene faction: while *ousia* is not used in Scripture, it is essential in order to safeguard the intention of the Scriptures regarding the Son's similarity to the Father. As such, Basil and George differentiate themselves from the view that the likeness of the Son to the Father is only a likeness in will.[139] However, their main target is the subordinationism of figures such as Aetius and Eunomius, repudiating their description of the Son as unlike the Father and challenging their prioritization of the language of unbegotten and begotten regarding Father and Son, again pre-empting what would become a standard pro-Nicene argument. Perhaps most significantly for subsequent theological developments, this letter uses the term *hypostasis* to refer to the discrete subsistence of the Father, Son and Spirit, clarifying that this does not imply three gods, but one divinity subsisting in three ways.[140]

However, the attempt to attach greater specificity to the Dated Creed by the introduction of *ousia*-language was rebuffed. When the twin councils met in 359, an unamended Dated Creed was presented.[141] The Western council met first and rejected the suggested confession on the grounds that there was no need to replace the Nicene Creed.[142] In response, Constantius relocated the Western council to Niké, where imperial pressure was successful[143] and the Dated Creed was ratified along with the small qualification that the Son was like the Father 'in all things'.[144] However, the embargo against *ousia* language was retained, and so the de facto departure from the Nicene confession was ratified.

137 Epiphanius, *Panarion*, 73.15. Cited from Behr, *NF*, 91.
138 Epiphanius, *Panarion*, 73.12. Cited from Ayres, *NL*, 159.
139 Epiphanius, *Panarion*, 73.13. Cited from Hanson, *SCDG*, 367.
140 Epiphanius, *Panarion*, 73.16. Cited from Behr, *NF*, 91–92.
141 Socrates, *Ecclesiastical History*, 2.39–40. Cited from Behr, *NF*, 92.
142 Letter recorded in Sozomen, *Ecclesiastical History*, 4.18.
143 Ibid. 4.19; Theodoret, *Ecclesiastical History*, 2.16. For Athanasius' account of the initial support of the Nicene confession and the following imperial pressure, see Athanasius, *Letter to the Africans*. In Theodoret, *Ecclesiastical History*, 2.18, NPNF II.3. See also Hanson, *SCDG*, 378.
144 See Kelly, *ECC*, 291–292; Ayres, *NL*, 160–161.

The Eastern council opened in the latter half of 359 – in the context of the expulsion of those who affirmed the *homoousion*[145] – and the Dated Creed did not have an easy route through the Eastern council, either.[146] Socrates describes the council as split between two unequal factions: the homoians, led by Acacius of Caesarea and the larger group of homoiousians, led by George of Laodicea (and later, Basil of Ancyra). Acacius' party was of the opinion that the Nicene Creed needed to be replaced and proposed a new confession to reflect homoian doctrine.[147] Acacius' proposed confession was rejected on the grounds that the homoiousian faction 'concurred in all the decisions of the council of Nicaea, but criticised its adoption of the term *homoousion*',[148] and called instead for a return to the second creed of the Dedication council.[149] With the council at a stalemate, delegations were sent to Constantinople to sue the emperor for support. The homoian faction were persuaded to sign the dated creed,[150] and Basil and his associates were compelled to ratify the Dated Creed on the final night of 359.[151]

The Dated Creed was formally ratified at the Council of Constantinople (360) at which all advocates of homoiousian theology were deposed,[152] securing the homoian victory. The Christological part of the confession is as follows:

> [We believe] in the Only-begotten Son of God, begotten from God before all ages and before every beginning, by whom all things were made, visible and invisible, and begotten as only-begotten, only from the Father only, God from God, like to the Father that begot Him according to the Scriptures; whose origin no one knows, except the Father alone who begot Him.[153]

The anathemas are as follows:

> But the name of 'Essence,' which was set down by the Fathers in simplicity, and, being unknown by the people, caused offense, because the Scriptures

145 Sozomen, *Ecclesiastical History*, 4.20.
146 See Hanson, *SCDG*, 372–380; Davis, *First Seven Ecumenical Councils*, 98–99.
147 Socrates, *Ecclesiastical History*, 40.
148 Ibid. 2.39.
149 Ayres sees this as indicative of divergent credal trajectories in the fourth century, with a family likeness between the Dedication and Nicene creeds contrasted to a different credal trajectory articulated here in the Dated Creed. In this, Ayres observes a disagreement regarding the process of credal development in the fourth century in which the homoiousian faction understood themselves, as opposed to disputants, to be in a positive relation to the Nicene confession. See Ayres, *NL*, 162–163. This insightful analysis provides further explanation as to how consensus formed between this faction and those who advocated the *homoousios*.
150 Socrates, *HE*, 2.41.
151 Theodoret, *Ecclesiastical History*, 2.23. Ayres, *NL*, 164.
152 Recorded in Socrates, *Ecclesiastical History*, 2.42. See also Hanson, *SCDG*, 380–382.
153 Athanasius, *Synods*, 30.

> contain it not, it has seemed good to abolish, and for the future to make no mention of it at all; since the divine Scriptures have made no mention of the Essence of Father and Son. For neither ought Subsistence [*hypostasis*] to be named concerning Father, Son, and Holy Ghost. But, we say that the Son is Like the Father, as the divine Scriptures say and teach; and all the heresies, both those which have been afore condemned already, and whatever are of modern date, being contrary to this published statement, be they anathema.[154]

The particular subordinationist character of the homoian theology expressed here is indicated by the fact that the Christological section undoes the compromise reached at Niké by removing the modifier that the Son is like the Father 'in all respects'. Also, as Ayres notes, the exclusion of the language of 'light from light' indicates a repudiation of the image theology of the homoiousians who, in their continued support for the Second Creed of the Dedication Council 'were making a claim on the past two decades of Eastern credal tradition'.[155] Moreover, the appointment of Eudoxius as Bishop of Constantinople indicates that a profoundly subordinationist doctrine of the Son was in the ascendency. It was in resistance to this that a pro-Nicene consensus of the homoiousian and homoousian factions began to gather around the figures of Athanasius and Basil of Caesarea.

[154] Ibid.
[155] Ayres, *NL*, 165.

6

'Genuine from the Father, as life from fountain, and radiance from light': from Nicaea to Constantinople (3)

Athanasius' alliance-building efforts

With the events in Constantinople alienating the significant faction gathered around Basil of Ancyra and George of Laodicea, Athanasius, along with Hilary, was alert to the possibility of a consensus between the homoousian and homoiousian factions. In this connection, Williams suggests that the Nicene consensus was formed by the homoiousian faction becoming convinced that their theological priorities would be better served by allying themselves with the pro-Nicene faction.[1] However, any alliance around the *homoousios* had significant conceptual barriers to overcome; namely, the associations between *homoousios* and modalism and the materialist connotations of the term *homoousios*.[2]

Anti-'Arian' polemic

Athanasius' polemical strategy was to gather together diverse strands of the broad non-Nicene tradition under the designation 'Arian', subjecting them to a sustained polemic, to situate advocacy of the *homoousios* as the only route to securing the essential likeness of the Son to the Father. So, in his *On the Synods* Athanasius locates the events surrounding the homoian creed of Constantinople (360) within a trajectory that began with Arius and continued through the Eusebians and the various confessional statements of the 340s and 350s. The intention is to present them all as part of one continuous 'Arian' tradition. As

1 Williams, *Arius*, 166.

2 Vaggione has explored the function of terminology in the fourth century as a tool to negotiate agreements between divergent traditions. See R. P. Vaggione, '*Ouk hōs en tōn gennēmatōn*: Some Aspects of Dogmatic Formulae in the Arian Controversy', *StPatr* 17 (1982), 181–187.

we have seen, these are a diverse range of confessional statements that can hardly be gathered under one classification, and they certainly do not represent the continuation of Arius' own distinctive theological ideas. Ostensibly, Athanasius' goal was not to re-present these statements, but to repudiate them.

This diversity, though, suited Athanasius' polemical strategy. By gathering a diverse and complex set of perspectives under the single banner of 'Arianism' Athanasius was able to present genuinely divergent theological perspectives as part of the same self-contradictory outlook.[3] The internal inconsistency of the 'Arian' faction, Athanasius argues, is proof that their convictions hold no truth,[4] are indicative of the pursuit of earthly power rather than fidelity to the gospel,[5] are the consequence of their faulty exegesis[6] and are borne out by their vexatious claims to historical precedent.[7] This is hardly a fair line of criticism given that very few of those who dissented from the Nicene statement thought of Arius as the founder of their intellectual position.

Beyond these personal attacks, Athanasius' polemic includes the critique that the core tenets of Arian theology are characterized by a number of theological impossibilities. First, Athanasius points to a logical problem inherent in Arius' doctrine. If it is the case, Athanasius asks, that creation cannot bear the direct hand of God and so requires an intermediary to enact God's creative and saving will, and, that the Son was brought into being from nothing, then how was the Son created? The creation of the Son would require the presence of a mediator, and another upon that and another upon that, and so on:

> For if it was impossible for things originate to bear the hand of God, and you hold the Son to be one of their number, how was He too equal to this formation by God alone? And if a Mediator became necessary that things originate might come to be, and you hold the Son to be originated, then must there have been some medium before Him, for His creation; and that Mediator himself again being a creature, it follows that he too needed another Mediator for his own constitution. And though we were to devise another, we must first devise his Mediator, so that we shall never come to an end.[8]

[3] See also K. D. Hill, *Athanasius and the Holy Spirit: The Development of His Early Pneumatology* (Minneapolis, Minn.: Fortress Press, 2016), 113–116. Gwynn drily describes this as 'Athanasian Arianism'. Gwynn, *Athanasius of Alexandria*, 76.

[4] Athanasius, *Defence Against the Arians*, 4.

[5] Athanasius, *Synods*, 39.

[6] Athanasius, *Opinions*, 2.

[7] Ibid. 3–4, 19.

[8] Athanasius, *Defence Against the Arians*, 8. See also Behr, *NF*, 235.

Beyond its logical impossibility, this 'Arian' proposition of the impossibility of God's direct action upon creation also impoverishes the doctrine of God. To say that God is not able to interact with that which is beyond him is not an affirmation of his holy transcendence; it is an accusation of incompetence![9]

Second, the doctrine that the Son was brought into being to facilitate God's creative work implies that the created order has a teleological superiority over the Son. This is a result of Arius' radical solution to the Alexandrian tension between the Son's existence *in se* and *pro nobis*. For Athanasius, this eradicates the central logic of the gospel. The Son of Arianism is contingent on God's will to create for his own existence. As such, the Son's relation to us is not out of his loving freedom, but rather is the result of his necessary orientation to creation.

Third, to deny the eternal existence of the Son is to impoverish the doctrine of God. If the Son, who is the Father's Word, Truth and Wisdom, is not eternal, then God was, for some interval, devoid of his Word, Truth and Wisdom: 'for if the Son was not before His generation, Truth was not always in God'.[10] Athanasius' target here is Arius' stronghold: the absolute primacy of God as unbegotten. God, the logic of Athanasius' argument runs, cannot be absolute and simple being if he is enriched by the bringing into existence of these properties. While immediately compelling, Athanasius was attacking a straw man on this occasion:[11] it does not follow that the denial of the distinct subsistence of the Son is equivalent to the denial of the property of wisdom being eternally true of God.[12] For Arius, the Son is identified as Wisdom on account of his participation in God's wisdom.

The fourth theological impossibility is the proposition that the Son is unlike in essence the Father of whom he is an image: 'for if He be not according to essence like, He is surely unlike: and the Unlike cannot be an Image'.[13] Moreover, continuing the theme of the third theological impossibility, this constitutes an impoverishment of the doctrine of God, for it deprives God of his own eternal image.[14] Beyond this, the disjunction of God and his image undermines the possibility of the knowledge of God because the one who reveals God is not ultimately grounded in the divine being: 'For if the Son be not like the Father in essence, something is wanting to the Image, and it is not a complete Image, nor a perfect radiance.'[15] This, Athanasius argues, leads to the detachment of

9 Athanasius, *Discourses*, 2.24–26. See also Anatolios, *RN*, 118.
10 Athanasius, *Discourses*, 1.20; *Defence Against the Arians*, 15–17.
11 Stead, 'Rhetorical Method in Athanasius', 121–137.
12 Athanasius, *Defence Against the Arians*, 16–17.
13 Athanasius, *Synods*, 38.
14 Athanasius, *Discourses*, 1.20.
15 Athanasius, *Synods*, 38.

human thought from the reality of God, thereby throwing human thought back upon itself in a form of madness.[16]

The compatibility of *homoousios* and *homoiousios*

In the texts *Defence of the Nicene Definition* and *On the Synods*, written in the period of homoian ascendency (355–61),[17] Athanasius formulated an account of the Nicene confession that was intended to explain its meaning in a way that emphasized the points of compatibility with the homoiousian faction.[18] He endeavoured to show that the best way to preserve the distinction between the Father and Son while also accounting for the Son's exact resemblance of the Father was by the *homoousion*.[19] The attempt was to demonstrate to Basil of Ancyra and his followers that their theological priorities would be better served by aligning themselves with pro-Nicene commitments. Similarly, Hilary's *On the Synods* was, in part, to demonstrate to the homoiousian faction that there was deep compatibility undergirding their respective theological modes of expression.[20]

Athanasius was aware of the scepticism that surrounded the designation *homoousios*. His strategy was to interpret *homoousios* as a clarification of the meaning of the proposition that the Son is 'from the essence of the Father',[21] and demonstrate that its purpose was to safeguard the doctrine that the generation of the Son is eternal and intrinsic to divine being.[22] Athanasius responds to the accusation that the *homoousios* is a philosophical innovation with an argument that runs in parallel to that of Basil of Ancyra: the Nicene Council adopted the unscriptural language of essence, as this was the only way to fix the sense of Scripture in the face of Arius' distortions of every biblical image.[23] It was not a departure from the Scriptures, but the way in which the meaning of Scripture could be stabilized and communicated:

> but if they still complain that such are not scriptural, that very complaint is a reason why they should be cast out, as talking idly and disordered in

[16] Athanasius, *Discourses*, 1.3; *Defence Against the Arians*, 1.15; *Synods*, 15.

[17] For the dating of Athanasius' works, see Hanson, *SCDG*, 417–421.

[18] Radde-Gallwitz describes Athanasius' intention as showing that the homoiousian 'position logically equates to the Nicene'. A. Radde-Gallwitz, *Basil of Caesarea: A Guide to His Life and Doctrine* (Eugene, Ore.: Cascade Books, 2012), 58.

[19] L. Ayres, 'Athanasius' Initial Defence of the Term *homoousios*: Rereading the *De Decretis*', *JECS* 12 (2004), 337–359.

[20] Weedman, *Trinitarian Theology*, 110.

[21] Athanasius, *Synods*, 40.

[22] See also Ayres, *NL*, 141.

[23] Athanasius, *Synods*, 36.

> mind. And let them blame themselves in this matter, for they set the example, beginning their war against God with words not in Scripture. However, if a person is interested in the question, let him know, that, even if the expressions are not in so many words in the Scriptures, yet, as was said before, they contain the sense of the Scriptures, and expressing it, they convey it to those who have their hearing unimpaired for religious doctrine.[24]

It is in this connection that the delegates of the Nicene Council 'were forced to express more distinctly the sense of the Son being "from God". All things are from God in some sense, but the Son is "from the essence of God".'[25] As *homoousios* with the Father, the Son is from the Father in such a way that the divinity of the Father is communicated to the Son:

> Accordingly, they wrote 'from the essence of God,' in order that 'from God?' might not be considered common and equal in the Son and in things originate, but that all others might be acknowledged as creatures, and the Word alone as from the Father. For though all things be said to be from God, yet this is not in the sense in which the Son is from Him.[26]

The Son is, in a manner of speaking, *caused*. However, he is not caused as things with an origin are caused. He is eternally begotten, while creation is made from nothing.[27] The logic of this distinction is explored in greater detail in the following chapter: while the Father–Son relation is intrinsic and necessary to divinity, the God–creation relation is extrinsic and contingent.[28] The term *homoousios* was introduced to 'collect the sense of the Scriptures' by fastening the meaning of 'from the essence' by an unequivocal affirmation of the continuity of divinity between Father and Son.[29]

Athanasius elucidates the meaning of the connection between *homoousios* and 'from the essence of the Father' by using the analogy of light and its radiance to clarify that the relation of the Father and Son is intrinsic to the divine being:

24 Athanasius, *Defence Against the Arians*, 21.
25 Ibid. 19, 22; *Synods*, 34.
26 Athanasius, *Defence Against the Arians*, 19.
27 Ibid. 20.
28 Athanasius, *Opinions*, 22.
29 Athanasius, *Defence Against the Arians*, 20.

> the Word [is not] related to God as fire kindled from the heat of the sun, which is commonly put out again, for this is an external work and a creature of its author, but they all preach of Him as Radiance, thereby to signify His being from the essence, proper and indivisible, and His oneness with the Father. This also will secure His true unchangeableness and immutability; for how can these be His, unless He be proper Offspring of the Father's essence? For this too must be taken to confirm His identity with His own Father.[30]

The point of the term *homoousios* is to 'preserve undivided the oneness of nature and the identity of light'.[31] The continuity of the one light in both the source and its ray is parallel to the continuity of the one divinity in both Father and Son. Hilary offers a very similar assessment of the meaning of *homoousios* and articulates it in concert with divine simplicity:

> [The Son] is not the Father, but the Son begotten of Him. He is not any portion of God, but is whole God. He is not Himself the source but the image; the image of God born of God to be God. He is not a creature but is God. Not another God in the kind of His substance, but the one God in virtue of the essence of His exactly similar substance. God is not one in Person but in nature, for the Born and the Begetter have nothing different or unlike.[32]

Here Hilary begins to articulate the grammar of a trinitarian doctrine of God. The Son is not a part of God (God is not a composite of the persons) or a unique instantiation of the divine being (God is not a genus with three members of that class), like a human person is a part of humanity and a unique instantiation of humanity. The Son is the one, undivided divine being subsisting in a particular way. This mode of subsistence is determined by the relation of being eternally begotten. The Son is not distinguishable from divinity, or a modification or multiplication of divinity. Instead, the Son is the divine essence subsisting as begotten from the Father.

From this basis, in *On the Synods* Athanasius makes a significant conciliatory move. Naming Basil of Ancyra, he says that the difference between them is in their favoured terminology, not in their theological convictions:

[30] Ibid. 23.
[31] Athanasius, *Defence Against the Arians*, 24.
[32] Hilary, *Synods*, 69.

> those, however, who accept everything else that was defined at Nicaea, and doubt only about the Coessential [*homoousios*], must not be treated as enemies ... [they] mean what we mean, and dispute only about the word. For, confessing that the Son is from the essence of the Father, and not from other subsistence, and that He is not a creature nor work, but His genuine and natural offspring, and that He is eternally with the Father as being His Word and Wisdom, they are not far from accepting even the phrase, 'Coessential.'[33]

Athanasius came to the remarkable volte-face that not all who demurred regarding the specific wording of Nicaea denied the divinity of the Son. The disagreement between Athanasius and Basil was not over *whether* the Son was God, but rather over *how* to describe the divinity of the Son. Accepting that the *homoousios* has troubling associations with Paul of Samosata, which explains his potential ally's reticence to accept it,[34] Athanasius explains that in substantial matters of doctrine he and Basil of Ancyra agree: the Son is from the essence of the Father and so there is a continuity of divinity between them in which the Son is intrinsic to the divine being and is not a work extrinsic to the divine being. In this, Athanasius appears to have 'grasped a central dynamic of Basil's argument',[35] and recognized its compatibility with his own understanding of the *homoousios*. Athanasius even goes so far as to say that Basil's description of the Son as 'like in essence' means the same thing as his unmodified acceptance of the Nicene *homoousios*.[36] Similarly, Hilary observes that the different terminology used by the *homoiousios* and *homoousios* factions masks the fact that 'our opinions are the same'.[37] Both factions shared the distinction between the generation of the Son and the making of creation,[38] alongside the view that the Son is 'genuine from the Father, as Life from Fountain, and Radiance from Light'.[39] However, Athanasius maintained that *homoousios* was a better term as it did not leave the conceptual space to assert the Son participates in divinity by grace.[40] So also, Hilary: 'Is not the meaning here of the word *homoousion* that the Son is produced of the Father's nature,

33 Athanasius, *Synods*, 41.
34 Ibid. 43, 45. See also Hilary, *Synods*, 81–82, 86.
35 Ayres, *NL*, 172.
36 Athanasius, *Synods*, 41.
37 Hilary, *Synods*, 81. See also Weedman, *Trinitarian Theology*, 110–115.
38 Hilary, *Synods*, 84.
39 Athanasius, *Synods*, 42.
40 Ibid. 53–54. See also T. G. Weinandy, *Athanasius: A Theological Introduction* (Oxford: Ashgate, 2007), 77–78.

the essence of the Son having no other origin, and that both, therefore, have one unvarying essence?'[41]

The gathering momentum of rapprochement

Constantius died in the autumn of 361, bringing about a new period of flux.[42] Constantius was succeeded by Julian, who was intent on restoring pagan worship to the empire.[43] This acted as a prophylactic against the consolidation of homoian theology. Julian restored the homoiousian and homoousian bishops exiled under Constantius 'not out of mercy, but that through contention among themselves, the churches might be involved in fraternal strife, and might fail of their own rights'.[44] Among the returning bishops was Athanasius, who re-entered Alexandria in the winter of 362.[45] However, rather than causing discord, this provided the opportunity for the dissenting pro-Nicenes to begin to organize themselves.[46] Just a few weeks after his return, Athanasius held a small but significant council that made some important progress in the attempt to forge a pro-Nicene consensus.

The Council of Alexandria (362)

The purpose of the Council of Alexandria (362) was, in part, to address the ongoing rift at Antioch and clear away the terminological barriers that had frustrated efforts to establish and maintain a consensus around the Nicene confession.[47] The developments made at this council, in which it was shown that different factions could use the same word (*hypostasis*) differently but still articulate the same doctrine, would be consolidated by Basil of Caesarea over the following decade. Also, as Socrates comments, this council 'asserted the divinity of the Holy Spirit and comprehended him in the consubstantial Trinity: they also declared that the Word in being made man, assumed not only flesh, but also a soul'.[48] In this, the council both looked forward and back: it looked

---

41 Hilary, *Synods*, 84.

42 Socrates, *Ecclesiastical History*, 2.47; Sozomen, *Ecclesiastical History*, 5.1.

43 Socrates, *Ecclesiastical History*, 3.1. For Julian's policies, see Sozomen, *Ecclesiastical History*, 5.3–5, 5.16–22; Socrates, *Ecclesiastical History*, 3.11–13; Theodoret, *Ecclesiastical History*, 3.3–4; G. Bowersock, *Julian the Apostate* (Cambridge, Mass.: Harvard University Press, 1978).

44 Sozomen, *Ecclesiastical History*, 5.5; Theodoret, *Ecclesiastical History*, 3.1.

45 Sozomen, *Ecclesiastical History*, 5.6; Socrates, *Ecclesiastical History*, 3.4. Fairbairn and Reeves, *SCC*, 68; Ayres, *NL*, 168–169; Hall, *Doctrine and Practice*, 148.

46 Ayres, *NL*, 170.

47 Socrates, *Ecclesiastical History*, 3.7.

48 Ibid.

forward to the coming transition of the dispute to the question of the divinity of the Spirit,[49] and it looked back to the old Lucianite proposition that the Son did not assume a full humanity, whereby his limitations could be ascribed not to his humanity but to his attenuated divinity.[50] Another significant question was over the propriety of *ousia*-language in theology. Socrates records that the council were mindful of the arguments against it but reaffirmed its usage, so best to defend the divinity of the Son and Spirit.[51]

Two documents that emerged from this council survive. The *Catholic Epistle* records the modest conditions the Council set for restoring communion with bishops who had been coerced to give assent to the confession of Constantinople (360), which was a doctrinal affirmation that the Son and Spirit, as God, cannot be creatures.[52] As Ayres points out, these modest requirements for reconciliation suggest that by 362 Athanasius had become increasingly aware that for a consensus to form around the Nicene confession, its interpretation would need to be spacious enough to receive a variety of theological emphases.[53]

> The symbol of our faith [is this: that] the Trinity [is] of one essence (*homoousios hē trias*), [that] true God became man of Mary. Whoever does not agree is anathematized. For this is what is intended by the letter of the great Council of Nicaea: that the Son is of one essence [*homoousios*] with the Father and the Spirit is co-glorified with the Father and the Son; that, true God, the Son of God became flesh.[54]

In defiance of the confession of Constantinople (360), this statement reaffirms the Nicene confession along with its controversial term *homoousios*. Importantly, however, it pairs this contentious Nicene watchword with an explicit affirmation of the three divine persons.

An example of Athanasius' growing tolerance of different theological terminology used in continuity with the Nicene confession comes in the *Tome to the Antiochenes*, the second document associated with the Council of Alexandria. In this letter, for the first time Athanasius accepts that the proposition that God has three hypostases does not imply three hierarchically differentiated entities,

49 Recorded in Sozomen, *Ecclesiastical History*, 3.22.

50 This also pertains to the growing problem of Apollinarius' Christology, which falls outside the parameters of this study. Here we are interested in a denial of the human soul of Christ in as much as it pertains to a denial of his full divinity. Apollinarius held a similar doctrine in such a way that maintained the Son as *homoousios* to the Father.

51 Socrates, *Ecclesiastical History*, 3.7.

52 Behr, *NF*, 97.

53 Ayres, *NL*, 173.

54 Athanasius, *The Catholic Epistle*. Cited from Behr, *NF*, 97.

but that it can refer to the one God's subsisting as Father, Son and Spirit.[55] This letter is so significant, Behr suggests, that it 'lays the foundation for the theological rapprochement that was to be accomplished in the following decades'.[56]

The broader context for this diplomatic letter is the long-standing factionalism in the episcopal area of Antioch with different factions supporting different episcopal claimants,[57] Paulinus and Meletius, both of whom were sympathetic to the Nicene confession.[58] Athanasius appeals for the groups to reconcile on their shared commitment to the Nicene confession, requiring them also to 'reject the proposition that the Holy Spirit is a Creature and separate from the Essence of Christ'.[59] Significantly, Athanasius also requires the recipients to give a joint statement against the doctrine that the Father, Son and Spirit are different names of one indivisible reality. In this way, Athanasius describes the Nicene confession as teaching both the unity of being of the Father, Son and Spirit alongside their personal distinction.[60]

With respect to the terminological development that would facilitate a pro-Nicene consensus, the most significant aspect of this document is the clarity it brings to the meaning of *hypostasis*. One cause of division in Antioch was the different ways in which this word was used. The group who supported Meletius were in the practice of speaking of three hypostases, while those who followed Paulinus used *hypostasis* as a synonym for *ousia* and so recognized only one *hypostasis*.[61] In many ways, this dispute gets to the heart of the problem facing the development of a pro-Nicene consensus. The homoiousian faction were fiercely antagonistic to any suggestion of Marcellian doctrine and so backed Meletius, whose mode of expression better reflected their own convictions. Meanwhile, there remained a group, including Athanasius, who continued to believe that describing God as one *hypostasis* was a necessary prophylactic against tritheism or Arianism and so supported Paulinus.

Athanasius records a conversation in which he interrogated the meaning of *hypostasis* among the Meletian faction. He put to them a number of possible meanings of this term including ontological gradation, material division and

55 Ayres, *NL*, 174.

56 Behr, *NF*, 99.

57 See Socrates, *Ecclesiastical History*, 5.5.

58 See ibid. 3.6, 9. For a study of Meletius of Antioch and his position in the complex field of fourth-century theology and ecclesial politics, see B. D. Daley, 'The Enigma of Meletius of Antioch', in R. J. Rombs and A. Y. Hwang (eds.), *Tradition and the Rule of Faith in the Early Church: Essays in Honor of Joseph T. Lienhard* (Washington, D.C.: Catholic University of America Press, 2010), 128–150.

59 Athanasius, *Tome to the Antiochenes*, 3, NPNF II.4.

60 Behr, *NF*, 97–98.

61 For the Marcellian legacy behind this miahypostatic theology, see Lienhard, '*Ousia* and *Hypostasis*', 107–110.

tritheism, asking what they meant by it.[62] The answer returned was acceptable to Athanasius, describing their meaning as asserting the distinct subsistence in reality (not only conceptually) of the Father, Son and Spirit:

> they believed in a Holy Trinity, not a trinity in name only, but existing and subsisting in truth, 'both a Father truly existing and subsisting, and a Son truly substantial and subsisting, and a Holy Spirit subsisting and really existing do we acknowledge,' and that neither had they said there were three Gods or three beginnings, nor would they at all tolerate such as said or held so, but that they acknowledged a Holy Trinity but One Godhead, and one Beginning, and that the Son is coessential with the Father, as the fathers said; while the Holy Spirit is not a creature, nor external, but proper to and inseparable from the Essence of the Father and the Son.[63]

Athanasius records a similar process of inquiry into the meaning of those who recognized only one *hypostasis*:

> we made enquiry of those blamed by them for speaking of One Subsistence [*hypostasis*], whether they use the expression in the sense of Sabellius, to the negation of the Son and the Holy Spirit, or as though the Son were non-substantial, or the Holy Spirit impersonal. But they in their turn assured us that they neither meant this nor had ever held it, but 'we use the word Subsistence thinking it the same thing to say Subsistence or Essence [*ousia*];' 'But we hold that there is One, because the Son is of the Essence of the Father, and because of the identity of nature. For we believe that there is one Godhead, and that it has one nature, and not that there is one nature of the Father, from which that of the Son and of the Holy Spirit are distinct.' Well, thereupon they who had been blamed for saying there were three Subsistences agreed with the others, while those who had spoken of One Essence, also confessed the doctrine of the former as interpreted by them.[64]

Athanasius' intention was to demonstrate that the two groups were articulating the same doctrine while using the available terminology in opposite ways. The content of their belief was that there is one God who subsists without

62 Athanasius, *Tome to the Antiochenes*, 5.
63 Ibid.
64 Ibid. 7.

multiplication or division as Father, Son and Spirit, but this doctrinal agreement was masked by their contrasting use of the term *hypostasis*.[65] Hanson's assessment is instructive: '[Athanasius] had signalled to his followers that *ousia* and *hypostasis* could be used in different senses, that it was possible to speak of *three hypostases* in an orthodox sense'.[66] For this reason, the *Tome to the Antiochenes* represents a significant step forward in terminological clarity and for the possibility of rapprochement with the homoiousian faction, demonstrating that advocates of the *homoousios* were not following the doctrine of Marcellus. However, as will be shown by the ongoing problems the Antiochene schism caused, despite Basil of Caesarea's efforts to strengthen communion with the West, personal and relational difficulties remained a significant inhibiting factor.

The councils of Antioch (363) and Lampascus (365)

After his death in 363,[67] Julian was succeeded by Jovian, whose support for Athanasius[68] led to the calling of a small council in Antioch. This attracted the apparently ever-vacillating Acacius of Caesarea to support the *homoousios*.[69] Along with the support of Basil of Ancyra, the council reaffirmed the Nicene confession and wrote of this decision to the emperor:

> we embrace and steadfastly hold the faith of the holy Synod formerly convened at Nicaea. Especially since the term *homoousios*, which to some seems novel and inappropriate, has been judiciously explained by the fathers to denote that the Son was begotten of the Father's substance, and that he is like the Father as to substance. Not indeed that any passion is to be understood in relation to that ineffable generation . . . it has been employed for the subversion of what Arius impiously dared to assert concerning Christ, *viz.* – that he was made of things 'not existing.' Which heresy the Anomoeans, who have lately sprung up, still more audaciously maintain, to the utter destruction of ecclesiastical unity.[70]

To the letter is appended the Nicene confession. It is significant that this letter recognizes and excludes the familiar negative associations of *homoousios* and

65 Anatolios, *RN*, 23.

66 Hanson, *SCDG*, 644.

67 Socrates, *Ecclesiastical History*, 3.21; Sozomen, *Ecclesiastical History*, 6.1–2; Theodoret, *Ecclesiastical History*, 3.20.

68 Sozomen, *Ecclesiastical History*, 6.5. Socrates relays the power struggle in which a number of bishops from different factions attempted to influence Jovian after his ascension. Socrates, *Ecclesiastical History*, 3.24.

69 Socrates, *Ecclesiastical History*, 3.25.

70 Ibid.

affirms instead that it was only intended to 'denote that the Son was begotten of the Father's substance, and that he is like the Father as to substance'.[71] Similarly, the presence of essence language is justified as a prophylactic against ahomoian hermeneutics, echoing Athanasius' explanation that a non-scriptural term was required in order to fix the meaning of the Scriptures.[72] In this connection, Zachhuber sees this council as a significant precursor towards the development of a 'neo-Niceneism' that affirmed the continuity of divinity between the Father and Son while being explicit regarding their distinct subsistence.[73]

The sudden death of Jovian in early 364 changed the landscape yet again,[74] with the newly proclaimed emperor, Valentinian, dividing the empire again between East and West, appointing his younger brother Valens as emperor of the East. For his part, Valentinian was sympathetic to the Nicene confession,[75] which reflected the theological consensus among Western bishops. Valens, like Constantius, saw the homoian creed of Constantinople 360 as the best ground on which to secure a broad consensus.[76] However, there are some suggestions that, given the strongly subordinationist bias of the homoian confessions of the late 350s, Valens himself was positively inclined to such a way of thinking.[77] For example, Socrates describes him as an Arian,[78] and, during his imperial reign, Eunomius was appointed Bishop of Cyzius[79] and a series of other measures were taken against those who adhered to the *homoousios*.[80]

However, underneath the sheen of homoian ascendency in the East, the homoiousian faction continued to meet in a succession of councils in 364 and 365.[81] A particularly significant example of this took place in Lampascus in 365, at which the Second Creed of the Dedication Council was affirmed and the Creed of Constantinople (360) was condemned.[82] The decision of the homoiousian faction to affirm the Creed of the Second Dedication Council indicates that

71 Ibid.

72 See also Behr, *NF*, 100.

73 J. Zachhuber, 'The Antiochene Synod of 363 and the Beginnings of Neo-Nicenism', *ZAC* 4 (2000), 83–101, at 85.

74 Socrates, *Ecclesiastical History*, 3.26.

75 Theodoret presents Valentinian as a champion of the pro-Nicene cause. Theodoret, *Ecclesiastical History*, 4.8–9.

76 For the pragmatic character of Valens' leadership, see Ayres, *NL*, 169–170. For a summary of Valens' pro-homoian policies, see Hanson, *SCDG*, 791–792.

77 Theodoret attributes this to the influence of Eudoxius and the wife of Valens. Theodoret, *Ecclesiastical History*, 4.11.

78 Socrates, *Ecclesiastical History*, 4.1–3.

79 Ibid. 4.7; Sozomen, *Ecclesiastical History*, 6.13.

80 Socrates, *Ecclesiastical History*, 4.8–9, 17, 21; Theodoret, *Ecclesiastical History*, 4.12.

81 Sozomen, *Ecclesiastical History*, 4.14.

82 Socrates, *Ecclesiastical History*, 4.4.

behind the division between the homoiousians and heterousians lay a deeper rift within the Eusebian faction along the lines of a participatory or otherwise account of image-Christology that reached back to the differences between Eusebius of Nicomedia and Eusebius of Caesarea. A faction remained within the Eastern bishops for whom the image-Christology of the Second Creed of the Dedication Council was most closely reflective of their convictions. From this ongoing unease in the East with the homoian theological settlement, there was growing awareness that an alliance with the pro-Nicenes would be the only way to secure the confessional account of the continuity of divinity between Father and Son. So, a delegation was sent west to Rome to seek the support of Emperor Valentinian and Liberius of Rome. The letter carried by this delegation proclaims their adherence to the 'catholic faith which was established in the holy council at Nicaea', affirming the inclusion of the *homoousios* in opposition to Arius.[83] The 325 confession of Nicaea is appended to the letter as a doctrinal statement reflective of its authors' convictions. Liberius' reply, which reaffirmed the supremacy of the Nicene 325 confession over all the subsequent doctrinal statements, was read out at the Council of Tyana in 366 alongside a formal endorsement of the Nicene Creed. However, the plans for Western and Eastern delegations to form a council in Sicily were blocked by Valens.[84] While this is insufficient to infer universal support for the Nicene confession among the homoiousian bishops,[85] it indicates that dissenters from the homoian ascendency recognized the Nicene confession as having a greater level of overlap with their own views, particularly with regard to a constitutive image-Christology.

Despite the changing political situation, significant theological developments had been made by 365, which set the foundation for the subsequent pro-Nicene consensus. The *homoousios* had been described in such a way that it was inseparable from the Son's generation from the essence of the Father. As such, it had been associated as a clarification on the doctrine shared by Athanasius, Hilary and Basil of Ancyra: that the Son's generation is intrinsic to divine being and as such is incomprehensible, beyond material associations (meaning the Son is absolute being as the Father is absolute being). Moreover, by aligning the *homoousios* with this, the significance of the generation of the Son as the ground of the continuity of divinity between the Father and Son was made more explicit. Pro-*homoousios* bishops had acknowledged the negative associations of the term and taken steps to ameliorate the concerns of the homoiousian

83 This letter and Liberius' reply is recorded in Socrates, *Ecclesiastical History*, 4.12. See also Sozomen, *Ecclesiastical History*, 6.11.

84 Socrates, *Ecclesiastical History*, 4.12; Sozomen, *Ecclesiastical History*, 6.12.

85 Ayres, *NL*, 170.

faction. Beyond this, a terminological basis was beginning to emerge by which the identity of essence between the Father and Son could be held alongside their real distinct subsistence. The stage was set for Basil of Caesarea.

Basil of Caesarea and the mechanics of a pro-Nicene consensus (359–78)

Basil of Caesarea was born in *c.*329 to a wealthy Christian family from whom he received a classical Hellenic education (grammar, rhetoric and philosophy).[86] He received the highest-quality education in these fields first in Constantinople (348/349) and then in Athens (355/356). Basil deployed this philosophical foundation to great effect in developing a coherent terminological framework acceptable to a range of different theological priorities. He was deacon to Basil of Ancyra at the Council of Constantinople in 360,[87] and, at that point, shared his master's preference for the description of the Son as like the Father according to essence. Basil was horrified when senior figures, such as Dianius of Caesarea, signed the confession of that council.

Disenchanted, Basil retreated from public activity to the ascetic life.[88] He would be drawn back to public office in 362 to assist Eusebius – the successor to Dianius – a role in which Basil excelled in both theological and administrative capacities (particularly during the famine of 369).[89] Basil, then, entered his ecclesial duties at around the time of the Council of Antioch (363) and so 'it is in the milieu of homoiousians allying themselves with the Nicenes' that we must locate Basil.[90] However, Basil was always characterized by a sensitivity to and aversion against modalism, which is indicative of his theological upbringing within a homoiousian perspective.[91]

Basil succeeded Eusebius in 370 and would prove to be a formidable bishop, who applied his significant theological, philosophical, political and personal qualities to the articulation and development of an alliance around a pro-Nicene theology. He exerted significant energy in establishing a theological consensus with the church in the West. Indeed, there seemed to be a solid

86 For what this would involve, see W. Jaeger, *Early Christianity and Greek Paideia* (London: Oxford University Press, 1961).

87 Socrates, *Ecclesiastical History*, 4.26.

88 Basil, *Ep*, 8–9.

89 Theodoret, *Ecclesiastical History*, 4.16.

90 Radde-Gallwitz, *Guide to His Life*, 62.

91 Christopher Beeley detects this sensitivity most clearly in Basil's pneumatology, which may account for why he preferred to speak of the Spirit as classified with the Father and Son, and existing with them in the community of being, over and above a clear affirmation of the Spirit as *homoousios* to the Father. C. Beeley, 'The Holy Spirit in the Cappadocians: Past and Present', *MT* 26.1 (2010), 95–116, at 93–94.

possibility of such a consensus being formed given Damasus of Rome's (who succeeded Liberius in 366) views. Damasus was an ardent pro-Nicene bishop, whose encyclical letter of the Council of Rome (368) adopts an explicitly Nicene formulation of the Father–Son relation.[92] For six years (371–7) Basil made several unsuccessful attempts to capitalize on this theological agreement.[93] Basil's efforts to strengthen communion with the West over a shared Nicene faith were made more complicated by the disputed episcopal see in Antioch, as Basil and Damasus supported different claimants. Basil supported Meletius,[94] while Damasus supported Paulinus,[95] whom Basil suspected of sympathy with Marcellus' doctrine of one divine reality.[96] This was not aided by an apparent mutual dislike between Basil and Damasus.[97]

However strained these interactions were, and however much the attempt to forge a pro-Nicene consensus was hampered by ongoing factional disputes, the theological compatibility of the prevailing theology in Rome and the pro-Nicene bishops of the East eventually prevailed. The Council of Rome (378) produced the *Tome of Damasus*, which is a catalogue of theological propositions the church in the West recognized were in error.[98] These included clear condemnations of Arius, Sabellius, Eunomius, Photinus and those who denied the divinity of the Spirit (the 'Macedonians'). Alongside this list, the *Tome of Damasus* makes a series of positive propositions of its own, including that the Father, Son and Spirit are eternally distinct and not only in God's mode of relation to creation.[99] As tortuous as it was, then, Basil's efforts with the West did lead to a document that would dispel many of the concerns held in the East that Latin theology was orientated to smudging the distinctions between the Father, Son and Spirit. Basil died in the late 370s, before the validation of the pro-Nicene consensus he was so influential in forming at Constantinople in 381. However, by the time of his death, he had provided a robust terminological framework for trinitarian doctrine, which it is the primary purpose of this section to describe.[100]

---

92 Theodoret, *Ecclesiastical History*, 2.22.

93 The four stages of these attempts are documented in Hanson, *SCDG*, 797–800. See also Ayres, *NL*, 224–229, and Behr, *NF*, 104–117.

94 Basil's letters to Meletius: *Epp*, 57, 68, 89, 120, 129, 216.

95 See Hanson, *SCDG*, 801–802, for a discussion of this dispute.

96 Basil, *Ep*, 263. Basil's role in the Antiochene schism is set out in Radde-Gallwitz, *Guide to His Life*, 133–136. On Basil's absolute opposition to the continued use of one *hypostasis* as part of his attempts to differentiate Nicene theology from Marcellian theology, see Lienhard, '*Ousia* and *Hypostasis*', 118–119.

97 Basil, *Ep*, 239, in which Basil describes Damasus as arrogant.

98 Recorded in Theodoret, *Ecclesiastical History*, 5.11.

99 See also Behr, *NF*, 116–117.

100 For biographical details, see Hildebrand, *Trinitarian Theology of Basil*, 18–29; Radde-Gallwitz, *Guide to His Life*, 22–42, 90–107.

Basil's changing attitude to the *homoousios*

Basil's early writings indicate that his thought was undergoing significant development through the 360s.[101] This personal intellectual development was central to the formation of a pro-Nicene consensus in that it contributed to the development of a terminological basis able to describe the continuity of divinity between the Father and Son in a way that is compatible with the distinct subsistence of the three.[102] In the midst of the councils of Neo-Arian ascendency (359), Basil – a member of the homoiousian faction – wrote to the influential advocate of *homoousios* Apollinarius to ask what he meant by his use of the controversial term.[103] Basil laid out in philosophical terms some theologically untenable meanings that could feasibly fall within the conceptual area defined by the word *homoousios*:

> Please give us a full discussion of the actual *homoousion* . . . What meaning does it bear? In what healthy sense can it be applied to objects as to which one can conceive no common genus transcending them, no material substratum pre-existing them, and no partition of the original to make the second. Pray distinguish for us fully in what sense we ought to call the Son of one substance with the Father without falling into any of the above notions.[104]

If *homoousios* means an abstract genus or a material substratum, then it is unacceptable because it would suggest that there is in some sense an impersonal divine essence preceding the Father, Son and Spirit in relation to which the Father, Son and Spirit share a common relation. If *homoousios* means the partition of the divine essence into distinct individuals, then it is equally unacceptable because the divine essence is not divisible.

Basil's questions do not indicate resistance to the idea that there is a continuity of divinity between the Father and Son, but rather to an uncertainty that *homoousios* is the best term to communicate that continuity. Basil goes on to explain his view as it was in 359, explaining that 'whatever one takes the substance [*ousia*] of the Father to be in basic reality, one is entirely bound to take the substance [*ousia*] of the Son to be that too'.[105] This is part of Basil's

101 Ayres, *NL*, 189.
102 Anatolios, *RN*, 23–26.
103 Basil of Caesarea, *Letter to Apollinarius of Laodicea*, tr. G. L. Prestige, *St Basil of Caesarea and Apollinaris of Laodicea* (London: SPCK, 1956).
104 Ibid.
105 Ibid.

standard homoiousian way of conceptualizing the likeness in essence through the divine procession of generation.[106] As part of this, he denies that this is best described by *homoousios* on the grounds that it would undermine the distinct subsistence of Father and Son, indicating his live anti-Marcellian concern.[107] For this reason they 'should rightly be described as precisely and undeviatedly similar in substance'.[108]

Apollinarius' response recognizes Basil's caution, clarifying that he does not mean any of the unsatisfactory notions Basil listed. Instead, in terms similar to those encountered with Athanasius and Hilary, he describes the Son as sharing in the divine nature *because he is begotten from the Father.* In other words, the divine nature is not some supra-personal reality, but is identified with the Father, who communicates it to the Son.[109] This does not, Apollinarius continues, mean the Father has become divided, as if he were some material entity, 'but the Son has come forth as a ray out of the Father's'.[110] For this reason, Apollinarius judges Basil's suggestion of 'similar in essence' to be unsatisfactory as it does not do justice to the unique character of being begotten from the Father's essence.[111] The designation of the Son as 'like' the Father in essence is simply not strong enough to convey the exact continuity between Father and Son.

Whether or not Apollinarius' letter was the primary catalyst for Basil's change of mind is not known. However, just one year later (360), Basil uses the mode of reasoning he learnt from Apollinarius in defence of the designation of the Son as *homoousios* to the Father:[112]

> We in accordance with the true doctrine speak of the Son as neither like, nor unlike, the Father . . . We, on the contrary, confess identity of nature and accepting the consubstantiality [*homoousios*] . . . God in substance, Who begat the Son, God in substance. From this the consubstantiality is proved. For God in essence or substance is co-essential or consubstantial with God in essence or substance.[113]

---

[106] Ayres, *NL*, 190.

[107] See ibid. Zachhuber has argued that Basil's concern here is not with Marcellian theology but with the notion of two distinct ultimate principles, following Eusebius of Caesarea's line of criticism. J. Zachhuber, *Human Nature in Gregory of Nyssa: Philosophical Background and Theological Significance* (Leiden: E. J. Brill, 2014), 25–28. This is very possible.

[108] Basil, *Ep*, 361. For this reason, Giulea is correct to describe the early Basil as receptive to a homoiousian position that asserted the continuity of divinity. D. A. Giulea, 'Basil of Caesarea's Authorship of *Ep*. 361 and His Relationship with the Homoiousians Reconsidered', *VC* 72 (2018), 41–70.

[109] Apollinarius of Laodicea, *Letter to Basil of Caesarea*, tr. G. L. Prestige, *St Basil of Caesarea and Apollinarius of Laodicea* (London: SPCK, 1956).

[110] Apollinarius, *Letter to Basil*.

[111] Ibid.

[112] See also Hildebrand, *Trinitarian Theology of Basil*, 76–82.

[113] Basil, *Ep*, 8, 3.

This is a pointed rejection of the Constantinopolitan confession of 360, which attempted to unite factions under the description of the Son as like the Father. Significantly, in another letter Basil argues that the terms *homoiousios* and *homoousios* conveyed the same meaning: 'the phrase "like in essence", if it be read with the addition "without any difference", I accept as conveying the same sense as the *homoousion*'.[114] Significantly, he draws on correlation of the continuity of the divinity between the Father and Son and the relation of begetting, parsing this using the familiar motif of light: 'it is impossible for anyone to entertain the idea of variableness of light in relation to light . . . or of the essence of the only begotten in relation to that of the Father'.[115]

Some ten years after this, in a canonical letter from the beginning of his episcopacy, Basil promoted the Nicene confession as the standard of orthodox teaching, with the proviso that it was supplemented by a statement about the divinity of the Spirit (more on which below).[116] This indicates a completed transition in Basil's thought, where he has left behind the language of *homoiousios* in favour of *homoousios*. However, Basil's instinctive sensitivity to a Marcellian interpretation of *homoousios* remained. In this connection, Basil attempts to clear away some of the misunderstandings around the term *homoousios*. First, he argues that this term does not mean the Father and Son are derived from some anterior impersonal essence (using the example of coins from a lump of bronze), for this would be to identify that the divine essence is logically prior to the Father, and it would establish the Father and Son as brothers, commonly descended from something else.[117] Instead, he reminds his readers that the Nicene confession employed this term to refute Arius' teaching:

> For after saying that the Son was light of light, and begotten of the substance of the Father, but was not made, they went on to add the *homoousion*, thereby showing that whatever proportion of light any would attribute in the case of the Father will obtain also in that of the Son . . . Since then the Father is light without beginning, and the Son is begotten light, but each of them light and light; they rightly said 'of one substance' in order to set forth the equal dignity of the nature.[118]

---

114 Ibid. 9.3.
115 Ibid.
116 Ibid. 52.
117 Ibid. 52.1.
118 Ibid. 52.2.

Basil also challenged the assertion that *homoousios* was tantamount to modalism. Instead, he argued that distinct subsistence belonged to the very logic of the designation 'for nothing can be of one substance with itself, but one thing is of one substance with another'.[119] For this reason, he observes that '[*homoousios*] has an excellent and orthodox use, defining as it does both the proper character of the *hypostases*, and setting forth the invariability of their nature'.[120]

Against Eunomius

Basil's early major theological work *Against Eunomius* (written in 364 or 365) addresses Eunomius' argument that the property of unbegotten is coextensive with the divine essence, with the implication that the Father alone is God. From his changing attitude towards the meaning of *homoousios* described above, we know that Basil was, by this point, active in defending the designation of the Son as identical in essence to the Father and the associated doctrine that the Son was from the essence of the Father. In other words, this text was written as by 'a supporter of the Nicene faith'.[121] In his response, Basil lays out that which is held in common between the Father, Son and Spirit and that which distinguishes them. This early theological work does not contain the terminological precision for which he is best remembered, but the force of Basil's argumentation lays the conceptual groundwork of his later terminological precision. Basil organizes several arguments against Eunomius.

First, against the proposition that unbegotten is the definition of divinity whereby the begotten Son cannot be divine,[122] Basil argues thought about God must be conducted with the proper epistemological humility in which created being is unable to comprehend fully the divine.[123] We do not know one property of God that is identical with his essence, but rather Scripture provides us with a plurality of titles and terms by which to think about God.[124] It is on this basis that it is appropriate to affirm the role of *conceptualization* (*epinoia*) in theology. By conceptualization, Basil meant the mental act by which humans develop a pattern of thought to discern something about the reality that is external to their thought, 'a sort of conceptual portrait painting'.[125] Theological concepts, therefore, are not coterminous with divine being, as indicated by the fact that

119 Ibid. 52.3.
120 Ibid.
121 Radde-Gallwitz, *Guide to His Life*, 57.
122 Basil, *AE*, 1.5, 16.
123 Ibid. 1.14. See also DelCogliano, *Anti-Eunomian Theory of Names*, 136–138.
124 See Radde-Gallwitz, *Transformation of Divine Simplicity*, 113–142.
125 Basil, *AE*, 1.6.

God's being is simple and thus incomposite, but we have a variety of different words we can attribute to God:[126]

> there is not one name which encompasses the entire nature of God ... Rather, there are many diverse names and each one contributes, in accordance with its own meaning, to a notion that is altogether dim and trifling as regards the whole but that is at least sufficient for us.[127]

They are useful in giving structure to our apprehension of God,[128] but God is not a concept. We have a variety of mental constructs about God, but none is identical with the divine essence; instead, they are modes of thought that give us some insight into who God is and his orientation to us.[129] In this way, Basil establishes some '"mental space" between name and referent',[130] which undermined the central heteroousian claim that the term 'unbegotten' was coterminous with the divine essence. Basil, with his presentation of conceptualization, would not allow any one term to have exhaustive explanatory power for the divine essence.

Second, on the strength of the first argument, Basil rejects Eunomius' claim that 'unbegotten' is the single authoritative designation for God, with its obvious implications for the Son who is begotten.[131] The term 'unbegotten', Basil argued, is just one of the terms available to us in our conceptual portrait painting, 'just as incorruptible is the name we give him because his life is without an end, so too is unbegotten the name given because his life is without a beginning'.[132] In part, Basil's arguments run in parallel to those of Athanasius on this issue (see chapter 7)[133]: 'unbegotten' is not a scriptural name and it is better to use the name 'Father', which implies the correlate relation of 'Son'.[134]

---

126 Ibid. 1.7.

127 Ibid. 1.10, 15.

128 See the helpful discussion in Ayres, *NL*, 191–198.

129 See also Radde-Gallwitz, *Transformation of Divine Simplicity*, 143–174. See also DelCogliano, *Anti-Eunomian Theory of Names*, 144–147, 169–171.

130 DelCogliano, *Anti-Eunomian Theory of Names*, 185.

131 M. V. Anastos, 'Basil's *Against Eunomius*: A Critical Analysis', in P. J. Fieldwick (ed.), *Basil of Caesarea: Christian, Humanist, Ascetic* (Toronto: Pontifical Institute of Medieval Studies, 1981), 67–136, at 94.

132 Basil, *AE*, 1.7.

133 The suggestion that Basil was heavily dependent on Athanasius has been challenged in recent scholarship. See Ayres, *NL*, 221; Hildebrand, *Trinitarian Theology of Basil*, 80, n. 10; DelCogliano and Radde-Gallwitz, 'Introduction', in *Against Eunomius*, tr. M. DelCogliano and A. Radde-Gallwitz (Washington, D.C.: Catholic University of America Press, 2011), 63–64. However, both in his arguments against the unique priority of the designation 'unbegotten' and in his exegetical procedure of correlate names there is significant overlap with Athanasius' thought. See M. DelCogliano, 'The Influence of Athanasius and the Homoiousians on Basil of Caesarea's Decentralization of "Unbegotten"', *JECS* 19.2 (2011), 197–223.

134 DelCogliano, 'Primacy of the Name', 57–68.

Therefore, far from being the definitive designation for God, 'unbegotten' is actually a restrictive term of reference in that it cloaks the relationality of divine being:

> The term 'Father' means the same as 'unbegotten', yet it has the additional advantage of implying a relation, thereby introducing the notion of the Son. For the one who is really Father is the only one who is from no other, and being 'from no one' is the same as being 'unbegotten'. Accordingly, we should not designate him the 'unbegotten' instead of 'Father', at least if we are not going to claim a wisdom superior to the teachings of the Saviour.[135]

Basil, consistent with a theological trajectory that runs from Origen through Alexander and to Athanasius, holds that divine perfection is constituted by the eternal Fatherhood of God: 'if being Father is good and fitting to the blessedness of God, how is that which is fitting for him not present from the beginning'.[136] Basil's argumentation is also concerned to defend the absolute character of the divine being. For Basil, however, this is not compromised by identifying the Son as identical in essence to the Father; it is compromised by suggesting that the being of God may be modified by the bringing into existence of the Son. Eunomius' formulation implies that Fatherhood is a modification of the unbegotten, suggesting that the unbegotten undergoes change and enrichment. In other words, the central appeal of Eunomius' theology – its insistence on the absolute and uncaused God – is not what it appears.

Basil's argument for the priority of the Father also proceeds along philosophical lines as he builds on his defence of conceptualization in theology. The term 'unbegotten' is not the definition of the divine essence, but is a human concept devised to refer to the difference between divine being and created being: strictly, that created being has a beginning and divine being does not.[137] Therefore, the term 'unbegotten' does not tell us what God is. Instead, it is the 'denial of what is incongruous with him',[138] by drawing a contrast between divine being and created being. Therefore, it is intended to delimit the divine being from created being rather than to give any positive account of its internal constitution or character. It is at this point that Basil's line of argument intersects with Athanasius': divine being is demarcated by negating the property of having

135 Basil, *AE*, 1.5.
136 Ibid. 2.12.
137 Ibid. 1.7.
138 Ibid. 1.10.

come into being, which is proper to created being alone.[139] On the other hand, positive knowledge of God is possible: Basil points to the scriptural designation of the Son as the image of the Father, through whom the Father is made known, continuing the polemic we have seen in Athanasius against the idea that the Son is an image unlike the Father.[140] This is a developing argument within a Nicene theological method that refuses to think of God in negative categories alone on account of the identity of essence between the Father and his Son, who is his image.

Third, having pushed the designation 'unbegotten' from its definitive position, Basil argues that there are scriptural ways of speaking about God that can be said of both the Father and the Son. The designation *light*, for example, is used of both Father and Son in different sections of Scripture. Such an overlap in scriptural designations, Basil asserts, is indicative of their 'commonality of substance' whereby the same 'formula of being' may be assigned to them.[141] That is, Scripture describes them in terms of a continuity of divinity whereby they may be spoken of in the same way as to their quiddity. Moreover, there is a unique way these designations are applied to the Father and Son, which is indicative of a certain order between them: the Father is the light and the Son the radiance. In this, Basil's line of argumentation begins to intersect once again with the idea of the continuity of being via derivation:

> It is impossible that the God of the universe has not co-existed from eternity with his image who has radiated light non-temporally . . . And so he is called the *radiance* that we may understand his connection [with the Father], and the *character of his subsistence*.[142]

As such, the Son is the radiance that eternally shines from the light that is the Father. Therefore, the Father is eternal and the 'Son is also from eternity, being connected in a begotten way to the unbegotteness of the Father'.[143]

Fourth, Basil establishes an important distinction between the essence held in common and the individuating features that differentiate it. In this way, Basil rejects the central doctrine of Eunomius, that name is identical with essence.[144] This is a central aspect of Basil's argument that the same formula of being may

139 Ibid. 1.16.
140 Ibid. 1.17–18.
141 Ibid. 1.19. See also Radde-Gallwitz, *Guide to His Life*, 67–68; Hildebrand, *Trinitarian Theology of Basil*, 160–170.
142 Basil, *AE*, 1.20; emphasis original.
143 Ibid. 2.17.
144 Radde-Gallwitz, *Transformation of Divine Simplicity*, 131–132.

be attributed to the Father and Son and yet they are distinct from each other. Basil posits the notion of individual terms of reference: names that are proper to one and not to the other. These individual terms of reference are related to the 'distinguishing marks' (*idiōmatōn*) of an individual,[145] but this individual term of reference does not refer to the essence.[146] For example, the Father and Son may be described with the same formula essence (terms that pertain to essence can be attributed to both of them), but each has distinguishing features by which they are differently named as individuals. The Father is the unbegotten source of the Son and the Son is begotten of the Father: 'begotteness and unbegotteness are distinctive features that enable identification'.[147] The Father has the property of Fatherhood and the Son the property of Sonship. These different properties are indicated by a term that is specific to that distinct, subsistent reality: 'In the case of both "Father" and "Son" the names do not communicate substance but instead are revelatory of the distinguishing marks [*idiōmatōn*].'[148] This is related to one of Basil's central theological claims: difference in names does not indicate a necessary difference in essence.[149] So, the continuity of essence is neither compromised by nor compromises personal distinction constituted by the particular relationship the Father has with the Son, and vice versa.

Basil elucidates this using the example of light, which is true of both Father and Son in different modes of existence:

> Begotten and unbegotten are distinctive features that enable identification and are observed in the substance [*ousia*], which lead to the clear and unconfused notion of the Father and the Son . . . The distinctive features, which are like certain characters and forms observed in the substance, differentiate what is common by means of the distinguishing characters . . . For example, the divinity is common, whereas fatherhood and sonship are distinguishing marks: from the combination of both, that is of the common and the unique, we arrive at a comprehension of the truth. Consequently, upon hearing 'unbegotten light' we think of the Father, whereas upon hearing 'begotten light' we receive the notion of the Son.[150]

The force of the argument is that the designation 'unbegotten' does not refer to the divine essence, but to the personal property of the Father that differentiates

145 Basil, *AE*, 2.3.
146 Ibid. 2.4.
147 Ibid. 2.29.
148 Ibid. 2.5. See also Lienhard, '*Ousia* and *Hypostasis*', 105.
149 Basil, *AE*, 2.4. See also Ayres, *NL*, 198–204.
150 Basil, *AE*, 2.28.

him from the Son and Spirit. Eunomius' error is to confuse the relative terms that pertain to the individuality of the Father, Son and Spirit with terms that pertain to the divine essence. Against this, Basil argues that there is one divine *ousia* that is beyond our knowledge, and this one divine *ousia* is common to the Father, Son and Spirit, who are differentiated from one another by their own unique property. This combination of a common essence and distinguishing features marks the basis of Basil's early trinitarian theology: the Father is God unbegotten, the Son is God begotten and the Spirit is God proceeding.[151] So, for the particular problematic of Eunomius' theology, Basil has shown that while 'ingenerate' may truly be said of God, it does not pertain to (and certainly is not identical to) the 'essence' of God. As such, it is wholly possible to attribute the terms 'unbegotten' and 'begotten' to God.[152] Here Basil anticipates what would become his clear terminological distinction between *ousia* and *hypostasis*.

Ousia and *hypostasis*

Basil's distinction between *ousia* and *hypostasis* undergirds his association between *homoousios* and the discrete reality of the three.[153] Among Basil's significant contributions is the clear distinction he drew between the common and the particular.[154] As Radde-Gallwitz puts it, 'what [Basil] develops, and bequeaths to subsequent pro-Nicene authors, is a way of classifying those terms which express the divine unity and those which express features distinctive of the persons'.[155] Basil's achievement is sometimes equated to the trinitarian formula 'one *ousia* and three hypostases' and described as the 'Cappadocian formula', a way to preserve monotheism alongside the distinct reality of the Father, Son and Spirit. However, as Lienhard has pointed out, this exact construction is rarely found in the writings of Basil and his associates Gregory of Nazianzus and Gregory of Nyssa (together known as the 'Cappadocian Fathers').[156]

One particularly good example of this distinction comes in a letter written towards the end of Basil's life (376):

151 For a fuller discussion of Basil's theory of proper names, see DelCogliano, *Anti-Eunomian Theory of Names*, 191–196.

152 See also Radde-Gallwitz, *Transformation of Divine Simplicity*, 141–142.

153 See also Hildebrand, *Trinitarian Theology of Basil*, 82–92.

154 Basil was far from pioneering this distinction in broader intellectual circles. Ayres lists five Christian sources for Basil's thought. See Ayres, *NL*, 202–204. Basil may be informed by Stoic (Hildebrand, *Trinitarian Theology of Basil*) or Aristotelian (N. Jacobs, 'On "Not Three Gods" – Again: Can a Primary-Secondary Substance Reading of *Ousia* and *Hypostasis* Avoid Tritheism', *MT* 24.3 [2008], 331–358) ways of thought.

155 Radde-Gallwitz, *Transformation of Divine Simplicity*, 169.

156 Lienhard, '*Ousia* and *Hypostasis*', 99–100.

> The distinction between the *ousia* and the *hypostasis* is the same as that between the general and the particular; as for instance between the animal and the particular man. Wherefore in the case of the Godhead, we confess one essence [*ousia*] . . . so as to not give a variant definition of existence, but we confess a particular *hypostasis*, in order that our conception of Father, Son and Holy Spirit may be without confusion and clear. If we have no distinct perception of the separate characteristics, namely fatherhood, sonship and sanctification, but form our conception of God from the general idea of existence, we cannot possibly give a sound account of our faith. We must, therefore, confess the faith by adding the particular to the common. The Godhead is common; the fatherhood particular.[157]

This way, Basil argues, it is possible to maintain the singularity of God and the plurality of the Father, Son and Spirit.[158] The *ousia*, as that which is common, may be spoken of only in the singular, but the Father, Son and Spirit are distinct from one another. In other words, God is one *ousia* and three hypostases.

It may appear that Basil's understanding of *ousia* is fulfilling exactly the role he argued against in his discussion of *homoousios*: that is, it is an anterior divine essence, a common genus shared by the Father, Son and Spirit. However, for Basil, there is no antecedent essence aside from the persons: the one divinity is communicated from the Father to the Son and Spirit. In the following passage from his *On the Spirit*, Basil explains the singularity of the divine essence with recourse to its primary association with the person of the Father:

> There is one God and Father, one Only-begotten, and one Holy Ghost. We proclaim each of the *hypostases* singly; and when count we must, we do not let an ignorant arithmetic carry us away to the idea of a plurality of Gods. For we do not count by way of addition, gradually making increase from unity to multitude . . . Worshipping as we do God of God, we both confess the distinction of the Persons and at the same time abide by the Monarchy. We do not fritter away the theology in a divided plurality, because one Form, so to say, united in the invariableness of the Godhead is beheld in God the Father, and in God the only-begotten . . . How, then, if one and one are there not two Gods? Because we speak of a king and of the king's image, and not of two kings. The majesty is not cloven in two,

157 Basil, *Ep*, 236.6.
158 See Lienhard, '*Ousia* and *Hypostasis*', 105–108.

> nor the glory divided. The sovereignty and authority over us is one, and so the doxology ascribed by us is not plural but one; because the honour paid to the image passes on to the prototype.[159]

Hypostasis, meanwhile, is defined as an individuated particular, which has its own real subsistence. In a statement of faith written in 373, Basil explains that the intended meaning of the Nicene confession had been subverted by Marcellus to deny the distinct subsistence of the three, using the *homoousion* and the synonymity of *ousia* and *hypostasis* to do so.[160] Against this, Basil writes that while the Father and Son are one essence, 'the Father [exists] in His own proper *hypostasis*, the Son in His, and the Holy Ghost in his'.[161] The distinction between the hypostases, Basil explains, is constituted by the properties that differentiate an individual as this or that.[162] In the case of the Father, Son and Spirit, the properties that delineate are the relationship each has to the other: 'the term *ousia* is common, like goodness, or Godhead, or any similar attribute; while *hypostasis* is contemplated in the special property of Fatherhood, Sonship, or the power to sanctify'.[163] The Father, Son and Spirit each have their own property that differentiates them from the others: the Father is unbegotten, the Son is begotten and the Spirit proceeds from the Father:

> The *ousia* has the same relation to *hypostasis* as the common has to the particular. Every one of us shares in existence by the common term *ousia*, and by his own properties is one such a one and such a one.[164]

The relationship between *ousia* and *hypostasis* is developed in one very significant letter written to his brother, Gregory of Nyssa.[165] For Basil, *hypostasis* as an individual carries the connotation of a concrete entity that has real subsistence.[166] Basil, for example, describes *hypostasis* as an 'existence proper and perfect in itself',[167] and not only having conceptual existence.[168] *Ousia*, meanwhile, does not have the concrete actuality that the specificity of *hypostasis*

159 Basil, *Spirit*, 44–45.
160 Basil, *Ep*, 125.1.
161 Ibid. 125.2.
162 Ibid. 38.5.
163 Ibid. 214.4.
164 Ibid.
165 Ibid. 38.
166 Ramelli, 'Trinitarian Meaning of *Hypostasis*', 312–314; Lienhard, '*Ousia* and *Hypostasis*', 120–121; Prestige, *God in Patristic Thought*, 173–178, 189.
167 Basil, *Ep*, 210.4.
168 Ibid. 210.5.

includes. This is the reason for Basil's play on words between *hypostasis* and *stasis*: '*hypostasis* is not the indefinite conception of *ousia* which, because what is signified is general, finds no standing [*stasis*], but the conception which by means of the expressed peculiarities gives standing [*stasis*] . . . to the general'.[169] In this sense Basil conceives of the common nature having subsistence in the *hypostasis*:

> Suppose we say 'a man'. The indefinite meaning of the word strikes a certain vague sense upon the ears. The nature is indicated, but what subsists and is specially and peculiarly indicated by the name is not made plain. Suppose we say 'Paul'. We set forth, by which is indicated by the name, the nature subsisting.[170]

As Zachhuber explains, 'for its concrete existence . . . nature (*ousia*) is dependent on individuals. In this sense, precisely, the latter are hypostases: they individuate the universal which without them would have no concrete existence of its own.'[171] Basil thus conceives of the one divine nature having three distinct and concrete modes of subsistence: God the Father, God the Son and God the Spirit.[172]

> In the case of the Godhead, we confess one essence . . . so as to not give a variant definition of existence but we confess a particular hypostasis, in order that our conception of Father, Son and Holy Spirit may be without confusion and clear . . . We must, therefore, confess the faith by adding the particular to the common. The Godhead is common; the fatherhood particular.[173]

Therefore, the unity of nature is not divided by appreciating the hypostatic distinction. Quite the opposite, in fact: the divine nature has existence only in its concrete subsistence as Father, Son and Spirit. Whether or not Basil's way of conceptualizing the oneness and threeness of God tends towards an idea of God as a composite of the common and particular (and so is ill at ease with the doctrine of simplicity) cannot be pursued in detail here. However, the notion

169 Ibid. 38.3. See also L. Turcescu, '*Prosōpon* and *Hypostasis* in Basil of Caesarea's *Against Eunomius* and the Epistles', *VC* 51.4 (1997), 374–395.

170 Basil, *Ep*, 38.3.

171 J. Zachhuber, 'Individuality and the Theological Debate About "*Hyopostasis*"', in A. Torrance and J. Zachhuber (eds.), *Individuality in Late Antiquity* (Farnham: Ashgate, 2014), 91–111, at 102.

172 Basil, *Ep*, 235.2.

173 Ibid. 236.6.

that the divine essence *requires* combination with the concretizing *hypostasis* implies some level of composite being, undermining the absolute primacy of divinity (as God's being appears to be dependent upon such a combination).

The Spirit

The growing significance of the question of the divinity of the Holy Spirit in the second half of the fourth century has already been indicated by the statements made at the Council of Alexandria (362) condemning the proposition that the Spirit is a creature. While Athanasius' dispute was with the *tropici* (discussed in the next chapter) Basil's was with the Macedonians, named after Macedonius of Constantinople (342–60), although the best-known exponent of this grouping was Eustathius of Sebaste, Basil's one-time mentor.[174] Given the loose association with Macedonius, the group is also known as the Pneumatomachians (the 'Spirit-Fighters').[175] The Macedonians were homoiousians with regard to the Son (the Son is like the Father according to essence) but heterousians with respect to the Spirit (the Spirit is unlike the Father according to essence).[176] As such, they did not worship the Spirit as they worshipped the Father and Son.

Notwithstanding this, Basil's earliest writings on the Spirit are part of his dispute with Eunomius. Eunomius argued that the Spirit was not divine but was rather to be thought of as a ministering spirit, who was tasked by God with teaching and sanctifying believers.[177] Basil's response pre-empts his later pneumatology: the Spirit's activity of teaching and sanctifying believers demonstrates that the Spirit is himself holy and light by nature and not by participation.[178] Basil lays out the fundamental distinction between God and creation, in which a central differentiating factor is that God is the active agent and creation the receiving agent.[179]

> It is said that there are two realities: divinity and creation, sovereignty and servitude, sanctifying power and sanctified power, that which has virtue by nature and that which achieves virtue by freewill. In which class shall we rank the Spirit? Among those who are sanctified? But he is sanctity itself. Perhaps among those who possess virtue by good deeds? But he is good by nature . . . So it is unrighteous either to say that he is our

174 Anatolios, *RN*, 25.
175 Hall, *Doctrine and Practice*, 153.
176 Socrates, *Ecclesiastical History*, 2.45.
177 Eunomius, *Apology*, 25, 27. Cited from Radde-Gallwitz, *Guide to His Life*, 81–82.
178 Ayres, *NL*, 216.
179 C. Beeley, 'The Holy Spirit in the Cappadocians: Past and Present', *MT* 26.1 (2010), 95–116, at 92–93.

> fellow-servant, as he is a leader by nature, or to number him along with the creatures, as he is counted in the divine and blessed Trinity.[180]

Basil illustrates this distinction between intrinsic and contingent possession through an analogy of iron in a fire:

> when iron is placed in the middle of fire, while it does not cease to be iron, it is nonetheless inflamed by the intense contact with the fire and admits the entire nature of fire into itself. And so in both outward appearance and activity it is transformed into fire. Likewise, the holy powers, from their communion with that which is holy by nature, possess a holiness that pervades their whole subsistence, and they become connatural with that which is holy by nature. The holy powers and the Holy Spirit differ in this regard: for the latter, holiness is nature, whereas for the former, being made holy comes from participation.[181]

Just as the fire has heat as an intrinsic property, but the hotness of the iron is contingent on its being placed in the fire, so also the Spirit has holiness as an intrinsic property but holiness of creation is contingent on the work of the Spirit. In terms later to be used by Athanasius, the Spirit is intrinsic to divinity, but creation is extrinsic and has its participation through God's kindness. Therefore, 'if holiness is the Spirit's nature, as it is for the Father and the Son, how does he have a nature that is third and foreign to theirs?'.[182]

Basil's letters also contain important comments on the divinity of the Spirit. In one, having described the Son in robustly Nicene terms as 'light from light, begotten from the *ousia* of the Father', Basil turns to the Spirit:

> The Holy Spirit, too, is numbered with the Father and the Son, because He is above creation and is ranked as we are taught by the words of the lord in the Gospel, 'Go and baptize in the name of the Father, and of the Son and of the Holy Ghost' . . . It is equally impious to reduce Him to the level of a creature, and to subordinate Him either to Son or to Father, either in time or in rank.[183]

180 Basil, *AE*, 3.2.

181 Ibid.

182 Ibid. 3.3.

183 Basil, *Ep*, 52.3. The ellipsis here marks several sentences in which Basil challenges the proposition that the Spirit is prior to the Father, corresponding to the understanding of *homoousios* that Basil is resisting here; namely, that there is some anterior divinity from which the Father and Son are commonly descended.

It should be noted that Basil did not articulate this view by explicitly describing the Spirit as God and he did not use the term *homoousios* as a way of describing the Spirit's relation to the Father. It is likely that Basil held back from doing so out of diplomatic caution: eager to establish a pro-Nicene consensus, he was minded to express his understanding of the Spirit in a way that was acceptable to a wide range of theological perspectives.[184]

Basil's views on the Spirit brought him into conflict with his one-time ascetic mentor, Eustathius of Sebaste. Eustathius was suspected by the pro-Nicene faction of not holding to the divinity of the Spirit, and Basil was under suspicion through association. Basil addressed the situation by writing a statement to be signed by him and Eustathius.[185] This doctrinal statement affirms the Nicene confession,[186] but recognizes that more needs to be said about the Spirit on account of the 'growing poison germs' that had led to his deity being denied.[187]

> They must anathematize all who call the Holy Ghost a creature, and all who so think; all who do not confess that He is holy by nature, as the Father is holy by nature, and refuse Him His place in the blessed divine nature. Our not separating Him from the Father and Son is a proof of our right mind, for we are bound to be baptized in the terms we have received and to profess belief in the terms in which we are baptized, and as we have professed belief in, so to give glory to Father, Son and Holy Ghost . . . We do not speak of the Holy Ghost as unbegotten, for we recognize one Unbegotten and one Origin of all things, the Father of our Lord Jesus Christ: nor do we speak of the Holy Ghost as begotten, for by the tradition of the faith we have been taught one Only-begotten: the Spirit of truth we have been taught proceeds from the Father and we confess Him to be of God without creation. We are also bound to anathematize all who speak of the Holy Ghost as ministerial inasmuch as they degrade Him to the rank of a creature.[188]

As with the Father–Son relation described in *Against Eunomius*, the Spirit shares the same formula of being as the Father and Son and so is to be described in the same terms. As holy in nature, the Spirit is the one who sanctifies and not the one who is sanctified. Therefore, the Spirit is to be classified with the

184 See Kelly, *ECC*, 343. See also Gregory of Nazianzus, *Or*, 31.5.
185 Recorded in Basil, *Ep*, 125.
186 Ibid. 125.2.
187 Ibid. 125.3.
188 Ibid.

Father and Son and so is to be worshipped. Basil develops his argument at this point to apply the notion of differentiation by the peculiar property of relation, with the Spirit differentiated as the one who proceeds from the Father. Like the Son, the Spirit derives from the essence of the Father, and so shares the divinity of the Father, but does so in his own specific way. Eustathius initially signed the statement but later retracted it and his personal relationship with Basil degenerated.[189]

Basil's mature theology of the Spirit is set out in his long treatise *On the Holy Spirit* (375). The catalyst for this text was a controversy surrounding his adaptation of the liturgy to ascribe glory to the Father *with* the Son *with* the Holy Spirit alongside the more traditional ascription of glory to the Father, *through* the Son, *in* the Spirit.[190] Basil sets out to demonstrate the legitimacy of worshipping the Spirit, arguing from the biblical presentation of the Spirit's activities that the Spirit is rightly classified with the Son and the Father. In other words, as Hildebrand observes, Basil 'argues from what the Spirit *does* to what he *is*'.[191] For Basil, then, the Spirit is to be classified with the Father and Son (and so glory is to be ascribed to the Spirit with the Father and Son) on the grounds that the Spirit participates in the activity of the Father and Son towards creation, operating with the principle that 'common activity demonstrates common essence'.[192] In this connection, the work of the Spirit is described as intrinsic to the work of God, in that the work of creation and salvation contain the element of perfection that is the specific work of the Spirit: 'the Spirit is third in the order of every divine action, completing and bringing to fruition what the Father accomplishes through the Son'.[193]

A particularly powerful example of this line of reasoning in Basil's *On the Holy Spirit* is the Spirit's role in illumining our minds and making the Father known through the Son. While all parties would accept the Spirit is the teacher, Basil parses this in terms of *what* the Spirit is. The Spirit is light in himself and it is in this light that we see the light of the Father in the Son:

> And when, by means of the power that enlightens us, we fix our eyes on the beauty of the image of the invisible God, and through the image are led up to the supreme beauty of the spectacle of the archetype, then . . . is with us inseparably the Spirit of knowledge, in Himself bestowing on

[189] See ibid. 99, 125, 130, 244, 266.
[190] Basil, *Spirit*, 27.68.
[191] Hildebrand, *Trinitarian Theology of Basil*, 178; emphasis original.
[192] Ayres, *NL*, 216.
[193] Ibid. 217.

> them that love of the vision of the truth the power of beholding the Image, not making the exhibition from without, but in Himself leading on to the full knowledge . . . as it is written 'in thy light shall we see light', namely by the illumination of the Spirit, 'the true light which lighteth every man that cometh into the world' . . . Thus the way of the knowledge of God lies from One Spirit through the One Son to the One Father, and conversely the natural Goodness and the inherent Holiness and the royal Dignity extended from the Father through the Only-begotten to the Spirit.[194]

Basil integrates the Spirit's role in the activity of revelation with a conception of the communication of the divinity of the Father. That is to say, the order of divine being, then, in which the glory of the Father is communicated to the Son and through the Son to the Spirit is reversed in the order of knowledge: by the Spirit, human souls are illumined to see the light of the Father in the Son:

> Just as the Father is seen in the Son, so is the Son in the Spirit. The 'worship in the Spirit' suggests the idea of the operation of our intelligence being carried on in the light . . . If you remain outside the Spirit you will not be able even to worship at all; and on your becoming in Him you will in no wise dissever Him from God any more than you will divorce light from visible objects. For it is impossible to behold the Image of the invisible God except by the enlightenment of the Spirit, and impracticable for him to fix his gaze on the Image to dissever the light from the Image, because the cause of the vision is of necessity seen at the same time as the visible objects. Thus fitly and consistently do we behold the 'Brightness of the glory' of God by means of the illumination of the Spirit, and by means of the 'Express image' we are led up to Him of whom He is the Express Image.[195]

Consolidation of Nicene ascendency

The death of Valens in the defeat suffered by the Roman army at the hands of the Goths at the battle of Adrianpole in 378 brought to an end the political ascendency of the homoian faction and also exposed Constantinople to the threat of attack.[196] The Western emperor, Gratian, who had succeeded Valentinian in 375, chose Theodosius – a military commander in his early thirties –

194 Basil, *Spirit*, 18.47.
195 Ibid. 26.64.
196 Socrates, *Ecclesiastical History*, 5.1.

as the successor of Valens in order to hold back the Goths.[197] Theodosius was immediately installed as commander of the army in the East before being proclaimed emperor in early 379. Valens' death opened the possibility of greater uniformity across the pro-Nicene West and the homoian East. To this end, in between Valens' death and Theodosius' accession, Gratian issued an edict allowing for all exiled bishops to return to their diocese, excluding only the followers of Eunomius and Photinus.[198]

The impression that a direct route to rapprochement was now open is strengthened by the Council of Antioch, called in the middle of 379. The purpose of this council was, ostensibly, to demonstrate to the new emperor that a pro-Nicene position could command a consensus both in the East and also across the two halves of the empire.[199] To this end, the *Tome of Damasus*, among other texts sent east by the Bishop of Rome, was accepted as orthodox. The council issued a statement of faith, which is now lost, but was pro-Nicene in content. It is also likely that it was this council that issued a request for Gregory of Nazianzus, the friend and theological ally of Basil of Caesarea, to be sent to Constantinople to teach pro-Nicene theology there.[200]

The opportunity for a shared theological settlement across the Eastern and Western parts of the empire was not lost on Theodosius, who, six months later, issued a pro-Nicene decree (the *Cunctos populous*). This decree indicates much about the religious policy of Theodosius. It declares Damasus of Rome (alongside Peter of Alexandria) as standard-bearers of the true faith of the church.[201] Alongside this, the edict includes the theological statement 'we should believe the sole divinity of the Father and of the Son and of the Holy Spirit within an equal majesty and an orthodox Trinity'.[202] By the end of 380, Theodosius had returned from his battles against the Goths and entered Constantinople, where the neo-Arian bishop Demophilus was deposed and Gregory of Nazianzus was installed as his successor.[203]

Gregory of Nazianzus' *Theological Orations* (380)

Following the synodal summons to Constantinople, Gregory was given a villa, where he lived and from which he taught.[204] In the summer of 380, some three

197 Ibid.; Sozomen, *Ecclesiastical History*, 7.2.

198 Socrates, *Ecclesiastical History*, 5.2; Sozomen, *Ecclesiastical History*, 7.1.

199 Behr, *NF*, 118.

200 Ibid.

201 Hanson, *SCDG*, 803–804.

202 *CT* 16.1.2. Cited from Behr, *NF*, 119.

203 Socrates, *Ecclesiastical History*, 5.6; Sozomen, *Ecclesiastical History*, 7.5.

204 See J. A. McGukin, *Gregory of Nazianzus: An Intellectual Biography* (New York: St Vladimir's Seminary Press, 2001), chs. 5–6.

or four months before his installation as Bishop of Constantinople, Gregory taught five sessions, which are known as his five *Theological Orations*. These five addresses were intended as a 'manifesto of Gregory's position' in his efforts to extend pro-Nicene theology in Constantinople,[205] and are characterized by a pronounced focus on the coherence of God's unity and plurality.

Gregory's *Theological Orations* begin with a close association between spirituality and the knowledge of God. The first discourse[206] is dominated by a consideration of the character of the theologian, whose life must be appropriate for the holy God whom he or she seeks to know.[207] So, as Gregory sets out to treat the theological substance of the *Theological Orations*, the unity and diversity of God are at the heart of this theological piety:

> let us now enter upon Theological questions, setting at the head thereof the Father, the Son, and the Holy Ghost, of Whom we are to treat; that the Father may be well pleased, and the Son may help us, and the Holy Ghost may inspire us; or rather that one illumination may come upon us from the One God, One in diversity, diverse in Unity, wherein is a marvel.[208]

As McGukin puts it, 'the apprehension of the deity, being pure spirit, is impossible for a materially based consciousness', requiring spiritual illumination.[209] Continuing the close association of spirituality and theology, Gregory uses the motif of the ascent of Sinai,[210] in which one's apprehension of the back parts of God are correlated to the incomprehensibility of the divine essence and our dependence on revelation, echoing Basil's epistemic humility in response to Eunomius:[211] 'What God is in nature and essence, no man ever yet has discovered or can discover.'[212] As is indicated in the passage cited above, the divine light can be known only through the illumination of our souls by the Spirit, who himself is light. However, this is firmly grounded Christologically

205 Ayres, *NF*, 244.

206 Gregory, *Or*, 27.

207 Ibid. 28.1. In Gregory, the Spirit is central to our epistemic connection with the Father through the Son. Gregory conceives of the Spirit as holy by nature, as the sanctifying agent, the light in which we see the light of the Father in the radiance of the Son. See C. Beeley, 'The Holy Spirit in Gregory Nazianzen: The Pneumatology of *Oration* 31', in A. B. McGowan, B. E. Daley and T. J. Gaden (eds.), *God in Early Christian Thought: Essays in Memory of Lloyd G. Patterson* (Leiden: E. J. Brill, 2009), 151–162; *Gregory of Nazianzus on the Trinity and the Knowledge of God: In Your Light We Shall See Light* (Oxford: Oxford University Press, 2013), 63–114.

208 Gregory, *Or*, 28.1.

209 J. A. McGukin, '"Perceiving Light from Light in Light" (*Oration* 31.3): The Trinitarian Theology of Saint Gregory the Theologian', *GOTR* 39.1 (1994), 7–32, at 13. See also Hanson, *SCDG*, 708–709.

210 Gregory, *Or*, 28.2.

211 Ibid. 28.3–5.

212 Ibid. 28.17.

in Gregory's vision of God that takes place with his being 'sheltered by the Rock, the Word that was made flesh for us'.[213] The inchoate trinitarian structure of Gregory's association of spirituality and theology is well drawn out in his fifth *Theological Oration*:

> The Father was the True Light which lightens every man coming into the world. The Son was the True Light which lightens every man coming into the world. The Other Comforter was the True Light which lightens every man coming into the world. Was and Was and Was, but Was One Thing. Light thrice repeated; but One Light and One God. This was what David represented to himself long before when he said, In Your Light shall we see Light. And now we have both seen and proclaim concisely and simply the doctrine of God the Trinity, comprehending out of Light (the Father), Light (the Son), in Light (the Holy Ghost).[214]

In this way, God's three-in-oneness is not ancillary to Gregory's theology, but is the precondition of our knowledge of him: the Father is the source of light, which shines to us in the Son, which we apprehend only in the light of the Spirit.

This focus on the harmony of God's unity and his plurality continues into Gregory's discussion of God's intrinsic generativity:

> Monarchy is that which we hold in honour. It is, however, a Monarchy that is not limited to one Person, for it is possible for Unity if at variance with itself to come into a condition of plurality; but one which is made of an equality of Nature and a Union of mind, and an identity of motion, and a convergence of its elements to unity – a thing which is impossible to the created nature – so that though numerically distinct there is no severance of Essence. Therefore Unity having from all eternity arrived by motion at Duality, found its rest in Trinity. This is what we mean by Father and Son and Holy Ghost. The Father is the Begetter and the Emitter; without passion of course, and without reference to time, and not in a corporeal manner. The Son is the Begotten, and the Holy Ghost the Emission.[215]

This passage interacts with earlier pro-Nicene theology in significant ways. On first glance, it may appear to be a departure from Basil of Caesarea's notion that

213 Ibid. 28.2. See also McGukin, 'Perceiving Light', 18–19.
214 Gregory, *Or*, 31.3.
215 Ibid. 29.2.

the unity of God is established on the person of the Father, who is the source of the Son and the Spirit. Here Gregory appears to describe the Godhead itself as the cause of the three.[216] There are other occasions in the *Theological Orations* in which Gregory appears to be describing the Godhead as the primal cause of the three persons.[217] However, later in the same treatise he describes the Father as the 'cause' of the Son.[218] Likewise, in other orations Gregory ascribes causality to the person of the Father alone.[219] The question of where Gregory locates the divine monarchy and his apparent inconsistency on this question has, understandably, been fertile ground for scholars to work out the puzzle of just how Gregory understood divine causality.[220]

In a study that provoked much of the recent scholarship, Meijering argued that Gregory attempted to locate the monarchy with the person of the Father, and that this is incompatible with their equality of nature. Driving this assessment is an opposition between emanation theories drawn from Plotinus' and Athanasius' doctrine of the eternal generation of the Son from the essence of the Father, which – according to Meijering – does not include a notion of causation. Meijering argues that to locate monarchy with the Father specifically is inconsistent with the equality of the Father and Son.[221] However, derivation and ontological identity are central to the logic of the Nicene confession in which the Son, as begotten from the essence of the Father, is intrinsic to the divine being and receives the divinity of the Father, maintaining their identity of essence and personal differentiation. The Son, although begotten, is God as the unbegotten Father is God. Moreover, beyond this, the proposal that Gregory

216 See also ibid. 31.14.

217 See ibid.

218 Ibid. 29.15.

219 Ibid. 29.3, 15.

220 Meyendorff considers Gregory to have meant that the Father is the cause of the divine nature. J. Meyendorff, *Byzantine Theology: Historical Trends and Doctrinal Themes* (New York: Fordham University Press, 1983), 183. Hanson, on the other hand, sees Gregory as locating the source of the Trinity in the divine nature from which persons are derived (Hanson, *SCDG*, 710). Torrance considers that the suggestion that the Son is caused by the Father implies the subordination of the Son to the Father and so considers Gregory to have held the divine nature to be the cause of the three. T. F. Torrance, *The Trinitarian Faith: The Evangelical Theology of the Ancient Catholic Church* (Edinburgh: T&T Clark, 1988), 319–322. Alternatively, Egan considers that Gregory does consider the Father the source of the Son but that this position is philosophically untenable as it requires causality to be equated to equality. J. Egan, 'Primal Cause and Trinitarian Perichoresis in Gregory Nazianzen's *Orations* 31.14', *StPatr* 27 (1993), 21–28. Cross, likewise, argues that while Gregory does sometimes teach that the Father causes the Son, he applies the term 'monarchy' to the divinity, which is common to the three. R. Cross, 'Divine Monarchy in Gregory of Nazianzus', *JECS* 14 (2006), 105–116. McGukin holds that Gregory locates monarchy with the person of the Father. McGukin, 'Perceiving Light', 27. Ayres and Behr take opposing perspectives on this question, with Ayres suggesting that Gregory might have allowed some inconsistency in his work, but that monarchy is located by him with the divine essence (Ayres, *NL*, 244–245). Behr, though, understands Gregory to locate the monarchy with the person of the Father (Behr, *NF*, 243–248).

221 Meijering, 'Doctrine of the Will', 103–113.

located the monarchy of God with the divine essence from which derive the three persons is an improbable departure from Basil's defence of the *homoousios* in that it did not imply some anterior substance from which the three were derived. It would welcome all the old accusations that the *homoousios* imposes materialist conceptions upon divine being.

In this connection, Christopher Beeley has recently offered a powerful rejoinder to Meijering, arguing that Gregory consistently locates the monarchy of God with the person of the Father and that this inclusion of derivation within the trinitarian relations is fully consistent with their identity of essence.[222] Indicative of this is an oration delivered shortly after his *Theological Orations* that includes a commissioning to teach the true faith, which he describes in the following terms:

> One God, unbegotten, the Father and One begotten Lord, his Son, referred to as 'God' when he is mentioned separately, but 'Lord' when he is named together with the Father – the first on account of the [divine] nature, the second on account of the monarchy; and One Holy Spirit, who proceeds or goes forth from the Father, 'God' to those who understand properly . . . Teach also that we must not make the Father subject to [another] source, lest we posit a 'first of the First' and thus overturn the [divine] Existence. Nor should we say that the Son or the Holy Spirit is without source, lest we take away the Father's special characteristic. For they are not without source – and yet in a sense they are without source, which is a paradox. They are not without source with respect to their cause, for they are from God even if they are not subsequent to them in time, just as light comes from the sun. But they are without source with respect to time, since they are not subject to time.[223]

Unequivocally, the monarchy of the Father is identified as essential to his personal distinction from the Son and Spirit and this is held alongside the full and equal divinity of the Son and Spirit. Both Son and Spirit are rightly described as God on the grounds that they fully receive the divine nature from the Father. The Son and Spirit are described as having a source in that their source is the

222 Beeley, *Gregory of Nazianzus*, 201–217. See also C. Beeley, 'Divine Causality and the Monarchy of God the Father in Gregory of Nazianzus', *HTR* 100.12 (2007), 205–206. See also B. Fulford '"One Conmixture of Light": Rethinking Some Modern Uses and Critiques of Gregory of Nazianzus on the Unity and Equality of the Divine Persons', *IJST* 11.2 (2009), 172–189. Fulford argues that locating divine monarchy with the Father is essential to ontological equality and maintaining the personal distinctions.

223 Gregory, *Or*, 25.15. Cited from Beeley, 'Divine Causality', 205–206.

Father and this derivation does not include a temporal or ontological interval. Driving Gregory's discussion is the logic central to the Nicene confession, which is that the Son is derived from the Father in such a way that only God can be: he is from the essence of the Father, and the divinity of the Father is communicated fully to the Son as God from God.[224] In this way, locating monarchy with the Father is foundational to Gregory's theology, for it is the basis of the oneness of God while affirming the Son and Spirit are God, for the Father fully communicates his divinity to both Son and Spirit. Moreover, it is the ground of personal differentiation, for the Father is the source, the Son is begotten and the Spirit proceeds from the Father.[225]

Locating monarchy with the Father is foundational to the Nicene logic in another way that relates to a further theological move Gregory makes in *Orations* 29.2 (cited above). Gregory is eager to describe the absolute harmony of God's unity and his plurality through God's threeness being the very expression of the perfection of the one God. In this, he continues a trajectory from earlier pro-Nicene thought regarding the movement of the Father–Son relation that is brought to rest in the Spirit. In Athanasius, as will be explored in the next chapter, the generation of the Son is parsed in terms of the expression of the Father's perfection. This duality is described by Gregory as motion as the perfection of the Father is communicated to and radiates in the Son. This motion, he suggests, is brought to rest in the Trinity. In this way, Gregory rejects the suggestion that God's triunity compromises the unity of the divine being and argues that it is its very expression as the perfection and completeness of what it is to be the one God. In this way, the sole monarchy of the Father is (1) the ground of personal differentiation as the Son and Spirit derive from him in their own respective ways, and (2) the ground of a relational construction of divine unity as the movement from the Father to the Son is brought to rest in the Spirit as the Spirit mediates the Son's return to the Father.[226] It is in these connections that Gregory developed beyond Basil in that the Spirit was not seen only as the perfecting agent of the work of God, but Gregory associated the Spirit rather with the perfection of the divine being itself, and this non-transitive identity is the basis of his work as the perfecter in God's transitive relations.[227]

224 Beeley demonstrates from a broader range of texts how Gregory consistently describes the Father as the only source of the Trinity and that this is the root of the oneness of God, the personal differentiation of the Father, Son and Spirit. Beeley, 'Divine Causality', 206–207.

225 Beeley, *Gregory of Nazianzus*, 219–221.

226 See Ayres, *NL*, 245–246.

227 Beeley, 'Holy Spirit', 100.

The Creed of Constantinople, 381

The context for Gregory's thought and work in Constantinople was Theodosius' own growing commitment to a pro-Nicene policy. Following his pro-Nicene *Cunctos populous*, Theodosius issued a further edict (*Nullis haereticis*) at the beginning of 381 in which 'heretics' were excluded from worship in the buildings of the church and from acts of worship within the walls of any town. Importantly, orthodoxy is described in relation to the Nicene faith:

> That man shall be accepted as a defender of the Nicene faith ... who confesses that Almighty God and Christ the Son of God are one in name, God of God, light from light; who does not violate by denial the Holy Spirit ... that man who esteems ... the undivided substance of the incorrupt Trinity, that substance which those of the orthodox faith call, employing a Greek word, *ousia*.[228]

This statement indicates Theodosius' growing confidence in using terminology drawn from the Nicene confession itself ('light from light'), perhaps influenced by Gregory's reflections on this theme. The suggestion that the Father, Son and Spirit are within the triune being is also a markedly Nicene sentiment in relation to its central claim that the Son is from the essence of the Father (this is drawn out through Athanasius; see the next chapter). Moreover, it affirms the Nicene use of *ousia*-language in an explicit departure from the homoian settlement of the Creed of Constantinople of 360.

Theodosius called a council to meet in Constantinople in May 381. The constitution of the council was made up of 150 Eastern bishops, none of whom held the proscribed opinions of Photinus and Eunomius.[229] As this was not an ecumenical council, minutes arising from it were not preserved.[230] The council was a rancorous affair, characterized by squabbling over the legitimacy of various episcopal appointments, with the Antiochene schism continuing to provide problems. Perhaps fittingly, then, Meletius of Antioch was appointed chair of the council. However, he died while the council was still in session. His place as president of the council was taken by Gregory, who had recently been appointed Bishop of Constantinople. Gregory's first problem was to appoint Meletius' successor in Antioch. Gregory chose Paulinus owing to an agreement

---

228 *CT*, 16.5.6. Cited from Ayres, *NL*, 252. See also Hanson, *SCDG*, 805.

229 Socrates, *Ecclesiastical History*, 5.8; Sozomen, *Ecclesiastical History*, 7.7–11; Theodoret, *Ecclesiastical History*, 5.6–8.

230 Kelly, *ECC*, 306.

made between Paulinus and Meletius that whoever of them died first, the second would assume the episcopacy of Antioch.[231] However, the council elected Flavian as a compromise figure to reconcile the factions in Antioch.[232] Exasperated by this, and by personal attacks made against his legitimacy (owing to a long-standing prohibition against bishops moving from see to see as Gregory had done[233]), Gregory resigned the chair and promptly retired as Bishop of Constantinople, returning to his country estate.[234] An unbaptized civil servant, Nectarius, was elected to take his place, was consecrated as bishop and took control of proceedings.[235]

Among other matters designed to address the ongoing factionalism and squabbling within and between episcopal sees[236] and assert the primacy of the see of Constantinople, second only to Rome,[237] the council affirmed the Nicene confession of 325 in its first canon. Included in this first canon is the proscription of a variety of factions including Eunomians, Arians, Sabellians, Photinians and Macedonians.[238] The fifth canon affirms a document from the Western bishops, which is likely the *Tome of Damasus*.[239] Finally, the council produced the Creed of Constantinople, which was very likely a statement intended to endorse the Nicene confession of 325,[240] while tightening other aspects of doctrine (specifically the doctrines of the Spirit, the church and of the unending rule of Christ) alongside producing a confession that reaffirms the core of the Nicene confession while articulating it in more readily useable liturgical formats.[241]

Upon the closure of the council at the end of July 381, a synodal letter was distributed in which the delegates describe themselves as contending for the faith received from the apostles through various persecutions. Included is a significant doctrinal statement:

---

231 Ayres, *NL*, 254.
232 Hanson, *SCDG*, 809.
233 Gregory was already Bishop of Sasima when he was appointed to Constantinople. Ayres, *NL*, 254.
234 Gregory, *Or*, 42. See Behr, *NF*, 120; Hanson, *SCDG*, 807, 809–810. Historical accounts of this are Socrates, *Ecclesiastical History*, 5.7; Sozomen, *Ecclesiastical History*, 7.7. For a discussion of the controversies around Gregory's episcopacy in Constantinople, see J. Torres and R. Teja, 'A Dispute of Episcopal Legitimacy: Gregory Nazianzen and Maximus in Constantinople', in A. Fear (ed.), *The Role of the Bishop in Late Antiquity: Conflict and Compromise* (London: Bloomsbury, 2013), 13–30.
235 Sozomen, *Ecclesiastical History*, 7.8.
236 See Hall, *Doctrine and Practice*, 165–166.
237 Hanson, *SCDG*, 808.
238 Ibid. 807; Kelly, *Creeds*, 306; Hall, *Doctrine and Practice*, 165.
239 Hall, *Doctrine and Practice*, 166.
240 Socrates, *Ecclesiastical History*, 5.8.
241 On the universality of the Constantinopolitan Creed as a baptismal and eucharistic confession, see Kelly, *ECC*, 344–357.

> According to this faith there is one Godhead, Power and Substance of the Father and of the Son and of the Holy Ghost; the dignity being equal, and the majesty being equal in . . . three perfect persons. Thus there is neither room for the heresy of Sabellius by the confusion of the essences or destruction of the individualities; thus the blasphemy of the Eunomians, of the Arians, and of the Pneumatomachi is nullified, which divides the substance, the nature and the godhead and superinduces on the uncreated consubstantial and co-eternal trinity a nature posterior, created and of a different substance. We moreover preserve unperverted the doctrine of the incarnation of the Lord, holding the tradition that the dispensation of the flesh is neither soulless nor mindless nor imperfect; and knowing full well that God's Word was perfect before the ages, and became perfect man in the last days for our salvation.[242]

The one divinity is common to the Father, Son and Spirit without interval, without multiplication and without inequality. This statement also includes a repudiation of the Christological convictions of Apollinarius, being that the Son did not assume a human soul or mind, but took the place of an animating force within human flesh. This would set the trajectory for the theological controversies of the fifth century; namely, the manner of the unity of the humanity and divinity in the person of Jesus Christ. For our purposes, this amounts to a rejection of the Lucianite/Arian doctrine that the limitations of Jesus of Nazareth are to be attributed to the muted divinity of the Son.

Theodosius issued a further edict (*Episcopis tradi*) confirming the authority of the Council of Constantinople. Significantly, this edict gave an unequivocal imperial stamp to the theology articulated in the Creed of Constantinople, making it the official religion of the Roman Empire:

> We command that all churches shall immediately be surrendered to those bishops who confess that the Father, the Son and the Holy Spirit are of one majesty and power, of the same glory, and of one splendour, to those bishops who produce no dissonance by unholy distinction, but who affirm the concept of the Trinity by the assertion of three persons and the unity of the Divinity.[243]

Ayres observes from the three edicts issued by Theodosius that the logic of three persons within one Godhead had become a 'fundamental identity marker' of a

242 Theodoret, *Ecclesiastical History*, 5.9.
243 *CT*, 16.1.3. Cited from Ayres, *NL*, 252.

pro-Nicene theology.[244] There is one divinity and the Father, Son and Spirit each have a distinct and true existence as the persons they are.

It is traditionally thought that the confession of Constantinople (381) is the confession of Nicaea (325) with a few additions designed to address various theological challenges that had arisen in the intervening decades. This is the understanding expressed at the Council of Chalcedon (451), which cites the confession and attributes it to the 150 bishops at Constantinople.[245] However, revisionist scholarship in the nineteenth and twentieth centuries has suggested that the relationship between them is not that straightforward. While there is a clear *theological* relationship between the documents, there are some discrepancies between the two confessions, which has led some to the conclusion that they are not *textually* related. The majority of these discrepancies are insignificant and so are not indicative of a purposeful departure from the Nicene Creed of 325, but are indicative of a different base confession.[246] For example, that the confession of 381 replaces 'things in heaven and things on earth' with 'maker of heaven and earth' had no bearing on the theological discussion. Moreover, differences in the order of words within clauses appear to have no theological significance.[247] Discrepancies such as these, which cannot be meaningfully explained as adaptations, are indicative that the 381 confession was not a modified version of the 325 confession.

There are also differences that have greater theological significance. For example, the 381 confession omits the central Nicene proposition that the Son is from the *essence* of the Father. This was a pivotal expression in the Nicene confession with the rest of the clause elaborating its meaning. It is hard to imagine that, given the intention of the Council of Constantinople was to affirm the theology of Nicaea, they would adapt the 325 confession by removing these words! Such a change would have to be predicated on a substantial shift in theology, whereby the Son's divinity was construed in terms of his sharing in a common (generic) divine nature, as opposed to sharing in the divinity of the Father. It is less problematic all round to suggest that the 381 confession appears to be of a different provenance, which was propounded by the delegates of Constantinople as 'Nicene' in its theological content.[248]

However, there are adaptations that do make sense within the traditional understanding of the relationship between Nicaea and Constantinople. For

244 Ayres, *NL*, 252.
245 Hall, *Doctrine and Practice*, 167.
246 A full list of the discrepancies can be found in Hanson, *SCDG*, 816–817.
247 See Kelly, *ECC*, 303–304.
248 Kelly, *ECC*, 322–331.

example, the expanded clause on the Spirit in which the theological commitments of Basil of Caesarea against the Macedonians are followed so closely (e.g. that the Spirit is to be worshipped *with* the Father and Son) is a development beyond the Nicene confession in the light of contemporary doctrinal disputes, albeit one that was consistent with its implicit trajectories. Similarly, the standard addition of the clause regarding the everlasting reign of Christ makes sense as an addition to the Nicene confession as a prophylactic against the Marcellian doctrine that the Son returns the kingdom to the Father as part of the conflation of the divine being after its economic expansion. However, there is no reason that these clarifications could have been made only on the Nicene Creed itself (these clarifications could have been added on to a different local confession). Perhaps most significantly, it is not clear that the Council of Constantinople had the authority to make such an amendment to the confession of an ecumenical council.

There is no good reason to think that the confession ratified at Constantinople is an adaption of the Nicene Creed. Instead, it appears that the doctrinal statement from the Council of Constantinople was a distinct confession, although still recognizably from within the Eastern family,[249] which was affirmed by the council on the grounds that they considered it wholly consistent with the 325 confession. Indeed, given that the Nicene Creed was never intended for liturgical or catechetical use, it is not unreasonable to infer that the confession validated at Constantinople in 381 was a local baptismal confession that had, at some point, been amended by the addition of phrases from the Nicene confession.[250] Such a theory accounts for the textual discrepancies, it is attentive to the purpose of the 381 council to affirm the Nicene confession in the East, and provides the requisite flexibility in which the theological convictions of the 325 confession could interact with questions such as the everlasting reign of Christ and the divinity of the Spirit.

One puzzling feature of this confession is its reluctance to attribute the *homoousios* to the Spirit. Some, including Gregory of Nazianzus, took this to be indicative of a capitulation to the significant Pneumatomachian delegation.[251] The confession uses exclusively scriptural categories of the Spirit's titles and activities in its propositions about the Spirit, in marked contrast to the philosophical terminology in the statements about the Son. The descriptor 'giver of life' is deeply Pauline in its provenance (Rom. 8:22; 2 Cor. 3:6, 17). Similarly, the

[249] In the view of Anatolios, the base confession is a pro-Nicene restatement of the Old Roman Creed. Anatolios, *RN*, 27.
[250] See also Ayres, *NL*, 256.
[251] Gregory, *Or*, 42. See Beeley, *Gregory of Nazianzus*, 155–185.

description of the Spirit as 'proceeding from the Father' emerges directly from the words of Jesus in John's Gospel (John 15:26). Within the logic of the confession, however, the Spirit's procession from the Father operates in conjunction with the Son as begotten from the Father to describe the Spirit's derivation from the Father in corresponding but distinct terms to that of the Son.

The confession opts for a proclamatory and doxological voice in affirming the divinity of the Spirit. In the proclamatory mode, the Spirit is described as 'Lord', both invoking the primary designation for God in the Septuagint and establishing a line of connection with the Son, who is so described and identified as identical in essence to the Father. In the doxological mode, the confession ascribes worship to the Spirit *with* the Father and Son. This is the direct application of the thought of Basil of Caesarea:[252] the suitability of the Spirit to be worshipped with the Father and Son is based on their identity of being. It could be that the clause regarding the Spirit does not contain an explicit statement of the divinity of the Spirit on account of Theodosius' desire to form a broad consensus, including those who denied the divinity of the Spirit.[253] This seems unlikely given that, even though the confession avoids identifying the Spirit as identical in essence to the Father, it still propounds the very doctrine the Macedonians rejected; namely, that the Spirit is to be worshipped with the Son and Father.[254] Finally, the synodal letter from a further council in Constantinople in 382 includes a more forthright statement of the Spirit's divinity: 'there is one Godhead, Power, and substance [*ousia*] of the Father and of the Son and of the Holy Spirit; the dignity being equal and the majesty being equal in three perfect *hypostases*'.[255]

252 Anatolios, *RN*, 27.
253 See Kelly, *ECC*, 343.
254 Hanson, *SCDG*, 818.
255 Theodoret, *Ecclesiastical History*, 5.9.

7
Athanasius of Alexandria: a theological study

John Behr writes of Athanasius that 'Nicene Christianity exists by virtue of his constancy and vision'.[1] Certainly, his theological conviction and personal resolution were instrumental in the development of a distinctive interpretation of the Nicene confession around which a consensus could be formed. Theologically speaking, at the heart of Athanasius' Nicene approach was a distinction between two different relations that are both true of God:

1 the intrinsic relations of Father, Son and Spirit, which Athanasius characterizes as eternal and necessary;
2 the extrinsic relation of God to creation as creator and redeemer, which Athanasius characterizes as temporal and contingent.

This chapter describes the dialectic in Athanasius' theology between the Father–Son relation and the God–creation relation and draws out its implications for his doctrine of God and the continuity of divinity between the Father and Son. This theme is consistent throughout his theological contribution, providing the grammar for his understanding of the gospel: the one who is the true Son shares in our humanity so we, who are extrinsic to God, might share in his relation to the Father as the adoptive children of God.

Athanasius was born in the late third century (*c.*290–95) and was adopted into the care of Alexander of Alexandria at a young age.[2] Athanasius' education was distinctive in that it was not steeped in the Hellenic educational system (in contrast to a figure such as Basil of Caesarea). Instead, he was incredibly well versed in the theological tradition of Alexandria. Even in his early years Athanasius was a powerful advocate of Alexander's theology and, when

[1] Behr, *NF*, 167.

[2] For brief biographies of Athanasius, see T. G. Weinandy and D. A. Keating, *Athanasius and His Legacy: Trinitarian-Incarnational Soteriology and Its Reception* (Minneapolis, Minn.: Fortress Press, 2017), 1–5; Weinandy, *Athanasius*, 1–7; Anatolios, *Coherence of His Thought*, 85–93; Gwynn, *Athanasius of Alexandria*, 1–54.

he was a little over 30 years old, succeeded him as Bishop of Alexandria in 328. His episcopal career would continue until his death some four-and-a-half decades later. His episcopacy was interrupted by five periods of exile (contingent upon the effectiveness of his opposition and the vacillating political situation), amounting to seventeen years in total. Athanasius' character has been subjected to focused examination, particularly regarding accusations made against the tactics he employed in defending the Nicene cause (Athanasius maintains that these accusations were part of an 'Arian' conspiracy led by Eusebius of Nicomedia).[3]

One of the characteristics of Athanasius' theological career was that his years of theological maturity (from the 340s) were largely committed to polemical works in response to the ascendency of a radical anti-Nicene theology. These polemical works inherited and developed the theological landscape he set out in his earlier two-volume work *Against the Greeks* and *On the Incarnation*, written in the years between his consecration and his first exile (328–35).[4] It is in these early texts, in which no mention of Arius or of the Nicene confession is made (although it is conceivable that these contain implicit attacks on lingering sympathy with Arius[5]), that his foundational understanding of the relationship between God and creation and the way in which this intersects with his understanding of the person and work of Christ is laid out. This provides the theological and cosmological framework in which his later pro-Nicene theological settlement was established.[6] As Anatolios puts it, the account of the relation between God and creation set out in these early works provides the 'architectonic centre' of his later works, which are more directly concerned with delineating the ontological status of the relations of the Father, Son and Spirit.[7]

God and creation: *Against the Greeks* and *On the Incarnation*

Gwynn contends that 'fundamental to Athanasius' entire theology is his conception of a complete ontological division between God and the world'.[8]

[3] See Hanson, *SCDG*, 239–262; D. M. Gwynn, 'Athanasius', in K. Parry (ed.), *The Wiley-Blackwell Companion to Patristics* (London: John Wiley, 2015), 111–125, at 113.

[4] For scholarship on dating these texts, see Anatolios, *Coherence of His Thought*, 26–27. For the genre of these texts, see Gwynn, *Athanasius of Alexandria*, 66–67.

[5] Anatolios, *RN*, 100–102.

[6] Behr, *NF*, 167.

[7] Anatolios, *Athanasius*, 39.

[8] Gwynn, *Athanasius of Alexandria*, 67.

However, unlike Arius, Athanasius did not consider this to mean that God and creation are locked in a relation of utter incompatibility that precludes God's involvement in creation.[9] This does not mean, however, that Athanasius has an impoverished doctrine of divine transcendence. Instead, as Anatolios has pointed out, Athanasius' theological vision includes a dialectic between God's transcendence and his loving-kindness (*philanthrōpia*):[10]

> For God Maker of all and King of all, that has His Being beyond all substance and human discovery, inasmuch as He is good and exceeding noble, made, through His own Word our Saviour Jesus Christ, the human race after His own image, and constituted man able to see and know realities by means of this assimilation to Himself, giving him also a conception and knowledge even of His own eternity, in order that, preserving his nature intact, he might not ever either depart from his idea of God, nor recoil from the communion of the holy ones; but having the grace of Him that gave it, having also God's own power from the Word of the Father, he might rejoice and have fellowship with the Deity, living the life of immortality unharmed and truly blessed.[11]

God and creation, then, are not at an utter disjunction, but neither are they elided. Athanasius reconciles these contrasting claims in the divine character and action: God, who is beyond all other being, becomes in his kindness the source of the life of creation, which he draws into communion with himself. In other words, the mediatorial work of the Son is not accredited to some attenuation of his divinity as is standard in the Lucianite theological vision. Instead, the incarnation of the Son is the truest activity of divinity.

That God, by kindness, transcends his own transcendence undermines the suggestion that the Son is begotten *pro nobis*: the existence of the Son is not contingent on bridging the ontological gulf between God and creation.[12] It is fundamental to Athanasius' soteriology that the Son has life in himself such that he may impart life to creation. This is grounded in a principle that serves as something of an axiom throughout Athanasius' theological contribution:

[9] T. F. Torrance, *Theology in Reconciliation: Essays Towards Evangelical and Catholic Unity in the East and West* (London: Geoffrey Chapman, 1975), 217–218, 224. See also Weinandy, *Athanasius*, 13–14, 21–23. Lyman has demonstrated that Athanasius' understanding of the relationship of God and creation pivots on the person of Christ, accounting for the twin emphases of God's transcendence over and transformation of creation. See R. Lyman, *Christology and Cosmology: Models of Divine Activity in Origen, Eusebius and Athanasius* (Oxford: Oxford University Press, 1993), ch. 4.

[10] Anatolios, *Athanasius*, 40–41; *RN*, 104; *Coherence of His Thought*, 32, 39–41. See also Behr, *NF*, 173.

[11] Athanasius, *Discourses*, 2, NPNF II.4.

[12] See Hanson, *SCDG*, 421.

divine being is self-existent, whereas created being is contingent and brought into existence from nothing.[13] As it has been created from nothing, created being always has – at the outer boundary of its existence – the possibility of collapsing back into the nothingness from which it was made: 'For the nature of created things, inasmuch as it is brought into being out of nothing, is of a fleeting sort, and weak and mortal, if composed of itself only.'[14] Created being, specifically because it came into being from nothing, is not the ground of its own existence or its continuation in existence.[15]

Both in its origin and its continuation created being is contingent on the will and act of God. This proposition becomes the starting point of *On the Incarnation*, in which the doctrine of God the Son's assuming flesh is nested in a theological metanarrative of creation and recreation.[16] The ongoing kindness of God through the Word is the only factor that stops created being collapsing back into the nothingness, whereby Athanasius' doctrine of the incarnation is located within his doctrine of God and his loving-kindness.[17] This becomes the guiding rationale of the incarnation, in which the Son shares the conditions of created being so that creation may share in the conditions of divine being:

> But God possesses true existence and is not composite, wherefore His Word also has true Existence and is not composite, but is the one and only-begotten God, Who proceeds in His goodness from the Father as from a good Fountain, and orders all things and holds them together. But the reason why the Word, the Word of God, has united Himself with created things is truly wonderful . . . Seeing then all created nature, as far as its own laws were concerned, to be fleeting and subject to dissolution, lest it should come to this and lest the Universe should be broken up again into nothingness, for this cause He made all things by His own eternal Word, and gave substantive existence to Creation, and moreover did not leave it to be tossed in a tempest in the course of its own nature, lest it should run the risk of once more dropping out of existence; but, because He is good He guides and settles the whole Creation by His own Word, Who is Himself also God, that by the governance and providence and ordering action of the Word, Creation may have light, and be enabled to abide always securely. For it partakes of the Word Who derives true

13 Athanasius, *AG*, 35.
14 Ibid. 41.
15 Athanasius, *On the Incarnation*, 3, NPNF II.4. See Anatolios, *Coherence of His Thought*, 35–38.
16 Behr, *NF*, 168.
17 See Anatolios, *Coherence of His Thought*, 42–44.

> existence from the Father, and is helped by Him so as to exist, lest that should come to it which would have come but for the maintenance of it by the Word, – namely, dissolution.[18]

Athanasius' conception of the Son is shaped by a commitment to divine simplicity. God, as absolute being, is not composite, as he would then be posterior to his parts. As such, the Son, who is the Word of God, is not a part of God but is fully God, subsisting as begotten. The Son is not in God as a quality of Wisdom, but is God as the Father is God; only his particular mode of subsistence is as God begotten.[19] As such, the Son is not among those things that have been brought into being from nothing. Nor does the Son participate in the divinity of the Father from the outside.[20] As begotten from the essence of the Father, the Son shares in the divinity of the Father, having life in himself as the Father has life in himself. The Son, who has 'true existence', and is not characterized by the same ontological instability as creation, unites himself to created being in order to maintain it in existence.[21] In this way, the divinity of the Son comes into the foreground of Athanasius' theology of creation, revelation and salvation.[22] If the Son were among the things brought into being from nothing, then his existence would be as unstable as ours and he would require it to be sustained by the agency of something more ontologically stable than himself. In this way, the eternal correlativity of the Father and Son is the grammar of the creative and salvific work of the Son: it is through the Son that the Father creates,[23] through the Son that the Father is made known,[24] and it is in the Son's offering to the Father that redemption is secured.[25]

Consistent with his comprehension of created being as dependent on the act and will of God for existence, Athanasius conceives of the structure of human being – the constitution of body, mind and soul – as specifically calibrated for assimilation with divine being as the ground of its existence.[26] His understanding of sin corresponds to this as the destructive about-turn from humanity's ground of existence. Sin, then, is an act of uncreation, a dissolution into nothingness:

---

18 Athanasius, *AG*, 41.

19 See S. J. Duby, *Divine Simplicity: A Dogmatic Account* (London: T&T Clark, 2016), 8.

20 Athanasius, *AG*, 46.

21 Ibid. 42.

22 Weinandy, *Athanasius*, 25, 31–35.

23 Athanasius, *Incarnation*, 5.

24 Ibid. 7.

25 Ibid. See also Anatolios, *Athanasius*, 7.

26 Anatolios describes Athanasius' anthropological framework in which the whole human person subsists in an orientation to communion with God. Ibid. 45–49. See also Athanasius, *AG*, 4–5.

> God has made man, and willed that he should abide in incorruption; but men, having despised and rejected the contemplation of God, and devised and contrived evil for themselves . . . received the condemnation of death . . . For transgression of the commandment was turning them back to their natural state, so that just as they have had their being out of nothing, so also, as might be expected, they might look for corruption into nothing in the course of time. For if, out of a former normal state of non-existence, they were called into being by the Presence and loving-kindness of the Word, it followed naturally that when men were bereft of the knowledge of God and were turned back to what was not . . . they should, since they derive their being from God who is, be everlastingly bereft even of being; in other words, that they should be disintegrated and abide in death.[27]

The only solution for this collapse into nothingness is the condescension of the Son, who participates fully in the divinity of the Father to return humanity to its ground of existence.[28] The agent of salvation must possess self-grounded existence to overcome created being's ontological fragility and orientation to non-existence.[29] God's loving-kindness, operative through the Word, both brought created being into existence from nothing and keeps it from its headlong plunge back into nothing.[30]

The way in which Athanasius has laid out the relation of God and creation, and the problem sin presents for existence, places emphasis on the full divinity of the Son. The incarnation is God the Son becoming human, condescending to the condition of created being to bring about such being's reversal from death and back towards the ground of its existence.[31] The Son's assumption of human nature into union with himself was the involvement of the Son, who has life in himself, in created being's collapse into non-existence such that through his voluntary death, death itself might be overcome.[32] If the Son were from nothing, he would not be able to liberate from the threat of nothingness:[33]

> by so ordinary a means things divine have been manifested to us, and that by death immortality has reached to all, and that by the Word becoming

27 Athanasius, *Incarnation*, 4. See also ibid. 5.
28 Athanasius, *AG*, 47; Gwynn, *Athanasius of Alexandria*, 69.
29 Anatolios, *Athanasius*, 12; Behr, *NF*, 185–186.
30 Athanasius, *Incarnation*, 8, 44. See also Behr, *NF*, 181.
31 Athanasius, *Incarnation*, 7. See also Athanasius, *Discourses*, 1.39; Anatolios, *Athanasius*, 43–44.
32 Athanasius, *Incarnation*, 13, 20–21, 27.
33 Ibid. 9. See also Behr, *NF*, 234; Hanson, *SCDG*, 451; Anatolios, *Athanasius*, 12.

> man, the universal Providence has been known, and its Giver and Artificer the very Word of God. For He was made man that we might be made God; and He manifested Himself by a body that we might receive the idea of the unseen Father; and He endured the insolence of men that we might inherit immortality.[34]

These are well-known lines from Athanasius and articulate his doctrine of salvation as 'deification', by which Athanasius did not mean to imply that humanity would become divine. This would compromise the single divine reality. Instead, it means that through human participation in divinity humanity is freed from sin, sanctified and given life.[35] This line of argument, especially the proposition that only that which is divine by nature can effect participation in divinity for another, would become integral to Athanasius' anti-Arian polemic, particularly through its more thorough working out in his trinitarian hermeneutic: in the power of the Spirit, we are included in the Son and participate in his relation to the Father.

Developing a trinitarian hermeneutic: *Discourses Against the Arians*

Athanasius' *Discourses Against the Arians*, written during his exile in Rome (339–45),[36] builds on the theological and soteriological landscape laid out in his early works, pursuing it in a more distinctively trinitarian direction. The content of Christian salvation is articulated as the eternally begotten Son becomes a human to include us in him through the power of the Spirit[37]: 'the Son Himself partakes of nothing, but what is partaken from the Father, is the Son; for, as partaking of the Son Himself, we are said to partake of God'.[38] The theological parameters of the relation of divine and created being continue to provide the basic structure of Athanasius' thought, but its implications for the character of divine being are laid out more completely in this later work in a way that anticipates most of the themes of Athanasius' later anti-Arian polemic.

[34] Athanasius, *Incarnation*, 54.

[35] See also Gwynn, *Athanasius of Alexandria*, 70, n. 23, for relevant scholarship on deification.

[36] Athanasius responds directly to their participative image-Christology of the Second Creed of the Dedication Council.

[37] Anatolios, *RN*, 124.

[38] Athanasius, *Discourses*, 1.16.

This text is an assault on the exegetical and hermeneutical foundations of the subordinationism of Arius and the Eusebians.[39] This anti-Nicene hermeneutic falls into two categories.[40] First, the contention that certain passages (e.g. Prov. 8:22) indicate that the Son was brought into existence. Second, passages interpreted as demonstrating the Son's inferiority to the Father (e.g. Mark 13:32). Athanasius is largely reactive to these categories, attempting to dismantle this 'Arian' hermeneutic and replace it with a 'trinitarian' hermeneutic. There are two parts to this:

1. A demonstration of the eternal correlativity of the Father and Son through overlapping scriptural designations, arguing that the pattern for naming the Father and Son points towards their necessary belonging to each other.
2. The application of what Behr has called 'partitive exegesis',[41] in which the scriptural descriptions of the Son are interpreted *either* with respect to his pre-incarnate or his incarnate existence. Scripture speaks differently about the pre-incarnate and incarnate Son, this distinction being essential to an understanding of Christ that does not distort this two-staged scriptural narrative. For example, the attributions of human limitation to the Son – his sufferings, for example – are applicable only to the Son as incarnate and not to his pre-incarnate state. In this way, Athanasius sought to preserve the reality of God the Son's sufferings with respect to his humanity without falling into the claim that this limitation can be applied directly to the Son's attenuated divinity.[42]

The following discussion takes these elements of Athanasius' trinitarian hermeneutic in turn.

Overlapping scriptural identifications

Athanasius argued that scriptural titles, names and designations (e.g. Word, Wisdom, Image, Power and Radiance) for the Son indicate his correlative relation to the Father. For Athanasius, these ways of referring to the Son are not modes of human conceptualization. Instead, they are directly *revelatory* in that they give insight (to the degree that is possible for humanity) into the divine

39 Ayres describes this text as 'one of the key early anti-Eusebian manifestos'. Ayres, *NL*, 117.
40 Anatolios, *RN*, 109.
41 Behr, *NF*, 213–215.
42 Anatolios, *RN*, 109–110.

being.[43] In other words, Athanasius thought of the words of Scripture themselves – particularly the names used for God – as a disclosure of the divine being. Rather than offsetting Scripture's revelatory function to its reference to God's act in history, Athanasius thinks of meaning as located within the text of Scripture itself. A premium, therefore, is placed on the relationship between disparate texts as a method of discerning meaning: Scripture is interpreted by Scripture. This is the basis of Athanasius' intertextual procedure of interpretation, which functioned by taking terms from their immediate context and tessellating them with related terms from other areas in Scripture. In doing this, Athanasius argued, there were interlocking fields of reference for the Father and Son that were indicative of the correlation between Father and Son. One example of this comes in a passage where Athanasius establishes a web of intertextual connections regarding a variety of scriptural designations:

> 'Who being the Brightness of His glory and the Expression of His subsistence,' and 'Christ the power of God and the Wisdom of God;' and another says in the Psalm, 'With You is the well of life, and in Your Light shall we see light,' and 'You made all things in Wisdom;' and the Prophets say, 'And the Word of the Lord came to me;' and John, 'In the beginning was the Word.' . . . All these passages proscribe in every light the Arian heresy, and signify the eternity of the Word, and that He is not foreign but proper to the Father's Essence. For when saw any one light without radiance? Or who dares to say that the expression can be different from the subsistence? Or has not a man himself lost his mind who even entertains the thought that God was ever without Reason and without Wisdom?[44]

The Son receives a designation that participates in the same field of meaning as terms applied to the Father: the Father is light (1 John 1:5) and the Son is radiance (Heb. 1:3). In one particularly clear example of this, Athanasius gathers together references to God as the foundation of wisdom and life:

> As He says by Jeremiah, 'They have forsaken Me the Fountain of living waters' and again '. . . they have forsaken the Lord, the Fountain of living waters '. . . – this implies that life and wisdom are not foreign to the Essence of the Fountain, but are proper to It, nor were at any time

43 Ibid. 110.
44 Athanasius, *Discourses*, 2.32.

> without existence, but were always. Now the Son is all this, who says, 'I am the Life.'[45]

In a later text, Athanasius would argue that 'Arian' exegesis avoids this correlative naming, and so in arguing that the Son came from nothing and is external to the Father they conceive of him no longer as the fountain of living waters but 'a sort of pool, receiving water from without' and unable to be the source of life for others.[46]

This correlative naming, however, does not obscure the distinction between the Father and Son. Designations are attributed to Father and Son in different ways: the Father is the source and the Son is that which comes from the source; the Father is the light and the Son the radiance; the Father is the speaker and the Son is the Word:

> Very Son of the Father, natural and genuine, proper to His essence ... not a creature or work, but an offspring proper to the Father's essence. Wherefore He is very God, existing one in essence with the very Father; while other beings, to whom He said, 'I said you are Gods,' had this grace from the Father, only by participation of the Word, through the Spirit. For He is the expression of the Father's Person, and Light from Light, and Power, and very Image of the Father's essence.[47]

The divine being exists as a 'dynamic outgoing movement',[48] as the Son radiates out from the Father. The problem with 'Arian' exegesis is that it does not reflect this movement within the divine being, conceiving of God as a pure, still and undifferentiated oneness. For Athanasius, the divine being is characterized by the flow from the source to that which comes from the source, the radiance eternally shining out from the light.

Partitive exegesis: the divinity and humanity of the incarnate Son

Within the Lucianite theological tradition, which included Arius as a particularly radical member, it was common to draw on scriptural descriptions of the limitations of the incarnate Son as indicative of the Son's attenuated divinity. The purpose of Athanasius' partitive exegesis was to account for how human

45 Ibid. 1.19.
46 Athanasius, *Defence Against the Arians*, 15.
47 Athanasius, *Discourses*, 1.9.
48 Anatolios, *RN*, 114.

limitations could be predicated of the incarnate Son without implying the divinity of the Son was less than that of the Father.[49] Central to the logic of this exegetical procedure is the proposition that there is one subject (the Son) to whom very different properties and experiences are able to be attributed owing to the two very different categories into which this subject's life can be organized: the pre-incarnate Son and the Son incarnate. To read Scripture correctly means to distinguish between these two categories while attributing them to the same single subject:[50]

> Now the scope and character of Holy Scripture, as we have often said, is this – it contains a double account of the Saviour; that He was ever God, and is the Son, being the Father's Word and Radiance and Wisdom; and that afterwards for us He took flesh of a Virgin, Mary Bearer of God, and was made man.[51]

Following this procedure, Athanasius insisted that the Son is not a lesser divinity who suffers alongside us and is subsequently glorified.[52] Instead, the Son is God as the Father is God, who enters our condition in its downward descent to death *for the purposes* of transforming the calamity of human existence.

One example of how Athanasius describes this scriptural double-speak for the Son comes in his exegesis of Proverbs 8:22. Athanasius distinguishes between that which is eternally true of the divine being and that which is true of God's economic activity to creation. Once this distinction is appreciated, the description of God's Wisdom as 'created' is attributed not to his essential mode of origination from the Father (as something pertaining to the divine being) but only with reference to God's activity towards creation:

> For the passage in the Proverbs, as I have said before, signifies, not the Essence, but the manhood of the Word; for if He says that He was created 'for the works,' He shows His intention of signifying, not His Essence, but the Economy which took place 'for His works,' which comes second to being.[53]

Behr summarizes the force of the argument very well: 'the point here is to demarcate very clearly what belongs to Christ himself – his being or essence,

[49] The following discussion is indebted to Behr, *NF*, 208–231.
[50] Anatolios, *RN*, 124.
[51] Athanasius, *Discourses*, 3.29.
[52] Ibid. 1.38–139. See also Anatolios, *RN*, 122–124.
[53] Athanasius, *Discourses*, 2.51.

what he always is – from what belongs to him by virtue of the economy, what he has done for us'.[54] The Son exists as the eternally begotten Son of the Father prior to this act of being 'created' as the Word incarnate.[55] The purpose of God's activity towards creation in which God the Son assumes humanity is explicitly the redemption of humanity: 'For the need of man preceded His becoming man, apart from which He had not put on flesh.'[56] This means that the human limitation of God the Son is not intrinsic to his divinity but becomes true of the Son through his loving action towards us. Understood in these terms, the incarnate Son's limitations are not indicative of his attenuated divinity but rather a manifestation of divine glory, which is his steadfast love.[57]

This opens up a paradox: it is true to speak of the Son as both eternally begotten and created temporally. This is the paradox in which the procedure of partitive exegesis is relevant as the single subject of the Son can be spoken of in different ways depending on whether one is speaking of his pre-incarnation or with respect to that which is true of him through the incarnation. In the assumption of human nature, humanity becomes proper to the Word, to whom properties and experiences of humanity may be attributed *with respect to that humanity*. All things that belong to human nature belong to the incarnate Son, without a change in his divinity.[58] This hermeneutic entails, then, a fiercely anti-Docetic Christology: the single subject, the Son, may be spoken of in human terms because he has really assumed human nature such that its conditions of being may be attributed to him.[59]

The point is that the Son is *one subject* to whom terms pertaining to divinity and terms pertaining to humanity can *both* appropriately be attributed:

> Whence it was that, when the flesh suffered, the Word was not external to it; and therefore is the passion said to be His: and when He did divinely His Father's works, the flesh was not external to Him, but in the body itself did the Lord do them ... These things were so done, were so manifested, because He had a body, not in appearance, but in truth; and it

[54] Behr, *NF*, 213.
[55] Athanasius, *Discourses*, 2.60.
[56] Ibid. 2.54.
[57] Anatolios, *RN*, 123–124. See also Athanasius, *Ep*, 10.9.
[58] Behr, *NF*, 216–217. Athanasius, *Incarnation*, 18.
[59] Athanasius' language of the Son's 'dwelling' in human flesh has been criticized as 'spacesuit Christology' by Hanson, *SCDG*, 446. Certainly, as the Council of Antioch of 268 suggests, it was not uncommon to hold that the Son replaced the human soul in the person of Jesus Christ. However, Anatolios, supported by Behr, has pointed to the flaws in attributing this doctrine to Athanasius. See Behr, *NF*, 216; K. Anatolios, '"The Body as Instrument": A Re-evaluation of Athanasius' "Logos-Sarx Christology"', *CCR* 18 (1997), 78–84.

> became the Lord, in putting on human flesh, to put it on whole with the affections proper to it; that, as we say that the body was His own, so also we may say that the affections of the body were proper to Him alone, though they did not touch Him according to His Godhead.[60]

The Son suffers, but not with respect to his divinity. Likewise, the Son performs the works of the Father, but not by his humanity. The Son is a single subject of whom both sets of properties can be predicated: the sufferings of Jesus really are the sufferings of the Son, and the perfect filial obedience becoming a lived reality in human flesh really is the act of the Son as a human.

This carries immediate implications for the doctrine of salvation: the incarnate Son receives and transforms the weakness and death of humanity:

> if the works of the Word's Godhead had not taken place through the body, man had not been deified; and again, had not the properties of the flesh been ascribed to the Word, man had not been thoroughly delivered from them . . . But now the Word having become man and having appropriated what pertains to the flesh, no longer do these things touch the body, because of the Word who has come in it, but they are destroyed by Him, and henceforth men no longer remain sinners and dead according to their proper affections, but having risen according to the Word's power, they abide ever immortal and incorruptible. Whence also, whereas the flesh is born of Mary Bearer of God, He Himself is said to have been born, who furnishes to others an origin of being; in order that He may transfer our origin into Himself, and we may no longer, as mere earth, return to earth, but as being knit into the Word from heaven, may be carried to heaven by Him. Therefore in like manner not without reason has He transferred to Himself the other affections of the body also; that we, no longer as being men, but as proper to the Word, may have a share in eternal life. For no longer according to our former origin in Adam do we die; but henceforward our origin and all infirmity of flesh being transferred to the Word, we rise from the earth, the curse from sin being removed, because of Him who is in us, and who has become a curse for us.[61]

God the Son participates in human suffering with respect to the human nature assumed into union with himself and redeems us from within ourselves.[62]

---

60 Athanasius, *Discourses*, 3.32.
61 Ibid. 3.33.
62 Ibid. 3.34.

The dialectic of the Father–Son relation and the God–creation relation

The different structural dynamics at work in the intrinsic Father–Son relation and the extrinsic God–creation relation are central to Athanasius' thought. The difference between these two relations enables us to gain an approximation of divine being as inherently generative and to define God's relation to creation from the ontological and logical priority of the Father–Son relation. These relations both have to do, in some sense, with derivation. The Son derives from the Father, and creation derives from God. However, the sense of derivation, to borrow a well-known phrase, is at an infinite qualitive distinction from the other.

Before he used the term *homoousios* to describe the Son in relation to the Father, Athanasius' favoured way of affirming the continuity of divinity between the Father and Son was to follow the clarification derived from a constitutive image-Christology: the Son is begotten *from the essence of the Father.* The derivation of the Son from the *essence* of the Father is necessary, timeless and intrinsic to divine being, whereas the making of creation from the *will* of the Father is contingent, sequential and extrinsic to divine being. The polemical force of this distinction is that 'begetting' implies an identity of essence, whereas 'making' implies a sharp difference.[63]

Necessity and the continuity of divinity versus contingence and the discontinuity of divinity

For Athanasius, the necessary relation of begotten from the essence is the ground of the continuity of divinity between Father and Son. By contrast, the contingent relation of that which is made from the will of the Father does not include such continuity. This is described through a distinction between *external* work and *proper* relation:

> a work is external to the nature, but a son is the proper offspring of the essence; it follows that a work need not have been always, for the workman frames it when he will; but an offspring is not subject to will, but is proper to the essence . . . But the Son, not being a work, but proper to the Father's offspring, always is; for, whereas the Father always is, so what is proper to His essence must always be; and this is His Word and His Wisdom. And

[63] 'It is this conception of the being of God as an act of eternal giving and responding that allows Athanasius to distinguish the relation of the Father and the Son decisively from that of God and the created order.' Widdicombe, *Fatherhood of God*, 186–187. See also Anatolios, *Coherence of His Thought*, 102–104.

> that creatures should not be in existence, does not disparage the Maker; for He has the power of framing them, when He wills; but for the offspring not to be ever with the Father, is a disparagement of the perfection of His essence. Wherefore His works were framed, when He would, through His Word; but the Son is ever the proper offspring of the Father's essence.[64]

The necessity of the Father–Son relation is underscored through the primacy of the designation 'Father' over 'unbegotten', which implies the relational correlate 'Son' and is, for this reason, indicative of their eternal correlation: 'But when we call God Father, at once with the Father we signify the Son's existence.'[65] Like Alexander before him, Athanasius identifies the Son as *proper* to the Father and so coeternal with the Father.[66] The correlate relation implied by the names 'Father' and 'Son' is of paramount importance to Athanasius, for it establishes the Son as 'offspring of [the Father's] essence',[67] whereby the Son shares in all the Father is, save for the Father's being the unbegotten cause of the Son: '[H]ow can a man consider that which is proper, as foreign and alien in essence?'[68] Crucially, unlike Origen, Athanasius does not extend this to the coeternity of creation. If he had, the central thrust of his Christology and cosmology would be compromised, eradicating the contrast between the Son, who is in an essential relation to the Father, and creation, which is a 'work made out of nothing'.[69]

This is a mode of reasoning that Athanasius would return to in his later works *Defence of the Nicene Definition* and *On the Synods*, in which he would work out more fully the connection between the controversial Nicene phrase *homoousios* and the proposition that the Son is begotten from the Father's essence:

> For if the Word be a work and foreign to the Father's essence, so that He is separated from the Father by the difference of nature, He cannot be one in essence with Him . . . On the other hand, if we confess that He is not a work but the genuine offspring of the Father's essence, it would follow that He is inseparable from the Father, being connatural, because He is begotten from Him. And being such, good reason He should be called Coessential [*homoousios*].[70]

64 Athanasius, *Discourses*, 1.29.
65 Ibid. 3.6.
66 Ibid. 1.14.
67 Ibid. 1.16.
68 Ibid. 1.20.
69 Ibid. 1.14.
70 Athanasius, *Synods*, 48.

Homoousios and 'from the essence' need to be understood in relation to each other. As Zachhuber has shown, Athanasius does not conceive of the *homoousion* as describing the Father and Son as 'ontologically co-ordinate collaterals', but rather grounds the *homoousion* in the derivative relationship.[71] The begetting of the Son from the essence of the Father is understood in terms of the perfect continuity of divinity between them.[72] This is undergirded by Athanasius' contrast between divine and human generation, whereby human generation involves temporal sequence (a human father *became* a father at a certain point) and divine generation is eternal, whereby God is eternally Father and Son.[73]

This raises the question of the sense in which Athanasius understood there to be one God. Athanasius correlates the oneness of God to the Father and the divinity of the Father is that which is communicated to the Son:

> the fullness of the Father's Godhead is the Being of the Son, and the Son is whole God. Therefore also, being equal to God, He 'thought it not a prize to be equal to God;' and again since the Godhead and the Form of the Son is none other's than the Father's, this is what He says, 'I in the Father.' Thus 'God was in Christ reconciling the world unto Himself . . . And thus he who looks at the Son, sees the Father; for in the Father's Godhead is and is contemplated the Son . . . And that propriety and Godhead which is from the Father in the Son, shows the Son in the Father, and His inseparability from Him; and whoever hears and beholds that what is said of the Father is also said of the Son, not as accruing to His Essence by grace or participation, but because the very Being of the Son is the proper Offspring of the Father's Essence . . .[74]

This does not imply the subordination of the Son or that the Son is initiated, as it were, into the one divinity from the outside. Athanasius is clear that the name 'Father' signifies the Son. It belongs to the one Father to be the source of the Son, who, given the essential character of that relation receives all that the Father is such that the divinity of the Son is the divinity of the Father:[75]

> Therefore also he who believes in the Son, believes also in the Father: for he believes in what is proper to the Father's essence; and thus the faith is

[71] Zachhuber, 'Antiochene Synod of 363', 91–92.
[72] Athanasius, *Defence Against the Arians*, 10.
[73] Athanasius, *Discourses*, 1.21.
[74] Ibid. 3.6.
[75] See Behr, *NF*, 241–242. Athanasius, *AG*, 1.45; 2.18. An excellent discussion of the image-theology of Athanasius can be found in Beeley, *Unity of Christ*, 146–151.

> one in one God. And he who worships and honours the Son, in the Son worships and honours the Father; for one is the Godhead; and therefore one the honour and one the worship which is paid to the Father in and through the Son.[76]

The irreducible oneness of God is the oneness of the Father. This one divinity is communicated to the Son, who is coeternal, such that the one divinity of the Father is true of both Father and Son. Athanasius explores this through the designation of the Son as the perfect image of the Father to whom the divinity of the Father is communicated[77] and through whom the Father is made known and who acts in divine power.[78] Athanasius even describes the Son as the image of God to the Father in whom the Father sees and delights in himself: 'When then did the Father not see Himself in His own Image? Or when had He not delight, that a man should dare to say, "the Image is out of nothing".'[79]

Returning to the primary theme, establishing the continuity of divinity on generation from the essence of the Father is central to the contrast between the Son and creation. This is the cornerstone of the proposition that the Son is derived from the Father and yet not among those things that have been brought into existence:

> a work is external to the nature, but a son is the proper offspring of the essence; it follows that a work need not have been always, for the workman frames it when he will; but an offspring is not subject to will, but is proper to the essence. And a man may be and may be called Maker, though the works are not as yet; but father he cannot be called, nor can he be, unless a son exist. And if they curiously inquire why God, though always with the power to make, does not always make . . . though God always had the power to make, yet the things originated had not the power of being eternal. For they are out of nothing, and therefore were not before their origination . . . But the Son, not being a work, but proper to the Father's offspring, always is; for, whereas the Father always is, so what is proper to His essence must always be.[80]

While creation is made from nothing by the will of God and is external to the divine being, the Son is begotten from the essence of the Father and is intrinsic

[76] Athanasius, *Discourses*, 3.6.
[77] Ibid. 1.9, 14–15, 19–20.
[78] Ibid. 1.61.
[79] Ibid. 1.20; 2.82.
[80] Ibid. 1.29.

to the divine being. Just as with the metaphor of the fountain and the life that springs from it or the radiance of the light,[81] the movement from Father to Son is intrinsic to the inherently generative divine being: 'it belongs to the Godhead alone, that the Father is properly father, and the Son properly son'.[82] This distinction between the continuity and discontinuity of divinity is grounded in the distinction between necessity and volition. The unity of the Father and Son is not contingent upon the will of the Father to beget; instead, it is a necessary unity of being, intrinsic to divinity itself.[83] Creation, as extrinsic to being, is not characterized by necessity:[84]

> God's creating is second to His begetting; for 'Son' implies something proper to Him and truly from that blessed and everlasting Essence; but what is from His will, comes into consistence from without, and is framed through His proper Offspring who is from it.[85]

As Behr observes, 'the existence of the Son does not depend on the volitional act of God, as if he might have chosen otherwise'.[86] The divine being is generative in and of itself, and there is no interval or element of contingence in the begetting of the Son.[87] This does not, however, mean that the generation of the Son is *against* the will of the Father. Athanasius' point is that the Father–Son relation is intrinsic to divine being, antecedent and *unrelated* to volition.

Intrinsically proper versus external participation

The dialectic between the Father–Son relation and the God–creation relation described above – structurally speaking – is the same as that which Athanasius laid out in *Against the Greeks* and *On the Incarnation*, only now parsed in terms with greater trinitarian resonance: it is as the Son and Spirit share by necessity and intrinsically in the divinity of the Father that creation, which is external to God, can participate in the divine life through the Son by the power of the Spirit.[88]

---

[81] Ibid. 3.66.
[82] Ibid. 1.21.
[83] Ibid. 3.60–64.
[84] See also Behr, *NF*, 245.
[85] Athanasius, *Discourses*, 2.2.
[86] Behr, *NF*, 238.
[87] Williams, *Arius*, 229.
[88] See Anatolios, *Coherence of His Thought*, 105: 'Athanasius insists that the Son is not related to God by participation as is the rest of creation, but rather creation is related to God through participation in the Son.'

Throughout the *Discourses Against the Arians* Athanasius delineates the distinction between the Son and creation by describing the Son as 'proper to' (*idios*) the Father, whereas creation is 'external' (*ektos*) or 'from outside' (*exōthen*) the Father.[89] Andrew Louth explains that this contrast between '*idios* and *exōthen* expresses the fundamental contrast between God and creature, between what belongs to the divine [essence] and what is created out of nothing':[90]

> When then was God without that which is proper [*tou idiou*] to Him? Or how can a man consider that which is proper, as foreign and alien in essence? For other things, according to the nature of things originate, are without likeness in essence with the Maker; but are external [*exōthen*] to Him, made by the Word at His grace and will, and thus admit of ceasing to be, if it so pleases Him who made them; for such is the nature of things originate. But as to what is proper to the Father's essence (for this we have already found to be the Son), what daring is it in irreligion to say that 'This comes from nothing,' and that 'It was not before generation,' but was adventitious, and can at some time cease to be again?[91]

Being from the essence of the Father, there is no temporal or volitional interval between the Father and Son. In short, the Son is 'proper' to the Father.[92] Athanasius contrasts this to the Arian notion that the Son is made from nothing and is adopted into participation with the Father by grace owing to some harmony of will,[93] a notion Athanasius describes in terms of externality. In this connection, Athanasius distinguishes between the two different senses in which the term 'Son' is understood.[94] First, the 'Arians' conceive of him as Son by adoption, meaning that he comes into existence from some other source outside

---

89 In this discussion, I have drawn on the analysis of Anatolios, *Coherence of His Thought*, 102–105.t

90 A. Louth, 'The Use of the Term *idios* in Alexandrian Theology from Alexander to Cyril', *StPatr* 19 (1989), 198–202. Transliterations are my own. For more on this, see Widdicombe, *Fatherhood of God*, 193–204.

91 Athanasius, *Discourses*, 1.20.

92 E.g. ibid. 1.9, 15–16. Radde-Gallwitz discusses this in terms of Athanasius' account of divine simplicity, arguing that Athanasius' description of the Father–Son relation is shaped by divine simplicity such that positing this as an internal relation (and so not separating the Father and Son to different levels of being) does not attribute composition to God. In this way, Radde-Gallwitz contends, Athanasius prioritizes the divine name 'Father' as naming the essence of God. As Father implies the correlate reality of Son, the Son is likewise an essential predicate. Fatherhood and Sonship, then, are not properties of the divine essence as such, but rather signify the divine essence. Radde-Gallwitz, *Transformation of Divine Simplicity*, 78–86. See also S. Wedgeworth, 'The Brightness of God's Own Light: Divine Simplicity in the Theology of Athanasius', in J. Minich and O. A. Kamel (eds.), *The Lord Is One: Reclaiming Divine Simplicity* (Burford: Davenant Press, 2019), 58–80.

93 Athanasius, *Discourses*, 1.5–6. See also Widdicombe, *Fatherhood of God*, 188–191.

94 Athanasius, *Defence Against the Arians*, 6–14.

God and is made Son 'by grace from moral improvement'.[95] Second, Athanasius' own doctrine is that he is begotten from the essence of the Father and shares the divinity of the Father.[96] As the Son is from the essence of the Father, he does not have some point of origin outside the Father and so does not come to participate in the divine being from something beyond himself.[97]

By contrast, created reality is external to God, parsed in the familiar terms of derivation from the will without a continuation of divinity. This externality is not indicative of the absence of relationship between God and creation, but rather of the *character* of the relationship as creation *participates in God by grace*. Our participation as contingent beings extrinsic to divinity has both a temporal and a volitional interval, which is God's freedom to create and redeem. Or, as Behr puts it, 'the starting point for [humanity's] participation in God is precisely the nothingness from which they were called into being'.[98] Our inclusion to share in the gift of God's being is itself a gift, a possibility that has come from outside the bounds of our contingent reality:

> For things originate, though they have an agreement with their Maker, yet possess it only by influence, and by participation, and through the mind; the transgression of which forfeits heaven. But the Son, being an offspring from the essence, is one by essence, Himself and the Father that begot Him.[99]

This is the application of a principle that Athanasius treats as a theological rule: it is only that which is necessarily God (and so does not participate from an external starting point through an intermediary) that can gift participation in divinity. In *On the Incarnation* only the one whose life is self-grounded (who was eternal by nature) could liberate humanity from death, and only the true image of God could renew humanity as the image of God. This takes an increasingly trinitarian grammar in *Discourses Against the Arians*:

> We are driven to say that what is from the essence of the Father, and proper [*idion*] to Him, is entirely the Son; for it is all one to say that God is wholly participated, and that He begets; and what does begetting signify but a Son? And thus of the Son Himself, all things partake according to

95 Ibid. 6.
96 Ibid. 11–13.
97 Anatolios, *RN*, 106–107.
98 Behr, *NF*, 237.
99 Athanasius, *Synods*, 48.

> the grace of the Spirit coming from Him; and this shows that the Son Himself partakes of nothing, but what is partaken from the Father, is the Son; for, as partaking of the Son Himself, we are said to partake of God.[100]

And again, in his later *On the Synods*:

> For by partaking of Him, we partake of the Father; because that the Word is the Father's own. Whence, if He was Himself too from participation, and not from the Father His essential Godhead and Image, He would not deify, being deified Himself. For it is not possible that He, who merely possesses from participation, should impart of that partaking to others, since what He has is not His own, but the Giver's; and what He has received, is barely the grace sufficient for Himself.[101]

Anatolios helpfully describes this as a 'chain of participation in which our participation of the Son amounts to a participation of the Father'.[102] Athanasius makes the corresponding argument with respect to the knowledge of God, grounding this likewise in the Son's continuity of the divinity with the Father: 'And beholding the Son, we see the Father; for the thought and comprehension of the Son, is knowledge concerning the Father, because He is His proper offspring from His essence.'[103] The Son, as intrinsic to divine being, is able to bring about our participation both salvifically and noetically.[104] Therefore, the mediatorial work of the Son (and the Spirit) is not the work of some intermediate being between God and creation; rather, their full divinity is the basis of their mediation.[105]

In part, this is an implicit reaction to Arian Christology and soteriology. For Arius, the Son is brought into being from nothing, and, by grace, is given some share in divinity through participation.[106] In other words, some interval is inserted between the divine being and the being of the Son, which is traversed by the moral commitment of the Son and the gift of the Father. For Athanasius, this rendered Arianism soteriologically impotent, as the Son would have no basis within himself to communicate the gifts of God. The pertinent question is how the *Son* participates in the life of God. If the Son does not share the

100 Athanasius, *Discourses*, 1.16.
101 Athanasius, *Synods*, 51.
102 Anatolios, *Coherence of His Thought*, 109.
103 Athanasius, *Discourses*, 1.16.
104 See Behr, *NF*, 236.
105 Athanasius, *Discourses*, 3.14. See Anatolios, *Coherence of His Thought*, 113–114.
106 Athanasius, *Discourses*, 1.15.

divinity of the Father, then some other contingent basis of his inclusion in the divine life (by which he may bring about our participation in it) must be established. In concrete terms, it would require the Father to bring into being some further intermediary to facilitate that participation and another upon that and another upon that, and so on. It is, in short, an infinite regress because things that are extrinsic to the divine being cannot gift communion with the divine being.[107] As Widdicombe puts it, 'if the Son participates in the Father in the same way in which we participate in the Son, then the Son would not be able to impart the Father to us'.[108] If the Son is extrinsic to divinity, then he shares in it by contingent participation and cannot be the agent to facilitate the participation of creation with the divine.

Describing creation as external to God and participating in God through the Son carries the important corollary that the Father–Son relation is constitutive for the God–creation relationship. This gives shape to Athanasius' doctrines of creation and salvation. As Torrance notes, 'for Athanasius the concept of God as Creator is wholly governed by the coinherent relation between the Father and the Son'.[109] Creation needs to be understood within the primacy of the Father–Son relation. The Son is proper to the Father, and intrinsic to the divine being, and so the divine being is understood to be inherently generative and fruitful.[110] As Widdicombe puts it, 'the word Father in Athanasius' theology is the word that identifies God's being as fruitful, inherently generative, relational, and dynamic'.[111] In other words, creation as a product of God's will has its ultimate basis in the Father–Son relation itself, which is not a relation of will but of being:[112]

> For if the Divine Essence be not fruitful itself, but barren, as they hold, as a light that lightens not, and a dry fountain, are they not ashamed to speak of His possessing framing energy? And whereas they deny what is by nature, do they not blush to place before it what is by will? But if He frames things that are external to Him and before were not, by willing them to be, and becomes their Maker, much more will He first be Father of an Offspring from His proper Essence.[113]

107 Ibid. See Behr, *NF*, 235–242.
108 Widdicombe, *Fatherhood of God*, 192.
109 Torrance, *Trinitarian Faith*, 77.
110 Athanasius, *Discourses*, 1.29. See Anatolios, *RN*, 115–116; Behr, *NF*, 245–246; Weinandy, *Athanasius*, 79–80.
111 Widdicombe, *Fatherhood of God*, 159.
112 Anatolios, *Coherence of His Thought*, 121–124.
113 Athanasius, *Discourses*, 2.2.

Irrespective of whether creation was brought into existence or not, God would be inherently generative and fruitful. The point is not only to assert the ontological primacy of the Father–Son relation to the God–creation relation; instead, it is to set the Father–Son relation as the necessary divine reality in continuity with which God chooses to create. This is not only a structural matter for Athanasius. The mutual delight between the Father and Son is of primary importance for understanding the character of God's relation to creation. Arguing again against the notion that the Son came into being, Athanasius argues for the eternal coexistence of the Son on the grounds that the Father has never been without joy:

> When then was it, when the Father rejoiced not? But if He ever rejoiced, He was ever, in whom He rejoiced. And in whom does the Father rejoice, except as seeing Himself in His own Image, which is His Word? And though in sons of men also He had delight, on finishing the world . . . For even thus He had delight, not because joy was added to Him, but again on seeing the works made after His own Image; so that even this rejoicing of God is on account of His Image.[114]

The mutual delight as the Father sees himself in his image and takes delight in him is the ground of the Father's love of creation, specifically humans, as those made in the image of God. As Anatolios puts it, God's delight in the world 'is derivative of the Father's delight in the Son'.[115]

Likewise, Anatolios observes, for Athanasius 'the content of Christian salvation involves being enfolded in the inner life of the Trinity'.[116] Athanasius' soteriology, which lays particular stress on our inclusion into the Son to share his relation to the Father lends a comprehensive coherence to his theological vision in that the source and telos of created being is to be enfolded in the Father's relation to the Son.[117] Once again, Athanasius' distinction between the Son as intrinsic and creation as extrinsic to divinity is applied: the Son, who is proper to the Father, shares in our creaturehood, which is extrinsic to God, so that we can participate in his relation to the Father:

> But this is God's kindness to man, that of whom He is Maker, of them according to grace He afterwards becomes Father also; becomes, that is,

[114] Ibid. 2.82.
[115] Anatolios, *Coherence of His Thought*, 124.
[116] Anatolios, *RN*, 125.
[117] See Anatolios, *RN*, 117–118; Athanasius, *AG*, 2.82.

> when men, His creatures, receive into their hearts, as the Apostle says, 'the Spirit of His Son, crying, Abba, Father.' And these are they who, having received the Word, gained power from Him to become sons of God; for they could not become sons, being by nature creatures, otherwise than by receiving the Spirit of the natural and true Son. Wherefore, that this might be, 'The Word became flesh,' that He might make man capable of Godhead.[118]

The Son, who is intrinsic to the Father, chooses to assume creaturely reality (which is extrinsic to God) into union with himself in order to bring us to share in his relation to the Father. We might say, the Son became an outsider to make us the children of the Father:[119]

> God, being first Creator, next, as has been said, becomes Father of men, because of His Word dwelling in them. But in the case of the Word the reverse; for God, being His Father by nature, becomes afterwards both His Creator and Maker, when the Word puts on that flesh which was created and made, and becomes man. For, as men, receiving the Spirit of the Son, become children through Him, so the Word of God, when He Himself puts on the flesh of man, then is said both to be created and to have been made. If then we are by nature sons, then is He by nature creature and work; but we become sons by adoption and grace.[120]

The God–world relation, then, is reconfigured as it comes to take its place in the mutual love and reciprocal delight of the Father and Son.[121]

The priority of Father over unoriginate

Hanson argues that Athanasius' attempt to describe the Son as intrinsic to the divine being and creation as extrinsic is hampered by a failure in *Discourses Against the Arians* to distinguish properly between the terms *agennētos and agenētos.*[122] Even though, in this text, Athanasius did arrange significant arguments against the prioritization of *agen(n)ētos*,[123] it was only by the time of writing *On the Synods* that Athanasius had learnt to distinguish between

118 Athanasius, *Discourses*, 2.59.
119 Ibid. 2.51.
120 Ibid. 2.61.
121 Ibid. 2.82. See Anatolios, *RN*, 153.
122 Hanson, *SCDG*, 433.
123 DelCogliano, *Anti-Eunomian Theory of Names*, 122.

agennētos and *agenētos* such that the Son can be rightly described as absolute; that is, without a beginning (*agenētos*) and yet begotten (*gennētos*).[124]

Athanasius' initial arguments against the priority of unoriginate as the primary designation for God can be found in *Discourses Against the Arians*, 1.30–34. Alongside being unscriptural, the term 'unoriginate' is not suitable as the primary designation of the Father, because understood as without a beginning (*agenētos*) it can apply to either the Father or the Son and so is imprecise. As such, Athanasius pressed for a distinction between that which has been brought into existence from nothing and that which is begotten from the Father:

> if they ask according as Asterius ruled it, as if 'what is not a work but was always' were unoriginate, then they must constantly be told that the Son as well as the Father must in this sense be called unoriginate. For He is neither in the number of things originated, nor a work, but has ever been with the Father ... When then, after failing at every turn, they betake themselves to the other sense of the question, 'existing but not generated of any nor having a father,' we shall tell them that the unoriginate in this sense is only one, namely the Father.[125]

Asterius' definition of unoriginated ('what is not a work but was always') can be applied to the Son, also. Therefore, as the primary designation for the Father, it is unsuitable.[126] However, if the term 'unoriginate' is clearly qualified as a meaning closer to unbegotten (rather than simply that which is without a beginning), then the term may be applied only to the Father.[127]

Beyond the problem of imprecision, Athanasius argued that the title 'unoriginate' was a poor signifier because it does not refer to that which is intrinsic to the divine being. Instead, it refers to God only in extrinsic terms through his difference from creation:

> [unoriginated] is not used in contrast with the Son, clamour as they may, but with things originated; and the like may be found in the words 'Almighty,' and 'Lord of the Powers' ... And therefore the Unoriginate is specified not by contrast to the Son, but to the things which through the

124 Athanasius, *Synods*, 46.
125 Athanasius, *Discourses*, 1.31.
126 See DelCogliano, *Anti-Eunomian Theory of Names*, 123.
127 See Behr, *NF*, 242–243.

> Son come to be. And excellently: since God is not as things originated, but is their Creator and Framer through the Son. And as the word 'Unoriginate' is specified relatively to things originated, so the word 'Father' is indicative of the Son. And he who names God Maker and Framer and Unoriginate, regards and apprehends things created and made; and he who calls God Father, thereby conceives and contemplates the Son . . . If they had any concern at all for reverent speaking and the honour due to the Father, it became them rather, and this were better and higher, to acknowledge and call God Father, than to give Him this name. For, in calling God unoriginate, they are, as I said before, calling Him from His works, and as Maker only and Framer, supposing that hence they may signify that the Word is a work after their own pleasure. But that he who calls God Father, signifies Him from the Son being well aware that if there be a Son, of necessity through that Son all things originate were created. And they, when they call Him Unoriginate, name Him only from His works, and know not the Son any more than the Greeks; but he who calls God Father, names Him from the Word; and knowing the Word, he acknowledges Him to be Framer of all, and understands that through Him all things have been made.[128]

Unoriginate is unsuitable as the primary mode of referring to God because it gives primacy to the God–creation relation. It describes God only by the difference between his eternity and those things that were brought into being. The result of this is that the primary designation for God is a correlate to contingent reality.

A superior designation for the unbegotten, unoriginated source of the Son, Athanasius argues, is 'Father', for then the God–creation relationship does not take primacy in our conception of the divine being. Instead, the intrinsic relation of Father and Son is given primacy:

> Therefore it is more pious and more accurate to signify God from the Son and call Him Father, than to name Him from His works only and call Him Unoriginate. For the latter title, as I have said, does nothing more than signify all the works, individually and collectively, which have come to be at the will of God through the Word; but the title Father has its significance and its bearing only from the Son.[129]

128 Athanasius, *Discourses*, 1.33. See also Widdicombe, *Fatherhood of God*, 165–167.
129 Athanasius, *Discourses*, 1.34.

Athanasius appeals both to the gratuity of divine self-naming as invitation (Jesus invites us to share his naming of God as 'Father'[130]) and to the practice of baptism, in which we are baptized 'not into the name of Unoriginate and originate, nor into the name of Creator and creature, but into the Name of Father, Son, and Holy Ghost'.[131] To refer to God as unoriginate is *impious* (or, at least, less pious) because it names God in such a way that ignores the invitation of the gospel.

Beyond this, to conceptualize divinity solely through contrast to contingent correlates is, in Athanasius' thought, idolatrous.[132] It is to define the divine by a logic that has created reality as its fundamental ground. Its impiety is compounded, within the logic of Athanasius' discussion of intrinsic belonging and extrinsic participation, by the association that this treats created reality as – in some sense – intrinsic to divinity. By contrast, to name God as Father is to name him from his relation to the Son, who is eternally begotten from the essence of the Father. This means God is named in such a way that is appropriate for his freedom from any creaturely correlate. In Athanasius' decentralizing of unbegotten, then, the divine being is not primarily described by its difference to created being (which implies some common genus within which divine and contingent being participate); instead, it is thought of primarily in terms of its self-grounded existence.[133] Athanasius refuses a way of thinking about God that is limited to extrinsic terms and insists on a way that is rigorous in following his revelation through which we are encouraged to think about God using these intrinsic terms of reference. This means that, before anything else, God must be spoken of primarily in terms of the Father–Son relation.[134] Widdicombe puts it well: 'Fatherhood, for Athanasius, is the divine attribute in relation to which all other attributions must be made.'[135]

The primacy of Father over unbegotten is a theme Athanasius returned to at some length in his later work *Defence of the Nicene Definition*, by which time Eunomius had come to lay greater stress on 'unoriginate' (*agen[n]ētos*) as the primary definition of the divine essence. Athanasius explains that the purpose of prioritizing the designation 'unoriginate' is to demonstrate that the Son, as begotten, belongs among those things that have been brought into existence from nothing.[136] Aware that this strategy operates through eliding the meaning

130 Ibid. See also Athanasius, *Defence Against the Arians*, 31.
131 Athanasius, *Discourses*, 1.34.
132 See Widdicombe, *Fatherhood of God*, 168.
133 Anatolios, *RN*, 129–130.
134 Ibid. 131; Hilary, *Trinity*, 3.22.
135 Widdicombe, *Fatherhood of God*, 170.
136 Athanasius, *Defence Against the Arians*, 28.

of terms, Athanasius carefully sets out the different meanings that *agen(n)ētos* may have:

1. that which does not yet exist but may come to be;
2. that which does not exist and does not have the potential to exist;
3. that which exists but whose existence is self-grounded and so does not have an origin or source of existence, so it is eternal.[137]

To say the Father alone is *agen(n)ētos* with the third meaning above implied (as was the case with Eunomius and Aetius) means that the begotten Son has no self-grounded existence and so is among the things brought into being (*gen[n]ētos*). While the term may appear to give honour to God as eternal and possessing life in himself, its effect is to recognize this as true of the Father alone.[138] In line with his argument that the term 'unoriginate' lacks specificity, Athanasius argues that when referring to the unoriginate in this third sense (God's self-grounded existence in contrast to the contingent existence of creation), this is true of both the Father and the Son.[139] By contrast, when referring to the unbegotten source of the Son, the designation 'Father' is to be preferred, as this recognizes the eternal correlate relation of the Son; it avoids the confusion between unbegotten and unoriginate and encourages speech of God that conceives of his intrinsic relations as constitutive.

The divinity of the Holy Spirit

Athanasius' foregrounding of the Son's generation from the essence of the Father, in contrast to the making of creation from nothing, may appear to be organized around the correlate Father–Son relation to the exclusion of the Spirit. However, developments in the middle decades of the fourth century led to the foregrounding of questions regarding the divinity of the Spirit. By the late 350s, Athanasius was once again in exile and in hiding among the monastic community in the Egyptian desert (356–62).[140] During this time, he was informed by a bishop loyal to him, Serapion of Thumis, of a faction who confessed the divinity of the Son but denied the divinity of the Spirit. Athanasius would come to ascribe the derogatory designation *tropici* (Metaphoricals) to this group, owing to their allegorical mode of interpreting Scripture.

137 Ibid.
138 Ibid 29.
139 Ibid.
140 Athanasius, *Letters to Serapion*, 1.33, tr. K. Anatolios, *Athanasius* (London: Routledge, 2004), 214–233.

The *tropici* accepted that the Father communicated his divinity to the Son but denied that the same communication of divinity held true for the Spirit's mode of procession from the Father. So, while the Father–Son relation is intrinsic to divine being, the God–Spirit relation is extrinsic. Proof-texts were advanced to support this doctrine, especially those that could be understood as describing the Spirit as created (Amos 4:13) and as an angelic being (1 Tim. 5:21). Athanasius' response to this faction, in several letters addressed to Serapion (written between 356 and 361), was significant in the formation of his mature trinitarian doctrine in as much as it involved the explicit extension to the Spirit of the arguments advanced for the divinity of the Son: the relations of Father, Son and Spirit are intrinsic to divine being.[141] Central to this, as Anatolios points out, is the confession of the full divinity of the Spirit alongside his real distinction from the Father and Son.[142]

The Spirit in *Against the Arians*

Athanasius' defence of the divinity of the Spirit in his *Letters to Serapion* is a development from his earlier thought. From the earliest examples, it was characteristic of Athanasius' thought to emphasize the saving effect of the union of the divinity of the Son with our humanity in the person of Jesus Christ: the Son shares in our condition so that we may share by grace that which he is by nature. As has been suggested above, in his *Discourses Against the Arians* this took a more high-resolution form after the manner of the dialectic between the Father–Son relation and the God–creation relation, with our incorporation by grace into the relation the Father and Son enjoy by nature.

The centrality of the Spirit in Athanasius' soteriology settles on the mediatorial work of Christ: the incarnate Son both gives the Spirit to humanity and vicariously receives the Spirit in humanity. The Son's anointing by the Spirit was not to impart divinity to the Son or to endue him with the office of kingship, for 'He had the Kingdom eternally, existing as God's Image.'[143] Instead, the Son receives the Spirit vicariously for the rest of humanity:

> But the Saviour on the contrary [the contrast is drawn to the anointing of Israel's kings], being God, and ever ruling in the Father's Kingdom, and being Himself He that supplies the Holy Ghost, nevertheless is here said to be anointed, that, as before, being said as man to be anointed with the

141 See Hill, *Athanasius and the Holy Spirit*, 133–135.
142 Anatolios, *RN*, 137–138.
143 Athanasius, *Discourses*, 1.56.

> Spirit, He might provide for us men, not only exaltation and resurrection, but the indwelling and intimacy of the Spirit.[144]

The Son's reception of the Spirit was not for his sanctification but for the sanctification of the humanity he shared with us:

> the Spirit's descent on Him in Jordan was a descent upon us, because of His bearing our body. And it did not take place for promotion to the Word, but again for our sanctification, that we might share His anointing.[145]

This is continuous with Athanasius' thought in *On the Incarnation*: by the assumption of humanity, human beings receive divine benefits through the humanity of God the Son. Here, though, what is received is the Spirit himself.[146]

Athanasius deploys the logic of his partitive exegesis: the single subject, God the Son, with respect to his divinity, is the distributor of the Spirit; with respect to his humanity he receives the Spirit as the anointed Son of God.[147] The salvific potency of the incarnation, then, is parsed through the perfect giving and receiving of the Spirit in the person of Jesus Christ: through whom should the Spirit 'be given except through the Son whose also the Spirit is? And when were we enabled to receive It [*sic*], except when the Word became man'?[148] The incarnate Son is the giver and recipient of the Spirit for the sanctification of humanity:

> but that the Giver of the Spirit, the Word Himself, hast spoken of Himself as anointed with the Spirit for us. And therefore have we securely received it [*sic*], He being said to be anointed in the flesh; for the flesh being first sanctified in Him.[149]

This is part of Athanasius' broader trinitarian framing of salvation. Athanasius describes salvation as our inclusion into the triune relations by our participation in the person of the Son, which is inseparable from our perfect reception of the Spirit through the humanity of the incarnate Son.[150] There is a dense web of interconnections whereby the very grammar of salvation is

144 Ibid.
145 Ibid. 1.57.
146 Anatolios, *RN*, 125.
147 See ibid. 134–137.
148 Athanasius, *Discourses*, 1.50.
149 Ibid.
150 Anatolios describes this as our being 'enfolded into the trinitarian life'. Anatolios, *RN*, 125.

inseparable from mutuality of the Father, Son and Spirit. Referring to John 1:12–13, Athanasius writes about the identification of humanity as the children of God through the reception of the Spirit of the Son:

> For God not only created them to be men, but called them to be sons . . . And here too the cautious distinction is well kept up, for first he says 'become,' because they are not called sons by nature but by adoption; then he says 'were begotten,' because they too had received at any rate the name of son . . . But this is God's kindness to man, that of whom He is Maker, of them according to grace He afterwards becomes Father also; becomes, that is, when men, His creatures, receive into their hearts, as the Apostle says, 'the Spirit of His Son, crying, Abba, Father.' And these are they who, having received the Word, gained power from Him to become sons of God; for they could not become sons, being by nature creatures, otherwise than by receiving the Spirit of the natural and true Son.[151]

Human participation in the divine life has its starting point in the humanity of Jesus Christ. God the Son receives the Spirit in our human being and we become co-recipients of the Spirit, through whom we are made participant members of the Son. By nature, human beings are creatures and not children, but we become children as we receive the Spirit of the Son, through whom we may fully share in the relation of Sonship. There is, then, a reciprocal balance between the Son and the Spirit in Athanasius' soteriology: the incarnate Son receives the Spirit vicariously for humanity by which we become co-recipients of the Spirit and through the Spirit our participation in the Son is secured such that we share by grace that which the Son is by nature. The Son shares our flesh, so that through his reception of the Spirit in our flesh we may be joined to him as his body.[152]

Letters to Serapion

These letters are the first extended discourse on the Spirit. It was characteristic of the *tropici*, against whom Athanasius was writing, to ridicule the proposition that the divinity of the Father is communicated to the Spirit just as it is communicated to the Son by asserting that this would mean that the Father had two sons, and that the Spirit was the brother of the Son.[153] Instead, they held that the Spirit lacks the sort of relation the Son has to the Father, and so does not receive the divinity of the Father. In refuting this, Athanasius drew on

[151] Athanasius, *Discourses*, 2.59.
[152] Hilary's doctrine of the Spirit bears similarities. See Ayres, *NL*, 184–185.
[153] Athanasius, *Letters to Serapion*, 15.

the same arguments he had used for the divinity of the Son, repurposing them for the Spirit. In this connection, Athanasius' arguments range from the overlapping scriptural designations to the trinitarian structure of salvation and the Christian life, and the perfection of divine being. In these letters the term 'Trinity' (*trias*) appears with greater frequency than in any of his other works.

Exegetical basis of attribution of divinity to Spirit

Athanasius' primary mode of refuting the *tropici* was exegetical.[154] First, Athanasius establishes the fact that the term 'spirit' is able to signify a number of different realities (the divine Spirit, wind, breath and human spirit). He isolates the presence of the definite article as central in discerning the true intention of the term: with the definite article, the reference is only to the divine Spirit. Texts, such as Amos 4:13, which the *tropici* claim to demonstrate the temporal creation of *the Spirit*, demonstrate only the creation of *human spirit*, and do not pertain to the Holy Spirit. By distinguishing the real intention of terms, Athanasius turns to consider the passages that refer to the Holy Spirit:

> Let us finally look at the sayings about the Spirit in the divine Scriptures taking them one by one, and like expert investigators let us determine well whether the Spirit has anything that belongs to creatures or whether it [*sic*] belongs to God.[155]

This, for Athanasius, indicates that the Spirit is fully divine along with the Father and Son, a claim Athanasius justifies with the following points.

Second, Athanasius extends his exegetical procedure for demonstrating the divinity of the Son to the Spirit. That is, he draws on the same methodological principle of intertextuality to show that there are scriptural designations for the Spirit that overlap with designations for the Father and Son, suggesting that the linguistic correlativity reveals their ontological correlativity.[156] This is demonstrated by Athanasius', characteristically, piling title upon title:

> Of course, the Lord is Son; but then the Spirit is called the Spirit of sonship. And, again, while the Son is Wisdom and Truth, it is written that the Spirit is Spirit of Wisdom and Truth. Yet again, while the Son is Power of

154 Weinandy enumerates ten scriptural and soteriological proofs that Athanasius offers in defence of the divinity of the Spirit. Weinandy, *Athanasius*, 114–117.

155 Athanasius, *Letters to Serapion*, 1.21.

156 See Anatolios, *RN*, 140–143.

> God and Lord of glory, the Spirit is said to be Spirit of Power and Spirit of glory.[157]

The procedure of tessellating diverse scriptural references that have overlapping conceptual ranges now extends beyond the Father–Son relation to include the particular way in which Scripture speaks of the Spirit. The driving logic, then, prioritizes the Father as the source and the Son as the outgoing radiance or manifestation of that source, while the Spirit is conceived of primarily as the application or accomplishment of that with respect to creation.[158] For example, the Father and Son are defined in relation to each other, and the Spirit is the one by whom we are made sons by adoption.[159] Again, the Father is the Light, the Son the Radiance and 'we may see the Son in the Spirit, by whom we are enlightened'.[160] Again, the Father is the source of life, the Son is the life and the Spirit is the one by whom we are made alive.[161]

The problem here is that the mechanism by which Athanasius demonstrated the ontological correlativity of the Spirit with the Father and Son also establishes the Spirit as a distinct entity more firmly within God's transitive relations. However, this is ameliorated somewhat by Athanasius' discussion of the Spirit as intrinsic to the perfection of God's triune being (see the discussion below). In part, the limitations of Athanasius' thought regarding the Spirit in this exegetical respect are a product of the order of the development of his thought: events demanded he begin with a focused defence of the divinity of the Son and so his foundational theological methodology is orientated in that direction. Beyond this is a more universal challenge facing Christian theology, which is that while the Father–Son relation includes within it a correlate relation whereby their coeternity and continuity of divinity are grounded in their very names, the Spirit does not contain such correlativity in the relation of derivation itself. This is a challenge that extends beyond this study and into the theological contribution of Augustine.[162]

Third, Athanasius returns to the fundamental distinction between divine and created being and draws together biblical texts that contrast the properties of divine being with those of created being, to demonstrate that Scripture repeatedly characterizes the Spirit as belonging to the category of divinity. In a passage that runs in parallel to his claims regarding the Son's generation from

157 Athanasius, *Letters to Serapion*, 1.25.
158 Anatolios, *RN*, 142.
159 Athanasius, *Letters to Serapion*, 1.19.
160 Ibid.
161 Ibid.
162 See Anatolios, *RN*, 143, 277–278.

the Father, Athanasius contrasts the eternal existence of the Spirit to the coming into being of created being:

> Creatures come into being from non-being and have a beginning of their coming into being . . . But the Holy Spirit is said to be from God, for it is said 'No one knows what pertains to a human being except the spirit that is in him. Likewise no one knows what pertains to God except the Spirit of God. We have not received the spirit of the world but the Spirit that is from God' (1 Cor 2.11–12). So on the basis of these words, what kind of kinship is there between the Spirit and creatures? Creatures used not to be, but God is the one who is (Ex 3.14), from whom also the Spirit is. But what is from God can neither be from non-being, nor a creature.[163]

The way in which Scripture identifies the Spirit aligns the Spirit unequivocally with the Father and Son, and not with created being.[164] Like the Son, the Spirit is from God and not among those things that have come into being from nothing. This establishes the Spirit's derivation from the Father as characterized by the same continuity of divinity as with the Son, in contrast to the extrinsic act of making, whereby creation does not share in that continuity of divinity.[165] The belonging of the Spirit with the Father and Son is complemented by the involvement of the Spirit in divine agency, which gives Athanasius' doctrine of salvation its distinctively triune structure.

The trinitarian structure of salvation

This distinction between divine being and created being is the locus for Athanasius' continued contrast between the Spirit and created being, for the Spirit is engaged in divine activity as opposed to creaturely receptivity.[166] Continuing his fundamental distinction between God and creation begun in his earliest theological works, Athanasius contends that in the work of creation and redemption God is active, while created being receives the act of God: creation is brought into being from nothing by the creative act of God and is held from a collapse into non-being by the redemptive act of God. The Spirit, acting towards the world for its sanctification, is involved in the one work of God towards creation.

163 Athanasius, *Letters to Serapion*, 1.22.
164 Anatolios, *Athanasius*, 82.
165 Athanasius, *Letters to Serapion*, 1.27.
166 See Anatolios, *Coherence of His Thought*, 76–80.

As with the Son, Athanasius explores this theme through the category of intrinsic belonging and extrinsic participation.[167] Just as the Spirit is not among those things that have come into being, but is proper to the Father and Son, so also the Spirit is not among those things that participate in divinity from the outside. Instead, as intrinsic to God, the Spirit is that through which created being participates in divinity:[168]

> How can that which is not sanctified by another and which does not participate in holiness but is itself participated – the one in which all of creation is sanctified – itself be one of the all? How can it be among those who participate in it? It would be necessary, then, for those who say this to say also that the Son, through whom all things come into being, is himself one of the 'all'.[169]

The Spirit does not participate in the holiness of divinity from the outside. The Spirit belongs intrinsically to divine being and so is holy not by participation but by nature. Therefore, the Spirit can enable created being to participate in the holiness of divinity through sanctification. The same logic is applied to Scripture's designation of the Spirit as life-giving: 'How can that which does not participate in life but is itself participated and in fact grants life to creatures have any kinship with things that come into being?'[170]

Clearly, there is continuity here with the line of argumentation Athanasius established with respect to the Son.[171] As we have seen, it is axiomatic for Athanasius that only that which is intrinsic to divine being can communicate participation in the divine life. So, likewise, the Spirit by whom also we participate in the holiness of divinity, is not himself the object of some other agency but instead 'belongs to the one Word, and accordingly belongs to the one God and is of the same being [*homoousion*]':[172]

> If we become sharers in the divine nature through participation in the Spirit, one would have to be crazy to say that the Spirit is of a created nature and not of the nature of God, for that is how those in whom the

[167] Hill, *Athanasius and the Holy Spirit*, 151–250.

[168] 'The Spirit, however, is always the same and is not among those who participate, whereas all things participate in it [*sic*].' Athanasius, *Letters to Serapion*, 1.27.

[169] Ibid. 1.23.

[170] Ibid.

[171] Hill, *Athanasius and the Holy Spirit*, 129–149.

[172] Athanasius, *Letters to Serapion*, 1.27.

> Spirit is become divinized. But if the Spirit divinizes, it is not to be doubted that it [*sic*] is of the nature of God himself.[173]

Again:

> The Spirit is not among the things that have come into being but belongs to the divinity of the Father, and is the one in whom the Word divinizes the things that have come into being. But the one in whom creation is divinized cannot be extrinsic to the divinity of the Father.[174]

As Anatolios puts it, 'the Spirit's capacity to effect our union with the Son and the Father presupposes its [*sic*] own natural unity with them'.[175] This insight is then applied in an emphatically trinitarian way:

> If the Son belongs to the being of the Father because he is from the Father, then necessarily, the Spirit also, who is said to be from God, belongs to the being of the Son . . . Therefore, it is in the Spirit that the Word glorifies creation and presents it to the Father by divinizing it and granting it adoption. But the one who binds creation to the Word could not be among the creatures and the one who bestows sonship upon creation could not be foreign to the Son. Otherwise it would be necessary to look for another Spirit to unite this one to the Word. But this is senseless. Therefore, the Spirit is not among the things that have come into being but belongs to the divinity of the Father, and is the one in whom the Word divinizes the things that have come into being. But the one in whom creation is divinized cannot be extrinsic to the divinity of the Father.[176]

The Spirit along with the Son glorifies creation, an act that rests upon the two Persons' necessary continuity with the Father.[177] The inseparability of the Son and Spirit, as those in whom creation participates in the blessing of divinity, is grounded in their one divinity and distinct relations of derivation from the essence of the Father. Therefore, it is nonsensical to affirm the divinity of the Son and not that of the Spirit also, for it is by the Spirit we are united to the Son. To deny divinity to one is to deny divinity to the other: 'for if the Spirit is

173 Ibid. 1.24.
174 Ibid. 1.25.
175 Anatolios, *RN*, 139.
176 Athanasius, *Letters to Serapion*, 1.25. This long ellipsis includes the overlapping scriptural designations used for the Son and Spirit.
177 This point is made with clarity by Behr, *NF*, 236.

a creature of the Son, it follows that they should say also that the Son is a creature of the Father'.[178] Moreover, it is to refuse their ability to unite creation to divinity.[179] As such, it is faith in the 'Trinity' that unites us to God, while he who holds a dyadic theology of the Father and Son 'receives nothing but remains empty and unsanctified'.[180] This is the reason that church praxis has always been to baptize in the triune name of God, for it is in the life-giving power of the Spirit that we share in the life of Christ that he receives from the Father. In this way, the trinitarian structure of salvation reveals that the perfection of divine being is triune.

The trinitarian structure of divine perfection

As early as his *Discourses Against the Arians*, Athanasius described the one divinity as being in triunity,[181] but it is in the *Letters to Serapion* that this designation becomes increasingly central. This is inseparable from the fundamental datum of the theology, being that which the Father has done through the Son and by the power of the Spirit: there is one divinity, which is that of the Father, which is communicated to the Son and Spirit through whom created reality is given some share in the blessing of divine being. In this way, the major elements of Athanasius' trinitarian theology are as follows:

1. A robust distinction between the creature and the creator, policed by different modes of derivation from the Father, with the Son's and Spirit's coming out from the Father's essence whereby they are intrinsic to divine being and share in continuity with the Father's divinity and creation being made from nothing and so extrinsic to divine being.
2. The resultant co-activity of the Father, Son and Spirit in the one work of God towards creation that is grounded ultimately on their continuity of divinity.
3. The distinct role of each within that co-activity.[182]

An example of this trinitarian thinking comes in Athanasius' comments on the connection between the indivisibility of the Father, Son and Spirit in nature and the one co-activity of God:

---

178 Athanasius, *Letters to Serapion*, 1.21.
179 Ibid. 1.30–31.
180 Ibid. 1.29.
181 See Athanasius, *Discourses*, 1.18; 3.15.
182 See Anatolios, *RN*, 144.

> The Trinity is holy and perfect, confessed as God in Father, Son and Holy Spirit . . . It is identical with itself and indivisible in nature, and its activity is one. For the Father does all things through the Word and in the Holy Spirit. Thus the oneness of the Holy Trinity is preserved and thus is the one God 'who is over all and through all and in all' (Eph 4.6) preached in the Church – 'over all', as Father, who is beginning and fountain; 'through all', through the Son; and 'in all' in the Holy Spirit. It is Trinity not only in name and linguistic expression, but Trinity in reality and truth.[183]

The one God is the Father, who is the fount of the Son and the Spirit. However, there is no interruption of being between them, for the Father communicates the one divinity to the Son and the Spirit as those who are derived from the essence of the Father. This unity does not eradicate the distinctions between them because the mode of sharing in the divinity of the Father are the relations of derivation that distinguish the Son and Spirit:

> God is not like a human being, nor does he have a partitive nature. Therefore, he does not beget the Son by way of partition, so that the Son may become the father of another, since the Father himself is not from a father. Neither is the Son a part of the Father. Therefore, he does not beget as he himself was begotten, but is the whole image and radiance of the whole. It is only in the Godhead that the Father is properly Father and the Son properly Son; in their case, the Father is always Father and the Son always Son. Just as the Father could never be Son, so also the Son could never be Father . . . So it is madness to speak and even to think in any way of a brother of the Son, and to name the Father a grandfather. Neither is the Spirit called Son in the Scriptures, so as to be considered as a brother, nor is it [*sic*] called a son of the Son, lest the Father be conceived as a grandfather. But the Son is said to be Son of the Father, and the Spirit of the Son is said to be of the Father. Thus, there is one Godhead of the Holy Trinity, unto which there is also one faith.[184]

Athanasius conceived of the Father, Son and Spirit as holding distinct and immutable identities grounded in their relations to one another. The Son and the Spirit are out from the Father in their own distinct ways. The Son is the *only-begotten* from the Father, whereas the Spirit 'is said to *proceed* from

---

183 Athanasius, *Letters to Serapion*, 1.28.
184 Ibid. 1.16.

the Father, since it [*sic*] shines forth and is sent and given by the Word who is confessed to be from the Father'.[185] Therefore, the Spirit is not to be called 'Son', even though like the Son he comes out from the essence of the Father:

> Even though it [*sic*] is not called 'Son' in the Scriptures but 'Spirit of God', nevertheless it [*sic*] is said to be in God himself and from God himself . . . If the Son belongs to the being of the Father because he is from the Father, then necessarily the Spirit also, who is said to be from God, belongs to the being of the Son.[186]

In this way, Athanasius described the essential unity of the three as intrinsic to divine being. The perfection of the divine life is not exhausted by the Father–Son relation alone but is completed in the Spirit.

185 Ibid. 1.20; emphases mine.
186 Ibid. 1.25.

Conclusion: working dogmatic comments

Transitive and non-transitive relations

In *On the Trinity*, Hilary writes, 'the very centre of our saving faith is belief not merely in God, but in God as Father; not merely in Christ but in Christ the Son of God'.[1] Similarly, Athanasius writes that 'it will be much more accurate to denote God from the Son and to call Him Father, than to name Him and call Him Unoriginated from His works only'.[2] This is a distinctively *Nicene* approach to theology, in which our thinking about God and his relations to us are to be controlled by the reality of God. In a Nicene frame, the way we are to conceptualize God and his transitive relations to us as creator and redeemer is grounded in the contemplation of the inner fullness of God's non-transitive relations as Father, Son and Spirit.

This does not mean to neglect the economy in favour of speculation into the immanent divine life. Nor does this mean that the external acts of God in the economy of salvation are confused with his intrinsic relations. Instead, it means that what it is for God to be redeemer and creator has its inner logic and grammar within the immanent relations of divinity. God's eternal life as Father, Son and Spirit is revealed in his loving outward actions to us. As it has been put by T. F. Torrance:

> It is distinctive of Christian theology that it treats of God in his relation to the world and of God in his relation to himself, not of one without the other. If it did not include the former, we who belong to the world could have no part in it, and if it did not include the latter, it could be concerned only with a 'knowledge of God' dragged down and trapped within the world and our relations with it.[3]

---

[1] Hilary, *Trinity*, 1.17.

[2] Athanasius, *Defence Against the Arians*, 31.

[3] T. F. Torrance, *Reality and Evangelical Theology* (Philadelphia, Pa.: Westminster Press, 1982), 21.

The divine life *in se* is the proper basis on which to understand God's activity *pro nobis*, but the immanent relations of God are not retroactively changed by his extrinsic relations to us. The following comments offer a brief exploration of this theme and are intended as indicative; tracing out a theological approach that arises from the Nicene Creed.

The order of the Nicene Creed is to declare faith in the immanent processions of God and then to declare faith in the corresponding external act in which that internal life is enacted in history. First, God the Father, who is eternally fruitful as the source of the Son and the Spirit and, second, the creator of all that is not God. First, the Son who is eternally begotten from the essence of the Father and, second, the Son who is sent from the Father into history. First, the Spirit who is eternally breathed out from the Father and, second, the Spirit who gives life to creation. The order of thought is always from the immanent to the economic, such that the non-transitive relations of God are the archetype from which God's transitive relations take their shape and their ultimate *theological* content. The creed models an approach to the task of theology that thinks about God in his relation to creation from the basis of the privileged insight we are given into the life of God by this saving self-revelation. In this, our theology is truly theological in that the reality of God, independent from our conceptual apprehension of him, governs that which can be said of God. The point is that God's actions in history are ontologically grounded in the intrinsic relations of God and take their potency and structure from that intra-divine reality.

In modern theology, this primacy of the non-transitive over the transitive has been laid out with particular insight by Paul Molnar. For Molnar, the formal primacy of the non-transitive relations means to protect the antecedent existence of God as Father, Son and Spirit irrespective of his relations to creation. God is who God is in the fullness of his triune relations, whether he chooses to create or not. Moreover, God does not become more himself through the course of his relations to us. While this could be parsed in the terms of classical theism (God's absolute being undergoes no modification or enrichment either as intrinsic and self-generated or as extrinsic and relationally determined), Molnar uses a trinitarian terminology, describing God's intrinsic relations as the immanent Trinity, which he views as distinct from, but related to, God's extrinsic activity in history (the economic Trinity).[4] While God's economic activity as creator and redeemer do not constitute God,[5] they do reveal and take their

[4] P. D. Molnar, *Divine Freedom and the Doctrine of the Immanent Trinity: In Dialogue with Karl Barth and Contemporary Theology*, 2nd edn (London: Bloomsbury, 2017), ix–xviii.

[5] See P. D. Molnar, 'The Function of the Immanent Trinity in the Theology of Karl Barth: Implications for Today', *SJT* 42.3 (1989), 367–399.

fundamental structure from the inner life of Father, Son and Spirit. From this insight, it follows that we truly do know God through his actions towards us – that what he is towards us in history, he is eternally and antecedently in himself – and that this knowledge takes the form of being drawn in as participants of an eternal knowing and being known that is quite independent from us. In this, Molnar is a powerful advocate of the freedom of God.

Similarly, John Webster has argued that the proper order of theology is first God's life in itself and then God towards the world: we consider the *agency* in the light of the *agent*. Webster does not mean this in terms of the priority of the one God over his triunity. As will be discussed below, the contemporary resurgence of *de Deo uno* over the *de Deo trino* does not, despite immediate appearances, consistently fulfil its promise to have proper regard for the unique transcendence of God. Instead, Webster lays out a theological vision that is in close correspondence to the Nicene approach in that the external divine relations (the economic missions of God) always follow after 'their origin in the eternal nature and personal properties of the agent'.[6] There is a continuity of identity between God's intrinsic life as Father, Son and Spirit and his external acts as creator and redeemer.

Likewise Karl Barth, in *Church Dogmatics* 2.1, argues for the primacy of God's intrinsic relations alongside God's givenness in his extrinsic relations. For Barth, our knowledge is grounded in God's givenness to us, but this is such that God is not collapsed into this self-revelation: 'the real knowledge of God is concerned with God in His relationship to man, but also in His distinction from him'.[7] God truly becomes the object of humanity as a knowing subject, and is antecedently and unchangeably the object to himself:

> As He certainly knows Himself first of all, God is first and foremost objective to Himself . . . In His triune life as such, objectivity, and with it knowledge, is divine reality before creaturely objectivity and knowledge exist. We call this the primary objectivity of Good, and distinguish it from the secondary, i.e., the objectivity which He has for us too in His revelation, in which He gives Himself to be known by us as He knows Himself. It is distinguished from the primary objectivity, not by a lesser degree of truth, but by its particular form suitable for us, the creature. God is objectively immediate to Himself, but to us He is objectively mediate.[8]

---

6 J. Webster, *God Without Measure: Working Papers in Christian Theology*, vol. 1: *God and the Works of God* (London: T&T Clark, 2016), 9.

7 Barth, *CD*, 2.1, 10.

8 Ibid. 16.

Using the language of subject–object epistemology, Barth lays out a similar methodological principle to that of Hilary and Athanasius. The character of God's primary objectivity is that immediacy which obtains between the Father and Son in the unity of the Spirit. The character of God's secondary objectivity is the mediate form, 'clothed under the veil of that which is different from Himself'.[9] So, even though the category of *encounter* is central to Barth's theology, that encounter is ultimately governed by the ontological reality beyond it. God may well be objective to us, *but he is not constituted by that secondary objectivity*.[10] For this reason, Barth parses our knowledge of God as obedience to God's self-truth and self-knowledge, in which we are made participants through the sheer gratuity of God:

> first of all, and in the heart of the truth in which He stands before us, God stands before Himself: the Father before the Son, the Son before the Father. And first of all, and in the heart of the truth in which we know God, God knows himself . . . This occurrence in God Himself is the essence and strength of our knowledge of God.[11]

Similarly, T. F. Torrance locates necessity only with God's intrinsic relations. This is the ground of God's radical 'ontological freedom',[12] meaning his self-caused fullness, from which his extrinsic relations are volitional and gratuitous rather than necessary (as if arising from some privation within the divine being). However, in the same gratuity God's saving revelation is a self-revelation. Given the ontological primacy of God's intrinsic relations, this extrinsic *self*-revelation does not constitute divine reality, but manifests it:

> We cannot think of the [immanent] Trinity as if it were constituted by or dependent on the economic Trinity, but must rather think of the economic Trinity as freely predetermined manifestation in the history of salvation of the eternal Trinity, which God himself was before the foundation of the world and eternally is.[13]

[9] Ibid.

[10] See Molnar, *Divine Freedom*, 141–150, and E. Jüngel, *God's Being Is in Becoming: The Trinitarian Being of God in the Theology of Karl Barth*, tr. J. Webster (Edinburgh: T&T Clark, 2001), 55–74.

[11] Barth, *CD*, 2.1, 49. This quotation has been selected as it seems to me to articulate Barth's point particularly well. The theme is explored throughout *CD*, 2.1, 3–128.

[12] Torrance, *Christian Doctrine of God*, 108.

[13] Ibid. 108–109.

In other words, God's extrinsic activity is not equivalent to his intrinsic relations but there is *correspondence*. God's extrinsic activity is a 'reflection' or is analogically related to his intrinsic relations:[14]

> Under the creative impact of his self-revelation the trinitarian pattern of his internal relations becomes imprinted upon the series of saving events proclaimed to us in the Gospel, and upon our knowing and speaking of him, under the constraint of his three-fold manifestation in those events as Father, Son and Holy Spirit.[15]

This is not the place for a consideration of how this informs Torrance's 'stratified structure' of theological knowledge, except to say that the triune structure of God's self-revelation, shaped by the triune reality of the divine being, shapes human thought such that, in our growing understanding of God's self-revelation, the deep trinitarian coherence begins to shape theology into a trinitarian logic.[16]

To prioritize the non-transitive relations is not to undermine the centrality of God's saving acts in history for our knowledge of God. It is only as those who are addressed and redeemed that we know God at all: we know him through his grace received in faith through the Spirit by Christ in whom we participate in faith through the Spirit. However, it is to say that God is *not* constituted by his outward acts to creation and that these transitive relations are themselves ultimately rooted in and correspond to the non-transitive divine relations. The relations of God *pro nobis* are the enactment of God's life *in se*. It is on this basis that the theological character of the divine economy is most readily engaged with: 'God's outer works are most fully understood as loving and purposive when set against the background of his utter sufficiency.'[17] In other words, the logic of the Christian confession is from the inside out, or from the immanent to the economic. God is not another historical agent who is in the process of becoming through that agency. He is not unanchored in himself such that his relation to us is constitutive of his reality. Instead, God's transcendent, self-grounded and self-caused life as Father, Son and Spirit, utterly distinct from creation, is the ground and grammar of his free self-involvement in creation.

---

[14] Ibid. 198.

[15] Ibid. 82.

[16] T. F. Torrance, *The Ground and Grammar of Theology* (Belfast: Christian Journals, 1980), 146–178; *Reality and Scientific Theology*, new edn (Eugene, Ore.: Wipf & Stock, 2001), 160–201. See my discussion in A. Irving, *T. F. Torrance's Reconstruction of Natural Theology: Christ and Cognition* (Lanham, Md.: Lexington Books, 2019), 46–51, 203–208.

[17] Webster, *God Without Measure*, 6.

This primacy of God as the absolute, free, self-grounded being provides the fundamental grammar for subsequent theological commitments. The remainder of this chapter offers some thoughts to this end.

Self-revelation

The Son and Spirit through whom the Father is made known and by whom we receive that knowledge do not participate in divinity in a contingent fashion. Their unity with the Father is not mediated by some other party. As from the essence of the Father, they are intrinsic to the divine being and do not receive divinity from outside themselves by participation (through whatever contingent mechanism that might be). Instead, they share fully, eternally and necessarily in the divinity of the Father. The knowledge of God we have through the incarnate presence of the Son and in the indwelling of the Spirit is not second-hand. In the categories of the fourth century, the Son is the very radiance of the light of the Father towards us, whom we see in the light of the Spirit.[18] In the categories of modern theology, the revelation of God is a *self*-revelation. God is both the subject and the object of revelation: God is revealed through God.

Nicene theology holds a constitutive image-Christology. The Son as the image of the Father is God as the Father is God. Primarily, this is an intra-divine event. The Son, as begotten from the essence of the Father, is God from God: he receives all the Father is – aside from being unbegotten – and reflects this to the Father. God in himself, in the perfection of his internal relations, involves the mutual delight of the Father and Son as the Father sees his likeness in the Son and takes joy in him. This non-transitive relation is the ground and the archetype of his self-revelation in his transitive acts towards creation. God the Son is the image of God on creation such that if we see him, we see the Father. The Son, as the eternal image of the Father to whom all the essence of the Father is given and received, knows the Father perfectly. Unlike the Arian Christ, whose attenuated divinity limited the Son's knowledge of the Father, the Nicene Christ knows the Father fully,[19] and makes his confession to the Father within our hearing and understanding (Matt. 11:27). God has held nothing back in his revelation. Had he revealed himself through some lesser intermediary, such a revelation would be like using a syringe in relation to the Atlantic Ocean, a syringe that could take in and give out only a tiny part of the whole.

18 Beeley, *Gregory of Nazianzus*, 194–201.

19 Athanasius, *Discourses*, 2.22.

This aspect of the Nicene faith has been seen with particular clarity by Torrance in his comments on the significance of the Son's identity of essence with the Father. Coordinating the Nicene faith to his own project of theological science, Torrance describes a realist bent of mind, of knowing 'only under the constraint of [a reality's] distinctive nature',[20] in which the reality external to and independent from the human knower shapes our thought such that we know 'strictly in accordance with [its] nature [which is] to know them in accordance with their truth or reality'.[21] This, he suggests, is intrinsic to the fidelity and godliness of our knowing God,[22] in that we do not defiantly or mythologically impose our own conceptions on to the divine but rather listen, receive and obey.[23]

From this perspective Torrance follows Athanasius and Hilary in prioritizing the internal relation of the Father and Son as the ground of our knowledge of God:

> the mutual relation of knowing and being between the Father and the Lord Jesus Christ constitutes the ontological ground for our knowing of God, for in and through it our knowledge of God the Father is objectively rooted in the eternal being of God himself.[24]

With regard to the mutual relation of *knowing*, our knowledge of God becomes inseparable from the mystical participation in the Son wherein we share in his knowledge and love of the Father,[25] and therefore from the doxological (and ecclesiological) activities in which that participation is effected, celebrated and lived within. In other words, the knowledge of God is inseparable from the category of relationship, and so from the moral and experiential associations this carries with it. With regard to the mutual relation of *essence*, there is no interval of essence between Father and Son. Torrance treats *homoousios* almost as a cypher for the identity of God and his outward activity:

> it expressed the fact that what God is 'toward us' . . . in and through the Word made flesh, he really is *in himself*; that is he is in the *internal relations* of his transcendent being the very same Father, Son and Holy Spirit that he is in his revealing and saving activity.[26]

20 Torrance, *Trinitarian Faith*, 52.
21 Ibid. 51, 54.
22 Ibid. 38.
23 Ibid. 43.
24 Ibid. 59.
25 Ibid. 55.
26 Ibid. 130. See also Torrance, *Theology in Reconciliation*, 223; emphases original.

The actuality of revelation as *self*-revelation serves as the ground of possibility for this Nicene approach in which the non-transitive relations take primacy over the transitive. Nicene theology is attentive to the fact of having been addressed and to the gratuitous character of that address. The task of theology, then, in serving the proclamation of the gospel is to allow this gratuity to inform the whole of our conceptual field. In what follows, this will be attempted first in relation to the contemporary resurgence of the primacy of the oneness of God over this threeness and then in relation to the twin doctrines of creation and redemption.

The oneness of God

The opening proposition of the Nicene Creed is the church's belief in the one God. In her recent influential work, Katherine Sonderegger has provided an insightful and far-reaching study in which she has set out to reverse the 'broad movement in present-day dogmatics that has pressed the treatise *De Deo Trino* to the fore [such that] it crowds out and supplants the exposition of the one God'.[27] In this, she argues for the primacy of the unicity of God over the multiplicity of God. This involves the prioritization of the scriptural language of the perfections of the divine being (oneness, his omnipresence, omnipotence, etc.), not as 'a pious livery for philosophical abstraction',[28] but rather to reflect what she considers to be the scriptural mandate to give reverence to the one God. In this, Sonderegger argues forcefully for a classical theism over against the contemporary variants of a theistic mutualism.[29] In this, Sonderegger's work is timely and significant. However, there follows a relocation and reconfiguration of the place and role of Jesus Christ in such a system of dogmatics, away from the all-determining centre. Instead, the one divine nature is placed at the conceptual heart. This involves replacing Jesus Christ as the primary ground of any analogy between God and creation with a broader analogical base established on a 'compatibilism' between God and the cosmos.[30] This compatibility, as Sonderegger envisages it, is governed by the divine perfections as God elevates nature in his gratuity. For example, in his omniscience the one God embraces our subjectivity and endues it

[27] K. Sonderegger, *Systematic Theology*, vol. 1: *The Doctrine of God* (Minneapolis, Minn.: Fortress Press, 2014), xiv.

[28] Ibid. xvi.

[29] See J. E. Dolezal, *All That Is in God: Evangelical Theology and the Challenge of Classical Christian Theism* (Grand Rapids, Mich.: Reformation Heritage Books, 2017), 1–8.

[30] Sonderegger, *Systematic Theology*, xviii–xix.

with his Spirit, illuminating us to a response in knowledge, prayer and worship.[31]

For Sonderegger, oneness is the foundational scriptural perfection that describes something of what kind of being God is.[32] More than that, to say God is one is to say he is *this* being rather than another. For Sonderegger, it refers primarily to the absolute singularity and unique transcendence of the holy God, 'the God who is unapproachable Light, Holy Fire and Goodness; around this One is thick darkness'.[33] The oneness of God is his incomparability: God is not within a wider class of beings to whom a degree of commonality can be asserted. In his *Proslogion*, Anselm described the incommensurability of God and creation in the following way: God is 'that than which nothing greater can be conceived'.[34] As McFarland puts it, this does not mean that God is the most perfect of beings, as this would locate 'God on the same metaphysical continuum as all other beings'.[35] God cannot be classified within a larger set of beings: *Deus non est en genere*, as the Thomistic principle runs.[36] God is not a species within a larger grouping because there is no higher genus within which God is limited. God's existence is not an instantiation of a more fundamental mode of being. There is no common class that obtains between divine and contingent being. Instead, God is wholly other, *transcendent*.[37] His mode of being is absolute as pure actuality in whom there is no passive potency; our mode of being is contingent, brought into being from nothing. Given this, any description within our conceptual realm would, by definition, be inappropriate in the theological lexicon if it were used with one overarching definition (univocally) with regard both to contingent reality and to the one God, as this would be 'to locate both within the same conceptual framework'.[38] Sonderegger characterizes this as the 'fundamental axiom' of theology,[39] suggesting that this requires us to adopt an apophatic theological method. However, it is here that Sonderegger's mode of conceptualizing divine aseity pulls against the conceptual content of the doctrine itself. That is, she describes God's absolute transcendence by negative correlation to contingent reality.

---

31 Ibid. xx–xi.

32 Sonderegger argues that oneness of God is a metaphysical predicate for God; i.e. that in revealing God to us as one, Scripture reveals the kind of being he is. Ibid. 3–21.

33 Ibid. 23.

34 Anselm, *Proslogion*, 2, in T. Williams (tr.), *Monologion and Proslogion with the Replies of Gaunilo and Anselm* (Indianapolis, Ind.: Hackett Classics, 1995).

35 I. A. McFarland, *From Nothing: A Theology of Creation* (Louisville, Ky.: Westminster John Knox Press, 2014), 29.

36 Sonderegger, *Systematic Theology*, 31.

37 Ibid. 33–35.

38 McFarland, *From Nothing*, 31.

39 Sonderegger, *Systematic Theology*, 26.

With Sonderegger, the oneness of God is inseparable from the scriptural witness to God. The God of Israel allows for no rival and demands his people's singular devotion (Deut. 6:4–5). Jesus reiterated this command to worship and serve the one God (Mark 12:28–34). Sonderegger's biblical and spiritual reverence for the one God is a helpful corrective to how the *homoousios* may be used to justify an overreaching theological epistemology that claims exhaustive knowledge of divinity. In this regard, it both holds us back from an 'immoderate confidence'[40] that treats God in overly familiar terms and it inspires our gratitude in the sheer gratuity of God in giving himself in his radical uniqueness to be known by strange creatures like us! Moreover, Sonderegger's fundamental conviction regarding the oneness of God is a helpful prophylactic against models of theism that envisage God as being in a reciprocal relation with creation: the one God is the God he is in himself and no new actuality or mode of being is given to him from beyond himself.

However, Sonderegger's reassertion of the primacy of the one God over and above his multiplicity is deeply problematic. First, God's triunity is more rightly considered without sequence. The Nicene confession does not follow its affirmation of the one God with an analysis of the divine perfections. Nicene theology always considers the one God inseparably from the Father: it is the divinity of the Father that is communicated with the Son and Spirit. In Athanasius, this was an integral part of distancing the *homoousion* from materialistic concerns. In Basil, this was an integral part of distancing the *homoousion* from equating the persons as equally derived from some free-standing *ousia*. Exploring the relation between the unity of God and his plurality in terms of *sequence* is the very theological move the Nicene approach is calibrated to resist. With one eye on Arius and the Eusebian faction, it resists the sequence of the one unoriginate to the Son with a subsequent volitional unity. With the other eye on Marcellus, it resists the sequence of the one God dilating to three. So, while Sonderegger is justified in her resistance towards the undermining of divine simplicity which is within any theological construction that views the divine being as composed of the communion of the three persons (for example, social trinitarianism), prioritizing the one divine essence aside from the three persons bears its own problems.

Second, where Sonderegger does establish some element of dynamic gratuity through the notion of spiritual illumination, it falls to the side of a distinctively Nicene approach that prioritizes the Father–Son relation as that in which we participate by the Spirit. Sonderegger calls up the image of the theologian on Sinai: 'we pray that God's entire Goodness may shield us and, in that shielding,

[40] Webster, *God Without Measure*, 10.

pass by so that we may know the mystery of this God'.[41] By contrast, Gregory of Nazianzus writes:

> I was running to lay hold on God, and thus I went up into the Mount, and drew aside the curtain of the Cloud, and entered away from matter and material things, and as far as I could I withdrew within myself. And then when I looked up, I scarce saw the back parts of God although I was sheltered by the Rock, the Word that was made flesh for us. And when I looked a little closer, I saw, not the First and unmingled Nature, known to Itself – to the Trinity, I mean; not That which abides within the first veil, and is hidden by the Cherubim; but only that Nature, which at last even reaches to us.[42]

While Sonderegger conceives of divinity itself as gratuitously shielding the human knower as the human soul and mind is illumined, Gregory conceives of our being shielded within the person of Jesus Christ, knowing God in his economic activity alone. Or, we could place it in a vicarious category: participating in the Son's knowledge of the Father. It is Jesus Christ, not the theologian, who ascends Sinai and it is in his face that we see the glory of the Father in the light of the Spirit (2 Cor. 4:5–6).

Third, and most significantly, Nicene theology does not approach the doctrine of God through negation. Instead, divinity is described using positive affirmations of God as Father, Son and Spirit. This is not simply a preference for relational language over metaphysical language. (Nicene theology is bold in its application of non-scriptural terms drawn from the surrounding philosophical context.) Instead, this is a genuine and consistent respect for divine oneness. This is counterintuitive: How does using familiar and familial terminology for the divine better respect his radical freedom from creation than the terminology of the wholly and holy other? It was characteristic of the broad tradition that objected to the Nicene confession to describe God by privation through a contrast to contingent being (*agen[n]ētos*). The Nicene faith, on the other hand, refers to God primarily in terms that have an immanent reference. This is the force of Basil of Caesarea's arguments against Eunomius and Athanasius' theological rule, that it is more godly and more accurate to call God 'Father' than to call him 'unoriginate'. The problem with taking unoriginate as the central designation for God is that it conceives of him solely by a contrast to contingent

41 Sonderegger, *Systematic Theology*, 23.
42 Gregory of Nazianzus, *Or*, 28.3.

being, and so God is described in a way he does not wholly control, but is controlled by the conditions of creaturely reality:

> if we try to reach knowledge of God from some point outside of God, we cannot operate with any point *in God* by reference to which we can test or control our conceptions of him, but are inevitably flung back upon ourselves. Even if we relate God negatively to what we are in ourselves, we are nevertheless quite unable to escape using ourselves as some sort of measure for what we think and say of him.[43]

In other words, the mode of thought that sought to respect the divine transcendence of the one unoriginate proves instead to undermine it by conceiving of God only in terms that have contingent existence as their correlate.

In the same way, far from securing the freedom of God in his difference from creation, Sonderegger's way of explaining unicity as the foundational predicate of God actually serves to bind God in correlation to the human conceptual field. Methodologically, this is indicated by Sonderegger's association between the theological rule that God is not in a genre and apophatic theology.[44] The problem with this is that God's transcendence is determined solely by his difference from contingent reality. The claim that 'the Lord's radical Uniqueness frees Him from all comparisons, all genus and likeness'[45] is incorrect in Sonderegger's way of viewing it. A revealing claim is the following: 'the negation of all creatureliness *must come first* in our praise and speech about God'.[46] For Sonderegger, the anti-idolatrous denial of any similarity to God becomes the affirmation of the one God such that the isolation of contingent reality from the realm of the divine is the primary mode of theology: 'the denial simply is the affirmation of Divine Unicity *under the conditions of creaturehood*'.[47] And again, 'By saying that creatures are not God, we affirm God's surpassing reality as the One Free God. And it is a glorious liberty.'[48] The grounding factor of all such theological constructions is not the free, transcendent God but the limitations of contingent reality.[49] Here the doctrine of God is grounded in

43 Torrance, *Trinitarian Faith*, 51; emphasis original.

44 Sonderegger, *Systematic Theology*, 27.

45 Ibid.

46 Ibid. 29; emphasis mine.

47 Ibid.; emphasis mine.

48 Ibid. 30.

49 Sonderegger's approach does not accord with the first of Kathryn Tanner's proposals for speech regarding a transcendent creator: 'for talk of God as transcendent beyond necessary relations of identity or difference with non-divine'. K. Tanner, *God and Creation in Christian Theology: Tyranny or Empowerment* (Minneapolis, Minn.: Fortress Press, 2005), 81.

correlation to contingent being, even if that correlation is negation. Sonderegger's account of the unique transcendence of the one God, then, is self-defeating and conceives of God only in terms of the ground of contingent, limited being. Divine perfection cannot have contingent imperfection as its ultimate ground, as it would then be a co-determinant of the conditions of created being.

A more satisfactory account of the one God in his unique transcendence from creation needs to be constructed in terms of triunity. Thought and speech about God must be undertaken primarily with reference to the non-transitive relations of Father and Son and Spirit. The transitive relation by which some analogy is established between this intra-divine reality and our human conceptualities is subsequent, derivative and gratuitous. This approach better reflects the theological rule that God is not in a genre.

For Webster, God's transcendent and unoriginate divinity cannot be properly thought of simply through a contrast between divine and contingent being: 'disorder threatens when that contrast is allowed to expand and fill the concept completely'.[50] The difference between God and creation is not constitutive of our apprehension of divinity, but is a corollary of it. Instead, God is to be thought of primarily in terms that are above comparative difference from contingent reality. That is, in terms intrinsic to divinity with this self-caused fullness God is the ground of his extrinsic relations to us in creation and redemption.[51] Webster's solution is to ground God's aseity – that is his self-caused existence as *autotheos* – in the doctrine of the Trinity: 'it is as Father, Son and Spirit that God is of himself utterly free and full, in the self-originate and perfect movement of his life: grounded in himself, he gives himself, the self-existent Lord of grace'.[52] In this sense, God's non-transitive relations entirely from within himself are the way to describe his oneness:

> Aseity is not to be defined merely in negative terms, as the mere absence of origination from or dependence upon an external cause. If this is allowed to happen, then a subordinate characteristic of aseity (God's 'not being from another') comes to eclipse its primary meaning (God's 'being in and from himself') . . . It is much more fruitful to understand aseity in terms of fullness of personal relations. Aseity is *life*: God's life *from* and therefore *in* himself. This life is the relations of Father, Son and Spirit. Crucially, therefore, aseity is not a property to be affirmed *de Deo uno* anterior to God's triune life, but indicates the wholly original character of

50 Webster, *God Without Measure*, 14.
51 Ibid. 13.
52 Ibid. 19.

> the inner relations which are God's life . . . The self-existence of the triune God is his existence in the personal internal activities of God. These activities are personal relations, that is, modes of subsistence in which each particular person of the Trinity is identified in terms of the other two persons.[53]

Divine aseity, then, is not the privation of derivation. Instead, aseity includes derivation, as the Son and Spirit are eternally derived *from the essence* of the Father within the being of God from and for himself. This is not a modification of divine being, but is intrinsic to what it is to be God. This approach takes seriously the notion that the Son and Spirit are *proper* to the Father and therefore constitute divine perfection: 'filiation [and spiration] is not a lack but a mode of God's eternal perfection, intrinsic to the wholly realized self-movement of God'.[54] Arising from this, it takes seriously the primacy of the terms that refer to God's intrinsic relations over and above terms that name him by difference from creation. In other words, God in his transcendent difference from creation is not constituted by that difference. Instead, God is who he is in the perfection of the mutual and loving relations of Father, Son and Spirit.

The triune creator and redeemer

This way of construing the self-caused divine perfection provides the proper grammar for God's extrinsic relations. God's self-causation is not only pertinent for his interior relations but for his external relations also. The non-transitive relations of Father, Son and Spirit are the structure of the enactment of the life of God in his transitive relations. Or, as Webster puts it:

> The movement of God's triune life has its perfection in and of itself, and is utterly sufficient to itself; but this perfect movement is not self-enclosed or self-revolving. In its perfection, it is also a movement of self-gift in which the complete love of Father, Son and Spirit communicates itself *ad extra* creating and sustaining a further object of love.[55]

God's perfection may be self-caused and self-contained but it is not *self-enclosed*. The character of the intrinsic divine relations is the ground and power of God's external relations to creation. The economic missions correspond to the

[53] Ibid. 19–20; emphases original.
[54] Ibid. 21.
[55] Ibid. 24.

immanent processions. We, therefore, understand God's extrinsic relations from the logical priority of the intrinsic relations, such that the force and content of God's external acts begin to be known when they are set in their proper foundation in God's life *in se*.

Creation

God's being is inherently generative, which makes creation an act (while not necessary) consistent with the very being of God. God's very being is as a fountain of life. The outward act of creation is a contingent and gratuitous overflow of the divine being to stand in relation to that which is external to himself. Out of that eternal and full delight of Father and Son, creation is made. In his recent account and defence of the doctrine of creation from nothing, Ian McFarland grounds the character of creation in certain qualities of divinity in order to show that 'God's work in and for the world (*ad extra*) corresponds to the eternal character of God's Trinitarian life (*ad intra*)'.[56] One such quality is that the divine being is *productive*: God eternally gives rise to God as the Father generates the Son and breathes out the Spirit.[57] Torrance takes this principle and applies it in his self-consciously Athanasian claim that 'it is as Father Almighty that God is Creator':[58]

> In virtue of his intrinsic and eternal Fatherhood God always had the power to create . . . Expressed otherwise, since God is Father in himself, as Father of the Son, he is essentially generative or fruitful in his own Being, and it is because he is inherently productive as *Father* that God could and did freely become Creator or Source of all being beyond himself. Creation arises, then, out of the Father's eternal love of the Son and is activated through the free ungrudging movement of that Fatherly love in sheer grace which continues to flow freely and unceasingly toward what God has brought into being in complete differentiation from himself.[59]

Here, not only is Torrance *not* naming God from creation and calling him the unoriginate cause of creation; he is naming God as Creator from God as Father of the Son![60]

56 McFarland, *From Nothing*, 42.
57 Ibid. 43.
58 Torrance, *Christian Doctrine of God*, 205.
59 Ibid. 209.
60 Torrance, *Trinitarian Faith*, 78–79.

This theological move has several implications. First, it means that the making of creation needs to be understood in relation to the fullness of the divinity. The work of God in bringing something into existence that is external to himself has to be understood as 'issuing from the infinite uncreated and wholly realized movement of God's life in himself'.[61] In other words, the Christian doctrine of creation is a derivative Christian doctrine rather than a source of our knowledge about God. We understand better the character and nature of created being within the knowledge of God. In this connection, Webster follows a profoundly Nicene line as he differentiates between the intra-trinitarian processions from the extrinsic act. The eternal, unique processions of the Son and the Spirit from the essence of the Father are qualitatively distinct from temporally bringing creation into existence by an application of will.[62] This distinction, he continues, is not a difference of degree but the incommensurable difference of that which is intrinsic and that which is extrinsic to divinity. Webster demonstrates that the act of God in creating needs to be understood on the basis of God's intrinsic, necessary and eternal fullness as Father, Son and Spirit: 'God is in himself replete, unoriginate love, the reciprocal fellowship and delight of the three and the utter repose and satisfaction of their love. God requires nothing other than himself. Yet, his unoriginate love also originates.'[63] This has been put with particular force by Barth:

> God did not need this otherness of the world and man in order not to be alone, single, enclosed within Himself, God did not need coexistence with the creature. He does not will and posit the creature necessarily, but in freedom, as the basic act of His grace. His whole relationship to what is outside Himself – its basis and history from first to last – rests on this fact. For everything that the creature seems to offer Him – its otherness, its being in antithesis to Himself and therefore His own existence in co-existence – He has also in Himself as God, as the original and essential determination of His being and life as God.[64]

From the eternal perfection of God's non-transitive relations, it is possible to say that creation is not necessary or intrinsic to him. This means creation might just as well not have existed without any change or detriment to God.[65]

---

[61] Webster, *God Without Measure*, 83.
[62] Ibid. 85–92.
[63] Ibid. 92.
[64] Barth, *CD*, 4.1, 201.
[65] G. Hunsinger, 'Election and the Trinity: Twenty-Five Theses on the Theology of Karl Barth', *MT* 24.2 (2008), 179–198, at 181. Molnar traces the recent challenges to this reading and reasserts just such an account. Molnar, *Divine Freedom*, 150–196.

Second, the making of creation needs to be understood in terms of absolute divine gratuity. The view of the existence of the world as a gift of God has been well described by Frances Young in her account of Basil of Caesarea's sermons on creation.[66] There is no necessity whatsoever in the act of creation, but only the absolute kindness of God in his freedom. To reorganize the furniture a bit, creation is made, not begotten. As Torrance writes, 'the universe did not come into existence through any inner compulsion in God's being. No, the universe flowed freely from and is unceasingly grounded in the eternal love that God is'.[67] Commonly, this divine gratuity and creaturely contingence are denoted by the doctrine of creation from nothing.[68] That creation is from nothing means it is brought into existence. It does not, in other words, exist necessarily or as intrinsic to divinity. That creation is from nothing is indicative of 'creation's status as an utterly gracious gift of God'.[69] McFarland understands this gratuity first from the Father–Son relation such that the proposition of the almighty creator is understood in correlation to the eternal begetting of the Son. Reflecting on John 5:19–23, McFarland notes that the 'Father's power takes the form of *giving* power to another . . . Viewed in its Trinitarian context, divine power is not a quantity that needs to be hoarded or guarded against encroachment by others.'[70] In this, the bringing into existence of creation from nothing through the Son is the faithful expression of God's own being in that, as Almighty Father, 'God is supremely powerful as the one who bestows power'.[71] As Kathryn Tanner has demonstrated, the structure of the creator–created relation operates through the gratuity of God as the giver of life and goodness to his creation, which introduces a notion of *progress*, as creation cannot receive all that God would give. This concludes in the person of Christ, the recipient of and witness to the covenantal love of God.[72]

Third, this gratuity is not arbitrary but is expressive of God's self-sufficiency as Father, Son and Spirit, which takes the form of mutual love and delight. In his retrieval of a Nicene doctrine of creation, Anatolios writes:

> There is an outflow, production and activity that is constitutive of divine being in the generation of the Son and procession of the Spirit and thus

66 Young, *God's Presence*, 46–48.
67 Torrance, *Trinitarian Faith*, 93.
68 Young, *God's Presence*, 52–58.
69 McFarland, *From Nothing*, 86.
70 Ibid. 95; emphasis original.
71 Ibid. 97. This perspective is shared by Kathryn Tanner, for whom 'God's creative agency is compatible with talk about the creature's own powers'. Tanner, *God and Creation*, 83.
72 See also K. Tanner, *Jesus, Humanity and the Trinity: A Brief Systematic Theology* (Minneapolis, Minn.: Fortress Press, 2001), 41–46.

> characterizes divine life as an eternal eventfulness. At the same time, the divine activity *ad extra* in bringing about creation from nothing is grounded in the inner fecundity of the intra-trinitarian life. Creation is not a necessary outflow of intra-divine generation, but neither is it an arbitrary act that 'gains' for God a communion that he does not inherently enjoy. Creation takes place within the mutual delight of Father and Son.[73]

The act of creation is a contingent and gratuitous overflow of what it is to be God. Alongside his intrinsic productivity, God is intrinsically *joyful*. The Father takes delight in his image in the unity of the Spirit. This eternal delight is the governing framework from which to understand creation. The act of creation is the manifestation of the Father's eternal delight in the Son. Creation as made through the Son, and particularly humanity in sharing in the image of God, is utterly contingent but not arbitrary: its purpose is the purpose of that which is delighted in by God.

Redemption

The full divinity of the Son and Spirit is integral to the grammar of a Nicene soteriology. If the Son and Spirit are not intrinsic to divinity, they cannot facilitate the participation of that which is extrinsic. Widdicombe has demonstrated that the concept of Sonship is central to Athanasius' soteriology as the one who is Son by nature becomes a human, receives the Spirit within our humanity and subsequently bestows the Spirit upon us, who unites us to the incarnate Son, such that we may become adopted as the children of God.[74] The ultimate end of Christian redemption, then, is to be incorporated into the mutual delight of the communion of the Father and Son, which is also our point of provenance.[75] To be saved, in other words, is to be joined to the Son's imaging of the Father in the power of the Spirit, whereby the Father's eternal delight in the Father is expressed over us also. This means that the grammar of redemption must be taken from the intrinsic divine relations.

This is a point seen particularly clearly by Barth. The doctrine of reconciliation articulated by Barth includes this grounding of the extrinsic saving works of God in the intrinsic divine reality. The incarnation and suffering of the Son (his way into the far country) is described in terms of his obedience to the Father and the associated humility. Barth is insistent that this not be understood simply as a human work, so that the reconciliation effected by Christ is

73 Anatolios, *RN*, 288.
74 Widdicombe, *Fatherhood of God*, 223–249.
75 See also Anatolios, *RN*, 289–290.

not denuded of its divine efficacy. As such, this obedience and humility must first be grounded in the being of God: 'if, then, God is in Christ, if what the man Jesus does is God's own work, this aspect of the self-emptying and self-humbling of Jesus Christ as an act of obedience cannot be alien to God'.[76] The grammar of the Christian doctrine of reconciliation must be established on a doctrine of God that contains the self-effacing deference to the other.[77] Engaging Athanasian categories, Barth distinguishes between creation that is extrinsic to God as a worldly counterpart to which there is an anterior counterpart structure intrinsic to the divine being itself that, while it includes subordination, as it is intrinsic to divinity, does not include inferiority:[78]

> In equal Godhead the one God is, in fact, the One and also Another, that He is indeed First and a Second, One who rules and commands in majesty and One who obeys in humility. The one God is both the one and the other. And, we continue, He is the one and the other without any cleft or differentiation but in perfect unity and equality.[79]

For Barth, the eternal mode of being of the Son as the one begotten from the Father is 'as the One who is obedient in humility'.[80] In becoming incarnate and enacting that obedient humility in our history, the Son's incarnate life corresponds to the eternal archetype. In this, the work of redemption does not need to be delegated to some inferior being who can actualize obedience among the disobedient human creatures: 'He does not change in giving Himself. He simply activates and reveals Himself *ad extra* in the world.'[81] This is the transitive and salvific enactment of the non-transitive relations in history.

The Nicene approach, then, does not encourage us to think of salvation in extrinsic categories. The Son and Spirit do not bring about our adoption to the Father from without. The Spirit effects our adoption by including us by grace in that which the Son is by nature. Certainly, this includes forensic categories of redemption. However, any account of the atoning work of Christ must account for the Nicene trajectory that the basis of the redemptive work of God is the reciprocal love of Father and Son and the overflow of that mutual delight in the form of unconditional gratuity towards and love of creation. The proper corrective to exemplarist doctrines of salvation, then, is not only to double

[76] Barth, *CD*, 4.1, 193.
[77] Ibid. 201.
[78] Ibid. 202.
[79] Ibid.
[80] Ibid. 203.
[81] Ibid. 204.

down on categories such as sacrifice, substitution, cleansing, penalty, and so on, which are important aspects of the saving work of Christ that are well founded in Scripture. The theological approach of Nicaea presses us to think in somewhat broader categories as well.[82] As the Father eternally sees himself in the Son and takes delight in the Son, so now the Son becomes one of us and lives the life of the image of the Father as one of us and for all of us: by the Spirit we are participants in him who is the bearer of our sin and the obedient Son of the loving Father, and it is as we share in his righteousness that we come before the Father.[83]

This cannot be developed fully here, but one or two indicative lines of thought can be traced out. First, invoking the seminal essay of J. B. Torrance, God's relationship to creation and his redemptive action should be understood primarily in *covenantal*, not *contractual*, terms:[84] 'God's primary purpose for humanity is "filial", not just "judicial", where we have been created in the image of God to find our true being-in-communion, in "sonship", in the mutual personal relations of love.'[85] In her insightful exploration of this theme, Alexandra Radcliffe comments that the priority in this way of thinking is not on *how* God acts in salvation, but on *who* God is and that we can better understand how God acts from this basis.[86] God does not relate primarily to creation as a lawgiver, but as a Father in whose gratuity creation exists and is sustained. The force of J. B. Torrance's distinction between a contractual and covenantal frame of the God–creation relationship is that in place of a relationship predicated upon the conditions of either side being met (a contractual relationship) is a relationship established on unconditional love and the decision to be God *for* us.[87] In these terms, salvation includes the eradication of sin and its legal charge made against us, but this is not the act of a merciful judge, but of a Father whose Son bears our part and makes our response of love, faith and obedience to the one who is faithful to us.

---

[82] Within Partee's distinction between three types of Calvinism, this approach would chart as something close to an 'Evangelical Calvinist' model. C. Partee, 'The Phylogeny of Calvin's Progeny: A Prolusion', in M. Habets and B. Grow (eds.), *Evangelical Calvinism: Essays Resourcing the Continuing Reformation of the Church* (Eugene, Ore.: Pickwick Publications, 2012), 23–66, at 26.

[83] See Young, *God's Presence*, 146–175, esp. 166–170.

[84] J. B. Torrance, 'Covenant or Contract? A Study of the Theological Background of Worship in Seventeenth-Century Scotland', *SJT* 23 (1979), 51–76.

[85] J. B. Torrance, 'The Doctrine of the Trinity in Our Contemporary Situation', in A. I. C. Heron (ed.), *The Forgotten Trinity: A Selection of Papers Presented to the BCC Study Commission on Trinitarian Doctrine Today* (London: British Council of Churches, 1991), 3–17, at 15.

[86] A. S. Radcliffe, *The Claim of Humanity in Christ: Salvation and Sanctification in the Theology of T. F. and J. B. Torrance*, PTMS 222 (Eugene, Ore.: Pickwick Publications, 2016), 22.

[87] J. B. Torrance, 'The Covenant Concept in Scottish Theology and Politics and Its Legacy', *SJT* 34 (1981), 143–162, 228.

Second, recognizing the church's part in the mediation of revelation in providing the framework within which the Scriptures are to be interpreted, a Nicene theological approach is compatible with some of the recent revisionist scholarship in Pauline theology. Richard Hays has suggested that Paul's phrase *pistis Christou*, typically 'translated as faith' in Jesus Christ, is better rendered as 'the faithfulness of Jesus Christ'.[88] As N. T. Wright comments, the force of this is that while

> Paul still clearly speaks of the faith of the individual believer, the weight of these particular passages falls, not on that individual faith, but on the accomplishments of Jesus Christ, or rather of God through Jesus Christ, and the 'faithfulness' of Jesus Christ to the purpose and will of God.[89]

The weight of the saving event is transferred from the pole of our subjective appropriation and on to the objective work of God undertaken on our behalf by Jesus Christ. Wright sees in this not only a focused exegetical matter, but a total reorientation of perspective on God's historical relations to Israel. The question is not so much 'Where do I find a gracious God?' (or 'How do I, a sinner, stand before a holy God?') but 'When will God fulfil his promises to Israel?' (or, 'When will God act to keep covenant both from his side and from ours?')[90]

This relates to Douglas Campbell's rereading of Paul's letter to the Romans, which decentres chapters 1–4 (and so the doctrine of justification by faith[91]), and suggests that chapters 5–8 better articulate the heart of Paul's witness to salvation.[92] In this, Campbell resets Paul's theology in this letter not on the question of how one might be saved from the wrath of God, but places it instead

---

[88] R. Hays, *The Faith of Jesus Christ: The Narrative Substructure of Galatians 3:1–4:11* (Grand Rapids, Mich.: Eerdmans, 2001).

[89] N. T. Wright, *Paul and His Recent Interpreters: Some Contemporary Debates* (London: SPCK, 2015), 96.

[90] Ibid. 96–97.

[91] Campbell is motivated to challenge the hegemony of a justification theory, which he believes has served as a distorting influence in the reception of Paul's thought. In his reception of Campbell's argument that Rom. 1 – 4 does not reflect Paul's own doctrine, but a legalistic doctrine of salvation against which Rom. 5 – 8 is established as an alternative, Alan Torrance draws on his father's opposition between covenant and contract, arguing that within the typical construction of the doctrine of justification by faith there is an implicit contractual model whereby humanity has fallen short of the conditions placed upon it such that the favour of God can be secured only through sacrifice. A. Torrance, 'A Review of Douglas Campbell's *The Deliverance of God from a Theological Perspective*', in C. Tilling (ed.), *Beyond Old and New Perspectives on Paul: Reflections on the Work of Douglas Campbell* (Eugene, Ore.: Cascade Books, 2014), 22–30, at 23–24.

[92] For Campbell's reception of *pistis Christou*, see D. A. Campbell, *Pauline Dogmatics: The Triumph of God's Love* (Grand Rapids, Mich.: Eerdmans, 2020), 297–316; 'The Faithfulness of Jesus Christ in Romans 3.22', in M. F. Bird and P. M. Sprinkle (eds.), *The Faith of Jesus Christ: Exegetical, Biblical and Theological Studies* (Milton Keynes: Paternoster Press, 2009), 57–71.

on the faithfulness of God expressed in his unilateral and unconditional act of sending the Son to include us in his life of faithfulness to the Father by the Spirit, through which we are liberated from the 'enslaved Adamic condition'.[93] Justification theory, as Campbell calls it, by contrast renders the human person as utterly introspective, aware of falling short of the standard God requires, which renders God opposed to him or her unless some price, penalty or sacrifice is paid. Salvation is effective by the human person having the requisite faith in the one who fulfils this condition on his or her behalf.[94]

This has a profound epistemological aspect. For Campbell, holding justification by faith as the organizing centre of theology applies a preconceived notion of God as lawgiver. This, in Campbell's view, is a naturalistic apprehension of the divine, not grounded in the reconciliation of the human mind to God in Christ but from a priori human ideas about the divine.[95] For Campbell, our thinking about God does not take place outside the context of his loving-kindness to us, but only within it. It is only as we are joined to the one who knows and loves the Father that we truly know God.[96] It is in this sense that Campbell describes the capture of Paul's thought by a methodological Arianism and insists instead upon an Athanasian mode of reading Paul.[97] The Arianism – although, it may be more accurate to call it Eunomianism – Campbell claims is a 'positing of an analogy for God in the pre- or non-Christian state', which is contrasted to an Athanasian approach that proceeds 'strictly from God's provision of the correct analogy in Christ'.[98] Indicative of this methodological Arianism is a naturalistic understanding of God. This leads to the reinterpretation of salvation in contractual – and so conditional – terms (with naturalistic ideas about justice being the core correlate for the divine).[99] By contrast, Campbell describes a methodological Athanasianism in which God's relationship to creation is understood in covenantal terms of unconditional faithfulness and love prior to all human activity.[100] Even though he himself does not frame it in this way, Campbell's rereading of Paul's theology has much to

---

93 D. A. Campbell, *The Deliverance of God: An Apocalyptic Rereading of Justification in Paul* (Grand Rapids, Mich.: Eerdmans, 2009), 63–73. See also Campbell, *Pauline Dogmatics*, 426–437.

94 Campbell, *Deliverance*, 28–34.

95 Ibid. 31–32.

96 Torrance, 'Review', 27–28.

97 D. A. Campbell, 'The Current Crisis: The Capture of Paul's Gospel by Methodological Arianism', in C. Tilling (ed.), *Beyond Old and New Perspectives on Paul: Reflections on the Work of Douglas Campbell* (Eugene: Cascade, 2014), 44–55. See also J. W. Smith, '"Arian" Foundationalism or "Athanasian" Apocalypticism: A Patristic Assessment', in C. Tilling (ed.), *Beyond Old and New Perspectives on Paul: Reflections on the Work of Douglas Campbell* (Eugene, Ore.: Cascade Books, 2014), 84–100.

98 Campbell, 'Current Crisis', 45.

99 Ibid. 46–48.

100 Ibid. 48–52.

commend it from the perspective of the core Nicene commitment that we know God as Father of the Son before we know him in correlation to our contingent mode of existence as the unoriginate.

A Nicene approach encourages us not to look to ourselves and become lost in our own attempts to be reconciled to the God we consider to be the eternal Whence or the uncaused ground of being. Instead, we look to God the Son, who became flesh and vicariously lived the life of the eternally obedient Son in whom the Father takes delight. It is the task of a genuinely Nicene Christology to trace the primacy of Jesus' vicarious and representative humanity more fully and have it inform the proclamation of the church as we call humanity to participate in the one who is Son by nature such that we may become by grace the children of God.[101]

101 Indicative of this approach in the form of a self-consciously introductory study is D. L. Migliore, *Faith Seeking Understanding: An Introduction to Christian Theology*, 3rd edn (Grand Rapids, Mich.: Eerdmans, 2014), 143–167.

Bibliography

Primary texts

Alexander of Alexandria, *Letter to Alexander of Byzantium (Hē philarchos)*, Urk 14, *NPNF* II.3.

____, *Letter to All Bishops (Henos sōmatos)*, Urk 4b, *NPNF* II.2.

Apollinarius of Laodicea, *Letter to Basil of Caesarea*, tr. G. L. Prestige, *St Basil of Caesarea and Apollinarius of Laodicea* (London: SPCK, 1956).

Arius, *Credal Letter to Alexander*, Urk 6, *NPNF* II.4.

____, *Letter to Eusebius of Nicomedia*, Urk 1, *NPNF* II.3.

Asterius, Fragments from Markus Vinzent, *Asterius von Kappadokien*; access through DelCogliano, *Anti-Eunomian Theory of Names*; Hanson, *SCDG*; Lienhard, *Contra Marcellum*.

Athanasius of Alexandria, *Against the Greeks*, *NPNF* II.4.

____, *The Catholic Epistle*; access through Ayres, *NL*; Behr, *NF*.

____, *Defence Against the Arians*, *NPNF* II.4.

____, *Defence of the Nicene Definition*, *NPNF* II.4.

____, *Discourses Against the Arians*, *NPNF* II.4.

____, *Epistles*, *NPNF* II.4.

____, *History of the Arians*, *NPNF* II.4.

____, *Letter to the Africans*, *NPNF* II.3.

____, *Letters to Serapion*; Anatolios, *Athanasius*, 214–233.

____, *On the Opinions of Dionysius*, *NPNF* II.4.

____, *On the Synods*, *NPNF* II.4.

____, *Tome to the Antiochenes*, *NPNF* II.4.

Augustine, *On the Trinity*, *NPNF* I.3.

Basil of Caesarea, *Against Eunomius*, tr. M. DelCogliano and A. Radde-Gallwitz (Washington, D.C.: Catholic University of America Press, 2011).

____, *Letter to Apollinarius of Laodicea*, tr. G. L. Prestige, *St Basil of Caesarea and Apollinaris of Laodicea* (London: SPCK, 1956).

____, *Letters*, *NPNF* II.8.

____, *On the Holy Spirit*, *NPNF* II.8.

Clement of Rome, 'The First Epistle of Clement to the Corinthians', in A. Louth (ed.), M. Stamforth (tr.), *Early Christian Writings: The Apostolic Fathers* (London: Penguin Books, 1987), 17–52.

Cyril of Jerusalem, *Catechetical Lectures*, *NPNF* II.7.

The Didache, in A. Louth (ed.), M. Stamforth (tr.), *Early Christian Writings: The Apostolic Fathers* (London: Penguin Books, 1987), 185–199.

Epiphanius, *Panarion*, tr. F. Williams, *The Panarion of Epiphanius of Salamis*, 2 vols. (Leiden: E. J. Brill, 1987); access through Behr, *NF*; Ayres, *NL*; Parvis, *Marcellus and the Lost Years*.

Epiphanius of Salamis, *Anacoratus: Die griechischen christlichen Schriftsteller* 25; access through Behr, *NF*; Hanson, *SCDG*; Ayres, *NL*.

____, *Panarion: Die griechischen christlichen Schriftsteller* 25; access through Ayres, *NL*; Hanson, *SCDG*.

'The Epistle of Barnabas', in A. Louth (ed.), M. Stamforth (tr.), *Early Christian Writings: The Apostolic Fathers* (London: Penguin Books, 1987), 153–182.

'The Epistle to Diognetus', in A. Louth (ed.), M. Stamforth (tr.), *Early Christian Writings: The Apostolic Fathers* (London: Penguin Books, 1987), 137–152.

Eunomius of Cyzius, *Apology*, ed. and tr. R. P. Vaggione, *Eunomius: The Extant Works* (Oxford: Oxford University Press, 1987); access through Ayres, *NL*; Radde-Gallwitz, *Transformation of Divine Simplicity*; Hanson, *SCDG*; Anatolios, *RN*.

Eusebius of Caesarea, *Against Marcellus*, ed. M. Vinzent, *Markell von Ankyra: Die Fragmente; Der Brief an Julius von Rom.*, supplements to *VC* 39 (Leiden: E. J. Brill, 1997); access through Hanson, *SCDG*.

____, *Demonstration of the Gospel*, GCS 6; tr. W. J. Ferrar, *The Proof of the Gospel: Being the Demonstratio Evangelica of Eusebius of Caesarea*, 2 vols. (London: SPCK, 1920); access through Ayres, *NL*; Anatolios, *RN*; Stead, *Divine Substance*; DelCogliano, 'Eusebian Theologies of the Son'.

____, *Ecclesiastical History*, ed. and tr. K. Lake, 2 vols. (Cambridge, Mass.: Harvard University Press).

____, *Ecclesiastical Theology*; access through Beeley, *The Unity of Christ*; Ayres, *NL*; Behr, *WN*; DelCogliano, 'Eusebian Theologies of the Son'; Lienhard, *Contra Marcellum*.

____, *Letter to Alexander of Alexandria*, Urk 7; access through A. J. West <https://www.fourthcentury.com/urkunde-7>, accessed 10 April 2020.

____, *Letter to the Diocese of Caesarea*, *NPNF* II.4.

____, *Letter to Euphration of Balena*, Urk 3; access through G. L. Thompson <https://www.fourthcentury.com/urkunde-3>, accessed 10 April 2020.

——, *Life of Constantine*, tr. G. Hall, *Eusebius: Life of Constantine* (Oxford: Clarendon Press, 1999).

——, *Preparation for the Gospel*, PG; access through Ayres, *NL*; Beeley, *Unity of Christ.*

——, *Proof of the Gospel*, PG; access through Ayres, *NL*; Beeley, *Unity of Christ.*

Eusebius of Nicomedia, *Letter of Recantation*, Urk 31, *NPNF* II.2.

——, *Letter to Paulinus of Tyre*, Urk 8, *NPNF* II.3.

Eustathius of Antioch, 'On the Soul Against the Arians'. Cited from Behr, *NF.*

Gregory of Nazianzus, *Orations*, *NPNF* II.7.

Hilary of Poitiers, *On the Synods*, *NPNF* II.9.

——, *On the Trinity*, *NPNF* II.9.

Hippolytus, *Apostolic Tradition*, tr. B. S. Easton (Cambridge: Cambridge University Press, 1934).

Ignatius of Antioch, 'The Epistle to the Ephesians', in A. Louth (ed.), M. Stamforth (tr.), *Early Christian Writings: The Apostolic Fathers* (London: Penguin Books, 1987), 59–68.

——, 'Epistle to the Smyrnaeans', in A. Louth (ed.), M. Stamforth (tr.), *Early Christian Writings: The Apostolic Fathers* (London: Penguin Books, 1987), 99–106.

——, 'The Epistle to the Trallians', in A. Louth (ed.), M. Stamforth (tr.), *Early Christian Writings: The Apostolic Fathers* (London: Penguin Books, 1987), 77–82.

Irenaeus of Lyons, *Against the Heresies*, ANF 1.

——, *Proof of the Apostolic Preaching*, repr. (Pickerington, Ohio: Beloved Publishing).

Justin Martyr, *Dialogue of Justin, Philosopher and Martyr, with Trypho, a Jew*, ANF 1.

——, *The First Apology of Justin*, ANF 1.

Marcellus of Ancyra, *Fragments*; Vinzent, *Markell von Ankyra*; access through Ayres, *NL*; Behr, *NF*; Hanson, *SCDG*; Anatolios, *RN*; Lienhard, *Contra Marcellum.*

Origen, *On First Principles*, tr. G. W. Butterworth (Notre Dame, Ind.: Christian Classics, 2013).

Philostogorius, *Ecclesiastical History*, GCS 21; access through Ayres, *NL*; Behr, *NF.*

Polycarp of Smyrna, 'Letter to the Philippians', in A. Louth (ed.), M. Stamforth (tr.), *Early Christian Writings: The Apostolic Fathers* (London: Penguin Books, 1987), 113–136.

Shepherd of Hermas, tr. J. B. Lightfoot (London: Macmillan, 1891).
Socrates, *Ecclesiastical History*, *NPNF* II.2.
Sozomen, *Ecclesiastical History*, *NPNF* II.2.
Tertullian, *Against Marcian*, *ANF* 3.
____, *Against Praxeas*, *ANF* 3.
____, *The Chaplet*, *ANF* 3.
____, *On the Prescription of Heretics*, *ANF* 3.
Theodoret, *Ecclesiastical History*, *NPNF* II.3.

Secondary texts

Alexander, M. E., 'G. H. Tavard's Concept of Tradition', in K. Hagen (ed.), *The Quadrilog: Tradition and the Future of Ecumenism* (Collegeville, Minn.: Liturgical Press, 1994), 287–311.
Anastos, M. V., 'Basil's *Against Eunomius*: A Critical Analysis', in P. J. Fieldwick (ed.), *Basil of Caesarea: Christian, Humanist, Ascetic* (Toronto: Pontifical Institute of Medieval Studies, 1981), 67–136.
Anatolios, K., *Athanasius* (London: Routledge, 2004).
____, *Athanasius: The Coherence of His Thought* (London: Routledge, 1998).
____, '"The Body as Instrument": A Re-evaluation of Athanasius' "Logos-Sarx Christology"', *CCR* 18 (1997), 78–84.
Anselm, *Proslogion*, in T. Williams (tr.), *Monologion and Proslogion with the Replies of Gaunilo and Anselm* (Indianapolis, Ind.: Hackett Classics, 1995).
Armstrong, J. J., 'From the *kanōn tēs alētheias* to the *kanōn tōn graphon*: The Rule of Faith and the New Testament Canon', in R. J. Rombs and A. Y. Hwang (eds.), *Tradition and the Rule of Faith in the Early Church: Essays in Honor of Joseph T. Lienhard* (Washington, D.C.: Catholic University of America Press, 2010), 30–47.
Atkinson, N., *Richard Hooker and the Authority of Scripture, Tradition and Reason: Reformed Theologian of the Church of England* (Milton Keynes: Paternoster Press, 1997).
Ayres, L., 'Athanasius' Initial Defence of the Term *homoousios*: Rereading the *De Decretis*', *JECS* 12 (2004), 337–359.
____, 'Irenaeus vs the Valentinians: Towards a Rethinking of Patristic Exegetical Origins', *JECS* 23 (2015), 155–169.
Ayres, L., and A. Radde-Gallwitz, 'The Doctrine of God', in S. A. Harvey and D. G. Hunter (eds.), *Oxford Handbook of Early Christian Studies* (Oxford: Oxford University Press, 2008), 864–885.

Barnes, M. R., 'The Fourth Century as Trinitarian Canon', in L. Ayres and G. Jones (eds.), *Christian Origins: Theology, Rhetoric and Community* (New York: Routledge, 1998), 47–67.

——, *The Power of God: Dynamis in Gregory of Nyssa's Trinitarian Theology* (Washington, D.C.: Catholic University of America Press, 2016).

Barnes, T. D., *Athanasius and Constantius: Theology and Politics in the Constantinian Empire* (Cambridge, Mass.: Harvard University Press, 2001).

——, *Constantine and Eusebius* (Cambridge, Mass.: Harvard University Press, 1981).

——, 'Review of N. Lenski (ed.), *The Cambridge Companion to the Age of Constantine* (Cambridge: Cambridge University Press, 2006)', *IJCT* 14 (2007), 197.

Barth, K., *Church Dogmatics: The Doctrine of God*, vol. 2, pt 1, ed. G. W. Bromiley and T. F. Torrance, tr. T. H. L. Parker, W. B. Johnson, H. Knight and J. L. M. Haire (Edinburgh: T&T Clark, 1957).

——, *Church Dogmatics: The Doctrine of Reconciliation*, vol. 4, pt 1, ed. G. W. Bromiley and T. F. Torrance, tr. G. W. Bromiley (Edinburgh: T&T Clark, 1956).

——, *Church Dogmatics: The Doctrine of the Word of God*, vol. 1, pt 1, ed. G. W. Bromiley and T. F. Torrance, tr. G. W. Bromiley (Edinburgh: T&T Clark, 1975).

——, *Church Dogmatics: The Doctrine of the Word of God*, vol. 1, pt 2, ed. G. W. Bromiley and T. F. Torrance, tr. G. T. Thomson and H. Knight (Edinburgh: T&T Clark, 1956).

——, *Göttingen Dogmatics: Instruction in the Christian Religion*, vol. 1, ed. H. Reiffen, tr. G. W. Bromiley (Grand Rapids, Mich.: Eerdmans, 1990).

Beatrice, P. A., 'The *Homoousion* from Hellenism to Christianity', *CH* 74 (2002), 243–272.

Beeley, C., 'Divine Causality and the Monarchy of God the Father in Gregory of Nazianzus', *HTR* 100.12 (2007), 199–214.

——, *Gregory of Nazianzus on the Trinity and the Knowledge of God: In Your Light We Shall See Light* (Oxford: Oxford University Press, 2013).

——, 'The Holy Spirit in the Cappadocians: Past and Present', *MT* 26.1 (2010), 95–116.

——, 'The Holy Spirit in Gregory Nazianzen: The Pneumatology of *Oration* 31', in A. B. McGowan, B. E. Daley and T. J. Gaden (eds.), *God in Early Christian Thought: Essays in Memory of Lloyd G. Patterson* (Leiden: E. J. Brill, 2009), 151–162.

———, *The Unity of Christ: Continuity and Conflict in Patristic Tradition* (New Haven, Conn.: Yale University Press, 2012).

Behr, J., *Irenaeus of Lyons: Identifying Christianity* (Oxford: Oxford University Press, 2013).

Blondel, M., 'Histoire et dogme: les lacunes de l'exégèse moderne', in *La Quinzaine* 56 (January and February 1904).

Bowersock, G., *Julian the Apostate* (Cambridge, Mass.: Harvard University Press, 1978).

Bray, G., *Creeds, Councils and Christ: Did the Early Christians Misrepresent Jesus*, rev. edn (Nairobi: Mentor, 2009).

———, *Synods* (London: Latimer Trust, 2019).

Calvin, J., *Commentary on 1 Timothy*, tr. W. Pringle (Grand Rapids, Mich.: Baker Books, 2005).

———, *Commentary on Galatians*, tr. W. Pringle (Grand Rapids, Mich.: Baker Books, 2005).

———, *Institutes of the Christian Religion*, ed. J. T. McNeill, tr. F. L. Battles (Philadelphia, Pa.: Westminster Press, 1960).

Campbell, D. A., 'The Current Crisis: The Capture of Paul's Gospel by Methodological Arianism', in C. Tilling (ed.), *Beyond Old and New Perspectives on Paul: Reflections on the Work of Douglas Campbell* (Eugene, Ore.: Cascade Books, 2014), 44–55.

———, *The Deliverance of God: An Apocalyptic Rereading of Justification in Paul* (Grand Rapids, Mich.: Eerdmans, 2009).

———, 'The Faithfulness of Jesus Christ in Romans 3.22', in M. F. Bird and P. M. Sprinkle (eds.), *The Faith of Jesus Christ: Exegetical, Biblical and Theological Studies* (Milton Keynes: Paternoster Press, 2009), 57–71.

———, *Pauline Dogmatics: The Triumph of God's Love* (Grand Rapids, Mich.: Eerdmans, 2020).

Clark, E. A., *The Origenist Controversy: The Cultural Construction of an Early Christian Debate* (Princeton, N.J.: Princeton University Press, 1992).

Congar, Y., 'Holy Writ and Holy Church', *Blackfriars* 41 (1960), 11–19.

———, *The Meaning of Tradition*, tr. A. N. Woodrow (San Francisco, Calif.: Ignatius Press, 1964).

———, *Tradition and Traditions: An Historical Essay and a Theological Essay* (London: Burns & Oates, 1966).

Crawford, M., 'On the Diversity and Influence of the Eusebian Alliance: The Case of Theodore of Heraclea', *JEH* 64.2 (2013), 227–257.

Cross, R., 'Divine Monarchy in Gregory of Nazianzus', *JECS* 14 (2006), 105–116.

Cullmann, O., *The Early Church* (London: SCM Press, 1956).

Cupitt, D., *Taking Leave of God* (London: SCM Press, 1980).

Daley, B. D., 'The Enigma of Meletius of Antioch', in R. J. Rombs and A. Y. Hwang (eds.), *Tradition and the Rule of Faith in the Early Church: Essays in Honor of Joseph T. Lienhard* (Washington, D.C.: Catholic University of America Press, 2010), 128–150.

Dam, R. van, *The Roman Revolution of Constantine* (Cambridge: Cambridge University Press, 2009).

Davie, M., *The Athanasian Creed* (London: Latimer Trust, 2019).

Davis, D., *The First Seven Ecumenical Councils (325–787): Their History and Theology* (Collegeville, Minn.: Liturgical Press, 1983).

DelCogliano, M., *Anti-Eunomian Theory of Names: Christian Theology and Late-Antique Philosophy in the Fourth-Century Trinitarian Controversy* (Leiden: E. J. Brill, 2010).

——, 'Basil of Caesarea and the Primacy of the Name "Son"', *RÉAug* 57 (2011), 45–69.

——, 'Eusebian Theologies of the Son as the Image of God Before 341', *JECS* 14.4 (2006), 459–484.

——, 'George of Laodicea: A Historical Reassessment', *JEH* 62.4 (2011), 667–692.

——, 'How Did Arius Learn from Asterius? On the Relationship Between the *Thalia* and the *Syntagmation*', *JEH* 69.3 (2018), 477–492.

——, 'The Influence of Athanasius and the *Homoiousians* on Basil of Caesarea's Decentralization of "Unbegotten"', *JECS* 19.2 (2011), 197–223.

——, 'Introduction', in *Against Eunomius*, tr. M. DelCogliano and A. Radde-Gallwitz (Washington, D.C.: Catholic University of America Press, 2011), 3–80.

——, 'The Significance of George of Laodicea in the Fourth Century Trinitarian Debates', *StPatr* 46 (2010), 307–311.

Dillon, J., *The Middle Platonists: 80 B.C. to A.D. 220*, rev. edn (Ithaca, N.Y.: Cornell University Press, 1996).

Dolezal, J. E., *All That Is in God: Evangelical Theology and the Challenge of Classical Christian Theism* (Grand Rapids, Mich.: Reformation Heritage Books, 2017).

Duby, S. J., *Divine Simplicity: A Dogmatic Account* (London: T&T Clark, 2016).

Dunn, J. D. G., *The Oral Gospel Tradition* (Grand Rapids, Mich.: Eerdmans, 2013).

——, *The Partings of the Ways: Between Christianity and Judaism and Their Significance for the Character of Christianity* (London: SCM Press, 1991).

____, *Unity and Diversity in the New Testament: An Inquiry into the Character of Earliest Christianity* (London: SCM Press, 1977).

Edwards, M., 'Alexander of Alexandria and the *Homoousion*', *VC* 66.5 (2012), 482–502.

____, 'The First Council of Nicaea', in M. M. Mitchell and F. M. Young (eds.), *The Cambridge History of Christianity* (Cambridge: Cambridge University Press, 2006), 552–567.

Egan, J., 'Primal Cause and Trinitarian Perichoresis in Gregory Nazianzen's *Orations* 31.14', *StPatr* 27 (1993), 21–28.

Elliot, T. G., 'Constantine and "the Arian Reaction After Nicaea"', *JEH* 43.2 (1992), 169–194.

____, 'Constantine's Preparations for the Council of Nicaea', *JRH* 17.2 (1992), 127–137.

Ferguson, E., 'Irenaeus' Proof of the Apostolic Preaching and Early Catechetical Instruction', *StPatr* 18.3 (1989), 120–133.

____, *Paradōsis* and *Traditio*: A Word Study', in R. J. Rombs and A. Y. Hwang (eds.), *Tradition and the Rule of Faith in the Early Church: Essays in Honor of Joseph T. Lienhard* (Washington, D.C.: Catholic University of America Press, 2010), 3–29.

Fleeseman-van Leer, E., *Tradition and Scripture in the Early Church* (Assen: Van Gorcum, 1954).

Florovsky, G., 'Creation and Creaturehood', in *Creation and Redemption: Volume Three in the Collected Works of Georges Florovsky Emeritus Professor of Eastern Church History* (Belmont, Mass.: Nordland, 1976), 43–78.

____, 'The Function of Tradition in the Ancient Church', *GOTR* 9 (1963), 181–200.

Fulford, B., '"One Conmixture of Light": Rethinking Some Modern Uses and Critiques of Gregory of Nazianzus on the Unity and Equality of the Divine Persons', *IJST* 11.2 (2009), 172–189.

Gaudium et Spes, ed. W. M. Abbot SJ, and tr. J. Gallacher, *The Documents of Vatican II: With Notes and Comments by Catholic, Protestant and Orthodox Authorities* (London: Geoffrey Chapman, 1967).

Geiselmann, J. R., 'Scripture and Tradition in Catholic Theology', *TD* 6 (1958), 73–78.

George, T., 'Evangelical Reflection on Scripture and Tradition', in C. Colson and R. J. Neuhaus (eds.), *Your Word Is Truth: A Project of Evangelicals and Catholics Together* (Grand Rapids, Mich.: Eerdmans, 2002), 9–34.

Giles, K., *The Eternal Generation of the Son: Maintaining Orthodoxy in Trinitarian Theology* (Wheaton, Ill.: IVP Academic, 2012).

Giulea, D. A., 'Antioch 268 and Its Legacy in the Fourth-Century Theological Debates', *HTR* 111.2 (2018), 192–215.

——, 'Basil of Caesarea's Authorship of *Ep.* 361 and His Relationship with the *Homoiousians* Reconsidered', *VC* 72 (2018), 41–70.

——, 'Divine Being's Modulations: *Ousia* in the Pro-Nicene Context of the Fourth Century', *SVTQ* 59.3 (2015), 307–337.

——, 'Reassessing Arianism in the Light of the Council of Antioch 268', *ETL* 95.1 (2019), 63–96.

The Gospel of Thomas, in A. Jacobs (tr.), *The Gnostic Gospels* (London: Watkins, 2006), Kindle edn.

Grech, P. S., 'The *Regula Fidei* as a Hermeneutical Principle in Patristic Exegesis', in J. Krašovic (ed.), *The Interpretation of the Bible: The International Symposium in Slovenia* (Sheffield: Sheffield Academic Press, 1998), 589–601.

Gregg, R. C., and D. G. Groh, *Early Arianism: A View of Salvation* (Philadelphia, Pa.: Fortress Press, 1981).

Grillmeier SJ, A., *Christ in the Christian Tradition: From the Apostolic Age to Chalcedon (451)*, vol. 1, tr. J. Bowden, 2nd rev. edn (London: Mowbrays, 1975).

Gwynn, D. M., 'Athanasius', in K Parry (ed.), *The Wiley-Blackwell Companion to Patristics* (London: John Wiley, 2015), 111–125.

——, *Athanasius of Alexandria: Bishop, Theologian, Ascetic, Father* (Oxford: Oxford University Press, 2012).

——, *The Eusebians: The Polemic of Athanasius of Alexandria and the Construction of the 'Arian Controversy'* (Oxford: Oxford University Press, 2006).

Hall, S. G., *Doctrine and Practice in the Early Church* (London: SPCK), 1991.

Hanson, R. P. C., *The Continuity of Christian Doctrine* (New York: Seabury Press, 1981).

——, *Tradition in the Early Church* (London: SPCK, 1962).

Hartog, P., 'The "Rule of Faith" and Patristic Biblical Exegesis', *TJ* 28 (2007), 65–86.

Hays, R., *The Faith of Jesus Christ: The Narrative Substructure of Galatians 3:1–4:11* (Grand Rapids, Mich.: Eerdmans, 2001).

Hildebrand, S. M., *The Trinitarian Theology of Basil of Caesarea: A Synthesis of Greek Thought and Biblical Truth* (Washington, D.C.: Catholic University of America Press, 2009).

Hill, K. D., *Athanasius and the Holy Spirit: The Development of His Early Pneumatology* (Minneapolis, Minn.: Fortress Press, 2016).

Holmes, S. R., *Listening to the Past: The Place of Tradition in Theology* (Grand Rapids, Mich.: Baker Academic, 2002).

——, *The Quest for the Trinity: The Doctrine of God in Scripture, History and Modernity* (Wheaton, Ill.: IVP Academic, 2012).

Hooker, R., *Of the Laws of Ecclesiastical Polity* (London: J. M. Dent, 1907).

Huby, P. M., and G. Neal (eds.), *The Criterion of Truth: Essays Written in Honour of George Kerferd* (Liverpool: Liverpool University Press, 1989).

Hunsinger, G., 'Election and the Trinity: Twenty-Five Theses on the Theology of Karl Barth', *MT* 24.2 (2008), 179–198.

Ihde, D., 'Text and the New Hermeneutics', in D. Wood (ed.), *On Paul Ricoeur: Narrative and Interpretation* (London: Routledge, 1991).

Inowlocki, S., and C. Zamagni (eds.), *Reconsidering Eusebius: Collected Papers on Literary, Historical and Theological Issues* (Leiden: E. J. Brill, 2011).

Irving, A., 'The Motherhood of the Church in John Calvin and Henri du Lubac', *IJSC* 18.1 (2018), 48–66.

——, *T. F. Torrance's Reconstruction of Natural Theology: Christ and Cognition* (Lanham, Md.: Lexington Books, 2019).

Jacobs, N., 'On "Not Three Gods" – Again: Can a Primary–Secondary Substance Reading of *Ousia* and *Hypostasis* Avoid Tritheism', *MT* 24.3 (2008), 331–358.

Jaeger, W., *Early Christianity and Greek Paideia* (London: Oxford University Press, 1961).

Janz, D., *Three Reformation Catechisms: Catholic, Anabaptist, Lutheran* (New York: Edwin Mellen Press, 1982).

Jedin, H., *A History of the Council of Trent*, tr. E. Graf, 2 vols. (Edinburgh: Thomas Nelson, 1967–71).

Jenson, R., *Canon and Creed: Interpretation: Resources for the Use of Scripture in the Church* (Louisville, Ky.: Westminster John Knox Press, 2010).

Jorgensen, D. W., *Treasure Hidden in a Field: Early Christian Reception of the Gospel of Matthew* (Berlin: W. de Gruyter, 2016).

Jüngel, E., *God's Being Is in Becoming: The Trinitarian Being of God in the Theology of Karl Barth*, tr. J. Webster (Edinburgh: T&T Clark, 2001).

Kant, I., *An Answer to the Question 'What Is Enlightenment?'*, tr. H. B. Nisbett (London: Penguin Books, 2009).

Kelly, J. N. D., *The Athanasian Creed* (London: A&C Black Publishers, 1964).

——, *Early Christian Creeds* (London: Longmans Green, 1950).

——, *Early Christian Doctrines* (New York: Harper Torchbooks, 1958).

Kinzig, W., and M. Vinzent, 'Recent Research on the Origin of the Creed', *JTS* 50.2 (1999), 535–559.

Kopecek, T. A., *History of Neo-Arianism* (Washington, D.C.: Catholic University of America Press, 1979).

Lane, A. N. S., *John Calvin: Student of the Church Fathers* (Edinburgh: T&T Clark, 1999).

——, 'Scripture, Tradition and Church: An Historical Survey', *VE* 9 (1975), 37–55.

Levering, M., *Engaging the Doctrine of Revelation: The Mediation of the Gospel Through Church and Scripture* (Grand Rapids, Mich.: Baker Academic, 2014).

Lienhard SJ, J. T., 'The "Arian" Controversy: Some Categories Reconsidered', *TS* 48 (1987), 415–437.

——, *The Bible, the Church, and Authority: The History of the Christian Bible in History and Theology* (Collegeville, Minn.: Liturgical Press, 1995).

——, 'Canons and Rules of Faith', in P. M. Blowers and P. W. Martens (eds.), *The Oxford Handbook of Early Christian Biblical Interpretation* (Oxford: Oxford University Press, 2019).

——, *Contra Marcellum: Marcellus of Ancyra and Fourth Century Theology* (Washington, D.C.: Catholic University of America Press, 1999).

——, 'Did Athanasius Reject Marcellus', in M. R. Barnes and D. H. Williams (eds.), *Arianism After Arius: Essays on the Development of the Fourth-Century Trinitarian Conflicts* (Edinburgh: T&T Clark, 1993), 65–80.

——, '*Ousia* and *Hypostasis*: The Cappadocian Settlement and the Theology of "One Hypostasis"', in S. T. Davis, D. Kendall SJ and G. O'Collins SJ (eds.), *The Trinity: An Interdisciplinary Symposium on the Trinity* (Oxford: Oxford University Press, 2002), 100–122.

Logan, A. H. B., 'Marcellus of Ancyra and the Councils of 325: Antioch, Ancyra and Nicaea', *JTS* 43.2 (1992), 428–446.

Louth, A., 'The Use of the Term *idios* in Alexandrian Theology from Alexander to Cyril', *StPatr* 19 (1989), 198–202.

Lumen Gentium, ed. W. M. Abbot SJ, and tr. J. Gallacher, *The Documents of Vatican II: With Notes and Comments by Catholic, Protestant and Orthodox Authorities* (London: Geoffrey Chapman, 1967).

Lyman, R., *Christology and Cosmology: Models of Divine Activity in Origen, Eusebius and Athanasius* (Oxford: Oxford University Press, 1993).

——, *Early Christian Traditions* (Boston, Mass.: Cowley Publications, 1999).

McFarland, I. A., *From Nothing: A Theology of Creation* (Louisville, Ky.: Westminster John Knox Press, 2014).

McGowan, A. T. B., *The Divine Spiration of Scripture: Challenging Evangelical Perspectives* (Nottingham: Apollos, 2007).

McGrath, A. E., 'Engaging the Great Tradition: Evangelical Theology and the Role of Tradition', in S. Grenz and J. G. Stackhouse (eds.), *Evangelical Futures: A Conversation on Theological Method* (Grand Rapids, Mich.: Baker Books, 2000), 139–158.

____, *Reformation Thought: An Introduction*, 2nd edn (Oxford: Blackwell, 1993).

McGukin, J. A., *Gregory of Nazianzus: An Intellectual Biography* (New York: St Vladimir's Seminary Press, 2001).

____, '"Perceiving Light from Light in Light" (*Oration* 31.3): The Trinitarian Theology of Saint Gregory the Theologian', *GOTR* 39.1 (1994), 7–32.

Mathison, K. A., *The Shape of Sola Scriptura* (Moscow, Ida.: Canon Press, 2001).

Meijering, E. P., 'The Doctrine of the Will and of the Trinity in the Orations of Gregory of Nazianzus', *God, Being, History: Studies in Patristic Philosophy* (Amsterdam: Elsevier, 1975).

Meredith, A., 'The Pneumatology of the Cappadocian Fathers', *ITQ* 48 (1981), 196–211.

Meyendorff, J., *Byzantine Theology: Historical Trends and Doctrinal Themes* (New York: Fordham University Press, 1983).

Migliore, D. L., *Faith Seeking Understanding: An Introduction to Christian Theology*, 3rd edn (Grand Rapids, Mich.: Eerdmans, 2014).

Molnar, P. D., *Divine Freedom and the Doctrine of the Immanent Trinity: In Dialogue with Karl Barth and Contemporary Theology*, 2nd edn (London: Bloomsbury, 2017).

____, 'The Function of the Immanent Trinity in the Theology of Karl Barth: Implications for Today', *SJT* 42.3 (1989), 367–399.

Molodet-Jitea, P., 'The Preamble of the Gospel According to John – Its Significance in the Hermeneutical Conflict Between the Bishop Irenaeus of Lyons and the Gnostic School of Valentinus', *Hermeneia* 17 (2016), 134–145.

Moran, G., 'Scripture and Tradition: A Current Debate', *ACR* 38 (1961), 14–22.

____, *Scripture and Tradition: A Survey of the Controversy* (New York: Herder & Herder, 1963).

Newman, J. H., *The Arians of the Fourth Century* (Notre Dame, Ind.: University of Notre Dame Press, 2001).

———, *An Essay on the Development of Christian Doctrine*, 2nd edn (London: James Toovey, 1846).

O'Collins SJ, G., *Retrieving Fundamental Theology: Three Styles of Contemporary Theology* (London: Geoffrey Chapman, 1993).

———, 'Revelation, Tradition and Scripture', in G. O'Collins SJ and M. Farrugia SJ (eds.), *Catholicism: The Story of Catholic Christianity* (Oxford: Oxford University Press, 2003).

Oden, T., *After Modernity . . . What? Agenda for Theology* (Grand Rapids, Mich.: Zondervan, 1990).

Olin, J. C. (ed.), *A Reformation Debate* (New York: Harper, 1966).

Optatam Totius, ed. W. M. Abbot SJ, and tr. J. Gallacher, *The Documents of Vatican II: With Notes and Comments by Catholic, Protestant and Orthodox Authorities* (London: Geoffrey Chapman, 1967).

Osborn, E., *Irenaeus of Lyons* (Cambridge: Cambridge University Press, 2001).

———, 'Reason and the Rule of Faith in the Second Century AD', in R. Williams (ed.), *The Making of Orthodoxy: Essays in Honour of Henry Chadwick* (Cambridge: Cambridge University Press, 1989), 40–42.

Outler, A. C., 'The Sense of Tradition in the Ante-Nicene Church', in E. Cushman and E. Grislis (eds.), *The Heritage of Christian Thought* (New York: Harper & Row, 1965), 8–30.

Ownes, G., 'Is All Revelation Contained in Sacred Scripture?', *Studia Montis Regii* 1 (1958), 55–60.

Partee, C., 'The Phylogeny of Calvin's Progeny: A Prolusion', in M. Habets and B. Grow (eds.), *Evangelical Calvinism: Essays Resourcing the Continuing Reformation of the Church* (Eugene, Ore.: Pickwick Publications, 2012), 23–66.

Parvis, S., 'Joseph Lienhard, Marcellus of Ancyra and Marcellus' Rule of Faith', in R. J. Rombs and A. Y. Hwang (eds.), *Tradition and the Rule of Faith in the Early Church: Essays in Honor of Joseph T. Lienhard* (Washington, D.C.: Catholic University of America Press, 2010), 89–108.

———, *Marcellus of Ancyra and the Lost Years of the Arian Controversy 325–345* (Oxford: Oxford University Press, 2006).

Patterson, L. G., *Methodius of Olympus: Divine Sovereignty, Human Freedom, and Life in Christ* (Washington, D.C.: Catholic University of America Press, 1997).

Pelikan, J., *Credo: Historical and Theological Guide to Creeds and Confessions of Faith in the Christian Tradition* (New Haven, Conn.: Yale University Press, 2003).

Prestige, G. L., *Fathers and Heretics* (London: SPCK, 1954).
____, *God in Patristic Thought* (London: William Heinemann, 1936).
Radcliffe, A. S., *The Claim of Humanity in Christ: Salvation and Sanctification in the Theology of T. F. and J. B. Torrance*, PTMS 222 (Eugene, Ore.: Pickwick Publications, 2016).
Radde-Gallwitz, A., *Basil of Caesarea: A Guide to His Life and Doctrine* (Eugene, Ore.: Cascade Books, 2012).
____, *Basil of Caesarea, Gregory of Nyssa and the Transformation of Divine Simplicity* (Oxford: Oxford University Press, 2009).
Rahner, K., 'Scripture and Tradition', *TD* 12.1 (1964), 3–7.
Ramelli, I. M., 'Origen, Greek Philosophy, and the Birth of the Trinitarian Meaning of *Hypostasis*', *HTR* 105.3 (2012), 302–350.
'The Report of the Theological Commission on Tradition and Traditions', *Faith and Order Paper* 40 (Geneva: World Council of Churches, 1963).
Ricoeur, P., *The Conflict of Interpretations*, ed. D. Ihde (Evanston, Ill.: Northwestern University Press, 1974).
____, *Time and Narrative*, vol. 2, tr. K. McLaughlin and D. Pellauer (Chicago, Ill.: University of Chicago Press, 1984–8).
Schilebeeckx, E., *Christ the Sacrament of Encounter with God* (London: Sheed & Ward, 1963).
Schleiermacher, F., *The Christian Faith*, repr. (London: T&T Clark, 2016).
____, *On Religion: Speeches to Its Cultured Despisers*, tr. J. Oman (San Francisco, Calif.: Harper Torchbooks, 1958).
Skarsaune, O., 'A Neglected Detail in the Creed of Nicaea (325)', *VC* 41 (1987), 34–54.
Slusser, M., 'Traditional Views of Late Arianism', in M. R. Barnes and D. H. Williams (eds.), *Arianism After Arius: Essays on the Development of the Fourth-Century Trinitarian Conflicts* (Edinburgh: T&T Clark, 1993), 3–30.
Smith, J. W., '"Arian" Foundationalism or "Athanasian" Apocalypticism: A Patristic Assessment', in C. Tilling (ed.), *Beyond Old and New Perspectives on Paul: Reflections on the Work of Douglas Campbell* (Eugene, Ore.: Cascade Books, 2014), 84–100.
Sonderegger, K., *Systematic Theology*, vol. 1: *The Doctrine of God* (Minneapolis, Minn.: Fortress Press, 2014).
Stead, C., 'Athanasius' Earliest Written Works', *JTS* 39.1 (1988), 76–91.
____, *Divine Substance* (Oxford: Clarendon Press, 1977).
____, '"Eusebius" and the Council of Nicaea', *JTS* 24.1 (1973), 85–100.

———, 'The Platonism of Arius', *JTS* 24 (1973), 85–100.
———, 'Rhetorical Method in Athanasius', *VC* 30 (1976), 121–137.
———, 'The *Thalia* of Arius and the Testimony of Athanasius', *JTS* 29 (1978), 20–52.
Studer, B., *Trinity and Incarnation: The Faith of the Early Church* (Edinburgh: T&T Clark, 1994).
Tanner, K., *God and Creation in Christian Theology: Tyranny or Empowerment* (Minneapolis, Minn.: Fortress Press, 2005).
———, *Jesus, Humanity and the Trinity: A Brief Systematic Theology* (Minneapolis, Minn.: Fortress Press, 2001).
Tetz, M., 'Ein enzyklisches Schreiben der Synode von Alexandrien (362)', *ZNW* 79 (1988), 262–281
Tilley, T., *Inventing Catholic Tradition* (New York: Orbis Books, 2000).
Tilling, C., 'Campbell's Apocalyptic Gospel and Pauline Athanasianism', ed. C. Tilling, *Beyond Old and New Perspectives on Paul: Reflections on the Work of Douglas Campbell* (Eugene, Ore.: Cascade Books, 2014), 56–83.
Torrance, A., 'A Review of Douglas Campbell's *The Deliverance of God from a Theological Perspective*', in C. Tilling (ed.), *Beyond Old and New Perspectives on Paul: Reflections on the Work of Douglas Campbell* (Eugene, Ore.: Cascade Books, 2014), 22–30.
Torrance, J. B., 'The Covenant Concept in Scottish Theology and Politics and Its Legacy', *SJT* 34 (1981), 143–162, 228.
———, 'Covenant or Contract? A Study of the Theological Background of Worship in Seventeenth-Century Scotland', *SJT* 23 (1979), 51–76.
———, 'The Doctrine of the Trinity in Our Contemporary Situation', in A. I. C. Heron (ed.), *The Forgotten Trinity: A Selection of Papers Presented to the BCC Study Commission on Trinitarian Doctrine Today* (London: British Council of Churches, 1991), 3–17.
Torrance, T. F., *The Christian Doctrine of God: One Being Three Persons* (London: T&T Clark, 2016).
———, 'The Deposit of Faith', *SJT* 36 (1983), 1–28.
———, *God and Rationality* (London: Oxford University Press, 2000).
———, *The Ground and Grammar of Theology* (Belfast: Christian Journals, 1980).
———, *Incarnation: The Person and Life of Christ*, ed. R. T. Walker (Downers Grove, Ill.: IVP Academic, 2008).
———, *The Mediation of Christ* (Exeter: Paternoster Press, 1983).
———, *Reality and Evangelical Theology* (Philadelphia, Pa.: Westminster Press, 1982).

——, *Reality and Scientific Theology*, new edn (Eugene, Ore.: Wipf & Stock, 2001).
——, *Royal Priesthood: A Theology of Ordained Ministry*, 2nd edn (Edinburgh: T&T Clark, 2003).
——, *Theology in Reconciliation: Essays Towards Evangelical and Catholic Unity in the East and West* (London: Geoffrey Chapman, 1975).
——, *Transformation and Convergence in the Frame of Knowledge: Explorations in the Interrelations of Scientific and Theological Enterprise* (Belfast: Christian Journals, 1984).
——, *The Trinitarian Faith: The Evangelical Theology of the Ancient Catholic Church* (Edinburgh: T&T Clark, 1988).
Torres, J., and R. Teja, 'A Dispute of Episcopal Legitimacy: Gregory Nazianzen and Maximus in Constantinople', in A. Fear (ed.), *The Role of the Bishop in Late Antiquity: Conflict and Compromise* (London: Bloomsbury, 2013), 13–30.
Trueman, C. R., *The Creedal Imperative* (Wheaton, Ill.: Crossway, 2012).
Turcescu, L., '*Prosōpon* and *Hypostasis* in Basil of Caesarea's *Against Eunomius* and the Epistles', *VC* 51.4 (1997), 374–395.
Ulrich, J., 'Nicaea and the West', *VC* 51 (1997), 10–24.
Vaggione, R. P., '*Ouk hōs en tōn gennēmatōn*: Some Aspects of Dogmatic Formulae in the Arian Controversy', *StPatr* 17 (1982), 181–187.
Vinzent, M. (ed.), *Markell von Ankyra: Die Fragmente; Der Brief an Julius von Rom.*, supplements to *VC* 39 (Leiden: E. J. Brill, 1997).
Webster, J., *Barth* (London: Continuum, 2000).
——, *God Without Measure: Working Papers in Christian Theology*, vol. 1: *God and the Works of God* (London: T&T Clark, 2016).
——, *Holy Scripture: A Dogmatic Sketch* (Cambridge: Cambridge University Press, 2012).
Wedgeworth, S., 'The Brightness of God's Own Light: Divine Simplicity in the Theology of Athanasius', in J. Minich and O. A. Kamel (eds.), *The Lord Is One: Reclaiming Divine Simplicity* (Burford: Davenant Press, 2019), 58–80.
Weedman, M., *The Trinitarian Theology of Hilary of Poitiers* (Leiden: E. J. Brill, 2007).
Weinandy, T. G., *Athanasius: A Theological Introduction* (Oxford: Ashgate, 2007).
Weinandy, T. G., and D. A. Keating, *Athanasius and His Legacy: Trinitarian-Incarnational Soteriology and Its Reception* (Minneapolis, Minn.: Fortress Press, 2017).

Wickham, L. R., 'The Syntagmation of Aetius the Anomean', *JTS* 19 (1968), 532–569.

Widdicombe, P., *The Fatherhood of God from Origen to Athanasius* (Oxford: Oxford University Press, 2001).

Wiles, M., *Archetypal Heresy: Arianism Through the Centuries* (Oxford: Clarendon Press, 1996).

———, 'Attitudes to Arius in the Arian Controversy', in M. Barnes and D. H. Williams (eds.), *Arianism After Arius: Essays on the Development of the Fourth Century Trinitarian Conflicts* (Edinburgh: T&T Clark, 1993), 31–43.

———, 'In Defence of Arius', *JTS* 13 (1962), 339–347.

Williams, D. H., 'Constantine and the "Fall" of the Church', in L. Ayres and G. Jones (eds.), *Christian Origins: Theology, Rhetoric and Community* (London: Routledge, 1998), 117–136.

———, *Evangelicals and Tradition: The Formative Influence of the Early Church* (Grand Rapids, Mich.: Baker Academic, 2005).

———, *Retrieving the Tradition and Renewing Evangelicalism: A Primer for Suspicious Protestants* (Grand Rapids, Mich.: Eerdmans, 1999).

Williams, G. H., *The Radical Reformation* (Philadelphia, Pa.: Westminster Press, 1962).

Williams, R., 'Angels Unawares: Heavenly Liturgy and Earthly Theology in Alexandria', *StPatr* 30 (1997), 350–363.

———, *Arius: Heresy and Tradition* (London: Darton, Longman and Todd, 1987).

———, 'The Logic of Arianism', *JTS* 34.1 (1983), 56–81.

Wolfson, H. A., *The Philosophy of the Church Fathers: Faith, Trinity, Incarnation*, vol. 1 (Cambridge, Mass.: Harvard University Press, 1956).

Woodbridge, J., 'Role of "Tradition" in the Life and Thought of Twentieth Century Evangelicals', in C. Colson and R. J. Neuhaus (eds.), *Your Word Is Truth: A Project of Evangelicals and Catholics Together* (Grand Rapids, Mich.: Eerdmans, 2002), 103–146.

Wright, N. T., *Paul and His Recent Interpreters: Some Contemporary Debates* (London: SPCK, 2015).

Young, F. M., *Biblical Exegesis and the Formation of Christian Culture* (Cambridge: Cambridge University Press, 1997).

———, *God's Presence: A Contemporary Recapitulation of Early Christianity* (Cambridge: Cambridge University Press, 2013).

———, 'Interpretation of Scripture', in S. Ashbrook and D. G. Hunter (eds.), *The Oxford Handbook of Early Christian Studies* (Oxford: Oxford University Press, 2008), 845–863.

____, *The Making of the Creeds* (London: SCM Press, 1991).
Zachhuber, J., 'The Antiochene Synod of 363 and the Beginnings of Neo-Nicenism', *ZAC* 4 (2000), 83–101.
____, 'Basil and the Three-Hypostases Tradition', *ZAC* 5 (2001), 65–85.
____, *Human Nature in Gregory of Nyssa: Philosophical Background and Theological Significance* (Leiden: E. J. Brill, 2014).
____, 'Individuality and the Theological Debate About "*Hyopostasis*"', in A. Torrance and J. Zachhuber (eds.), *Individuality in Late Antiquity* (Farnham: Ashgate, 2014), 91–111.

Index